DATE DUE

"*The Bible, in both Old and New Testaments, may be read in many ways. For some it constitutes divine teaching. For others it is the purest literature we have in the English language. For still others, it is a compendium of information on suffering, struggling, rejoicing human nature.*"

—PEARL S. BUCK

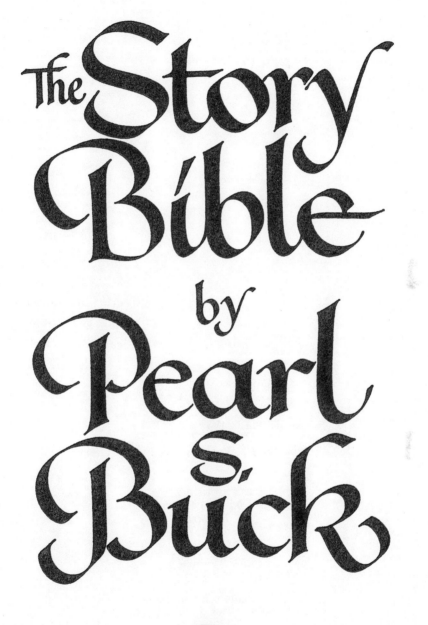

The Story Bible
by Pearl S. Buck

BARTHOLOMEW
HOUSE
LTD

BARTHOLOMEW HOUSE LTD.

© 1971 by Pearl S. Buck and Lyle Kenyon Engel

THE STORY BIBLE
Produced by Lyle Kenyon Engel
Editors:
Valerie Moolman
Marla Ray
George Engel

CONTENTS

FOREWORD

When I was a child growing up in China in the household of my American parents, I was not encouraged to read the Bible. My father, scholar in Hebrew and Greek, considered the translation of the Old and New Testaments inadequate renderings of the ancient texts and, irritated by what he considered downright mistakes in the use of words, he ignored the English version and read the Scriptures in the original languages. Since he did not teach me either Hebrew or Greek, I was reduced to English, but without encouragement I did not read the Bible. True, I heard it read for brief periods, night and morning, when my father summoned the household to family prayers. In the morning he read in English a few verses chosen by him for the benefit of his American family and in the evening he read another few verses in Chinese for the benefit of our Chinese servants. Beyond this my knowledge of the Bible was limited to the memorizing of the Beatitudes and Psalms and parts of the old prophets as Sunday occupation and to the reading—with much pleasure, I might say—of a very fat volume in a brown cloth cover entitled *Stories of the Bible* in worn gilt letters. My mother, who delighted in the English language, required me to memorize those parts of the Bible which she considered most beautiful and poetic, and to assuage my undying thirst for stories she found the fat volume for me.

Now as everyone knows who has read the Bible, there is not a better source for story than this vast collection of verse and prose, song and lamentation, love and death, sin and punishment. The scriptures of any religion are a fascinating and profound revelation of the struggle of the souls of men and women to find the source of their being and the cause of life and death. In recent years, for example, the sacred books of the Sikh religion in India have been beautifully translated into English and to my joy copies of these two volumes were presented to me on a recent trip to India. Reading them, I discover the same spiritual urgency that inspired my own youthful soul when I began to read the Bible for myself. Thus it is with other scriptures, wherever they are found. The books of Buddhism, the richly colored tales of Hinduism, the pantheons of Greece and Rome share with the Hebrew and Greek Testaments the stories of man's yearning to penetrate the Beyond. All have certain stories in common. The virgin birth is not unique to Christianity and it loses nothing of its importance thereby. The story of the great flood and Noah's ark is to be found in more than one literature. Reared as I have been in Asia, I find one religion enhances and deepens another by correlation and corroboration.

It is not as religion, however, that the stories contained in this volume are presented. I remember simply that I derived great pleasure and profit from reading that earlier volume of *Stories of the Bible*, and since I do not see its duplicate, it may be that this collection will take its place for today's readers.

The Bible, in both Old and New Testaments, may be read in many ways. For some is constitutes divine teaching, and it does contain this element. For others it is the purest literature we have in the English language. For still others it is a compendium of information on suffering, struggling, rejoicing human nature. For children, it is a story book. May they read it as I read it long ago in a Chinese house on a Chinese hillside!

Yet stay—as I write it occurs to me that the Bible has another meaning. It is an Asian book, for Christianity came out of the

East. It seems a contradiction that today the West, facing conflict with the East, should nevertheless find its own source of spiritual life in a volume of Asia, centering about the Jews, who, though they have wandered far, nevertheless remain in many ways true to their ancient history which is Asian. It may be that in this very fact we shall find the means of a common understanding, a basic agreement on the constitution for a peaceful world.

THE CREATION OF THE WORLD

*J*n the beginning God created the heaven and the earth.

At first there was nothing: neither earth nor sky, nor light, nor sound, nor any living thing. All was darkness and silence.

And then the Spirit of God came into the emptiness to give it form and bring it life.

God said: "Let there be light," and the first dawn of time brought light into the world. God looked upon his work and found it good, and divided the light from the darkness. "Let the light be called Day," he said, "and the darkness be called Night." So ended the first of all the days of the earth.

On the second day, God said: "Let there be a sky as a roof over the world, and let it be called Heaven." And it was so. God made the sky and the rainclouds and placed them high above the waters of the deep.

On the third day God said: "Let the waters under the heaven be gathered together into one place, and let the dry land appear." And it was so. Mountains and plains and valleys rose out of the waters, so that now there were great stretches of dry land divided by vast expanses of deep water. God called the land Earth, and the waters he called Seas. Then God said: "Let the earth bring forth herbs and grass, and flowers and trees, each yielding seed of its own kind so that the earth will never cease to yield." And it was so. Soft grass carpeted the land. Plants sprang up and bore flowers and seeds. Trees grew and yielded fruit, each according to its own kind; and the seeds of the new growth spread across the earth.

On the fourth day God said: "Let there be lights in the heavens to mark the seasons and the days and the years, and to give light upon the earth." And it was so. God made the sun and the moon and the stars, and they shone down upon the earth. Of the two greatest lights, he made the sun to rule over the day and the moon to rule the night.

On the fifth day God said: "Let the waters bring forth living creatures and may birds fly above the earth in the heavens." And it was so. God created great whales and tiny fishes and all the living things of the sea, and great hawks and tiny sparrows and all the birds of the air. Now there was life in the waters and the heavens, and the silence was gone from the world. By the end of the fifth day there was birdsong in the land.

On the sixth day God said: "Let the earth bring forth living creatures, cattle and creeping things, and beasts that walk on legs." And it was so. God made the cattle and the creeping things and all the beasts that live on the land. But as yet there was no being in the likeness of God.

And God said: "Let us make man in our image, after our likeness, and let him have dominion over the fish of the sea, and over the fowl of the air, and over the cattle and beasts, and over every creeping thing, and over all the earth."

And so it was that God created man in his own image. From the dust of the earth he shaped man's form, and into man's nostrils he breathed the breath of life; and man became a living soul. God called him Adam, and gave to him every herb and fruit that was upon the earth, every lovely flower and shady tree, every bird in the air, and everything that walked and crept upon the land.

Now it was for Adam to enjoy the fruits of the earth and rule over all its creatures. He looked upon all the birds and beasts and gave names to all of them; but among them there was not another like himself to be his true companion.

And then God said: "It is not good that the man should be alone. I will make a helpmeet for him." God caused Adam to fall into a deep sleep. While the man slept, God took a rib from Adam's body and closed up the flesh in its place. And from Adam's rib the Lord God made a woman.

Now the first man had a wife.

Adam named her Eve and loved her deeply. They began their life together in a garden paradise the Lord had planted for them in the loveliest part of the newborn world. It was a land of rivers and precious stones, of flowering trees and abundant fruit; and its name was Eden.

God saw everything that he had made, and it was good. The heavens and the earth were finished, and living creatures in his likeness walked upon the earth according to his plan.

So ended the sixth day.

On the seventh day God rested from his work.

THE GARDEN OF EDEN

*A*dam and Eve were content in their garden home. The Lord had given them everything they could want for their food and pleasure. Brightly colored birds flitted from flower to flower and from branch to branch, singing sweet songs that rose high into the heavens. The river splashed and whispered through the land, watering the earth so that all plants but weeds and thistles grew easily in the fertile soil. It was the lightest of labors for Adam to look after the garden, for the Lord had not meant him to spend his days in toil.

There were trees of every kind, beautiful in all seasons but especially lovely when their leaves were a young green and blossoms brightened the boughs; and there was fruit to eat in plenty. In the midst of the garden stood the Tree of Life, and also the Tree of Knowledge of Good and Evil. But Adam and Eve knew nothing of evil. Their world was all good, and in it they were as free and unafraid as the birds of the air and the animals that roamed the woods and fields. God himself would walk on earth and talk to them in the cool of early evening, and then their happiness was complete.

The Lord asked only one thing of them, and that was to obey. "Of every tree in the garden," he told Adam, "you may eat freely, except of the Tree of Knowledge of Good and Evil. The day that you eat of that tree, you will surely die."

Adam gave his promise readily. There was no need to eat of that tree; there were many others. And even though he did not know what it meant to die, he knew that he must obey and love the Lord who had created him.

Even for the woman it should not have been hard to avoid picking from that one tree and eating its fruit. But the serpent was the most cunning of any of the beasts of the field, as well as one of the most beautiful. He knew that he could make the fruit of that tree seem desirable above all others simply because it was forbidden, especially if he approached the woman in his most persuasive manner. So he appeared before Eve, tall and handsome in his multicolored coat.

"God has told you that you shall not eat of every tree in the garden, is that not so?" he began slyly.

"We may eat the fruit of every tree but one," Eve answered. "Of the tree in the middle of the garden, God has said that we should neither eat of it nor touch it, or we will surely die."

"You will *not* surely die," the serpent said. "God has told you that you will die so that you will be afraid to eat of the fruit, for he knows that if you do your eyes will be opened, and you will be as wise as the gods, knowing good from evil."

Eve took another look at the tree. It was pleasant to the eye, and the fruit looked good. If it was true that eating of it would make her wise, it was indeed a desirable tree. She did not realize how subtly she was being tempted by the wily beast. Her hand reached out and her fingers plucked the fruit. She tasted it; she began to eat. The serpent left her to her meal.

She shared the whole world with her husband, so now she shared the new thing she had discovered. The fruit was pleasant to the taste, and Adam must have some of it, too. Eve gave some to her husband; and Adam also ate of the forbidden fruit.

It was true that they did not die at once, but by their disobedience they had denied themselves eternal life. It was true, too, that their eyes were opened, and now they were aware of things they had never known before. For the first time they realized that they were naked, and for the first time they felt shame. They knew they had done wrong. They sewed fig leaves together into clothes to cover their nakedness; and when that was not enough to shield them from their shame and fear they hid themselves among the leafy trees.

Then they heard the voice of the Lord as he walked in the garden in the cool of the day, and they went deeper into the woods to hide from him.

"Adam! Where are you?" the Lord God called.

"I am here, Lord," Adam answered. "I heard your voice in the garden, and I was afraid because I was naked, so I hid myself."

"How do you know you are naked?" asked the Lord. "Have you eaten the fruit of the forbidden tree, that you should have such knowledge?"

"It was the woman," Adam said. "She gave me some of the fruit, and I did eat."

The Lord God turned to Eve. "What is this that you have done?" he asked her sorrowfully.

"It was the serpent," said the woman. "The serpent tempted me, and so I ate."

Adam and Eve had been wrong to disobey. The Lord had asked only for obedience, and they had failed him. Yet the serpent had also done wrong in tricking Eve, and God's first words of punishment were for the beautiful beast.

"Because you have done this," the Lord God said to him, "you are cursed above all cattle and above every beast of the field. Upon your belly you will crawl, and dust you will eat all the days of your life. You and the woman, and your children and her children, shall be enemies forever."

The serpent no longer stood upright and proud but lay upon the ground lower than any other beast on earth. And it crawled away with its belly in the dust.

"For you," the Lord God said to Eve, "there will be pain and suffering, and in sorrow will you bring forth children. No longer are you equal to the man, for he shall rule over you."

And to Adam he said: "Because you listened to your wife and ate the fruit you were commanded not to eat, the ground will no longer bring forth only good things but also thorns and thistles. You will eat of the herb of the field, but food shall not be yours only for the taking. From now on you will work and earn your bread by the sweat of your brow, and this you will do until you return to the earth from which you were made."

Here, then, was the promised death. But it was not to come for many years, and during those years Adam and Eve would have children and Eve would be the mother of the world.

Then the Lord God made coats of skin for Adam and his wife, and clothed them with his goodness. And he said to himself, "It is enough that the man knows good and evil. Now unless they leave this place, he may put out his hand and eat also of the Tree of Life, and live forever. And that he shall not do."

Therefore the Lord God sent Adam and Eve away from the garden and out into the world to make a new life for themselves. At the east of Eden he placed angels to watch over the garden, one of them with a flaming sword which turned in all directions to guard the pathway to the Tree of Life. It was the end of perfection in the world, for Adam and Eve had disobeyed. No longer would they know a paradise on earth. But they left Eden with God's promise that some day a savior would appear among their children's children to wash all sins away.

CAIN AND ABEL: The First Murder

*L*ife was very different now for Adam and Eve. Instead of tending a fertile garden and picking fruit when they were hungry, they had to work hard to wrest a living from the soil. Instead of feeling safe and free from fear, they had to find shelter against the wild animals that had once been their companions. The ease and beauty of their former life were gone forever. As God had warned them, they knew both suffering and sorrow; and God himself no longer walked upon the earth to talk to them.

Yet there was still goodness in the world. God loved Adam and Eve, and they loved him in return. Adam learned how to till the soil so that the crops would grow and there was food to eat; and Eve learned how to make a home for her husband and herself. Even though they could no longer talk directly to their Lord, they could still keep close to him by offering him their gifts of love. Upon the rough stone altars that Adam built they would place the fruits of their harvest and the lambs of their flock as tokens of their faith. Because their love was great, so were their gifts. It was to show that they were willing to offer everything they had that they brought not only the food they grew from the soil but also creatures of flesh and blood to the altar of their Lord.

As time went by Eve gave birth to the first baby in the world, a sturdy little boy whom she and Adam named Cain. Before long a second baby came, and they called him Abel.

As the boys grew up they began to help their father on the land. Cain, like his father, preferred to work in the fields, tilling the soil and looking after the crops. Abel liked to tend the flocks, so he became a shepherd.

In time it came to pass that the two young men built altars of their own to bring gifts to the Lord. Cain brought the fruits of the field for his offering, and Abel brought the young lambs of his flock. God was pleased with Abel and his offering, because the younger brother was giving him creatures who lived and breathed even as Abel did. It was almost as if he were giving himself to God. But God was not pleased with Cain. The older brother was not giving freely of himself, and so was not offering all that God desired of him.

Cain felt God's displeasure, and he became angry because it seemed to him that he had done his best. After all, he had brought the fruits and grains he had grown with his own hands. Surely no more could be expected of him! His face fell, and he raged inside himself. God saw his sullen look and the anger burning in him.

"Why are you angry?" said the Lord to Cain. "And why is there a frown upon your face? If you do well, you will be accepted. And if you do not, you must know that you are in the wrong. It is for you to master sin, not to give in to it."

But Cain would not try to please the Lord. Instead, he let his anger grow until it took command of him. Why should Abel be more favored than he, and why should not the Lord place an equal value on his offering?

The two brothers went together into the fields and talked. Cain's rage was growing, and the talk grew into a quarrel that became so fierce that Cain's anger overflowed. He sprang at Abel and attacked him bitterly, and when the sudden assault was over Abel lay dead in their father's fields. Cain left him lying there.

The Lord spoke to him again. "Where is your brother Abel?"

"I don't know," Cain lied. "How should I? Am I my brother's keeper?"

God knew that Cain was lying. "What have you done?" he said. "The blood of your brother cries out to me from the ground. Because of that, the earth that drinks the blood shed by your hand shall forever curse you. When you till the soil it will not yield its crops for you; from this day on you will be a wanderer and a fugitive throughout the land."

At last Cain was afraid.

"My punishment is more than I can bear!" he cried. "You have driven me away from yourself and from the company of men, and nowhere on the face of the earth will I find a home. Where shall I go? I shall be a homeless vagabond, and every man's hand will be against me as I wander. Any man who finds me will surely try to kill me."

Then the Lord said to him: "Whoever kills Cain will be punished seven times over. I will put a mark upon you so that you will be known wherever you go as a man to whom no harm shall come. You will not be killed by anyone who finds you."

So Cain left the land of his parents and wandered into a far country called Nod. He no longer spoke to God, yet God did not forsake him. Although Cain had killed his brother, God let him live to build a city and find himself a wife; and in time Cain's family became great in numbers and rich in worldly goods. But they did not worship God.

NOAH AND THE FLOOD

*A*dam and Eve went on living for a long time after losing their first two children, for people lived many hundreds of years when the world was new. Their hearts were sad because their sons had left them in such a tragic way, but they did not give in to sorrow. In time they had many more children, the first of whom was a boy very much like Abel. They called him Seth. When Seth grew to manhood he himself married, and established a branch of the family that went down through the centuries to produce a man who was to save the world from the judgment of the Lord.

When at last Adam and Eve died, eight hundred years after the birth of Seth, their family had grown into a vast tribe of people. The earth on which they had lived and toiled was no longer a lonely wilderness but a productive land teeming with their children, their children's children, and great-great-great-grand children who themselves were grown and had children of their own. It should have been a good and wonderful world.

But it seemed that the more people there were the more wickedness there was upon the earth. Among them all there were only a few who found favor in the eyes of the Lord because of their love for what was good and right. These few were descended from Seth. One of them was Enoch, who walked and talked with God as Adam had done in the days of Eden. Another was Enoch's son Methuselah, a man who lived longer than any other man in the world, and who produced a great many sons and daughters in the course of his nine hundred and sixty-nine years on earth. Among his several sons was Lamech, who had a son of his own who proved to be among the most outstanding of the descendants of Seth. That son's name was Noah.

Men multiplied on the face of the earth, working and playing and having families, and forgetting all about their Lord. God looked down and saw a few men like Noah working hard in their fields and dealing honestly with their fellow men; and he saw many men, such as the descendants of Cain, becoming wealthy in their cities and worshiping the things that they had made with their own hands. Scarcely any man or woman gave thought to the Lord who had created them. People seemed to have forgotten how to be good to one another, much less love their Lord. They had become so thoughtless that they no longer knew what was right; nor did they seem to care.

Something had to be done. The Lord gave warning: "My spirit shall not strive forever with the people of the earth. The days of man shall be no more than a hundred and twenty years if his wickedness does not pass."

But it was as if they did not hear him. The people did not heed the warning of the Lord. Instead of changing for the better they became even worse. And God saw that the world was full of evil and wrongdoing. Not only were man's deeds wicked, but his thoughts were evil and there was evil in his heart continually.

The Lord was grieved at what he saw, and he regretted that he had ever placed man upon the earth. In sorrow, he said: "I will destroy man, whom I have created, from the face of the earth; not only man, but all the beasts and creeping things, and the fowls of the air; for I repent that I have made them."

But even in those bad days there was one man who found grace in the eyes of the Lord, and that was Noah. Like his great-grand-father Enoch and his first ancestor Adam, Noah was a just man who walked and talked with God. In the midst of all the world's wickedness he alone was truly righteous, and he alone tried to keep his family in the ways of God. He had three sons, Shem, Ham, and Japheth, and there was good in them as well.

God spoke to Noah. "The time has come to make an end of all this violence and evil," he said. "I will destroy all living things, and the whole earth with them. But you, Noah, must build an ark of gopher wood. You will make rooms in it, and line it with pitch inside and out so that no water can enter in. The ark shall have three levels: a lower, a second, and a third; and it shall be forty-five feet high. The length of it should be four hundred and fifty feet, and it must be seventy-five feet wide."

Noah listened with growing wonder as God spoke to him. He had never built a boat, for he lived far from the coast and had never needed one. Certainly, he had never imagined building a boat of such great size. But God was telling him how it should be done. It was to be very strongly built with a sturdy wooden frame and a sound, stout roof to keep the water off the decks, and there would also be a window and a single wide door set into the side. When it was finished it would look like a great houseboat. But what was it for?

The answer was soon coming. "There will be a flood of waters upon the earth," said the Lord, "and everything under heaven shall die. But to you, Noah, I make a promise. When you have finished building you will go into the ark, you and your wife and your three sons and their families, for I have seen that you are a righteous man and I will save you. And of every living creature, excepting only man, you shall bring two of every sort into the ark to keep them alive with you. Each pair shall be male and female. Of every fowl of the air and every beast that is greatly needed by man, such as sheep and cattle, you shall take in sevens of pairs, so that all such shall be reborn upon the earth in good quantities when the flood has passed away. And you shall gather every kind of food and place it on board for yourselves and all the animals and birds and creeping things that will be with you in the ark."

It was a strange thing for Noah to have to do, but he did as he was commanded because he believed in God. It was a long task to build the ark, to round up all the animals, to gather and store the food, and it was made no easier by his mocking neighbors. He warned them of the oncoming flood, and begged them to repent and save themselves, but they laughed at him and his enormous boat so far from the sea and would not believe that they were in any danger from the Lord. They could not believe, because they did not believe in God. And they could not imagine a flood so bad that it would destroy everything they had, including their own lives. Therefore they kept on laughing and they kept on with their evil ways.

But Noah went on building, while his sons collected animals and food.

The time came when God told him he should load the ship. "In seven days," said the Lord, "I will cause it to start raining upon the earth. And it will rain for forty days and forty nights. Take the beasts, two by two, into the ark, and your family also. Whatever living thing is not upon the ark will be washed from the face of the earth."

Noah went into the ark with his sons and his wife and the wives of his sons. Two of every bird and beast and every creeping thing, the male and female, followed the human family into the ark. Then Noah closed the door and waited.

He did not have long to wait. It came to pass after seven days from God's final warning that the waters of the flood were upon the earth. It was in the six hundredth year of Noah's life, on the seventeenth day of the second month, that the fountains of the great deep were broken up and the windows of heaven were opened.

Water poured down from the sky. People ran from the drowning lands into their homes to keep dry, and when that did not help them they climbed the hills and mountains to escape.

There was no escape. The rivers swelled and rose until they broke their banks and washed across the lands. Great pools of water joined together into even greater pools, and the water level slowly rose. The ark rose steadily with the rising waters, and the rain lashed down upon its pitch-lined roof. Inside, the good man Noah and his family were safe and dry, and with them were the many pairs of animals of every kind. They alone floated above the flood, and although they were cut off completely from the land, they had with them enough food to last for many months if that were needed.

For forty days and forty nights, it rained.

Outside the ark, small streams grew into rushing rivers, the rivers into walls of water that turned the land into a vast lake dotted with small islands which had once been high land. Rain water joined with sea to wash away the coastline and the valleys, and the hills shrank down beneath the growing seas. Higher and higher rose the waters, until all the high hills under the whole heaven and even the tall mountains were covered. There was no longer anywhere to run for safety. Every man and all the cattle, all the birds of the air and every creeping thing, all were washed away by the flood, until there was nothing left in the world but a great sheet of water and one wooden boat bobbing on the face of the deep.

And then the rain stopped. At the end of forty days and nights God remembered Noah and every living thing that was with him in the ark. And God made a wind to pass over the earth so that the waters were quieted. He stopped the fountains of the deep and closed the windows of heaven, and he held the rain back from the sky. The great sea over the land began subsiding gradually. For six months and more the ark went on floating on the silent sea, the only life in all the world. Slowly, day after day for a hundred and fifty days, the waters drained away. On the seventeenth day of the seventh month after the rain the ark came to rest upon the mountain of Ararat in Mesopotamia. And on the

first day of the tenth month, the tops of distant mountains could
be seen from the ark.

At the end of forty days of receding waters Noah sent out a
raven from the window of the ark and watched it fly back and
forth across the lonely sky. It was the only living thing outside the
ark; and though it scouted for dry land, it found none. Noah also
sent a dove, knowing that the dove would light on land if any
land there was. But the dove came back, and Noah reached out
his hand and took her into the ark. Seven days later he sent the
dove out once again. This time she came back to him in the evening with a fresh young olive leaf in her mouth. Now Noah knew
that the waters had drained away from the earth enough to
permit life on the land, and that, somewhere, living trees had
raised their heads above the immense lake. He waited yet another
seven days, and then sent the dove out once again. She did not return at all.

And so it was that, on the first day of the first month of Noah's
six hundredth and first year of life, the waters were dried up from
the earth. Noah removed the covering of the ark and looked out
upon a strange yet promising world. He was no longer in his own
country; but the face of the ground was dry. God spoke to him
again, saying: "Go out of the ark, and take with you your wife,
your sons, and your sons' wives, and all the fowl and cattle and
the creeping things, and put them back upon the land so that they
may breed, and be fruitful, and multiply upon the earth."

Then Noah opened the great door of the ark, through which his
strange crew had trooped more than a year before, and each and
every pair followed Noah and his family onto the wonderful dry
land. At last the world was alive again.

As soon as all were on dry land Noah built an altar of thanksgiving to the Lord to show his gratitude for having been saved.
Upon the rough stones he made burnt offerings to the God who
loved him, and gave thanks for the new hope in the world.

The Lord smelled the sweet savor of Noah's offerings and was
pleased with what was in the good man's heart, and he vowed in

his own heart that he would never again curse the ground to punish man or destroy all life on the earth. "While the earth remains," he promised, "seedtime and harvest, and cold and heat, and summer and winter, and day and night shall not cease to be." God then blessed Noah and his sons, and said to them: "The earth is yours. Be fruitful, have many children, and replenish it." He gave to them the earth and every living thing upon it.

Then he caused a great arc of lovely colors to vault the sky. "This is a token of the vow between us," he declared. "I make my promise to you and all the living creatures you have brought with you, and to your offspring for all time. I do set my rainbow in the sky as a reminder of my covenant with every living thing on earth. When you see it, you will remember what I say to you, and know that I remember. And this is my everlasting vow: The waters shall no more become a flood to wash all living things away. Never again will there be a flood to destroy man from the earth."

THE TOWER OF BABEL

*T*he three sons of Noah were to be the founders of a new human race, one that would start afresh in a world washed clean by the flood. After leaving the ark and receiving God's blessing, they made new homes for themselves, and it was not long before sons were born to their wives. The family of Noah increased greatly, generation after generation, so that in the course of time the world was indeed replenished through Japheth, Shem, and Ham.

Noah himself lived on for three hundred and fifty years after the flood, his boat-building days over forever. He farmed his lands, worked in his vineyards, and watched his huge family grow. At the age of nine hundred and fifty years, he died, knowing that his sons were the fathers of the nations of the world.

From Japheth's seven sons came the Gentiles, or the non-Jewish nations. Shem's five sons were to be the fathers of the Shemites, or Hebrews; and from his line would spring two upright men called Abram and Lot. Ham's four sons would go forth and people Africa, and would also be the fathers of the non-Hebrew inhabitants of Canaan. Eventually the descendants of Shem, later to be called the Israelites, would be in constant battle against the

Canaanite descendants of Ham, but this was not to be for many, many years after the death of Noah.

Thus were the families of the sons of Noah separated into the nations of the world. And the whole earth, with all its nations, was of one language and of one speech.

The descendants of Noah left the region of Mount Ararat and traveled south into the valley of the Euphrates. They found a fertile plain in the land of Shinar, which was part of the country of Babylonia, and settled down to live there.

"Let us make bricks and mortar," they said to each other, "and let us build a city in which we can live together. And let us build a tower, so great and tall that its top will touch the skies. We will make a name for ourselves with our tall tower, and we will be a nation instead of being scattered abroad over the face of the whole earth."

They set to work, and it must be said that they labored with all their strength. They made bricks and more bricks, and carried heavy loads to the building site; they piled brick and mortar higher and higher until the tower grew to be as tall and magnificent as a temple to a pagan god. And still they went on building. They had no need for a tower so elaborate and vast, but they wanted theirs to be the greatest building in the world so that they could point to it with pride in their accomplishment.

And then the Lord came down to see the city and the tower which the children of men were building. He did not like the tower and what it told him of their pride. "The people of the earth are only one people," he thought, "and they have only one language. And even so, they are doing this to keep themselves together. If they can do such a thing as this, surely nothing will keep them from doing anything they dream of doing. But their pride is sufficient sin." For it looked, indeed, as though they had again forgotten all about God and were beginning to worship the creations of their own hands. "Let us go down there and confound their language," said the Lord, "so that they may not understand each other's speech."

And suddenly the builders of the city and the tower could not understand each other. Work stopped at once. It was impossible to go on building when the workmen all spoke different languages. It was the same thing throughout the city. Those who could understand each other came together and moved away to stay together. Soon little pockets of people speaking their own language appeared throughout the earth. Whoever was left in the city gave up building altogether because most of the citizens had scattered far and wide. And that is why the city is named Babel; it was there that the Lord confused the language of all the earth, and from there that the people scattered to the far corners of the earth to form separate nations, each with a language of its own.

THE JOURNEY OF ABRAM AND LOT

*O*ne of the descendants of Shem, a man by the name of Terah, made his home not far from Babel in a great city called Ur in the land of the Babylonians, or Chaldeans as they were also called. He had three sons, and their names were Abram, Nahor, and Haran.

Now Ur at this time was a very beautiful and very wealthy city, but its inhabitants did not pray to the God of the Hebrews. Many people in those days bowed down to the sun or the moon or the stars, or even the great rivers and the mountaintops. The people of Ur made idols and worshiped them, believing themselves to be especially favored by the moon-god. Terah himself had forgotten how to pray to the true God of his own people, but he did not feel completely at home in the city of Ur. He was a simple man and a farmer, and city life was not for him. When his sons had grown to manhood he decided to leave Ur and go to the land of Canaan. By the time he was ready to go, one of his sons, Haran, had died in Ur, so Terah took with him Haran's son Lot, Abram his own son and Abram's wife Sarai, and his second son Nahor and Nahor's wife Milcah.

Together they journeyed up along the course of the river Euphrates in search of a better land. Instead of turning south and going into the land of Canaan, which the people of today call Palestine, they veered north and settled in a place called Haran in the district of Padan-Aram.

Terah had been quite rich in cattle and sheep even before leaving Ur. Now, in Haran, he soon established himself as a wealthy shepherd-farmer and the respected head of a growing family that worked hard and added steadily to the wealth. In time Terah died, and Abram became the head of the family and all the people who had joined their settlement to work in the household or among the flocks.

When Abram was seventy-five years old he heard the voice of the Lord say to him: "Leave your country and your kinsmen and your father's house, and go to a land that I will show you. I will make of you a great nation, and I will bless you and make your name great. Through you shall all the families of the earth be blessed."

And Abram, even though he was no longer young and still without a son to help him, listened to the voice of the Lord and gathered his people together. His wife Sarai would of course go with him at his side. Nahor and his family decided to remain at Haran. Lot elected to go with Abram. Abram was glad that Lot chose to make the journey, because it meant that the two of them could share the leadership of the expedition. As soon as all was ready, Abram's caravan of shepherds and cattlemen and household retainers traveled away from the great river Euphrates toward Canaan in the southwest. With them they took all their sheep and cattle and their household goods, and they followed Abram and Lot and Sarai into the land the Lord had spoken of.

They journeyed on until they came to a place called Sichem on the plain of Moreh, which was in the land of Canaan. Here the Lord appeared to Abram and said: "To you and your children shall I give this land." Abram halted his caravan while he built an altar there to thank the Lord, and then went on with all his followers to a mountain on the east of Bethel. Here he pitched his tents so that all might rest a while, and he built another altar in praise of his Lord. Again he moved, journeying steadily toward the south, for he was not a city-dweller who would plant his roots deeply in one place but a tent-dweller and an animal farmer who needed to move where the pastures were rich.

The time came when the rivers dried up and there was a famine in the land. Abram needed water and fresh grass to pasture his herds and also to feed his people, so he and his train of followers went down into the well-watered land of Egypt to live there until the famine should pass. When at last it did he took Sarai and Lot and his whole caravan back into the land of Canaan, back to Bethel where he had pitched his tents before.

Life was good to them in the land the Lord had shown them, and Abram became rich not only in cattle but also in silver and gold from the land of Egypt. His flocks increased greatly, so that as the years passed he needed more pasture for them and more shepherds and herdsmen to look after them. Lot also had done well; he, too, had flocks and herds and tents and many people working for him. In fact, Abram's settlement was now so large that the land could not support all the living things that were upon it. The family and their serving men lived in a cluster of tents as large as a small city, while the sheep and cattle roamed far into the countryside in search of grazing ground.

It became a contest between the men of Abram and the men of Lot to find the best pastures for their herds when there was really only enough for one group or the other in the region of Bethel. The herdsmen began to quarrel among themselves. Abram called Lot aside and spoke to him about the arguments between their men. "Let there be no strife, I pray you," he said, "between the two of us or between our herdsmen. It is true, there is not room for both of us in this one place. But does not the whole land lie before us?" As they spoke they stood high upon the mountainside, and they could see the land below them stretching in all directions. "Let us separate, I beg you," Abram said. "Choose which way you will go. If you will go north, I shall go south; if you

choose the east, I shall go west. Choose what you will, but let us
not quarrel."

Lot surveyed the land below. Some of it was semi-desert plain
and forbidding mountain; some, to the east, was green and fertile,
as well-watered and productive as the garden of the Lord or the
land of Egypt where they had escaped the famine. It was the
plain of Jordan; and he knew that he could do well there with his
flocks. He also knew that it was Abram's right to make the choice
and take the fertile eastern lands. But Abram had offered that
right to him, and so Lot took it.

"I shall go east," he said, and chose for himself all the gentle
plain of Jordan.

They separated, then, and Lot journeyed into the eastern plain
with his family and flocks. Abram stayed in the land of Canaan,
content with whatever lands his nephew Lot had left him. Lot
traveled on toward the cities of the plain, and eventually he
pitched his tents and pastured his flocks near the city of Sodom. It
was a good land for a farmer, and it was also convenient for Lot to
be near a city of some size. But the men of Sodom were exceedingly wicked, and they sinned against the Lord continually.

After Lot had made his choice and left, the Lord spoke again to
Abram.

"Lift up your eyes, Abram. Look northward from where you
stand, and southward and eastward and westward. All the land
that you see I will give to you and your children, and your
children's children, forever. I will give you many descendants, as
many as there are grains of dust upon the earth. Arise, walk
through the land, across the length of it and the breadth of it, for I
will give it all to you."

Then Abram moved his tents and journeyed through the land
to see what God had given him. When he had had enough of
travel he halted on a plain called Mamre, and pitched his tents
among the tall oaks near the city of Hebron. Here he built another altar to the Lord who had guided him and given him so
much. He and his wife Sarai prospered, although they did not yet

have any of the children the Lord had promised Abram, and were happy with their simple way of life. But Lot had grown to enjoy the pleasures offered by the cities of the plain, and had moved his family into the city of Sodom.

THE CAPTURE OF LOT

The city of Ur in Babylonia had been a godless place, but Sodom was even worse. Its people thought of nothing but their own pleasures and the pursuit of wealth. Nor was Sodom the only city of its kind; the neighboring town of Gomorrah was equally bad. Both Sodom and Gomorrah were known throughout the land for the evil deeds of their inhabitants.

These two cities and three others lay in the vale of Siddim near an inland sea called the Dead Sea, or the Salt Sea. The five of them were long-time enemies of the mighty king of Elam and his three powerful allies, and in fact had lost in battle to them and were obliged to pay tribute to their conquerors for many years. The tax was a burden to them, but it was not so heavy that they could not still afford to live in luxury. As long as they could go on enjoying themselves, they would rather pay the tribute money than fight to free themselves.

When at last they rebelled against the king of Elam and refused to go on serving him, they were so softened by easy living that they had almost forgotten how to fight. The forces that faced them were smaller than their own but at full fighting strength, and the war went badly for the people of Sodom and Gomorrah.

Four kings fought with five in the vale of Siddim, and the five kings fled before the king of Elam and his fighting friends. They turned and ran, with all their soldiers, into the mountains and the valleys, and left their cities open to the mercy of the enemies.

The conquering soldiers swarmed into the cities of Sodom and Gomorrah, looking for the gold and silver they knew were hidden in the houses of the wealthy, and looting everything they could find in the homes and market places. They took goods and food and captives, and went back to their camp with all that they had taken. And with them they took Lot, Abram's brother's son, and all Lot's goods, and they held him in captivity with many other men and women whom they had taken for their slaves.

But one man managed to escape from the enemy camp. He broke loose from his captors and fled across the country to find Abram in the plain of Mamre, and when he had found him he told Abram about the awful battle and the fate of Lot. Abram was a peaceful farmer-shepherd and not a fighting man, but when he heard what had happened to his nephew Lot he knew at once that he must rescue him. With the help of a few friends who lived near him, he gathered together his band of herdsmen and the servants of his household, and he swiftly formed them into a well-armed fighting force. There were three hundred and eighteen of them, all born to his household, and all trained men who knew well how to defend their flocks and pastures from attack. This time they would be the attackers; and Abram knew that they would fight with him to save his kinsman with all their strength and loyalty.

Abram placed himself at the head of his small army and went off in hot pursuit of the forces who held his nephew Lot. Far to the north, at a place called Dan, he came upon the enemy camp at night and launched a swift attack. It was so sudden and so unexpected that the enemy broke camp and ran. Abram's forces pursued them almost to Damascus, attacking all the way, before letting the remnants of the Elamite forces straggle away into the hills of their homeland.

And Abram rescued all the captives and their stolen possessions, all the men and women and their goods; and his nephew
Lot, and all his goods. Lot was a grateful man that day; and grateful, too, were all the people of the ransacked cities. But though
Abram could have made himself a very rich man indeed by
keeping the goods he had recovered, he would take no reward
from their kings for what he had done. Instead, he returned the
goods to the people and the people to their cities, accepting nothing in return but the food he needed for the young men of his tiny
army. Lot and his family went back into the city of Sodom, which
had become no less wicked for having been saved by Abram; and
Abram went back to the quiet life of his tent home on the plain of
Mamre.

GOD'S PROMISE TO ABRAM

*T*hus, although it was the custom for the conqueror to keep the spoils of battle, Abram accepted no reward from man. But soon after the rescue of Lot, Abram heard the voice of the Lord saying: "Fear not, Abram, I will protect you and reward you greatly for your righteousness."

Now Abram had everything he wanted out of life but for one thing; and the lack of that one thing was a cause of sadness to him.

"Lord God, what is my reward?" he asked. "I still have no child of my own. Eliezer of Damascus, who is the steward of my household and watches over everything I own, was born in my house and is a good man. Should he be my heir?"

"He shall not," the Lord told him. "Your own son shall be your heir. Look up at the stars, Abram. See if you can count them. As many stars as there are up in the heavens, so many will be the children of your family. I am the Lord who brought you out of Ur to give you this land to inherit. I give it to you, and the children of your children, and not to someone else born in your house." And Abram, although he was old and still without a son, believed in the Lord's word.

God also told him something of the far-off future, when the

Hebrews would suffer hard times but would overcome their sorrows. In a distant time, God told the faithful Abram, the children of his family would be strangers in a strange, unfriendly land for four hundred years. They would be slaves to the people of that nation, but when they left it they would become a great people in their own right and they would possess the land of Canaan for themselves.

And eventually it did happen that the descendants of Abram became slaves in the land of Egypt, and that they left the country of the Pharaohs and journeyed slowly back to the promised land. But it would be many years before this came to pass, and Abram himself was not to see it happen. While he still lived in Mamre near the great oaks of Hebron, not only Abram but his wife Sarai continued to think about the children that they did not have.

Sarai thought about it for a long time, for she wanted children very badly. Even though she knew of God's promise to her husband, time was passing by and she could no longer believe that she would ever have a baby of her own. One day she said to Abram: "The Lord has not let me have a child. Go to my hand-maid, Hagar. Take her to yourself; in that way I may have a child through her." Now Hagar was an Egyptian maidservant who had become attached to Abram's household during his journey to Egypt at the time of the famine in Canaan. In those days it was not unusual for a man to have more than one wife, or for a wife to give her handmaid to her husband. Sometimes childless women like Sarai would ask their husbands to produce children through a trusted handmaid, and then the wife would be thought of as the mother of the handmaid's children.

Abram agreed to Sarai's request, and Sarai gave the handmaid Hagar to him so that she might bear a child.

It was not long before Hagar knew that she was going to have a baby. She was proud of it, and she began to mock her mistress because Sarai had not been able to have a child of her own. This was not at all what Abram's wife had hoped for, and she was most unhappy. Instead of feeling like a mother herself, she felt she was a failure as a wife. And Hagar let her feel it; Hagar despised her openly.

"I was wrong to do what I did," Sarai said sadly to Abram. "It was a mistake, for now I am despised in Hagar's eyes. Tell me, what should I do now?"

"She is your maid," Abram replied. "Do with her what you will."

And Sarai was hard on the mocking Hagar; she treated her so severely that Hagar could no longer bear it, and ran away into the wilderness. It was not long before she tired and was obliged to rest. She stopped by a fountain of water on the way to Shur, and it was here that the angel of the Lord found her in the wilderness.

"Hagar, Sarai's maid!" he said. "What are you doing here, and where are you going?"

"I am running from my mistress Sarai," she replied.

"Return to your mistress," said the angel of the Lord, "and obey her. God has seen your suffering. You will have a child, and he will grow up to be a strong and mighty man who will dwell in the wilderness. Through him you will have a great family of your own. But now you must go back, Hagar. The Lord sees you, and is with you."

Hagar returned to the tents of Abram and Sarai. When her time came she bore a son to Abram, and they called him Ishmael. Abram was eighty-six years old, and proud to have a son even though it was not Sarai's; but Sarai could never bring herself to forgive Hagar or to accept Ishmael as her own beloved son.

And it was true that Ishmael was not the child that God had promised Abram. He grew into a strong, wild lad, loved by Abram and disliked by Sarai; and Abram and Sarai kept on growing older.

When Abram was ninety-nine years old and Sarai herself, though younger, was past the age when she might have a child, the Lord appeared again to Abram and said: "I am the Almighty God, and I shall make a covenant with you. You have been faithful and have served me well; and you will be the father of many nations. From your children, and your children's children, there will come great men and kings, and all the land of Canaan will be theirs forever." And because Abram was to be the father of many nations, the Lord told him that his name would change. Instead of being Abram, which meant "exalted father," he would become Abraham, which meant "father of a multitude." Sarai, too, must change her name. Her new name would be Sarah, meaning "queen," for she would be the mother of nations and from her would come men who would be kings.

Then Abraham, who had believed the Lord all the years of his life, hardly dared to believe what he was hearing now. That he would still have his own child was so incredible to him that he laughed, and in his heart he said: "Shall a child be born to a man who is nearly a hundred years old? And to a woman who is ninety?" And he thought of the one son he did have, and whom he loved even though the boy was not Sarah's child. Abraham wanted good things for him, too. "O Lord, what of Ishmael?" he asked.

And God said: "I have blessed Ishmael. He, too, will have many children. Twelve princes will descend from him, and I will make of him a great nation. But my covenant is not with him but with the son of Sarah. For Sarah shall indeed bear a child, and you will call him Isaac. I say to you now that Sarah shall have a son at this same time next year."

Yet it was still hard for Abraham to believe, and harder still for Sarah.

THE VISIT OF THE STRANGERS

*O*ne day the Lord appeared to Abraham as he sat in the shaded doorway of his tent in the heat of the day. The old man looked up and saw three strangers walking toward him through the tall oak trees that gave cool shade to the camp, and he knew at once that they were from a very far country. In his heart he was sure that the Lord had come to him in the form of three angels from heaven. Whether they were angels or ordinary travelers through the desert, they would be well received by the hospitable Abraham; but somehow he knew that there was nothing ordinary about them.

He ran to meet them from the tent door and bowed low toward the ground. "My Lords," he said, "if I have found favor in your sight, do not travel on. Stay here, I pray you, and I will have water brought to you so that you may wash your feet. Do rest yourselves beneath the shady trees, and I will fetch a morsel of food so that you may refresh yourselves before you go upon your way."

They thanked him and accepted. "Do as you have said," they answered. "We will rest here with you."

So Abraham brought them cool water for their feet, for it was the custom that wayfarers should wash their feet and rest them as they paused upon their way. Then he hurried into the tent to find Sarah, and said: "Quickly, prepare three measures of fine meal, and knead it, and make cakes upon the hearth."

She set to work at once and without question while Abraham ran to the herd and chose a calf, a good young one and tender, which he gave to a young manservant to prepare and roast. When all was ready he took butter, milk, baked cakes, and roasted calf to the waiting strangers, and placed the food before them under the shade of a large tree. He stood by them beneath the tree while they were eating; and when they were rested and refreshed they talked to him.

"Where is your wife Sarah?" they asked, for their backs were toward his tent and they had not seen her yet.

"She is in the tent," said Abraham.

"The Lord shall bless her," said one, the one whom Abraham thought must be the Lord himself. "Sarah your wife will have a son at the appointed time, as I did promise."

Now Sarah stood hidden within the doorway of the tent, and she heard this, and she laughed. Many times before she had heard about this promise, and now it was much too late for it to come true. Both she and Abraham were very old: he was a hundred years, and she was ninety, well past the age when she could have a child. Therefore Sarah laughed silently within herself.

And the Lord, who was indeed among the strangers, said: "Why did Sarah laugh, and think to herself that she is too old to bear a child? Is anything too hard for the Lord? At the time appointed I will return to you and Sarah, and she will surely have her son."

Sarah heard this, and suddenly she was afraid. How could someone have heard her silent laughter and her innermost thoughts? "I did not laugh," she denied, looking out fearfully from the tent door.

"But you did laugh," said the Lord. Yet he was not angry, for he could understand her doubts.

Then the three men, with the Lord among them, rose from beneath the tree and looked toward Sodom, for it was toward the city that they were making their way. Abraham went with them for a short distance to show them the right road, and as he led them to the road to Sodom he wondered to himself what their business could be in that wicked city. His nephew Lot still lived there, and Abraham had heard many tales about the growing sinfulness among the people of the town. Again it seemed as though the Lord had heard his thoughts.

"Shall I hide from Abraham the thing I am about to do?" said the Lord. "No, because I know you, Abraham. I know that you will become a great and mighty nation, and that you will teach your children and your children's children to be righteous and keep the ways of the Lord. So I will tell you what I am going to have to do. I am going now to Sodom, because the people there are full of sin. The two cities, Sodom and Gomorrah, cry out their evil to the skies. I shall go first to Sodom, to see for myself if they are as bad as the report that has been brought to me, and I shall learn if these cities can really be as wicked as they seem. I shall know when I see them. And I will know what I must do with them."

Abraham stopped in the road and stood before the Lord. He knew what those words meant. He thought of Lot in Sodom, and other men who perhaps did not deserve to die. The two men with the Lord turned away and went on toward the wicked city, but Abraham still stood before the Lord.

"But surely you will not destroy the righteous with the wicked?" he said anxiously. "Perhaps there are fifty good people within the walls of Sodom. Would you also destroy them with the city, or would you spare the place because of them? It would not be like the Lord to slay the righteous with the wicked. It would not be right. And shall not the Judge of all the earth do right?"

The Lord felt pity for Abraham and all the people of the city. "If I find fifty righteous people in Sodom," God said to Abraham, "I will not destroy the people or the city. All Sodom will be saved because of them."

Abraham thought this over. He felt that he was taking too much upon himself to talk in this way to the Lord of all the earth, but he had to try again. He wondered if the number of fifty was not too much to hope for. "Perhaps there will be a few less than fifty," he suggested. "Perhaps five less. Would you destroy the whole city for the lack of five good men to make up fifty?"

The Lord said, "If I find but forty-five good men, I will not destroy the city."

But Abraham still felt troubled. He did not want any good men to be destroyed along with the bad, but from all accounts that he had heard of Sodom it was not likely that as many as forty-five righteous people could be found there. "Perhaps there will be no more than forty," he said hesitantly.

The Lord was patient with him, for the Lord himself did not want to destroy good men. "For the sake of forty I will not destroy the city," he told Abraham.

Forty seemed rather a lot to expect in a town like Sodom. Abraham went on pleading. "Oh, do not be angry with me, Lord, but what if there are less than forty? No more, perhaps, than thirty?"

"Then I will not do it," the Lord answered. "If I find thirty good souls there, I will not do it."

"Lord," said Abraham, "now that I have taken it upon my humble self to speak to you in this way, I cannot help going on. May I ask what will happen if there are twenty good men found in Sodom?"

"I will spare the city for the sake of twenty."

But perhaps there would be fewer than twenty good men found in Sodom, and one of them his nephew Lot. "Oh, please do not be angry, Lord," Abraham begged him. "This is the last time I will speak. What if there are only ten?"

"If there are ten good men, then for the sake of ten I will not destroy it," the Lord assured him, and went upon his way. Abraham watched him walk off into the distance toward the wicked city, and then returned to the place of his tents to think about the fate of Sodom and his brother's son.

He could only hope that the angels of the Lord would find ten good men in the midst of all that wickedness so that they and their city could be saved.

THE FATE OF SODOM

*O*f all the five cities in the vale of Siddim near the Salt Sea, the city of Sodom and the neighboring town of Gomorrah were the worst in sinfulness. Yet Lot had freely chosen to make the city of Sodom his home, knowing that he could make a good living by supplying the townspeople with fresh meat from his herds and believing that their wickedness would have no effect upon him. In spite of their evil ways, the people of Sodom had enough respect for Lot to allow him to become a great man in their city, and as time passed they came to regard him as one of their judges or wise men. And as a wise man he became accustomed to sit at the main gate of the city where he could be easily found when people sought his advice in settling their quarrels.

On the evening of the day during which Abraham had been visited by the two angels and the Lord, Lot was sitting in his usual place near the gate of Sodom when two strangers approached and entered through the gate. Lot knew how the people of Sodom were used to treating strangers; instead of offering friendly greetings they would make sport of newcomers, and instead of offering food and rest they would offer brutality and cruel harm. Lot quickly rose to meet the two men, unaware that they were angels of the Lord come to see the wickedness of Sodom for themselves, and he bowed low toward the ground.

"I greet you, my Lords," he said. "Come into my house, I pray you, and refresh yourselves, and stay the night. Rise up early if you wish and then go on your way, but do not try to go further in the city tonight."

"No, we thank you," the two men answered Lot. "We will spend the night in the street."

"No, my Lords," Lot said firmly. "You shall not stay here in the street." He was sure that the strangers would not be safe unless he offered them protection from the people of Sodom. "I beg you to join me in my house." As the two men looked around and saw the filth of the streets and the leering faces of the people who were crowding around, they began to think that perhaps they would be better off to accept Lot's invitation. But they were there to see what Sodom was like and so they hesitated, looking carefully at the people who stared back curiously and talked excitedly among themselves about how they might rob and hurt the strangers.

Lot pressed them. He insisted. They must please come with him to his house, he said. Finally they nodded and followed him into his home. As darkness fell upon the city they went with Lot to wash their travel-weary feet and rest within his house. Lot made a feast for them, and they ate gratefully. Soon they would lie down to sleep.

But before they could lie down there came a loud knocking at the door. The word of Lot's two visitors had spread throughout the town, and the people of Sodom wanted to amuse themselves by tormenting the two strangers. Young and old, and from every quarter of the city, they swarmed around Lot's house and demanded that he let them in or turn his guests over to them so that they could have their awful fun. "Where are the men who came to your house tonight?" they shouted to Lot as they battered against the doors and windows. "Bring them out to us!"

Lot went out of his house alone and stood with his back against the door.

"I pray you, my brothers," he said quietly, "stop your wickedness. Leave these men alone. Do what you like to my family, but spare the strangers in my house. They came under my roof for shelter, and shelter they shall have." But his words did nothing to change the men of Sodom except to make them even more angry and excited. "Stand aside!" they shouted. "You are nothing but a stranger here yourself, and you have made yourself a judge over us. If you do not get out of our way we will deal worse with you than with those other men!" They crowded rudely against him, pushing him brutally and almost succeeding in breaking down the door. But the two men inside quickly reached out their hands and dragged Lot into the house with them and firmly shut the door.

The door shuddered and creaked, and almost splintered inward under the savage battering of the Sodomites. But suddenly the heavy pounding stopped, and instead of howling for the blood of the two strangers the men of Sodom howled with fear. Each one of them, the great ones and the small alike, had been struck blind by a power they could not understand, and they could no longer even find the door to hammer on it. At last Lot realized that he was harboring angels in his house, for it was they who had struck the men outside with blindness.

The heavenly agents had seen for themselves that Lot was a good man who would risk his own life to save theirs, but it was clear to them that it was unlikely they would find as many as nine other good people in this terrible town.

And they said to Lot: "Do you have any other family in this town? Sons, daughters, sons-in-law, or anyone else? If you have, get them out of Sodom, for this place is about to be destroyed. It is evil altogether, and the Lord himself has sent us to destroy it."

Lot hurried off to speak to his sons-in-law, and said to them: "Get up! Get out of this place! Listen to me and go, for the Lord is about to destroy the city." But he could not make them understand that he was serious, and they would not believe that Sodom would be destroyed. They laughed, and made no move to leave.

Very early on the following morning, before the sun had even touched the sky, the angels aroused Lot and begged him to hurry away. "Arise!" they said urgently. "Take your wife and the two daughters who live with you, and go quickly from the city or else you will die with it."

It was hard for Lot to leave. Sodom had been his home for many years. If he fled now, after so little preparation, he would be leaving much behind: his home, his lands, his riches, even part of his family. And so he lingered, casting longing eyes at the things he did not want to leave. But the Lord was merciful to Lot and did not let him stay. As he lingered, the angels of the Lord took hold of Lot, his wife, and their two daughters, and dragged them away by the hand until they were well outside the city walls. "Now you must run for your lives," the Lord said through his angels. "Do not look back, and do not stay here in the plain. Go to higher ground; escape to the mountain, or you will perish with all the people of the plain."

"Not the mountain!" pleaded Lot. "My Lord, you have shown me great mercy by saving my life. I beg you, show me more mercy yet. I cannot escape to the mountain, for some evil might overtake me and I shall die. There is a small city nearby that we may flee to. It is much closer than the mountain, and it is only a little city so it cannot be too bad and it is not much to save. Is it not a little one? Spare that little city, Lord, I beg you, and let us escape to it and go to live there."

He was talking about the city of Zoar, one of the five cities of the plain that lay near the Salt Sea. Although its reputation was not so good as it might have been, the Lord decided to save it and thus make escape easier for Lot.

And through one of his angels he said to Lot: "I will do what you ask, and I will not overthrow the city of Zoar. But you must hurry. Escape to it quickly, and do not waste time by looking back. There is no longer any time to lose."

Lot hurried toward the tiny city. The sun was rising just as he and his daughters entered Zoar, and all at once the earth began to tremble and quake and the sky was red with an ugly light. Behind

them, the ground split open with a rumbling sound that was like
the loudest thunder, and the plain heaved mightily. Fire and
sulphur seemed to pour down from the very heavens themselves,
and the waters of the Salt Sea churned and boiled. Buildings
shook and flew apart, and the earth crumbled. Hot ash and blazing fire, flying sulphur and streams of scalding water rained down
upon Sodom and Gomorrah and the neighboring cities of the
plain; and the Lord overthrew those cities and the people in
them. The plain itself was swamped with the fire from above and
the walls of salty water that were thrown out by the churning sea,
so that everything that lived and grew upon it was destroyed.
Nothing was left undamaged on the plain of the Salt Sea but the
little town of Zoar. Its people were unhurt; Lot and his daughters
were safe.

But not Lot's wife! She was behind her husband and daughters
as they ran, because she had been slow to tear herself away from
the city that had been her home, and when the earth began to
quake and roar she was still behind him; and she did look back.
She paused for a moment too long. There in the vale of the Salt
Sea she was engulfed by the waters that boiled and plunged beneath the fiery heavens, and she was caught there on the plain.
And she herself became a pillar of salt.

Early that same morning Abraham left his tent and went to the
place where he had stood before the Lord and pleaded for Lot
and the people of Sodom. The distant sky was a strange color and
the winds brought back to him the smell of sulphur. So there had
not been ten good men, he thought.

But God had remembered Abraham, and had sent Lot safely
out of the midst of the giant upheaval that was still overthrowing
the cities of the plain. As Abraham looked across the plain toward
Sodom and Gomorrah he could see the smoke of the country
rising like the smoke of a furnace. His heart grieved for all the
people, wicked though they had been. He watched in sadness for
a while and then went back to his tent beneath the trees near
peaceful Hebron.

Lot was not happy in the town of Zoar; somehow he no longer felt safe upon that devastated plain. In his fear he decided to leave town. With his two daughters he went up into the mountain that he had avoided before, and the three of them lived in a cave without any of the comforts they had been used to all their lives. Gone were all the sheep and cattle; gone were all the riches; gone Lot's wife, and gone the sons-in-law; and all because in earlier years Lot had chosen to pitch his tent near Sodom. But at least he was alive.

Years later, Lot's older daughter had a son whom she called Moab, who became the father of the Moabites; and Lot's younger daughter bore a son called Ben-Ammi, whose descendants were the Ammonites. Both the Moabites and the Ammonites were to cross the lives of the Hebrews in the land of Canaan throughout the years to come.

But that was far into the future, and in the meantime Lot lived almost like a hermit in his cave. And Abraham and Sarah were still waiting for their dreamed-of child.

THE SONS OF ABRAHAM
(The Story of Hagar and Ishmael)

*A*braham was a hundred years old when his son Isaac was born to him and Sarah. For the Lord did visit Sarah as he had said he would, and he did fulfill the long-awaited promise. And thus did Sarah bear Abraham a son in his old age, at the very time of which the Lord had spoken.

Sarah remembered how she had laughed when she had overheard the prophecy of the stranger resting underneath the trees. Then her laughter had held the bitterness of disbelief, but now she could laugh with a heart full of happiness. "God has given me reason to laugh, so that all that hear will laugh with me," she said joyfully. "Who would have thought that Sarah should have given a child to Abraham, and both of us so old?"

The baby Isaac grew and left his mother's arms. When he was barely past babyhood and only just big enough to explore the settlement of large tents and shady trees for himself, Abraham decided that his son was old enough to be shown off to their friends and relatives in the neighboring tent towns. He gave a great feast in celebration; and the two old parents were filled with quiet pride in their young son. It was a wonderfully festive occasion, but something happened to spoil it for the people who had most reason to be happy. Sarah saw the son of Hagar, the Egyptian woman, making fun of little Isaac. Ishmael was a lad of four-teen by this time, and Sarah did not like the way he treated her small boy.

Angrily, she said to Abraham: "Send away this Egyptian woman and her son! My son shall not grow up with that boy, and that woman's son shall not be heir with Isaac. Send them both away from here!"

This was a hard thing to ask of Abraham, who himself asked little of life but that everyone should live in the ways of God and be content. He loved his Sarah deeply and would do anything in his power to make her happy. Yet he also loved his son Ishmael and did not want to send him away, perhaps even into danger, for in those days people who lived or journeyed without protection were almost certain to run into trouble of some kind. Even if there were no question of danger, he did not want to be unfair to Hagar and her boy. And he would miss his firstborn son. Therefore Abraham was exceedingly unhappy.

God saw his sorrow and told him not to grieve. "Listen to Sarah," said the Lord. "Do whatever she says. And do not grieve because of the lad, or because of the woman. It is with Isaac that I have my covenant, and it is through Isaac that your name shall be forever known and your family shall be blessed. As for the son of the Egyptian woman, I will also make a nation of him, because he is your child. Therefore, have no fear for Ishmael and Hagar."

Abraham was still grieving in his heart when he arose very early the next morning to say farewell to Ishmael and the woman from Egypt who had borne him, but his pain was less and he no longer feared for them. He took food from his supplies and gave it to Hagar and placed a bottle of water on her shoulder; and he sent her away with her child.

Hagar took the boy from Abraham's home and walked for many days, heading for her own distant homeland of Egypt through the wilderness of Beersheba. And there in the wilderness the two of them wandered alone and without help, meeting no one on the way to offer them food or a place to rest. The day came when their food ran out and the water bottle was drained of its last drop. They went on walking, more slowly all the time, looking for a well or spring so that they might at least be able to drink. But there was no water in sight; nothing but the hot sun blazing down on them, the burning desert shimmering with the heat, and the low shrubs that gave off scarcely any shade and not a drop of moisture.

Together they stumbled on as long as they could move, still hoping that help would come from somewhere. At last Hagar could go on no longer. She and young Ishmael were faint for the lack of food and water, and tired of the endless walking with nothing to sustain them. Their hope gone and their bodies weak, they stopped where they were and sank down onto the burning sand. Hagar rested for a moment and drew breath for what she had to do. Lovingly, and with a heart that was near to breaking, she laid her son beneath one of the small shrubs so that he would have its scant shade to comfort him if nothing else. Then she turned and walked away as far as she could go; as far as an arrow shot from a bow, but no more, for she was deadly tired and heartsore and could go no further. Yet she could not bring herself to stay beside that small shrub and watch the suffering of Ishmael. She sat down, then, and the tears trickled down her face. "I cannot bear to see the death of the child," she wept, and turned her head away. In her heart she was sure that he would not last long, and that she would follow soon after.

But God had not forgotten her, or his promise to both her and Abraham; and they were not alone and lost in the wilderness. He heard their voices, and he answered.

"Hagar! Do not be afraid, for I have heard the cry of the lad where he lies. Arise! Lift up the boy and take him by the hand, for you shall both be saved and I will make of him a great nation."

And God opened her eyes, and she saw a well of water. With new strength she rose and filled the bottle with water, and gave it to the lad to drink. They went on then, the woman and the boy, but not as far as Egypt. Hagar made an end to their wanderings when they came to the Wilderness of Paran, and made a home for the two of them in the wild country. God watched over them in their lonely home and saw that no harm came to them. The boy grew tall and strong, and became a man skilled in hunting with the bow and arrow. His mother took him a wife out of the land of Egypt, and soon Ishmael had children of his own. His sons were strong, rough men of the outdoors even as he; and *their* sons counted among them twelve princes and twelve mighty tribes. And thus, out of Ishmael, there came a nation.

THE SACRIFICE OF ISAAC

*A*s the years passed Isaac grew into a fine young lad who loved his father as much as Abraham loved him. Just as Abraham obeyed the Lord, so did Isaac trust and obey his father Abraham in every way. God watched over them both, never forgetting his promise that Abraham would become the father of a multitude through his son Isaac.

Yet God had one more test for Abraham, and it was a very difficult one. The Lord had taught his people that he required their complete faith and love, even their lives, and that they should be willing to offer everything to him. And yet at the same time he had said that no man should shed another's blood. A burnt offering from a man's flocks, given freely and with all his heart, was enough to show a man's desire to offer all he had. The sacrifice of a man himself, or of a beloved child, was wrong in the eyes of God. And the Lord wanted to be sure that Abraham understood this even while he proved his love and faith.

And so he tested Abraham, the founder of the Hebrew race from which the savior of the world would come.

"Abraham!" he called.

"I am here, Lord," Abraham answered.

And God gave him a terrible command that would require a special kind of obedience and trust from Abraham.

"Take your son," said God, "Isaac, your only son, and bring him with you into the land of Moriah. There you will give him up to me as a burnt offering upon a mountain that I will show to you."

Abraham did not question God. He, too, remembered God's promise that his family, through Isaac, would be great and blessed. If he wondered at all at God's command, he wondered how the promise could possibly come true if he gave up Isaac as an offering. And yet he did believe the promise. He had faith, and he obeyed.

He rose early in the morning and made ready to go. It was a long way to the land of Moriah and he could not walk the whole way with the boy's hand held in his. So he called two of his young menservants to him, saddled his donkey, and cut wood for the fire he would build upon the mountain. When the donkey was laden with the wood he sent for Isaac; and then they left on their long journey.

On the third day he saw the place from afar, the place that God had told him of. As they drew near Abraham said to the young men: "Stay here with the donkey while the boy and I go up into the mountain and worship. Wait, and we will come back to you when we have made the offering." For his love was so great and his faith was so strong that even while he was prepared to give up Isaac to his Lord he was sure in his heart that God would somehow return his son to him.

He took the wood for the burnt offering and laid it on Isaac's shoulder to carry, and he himself took the fire and a knife. Father and son went off together to climb the mountain where the offering would be made. As they climbed Isaac began to wonder why they had not brought anything to offer on the altar.

"Father?" he asked, looking at the things Abraham carried in his hands.

"I am here, my son."

"I see the wood and I see the fire, but where is the lamb for the offering?"

"My son," said Abraham, "God will provide himself a lamb for a burnt offering." That was enough for Isaac, for he trusted in his father and his father's God. They went on climbing together.

When they came to the place on top of the mountain that God had told him of, Abraham built an altar of stones and laid the wood upon it. Isaac looked around; he still could see no lamb.

Abraham reached gently for his son and bound his hands and feet. This time Isaac asked no question. Then Abraham laid his son upon the wood of the altar and reached out his hand for the knife. He raised it slowly, still willing to give everything to God and still believing that God would not take his son from him forever.

He brought the knife up high, ready for the downward plunge.

"Abraham! Abraham!" a voice called out. He stopped. It was the angel of the Lord calling to him out of heaven. Abraham turned the knife aside and listened. "Here I am," he said.

"Do not lay your hand upon the lad," said the angel of the Lord. "Do no harm to Isaac. Now I know that your love for God is deep and true and that you are obedient, seeing that you did not withhold your son, Isaac your only son, from him. Lift up your eyes!"

And Abraham lifted up his eyes and looked around him. As he turned he saw behind him a ram caught in the bushes by its horns. Quickly, he untied his son, rejoicing in his heart. He went and took the ram from the thicket, and offered it up on the altar for a burnt offering in the place of his beloved son. It was all that God required; Abraham had already proved not only his obedience but his trust.

When he and the boy had worshiped God and completed the offering, Abraham gave a name to the place where he had been prepared to give up Isaac, and where he had told his son that God would provide himself a lamb. He called it Jehovah-jireh, meaning "The Lord will provide." Now he knew even better than before that God would provide for those who truly loved him. And he also knew that God did not want his people offered to him as gifts on blazing altars, for those whose faith and love was strong already belonged to God with their hearts and souls.

Father and son walked together down the mountainside and returned, as Abraham had said they would, to the young men who were waiting.

REBEKAH AT THE WELL

Sarah died when she was a hundred and twenty-seven years old. Abraham wept for her and mourned his loss; but their life together had been long and good and she had given him a son to comfort him. Because the land of their forefathers was so far away, Abraham bought a burial plot from one of his neighbors, one Ephron of the Hittite tribe. Ephron's field was called Machpelah, and on it there were many trees and a cave that would serve well as a burial place. Therefore Abraham laid his wife to rest in the cave of Machpelah, close to the plain of Mamre where they had lived together for so many years. Thus Sarah became the first of all the Hebrew people to die and be buried in the land of Canaan, the land that God had promised to the descendants of Abraham.

Isaac was a grown man and Abraham was very old; but the Lord had blessed him in all things. When the loss of Sarah had become less painful to him he began to think of Isaac's loneliness, for it was time that Isaac should take a wife. Now, though Abraham was friendly with his neighbors and respected by them, he did not wish his tribe to merge with theirs. It was necessary, he felt, to find a Hebrew maiden for his son to marry. And he remembered that his brother Nahor and his wife Milcah had remained, years earlier, at Haran in the district of Padan-Aram, and he had heard that their family now was large with children and their children's children. It would be most desirable, Abraham believed, if Isaac were to marry a cousin from Padan-Aram. But he did not want Isaac to leave Canaan himself and go back into the land the Lord had commanded him to leave.

Therefore he called to him one day the oldest steward of his house, the one who ruled over everything he had, and gave to him the task of finding a suitable wife for Isaac. "Give me your hand and swear to me," he said, "by the Lord who is the God of heaven and earth, that you will not take a wife for my son from the daughters of the Canaanites among whom I dwell, but that you will go back into my old country to look among my kinsmen for a wife for Isaac."

The steward felt that this would be no easy task. "Perhaps," he said, "the woman I choose will not be willing to come with me from her land to ours. And perhaps your son Isaac will not approve my choice. Should I not take him back into the land from which you came so that he might make his own choice?"

But that was not what Abraham wanted. And he said: "No, you shall not take my son with you into that land. The Lord God of heaven, who took me from my father's house and promised this land to me, will surely send you his angel to guide you, and you shall choose a wife for Isaac according to his guidance. Give me your oath that you will do as I ask. If the woman is not willing to follow you, then I shall free you from the oath and not blame you. Only do not take my son back to that place. Now swear to me."

"I do swear it," the trusted servant said, and gave his hand to Abraham. "I shall go and do as you say."

He took ten of his master's camels and loaded them with goods for gifts. Then he departed, taking with him several of Abraham's men to help him with the camels, and traveled for many days across the plains and deserts to the land of Mesopotamia where Abraham's brother had made his home. At last he stopped at a well outside the city of Haran in the district of Padan-Aram and waited for the guidance that would lead him to the family of Nahor and a wife for Isaac.

It was evening when he arrived, and it was the time when the women of the town came out to draw water from the well. The steward watched them as they drew near, and he made his camels kneel beside the well. He did not know what he could do but put his trust in God. Therefore he prayed within his heart. "O Lord God of my master Abraham, I pray you, help me this day and show kindness to my master Abraham. Behold, I stand here by the well, where the daughters of the men of the city come out to draw water for their houses. Give me, I pray, a sign. Let it be that the young woman I shall ask for water to drink from her pitcher will say to me, 'Drink, and I will give your camels drink also.' Let her be the one whom you have chosen for your servant Isaac. By this sign shall I know her, and know that you are showing kindness to my master."

Even before he had finished speaking in his heart, a young woman came down to the well with her pitcher on her shoulder. The maiden's name was Rebekah, and she was very fair to look upon and not yet married. She lowered her pitcher into the well and brought it up brimming with cool water. The steward watched her, wondering if she might be the one. He went to meet her, and asked the question he had planned to ask. "Let me, I pray you, drink a little water from your pitcher."

And she said, "Drink, my lord." And although he was a stranger she was courteous to him, lowering her pitcher at once into her hand and offering it to him so that he might drink. When his thirst was quenched she said: "I will draw water for your camels also, until they have had enough to drink." As she spoke she emptied the pitcher into the drinking trough, and hurried to the well to draw more water so that all the camels might drink their fill. The man wondered at her, but he held his peace. It was the sign that he had been praying for, yet he still could not know for certain whether the Lord had made his journey a success or not.

He would know only when he had found out who this kindly maiden was.

When the camels had finished drinking, the man took from a satchel a golden earring and two gold bracelets as a gift of thanks. He gave them to the girl and asked: "Whose daughter are you? And tell me, I beg of you, is there room in your father's house for us to lodge in?"

And she said to him: "I am the daughter of Bethuel, who is the son of Milcah and Nahor. There is room for you to lodge in, and both straw and feed enough for all the camels. I will tell my father that you are here."

She smiled and turned away. Abraham's steward bowed his head and worshiped God. The granddaughter, her very self, of Abraham's brother Nahor! "Blessed be the Lord God of my master Abraham," the man prayed thankfully. "You have been merciful to my master and answered my prayer, for you have led me to the house of my master's brother."

Rebekah ran to her family's house to tell them about the friendly stranger at the well. Now Rebekah had a brother named Laban, and when he heard Rebekah's story and saw the golden gifts in his sister's hands, Laban went out to meet the man who was standing with his camels at the well.

"Come in, you blessed of the Lord," he said, with welcome in his voice. "Why do you stand outside? For the house is ready for you, and there is room for the camels. Come!"

So Abraham's servant and the men who had come with him went into the house of Bethuel the son of Nahor, Abraham's brother, and they were received with kindness even though the family did not yet know who this stranger was. Laban brought water for the travelers' feet and himself attended to the camels, unharnessing them and giving them their feed and straw. When that was done he saw to it that food was set before his visitors to eat; but Abraham's head servant would not eat until he had explained his errand. "First let me tell you why I have come to you," he said.

"Very well, speak on," said Laban. He and his father listened courteously and with growing interest while the steward spoke.

"I am Abraham's servant," he began. "The Lord has blessed my master greatly, so that he has become great himself. God has given him flocks and herds, and silver and gold, and menservants and maidservants, and camels and donkeys. Sarah, my master's wife, bore him a son when she was old, and that son Isaac is heir to everything that Abraham has. But Isaac is not yet married, so my master sent me to find a wife for him among his own people, for he would not have Isaac marry a daughter of the Canaanites." Then Abraham's servant explained how his master had made him swear an oath and sent him off with a promise that an angel would guide his choice at the proper time; and how Rebekah, in answer to his prayer, had offered water not only to him but to his thirsty camels. "Now tell me," he finished, "if you will deal kindly and truly with my master, or if you will not, so that I will know which way to turn and what is right."

Then Laban and his father Bethuel answered: "This has come to us from the Lord, and it is not for us to say whether it is good or bad. See, Rebekah is here. Take her and go, and let her be the wife of your master's son, as the Lord has spoken." For they truly believed that it was the Lord who had sent them Abraham's servant, and that the Lord desired Rebekah to go.

When Abraham's servant heard their words he was deeply thankful to the Lord who had guided him to the family of Nahor. He bowed down to the earth and worshiped, with a grateful heart, the God who had helped him in his task. Afterward he brought forth from his satchels the riches he had brought from Abraham: jewels of silver and of gold, earrings, bracelets, goblets, cloth, and beautiful clothes from the far-off land of Canaan; and he gave them to Rebekah. He also gave her brother Laban and their mother many precious things that pleased them and showed to all that Abraham and Isaac were men of wealth and standing.

When he had told his story and given to all the rich gifts from Abraham, he at last consented to eat. He and the men who had come with him on the journey ate and drank, and spent the night resting at the house of Bethuel, the father of Rebekah.

When they rose in the morning the steward said: "Now I must return to my master with the girl Rebekah."

But his visit had been so unexpected that the family of the girl had had no time to get used to the idea of saying goodbye to her and watching her go far off into a strange land. Laban and his mother did not want her to leave so suddenly, so soon. "Let her stay with us for a few days, ten days at least," they asked the steward. "After that time she shall go with you."

Yet the steward had completed his mission and was eager to be on his way. "No, do not hinder me," he said. "The Lord has made my journey a success, and now I must go back to my master with the maiden!"

They hesitated still, for they did not know how Rebekah felt about hurrying off with scarcely time to catch her breath. "We will call the girl and ask her what she has to say," they said. They called her and she came at once. "Will you go with this man?" they asked her. For they loved her and wanted to be sure that she was doing what she wished.

"I will go," Rebekah said.

So they blessed her lovingly, and helped her to prepare the things she needed for her journey. And they sent her away, Rebekah their sister and her nurse and several handmaidens, with Abraham's head servant and his men. The steward rode ahead to lead the way, and behind him rode his men and all the women of Rebekah's party. Bethuel and his family watched them ride off on their camels until they were no more than dots upon the desert.

They rode for many days, following much the same route as that taken by Abraham a long, long time before when he had left his brother Nahor in Haran to venture, with Lot, into the promised land of Canaan. Rebekah traveled with her face uncovered, looking at the new country from her camel's back and wondering all the time what manner of man her husband would turn out to be.

At last they reached the south country where Isaac lived with Abraham. It was evening, and Isaac was walking in the fields and meditating as the sun dipped low over the land that belonged to him and Abraham. He lifted up his eyes and saw the caravan of camels coming from a distance, and he started walking toward the distant dust.

Rebekah also lifted up her eyes. When she saw the man in the distance she got down from her camel, for she felt who the man might be and wanted to meet him on foot.

"Who is that man who is walking in the field to meet us?" she asked the steward.

"It is my master Isaac," he told her.

Thereupon Rebekah took a veil and covered her face, as was the custom among the women of her people. Later, when they had properly met, she would unveil and he could see her. But it was not yet time for that.

Isaac and the camel caravan came together near his dwelling place, and both halted. The servant told Isaac everything that he had done, and how the Lord had guided him to the daughter of Bethuel; and Isaac was well pleased.

A while later he took Rebekah into his mother Sarah's tent and made it into a home for her. She became his wife, and they loved each other deeply. And thus was Isaac comforted after his mother's death.

ESAU LOSES HIS BIRTHRIGHT

*A*braham himself was not too old to require comfort. He took another wife, whose name was Keturah, and she bore him six fine sons. The old man was fond of them and gave them many gifts, but he still remembered that God's promise would come true through Isaac and he was determined that Isaac should be his only heir. He sent his young sons away to live in the east country, while he and Isaac remained in the southland, and apart from the gifts that he had given the six boys he gave all he had to Isaac.

Then Abraham died at a good ripe age, a man full of years. He was one hundred and seventy-five years old when he was gathered to his people. Ishmael, the son of Hagar, came from the wilderness to say farewell, and he and Isaac buried the old man in the cave of Machpelah near Mamre, where Abraham's wife Sarah had been laid to rest more than forty years before.

Isaac and Rebekah made their home at Beersheba, where Abraham had once dug a well of water and planted a grove of trees. Years passed, and it began to look as though Rebekah would not have a child. Then Isaac prayed to the Lord for his wife, and the Lord granted his prayer. There was something that troubled Rebekah, though, and she inquired of the Lord why she felt as she did.

And the Lord said to Rebekah: "Two nations are within you, and two kinds of people. The one shall be stronger than the other, and the elder shall serve the younger."

When her time came Rebekah gave birth to twin sons. The first to be born was redheaded and hairy, and they named him Esau; the second was smooth-skinned and more slight of build, and they called him Jacob.

And the boys grew.

Esau was the rough and hearty one. He was strong and swift of foot, a wily hunter and man of the outdoors who lived among the birds and beasts of the field. Jacob, the younger by little more than seconds, was a plain man and a quiet one who dwelled in the tents and preferred to stay close to home minding his father's flocks. Isaac loved both his sons, but he loved Esau the more because he was so very strong and manly, and because when he came from the hunt he brought venison that he prepared in just the way to delight his father. But Rebekah loved Jacob, the quiet man of dignity. Isaac's family was rich, important in the district and destined to be great, and Rebekah's feeling was that Esau was not the proper man to be Isaac's heir.

Because of Rebekah, Jacob came more and more to think about his misfortune in being born after his brother. As the elder son, Esau had the birthright. That meant, among the people of those lands and those times, that when Isaac died Esau would inherit a double portion of whatever his father left. It also meant that he would become the head of the family with all the patriarch's rights and responsibilities, and with certain priestly privileges and duties. In the case of the family of Abraham and Isaac, the birthright was even more than usually important: Esau, as the oldest son of Abraham's son, was in line to receive great blessings from the Lord who had made the promise of greatness to Abraham and Isaac. But Esau did not seem interested in the honor of having such a precious birthright. He was in love with the outdoors and the simple things of life, and he gave not a thought to the question of his birthright and his future as the head of the family. He knew he was the elder son. Why should he spend his days thinking about it?

But Jacob and Rebekah thought about the birthright. Many times did Rebekah recall the words of the Lord, spoken before her children were born. Certainly they were different, and one was surely stronger than the other, at least in terms of physical strength. Possibly Jacob would turn out to be the stronger in other ways. But the last part of the prophecy was especially puzzling. "The elder shall serve the younger." What could it mean? Rebekah wondered.

Jacob went on thinking about the birthright, and Esau went on forgetting about it.

One day, much like so many other days, Esau was out in the woods and fields and Jacob was among the tents. But this day Esau's hunt was long and unsuccessful, and he came home ravenous after his hard and useless work. The first thing he noticed was a delicious aroma of food. Jacob had been making a tasty lentil soup; and Esau had not found a deer all day. Esau sniffed hungrily. He was tired, and he was as hungry as a bear. He had been hunting all day for nothing, and he needed food.

"Feed me, I pray you," he begged his brother Jacob. "Give me some of that pottage, for I am faint with hunger."

Jacob turned and looked at him thoughtfully. "I will, if you sell me your birthright this day."

"I am starving to death!" said Esau, in his rough way. "What good will a birthright do me if I die of hunger?"

"Swear it to me!" said Jacob. "Swear that you will sell it to me if I give you food this day."

"I swear, I swear! The birthright is yours. Only give me the food before I drop."

And he sold his birthright to Jacob, and Jacob gave his brother Esau bread and lentil soup in exchange for all the rights of an elder son. Esau ate and drank and went upon his way, satisfied with his meal; and not until long afterward did he give any thought to the bargain he had made.

And thus did Esau throw away his birthright.

JACOB TRICKS HIS FATHER

*I*saac continued to prosper as he grew to old age. The Lord blessed him with great riches: abundant lands that gave forth plentiful crops; huge flocks and herds; and a multitude of servants. Some of his neighbors among the people of Canaan were envious of his wealth and alarmed because of his growing power in the land, yet they could not succeed in making war with him. The most unfriendly of his rivals were the Philistines who lived in the coastal lands of Canaan and repeatedly made trouble for Isaac as he dug wells in the desert in times of drought and famine, for they thought he was trespassing on their property and they feared his power. The more wells he dug the more anxious they became. They envied him his great wealth and his many servants, and because they themselves were accustomed to fighting for what they wanted to take they were afraid that he, with his ever-growing strength, would do the same to them. But Isaac was a man of peace, and eventually he managed to persuade even the Philistines that he had no wish to steal their lands or harm their people. He became known among all his neighbors as a peaceful, God-loving man blessed by the Lord.

After Isaac came to his understanding with the Philistines, life at Beersheba was peaceful and without event for several years.

And then, without consulting his father, Esau took two wives. Rebekah and Isaac were deeply distressed, not because their elder son had taken two wives but because the women were Hittites and not acceptable to a Hebrew family. But Isaac was forgiving, and his love for Esau did not lessen.

It came to pass that, when Isaac was old and his eyes were dim so that he could not see, he began to think of the day of his death and of the blessing that he must give his firstborn son before he died. The blessing would confirm the birthright and grant rights and riches to the blessed one, and was thus of great importance to the elder son. Isaac therefore called to Esau. "Come to me, my son," he said. And Esau came to him, saying, "I am here, my father."

"Look now, I am old," said Isaac. "I do not know when I shall die; it may be soon. Take your weapons, your quiver of arrows and your bow, and go out into the fields. Hunt the deer for me once more. Bring me some venison and prepare for me the savory meat such as I love. Give it to me then that I may eat; so that my soul may bless you before thy Lord before I die."

Esau left at once and went into the woods and fields to hunt for deer so that he might bring his father the tasty venison of which the old man was so fond.

But Rebekah had heard Isaac speaking to Esau, and she did not want the elder son to receive the blessing that was his right. She called her favorite son, Jacob, and told him what she had overheard and how Isaac wanted to bless Esau before he died. And then she said: "Now therefore, my son, obey my voice and do as I command you. Go to the flock and get me two young goats, kid goats that are good and tender, and I will prepare them in such a way that the meat will taste like the savory venison that Esau prepares. Then you will take it to your father so that he may eat the meat he loves, for he will not know the difference, and he will bless you before he dies. He will not see that you are Jacob, for his eyes are dim."

But Jacob was afraid that Isaac would not be so easily

deceived. "Yes, but my brother Esau is a hairy man," he told his mother, "and I am smooth. What if my father reaches out and touches me? Then he will feel that I am not hairy, and I shall seem to him as a deceiver. I will bring a curse down upon myself, and not a blessing."

"The curse will be on me, my son, not you," Rebekah said. "Only obey my voice and bring me the young kids."

Jacob went to the flock and picked out two tender young goats and brought them back to his mother. Skillfully she prepared the meat with herbs and spices so that it tasted like the venison Isaac enjoyed so much, and set the skins aside for later use. When the food was ready she took some of Esau's clothes and put them upon her younger son. Next, she covered Jacob's hairless hands and the smoothness of his neck with the soft, hairy skins of the young kids, and she gave to him the savory meat and bread that she had prepared. "Go to your father," Rebekah said.

And Jacob, in his borrowed skins and clothes, took the savory food to his father Isaac.

"I am here now, my father," he said, trying to sound like Esau.

"Who are you, my son?" said Isaac, uncertain of that voice.

"I am Esau, your firstborn," answered Jacob, "and I have done what you asked. Arise, I beg of you; sit up and eat the venison I have prepared for you, so that your soul may bless me."

Isaac was puzzled by the voice and by his son's unusually swift return from the hunt. "How is it that you found the meat so quickly, my son?" he asked.

"The Lord your God led me to it," answered Jacob.

Isaac was still not completely satisfied. "Come near to me, I pray you," he said, to this son he could not see. "Let me touch you, my son, so that I may know for certain that you are Esau."

Jacob went close to the old man and let him feel the false hairiness of his body. Blind Isaac touched the goat-skin-covered hands and neck of his younger son and wonderingly said: "The voice is Jacob's voice, but the hands are the hands of Esau." And

Isaac did not discover the deception, for Jacob's hands felt as hairy as his brother Esau's hands.

Isaac said again, "Are you truly my son Esau?"

"I am," said Jacob.

"Then bring the food to me," the old man said. "Bring, and I will eat of my son's venison, so that my soul shall bless you."

And Jacob brought it to him. Isaac ate the meat, and found it savory and delicious, and Jacob brought him wine to drink with it.

When Isaac had eaten the meal which he had asked from Esau and received from Jacob, he was ready to pronounce the precious blessing.

"Come near now and kiss me, my son," he said. Jacob drew close and leaned down for the kiss that went with the blessing. Isaac smelled the good smell of Esau's clothes, that carried with them the fragrance of the out-of-doors, the tang of the hunter and man of the soil, and the clean smell of the woods and fields. And Isaac blessed the younger son, saying: "See, the smell of my son is as the smell of a field which the Lord has blessed. Therefore, God give you of the dew of heaven, and the fatness of the earth, and plenty of corn and wine. Let people serve you, and nations bow down to you; be lord over your brothers, and let your mother's sons bow down to you. Cursed be every one that curses you, and blessed be every one that blesses you."

It was done. Jacob had deceived his father and once again tricked his brother Esau.

Now it happened, as soon as Isaac had finished blessing Jacob, and Jacob had scarcely left the presence of his father, that Esau returned from the hunt with venison. And he also made savory meat and brought it to his father.

"Rise up, my father, and eat of your son's venison," said Esau, "and then let your soul bless me as you have said."

Isaac sat up in great surprise. "Bless you? Who are you, then?"

"I am your firstborn son, Esau," said the hairy man.

And Isaac's old body started trembling all over. Something here was very wrong, and his distress was great.

"Who? Esau? Then who was it that prepared the venison and brought it to me before you came? For I have already eaten, and I have blessed the one who brought it. And the blessing remains his; blessed he shall be."

When Esau heard the words of his father he cried out with a great and bitter cry, for he knew at once that it was Jacob who had received the blessing meant for him. "Bless me, too, my father!" he pleaded.

Isaac was sorely troubled, for blessings were not given lightly and could not be taken away. "Your brother came to me with subtlety," he said sorrowfully, "and he has taken away your blessing."

Esau groaned with deep dismay. "My brother! Is he not rightly named Jacob, 'the supplanter'? Twice he has taken my place; twice he has used trickery to take something that is mine. He took away my birthright; and now he has taken away my blessing. Oh, my father! Have you not saved any blessing for me?"

And Isaac answered, saying: "How can that be? I have made him lord over you, and I have given all his brothers to him as his servants so that they will all serve him. With corn and wine in plenty have I provided him; and I have given to him all the blessing that is mine to give. What can be left that I may now do for you, my son?"

"One blessing only!" Esau begged. "Have you only the one to give? Oh, bless me, too, my father!" And Esau lifted up his voice and wept, for his loss was very great.

And Isaac his father, grieving, answered and said to him: "A blessing I shall give you, but it cannot be what I have already given Jacob of my own. Your dwelling shall be the richness of the earth and of the woods and fields you love, and of the dew of heaven from above. You will live by toil and by the sword, and you will serve your brother. But the day will come when power shall be yours, and then you will break his yoke from off your neck."

It was not so much a blessing as a promise for the future; and Esau hated Jacob because of the lost blessing. In his heart he swore that he would have revenge. "Not yet," he told himself. "Not while my father lives. But he is old and soon will die. When the days of mourning are over, I will surely kill my brother Jacob."

JACOB'S LADDER

*E*sau did not speak of his rage and hatred to his father, but neither did he keep it to himself. The news of his great anger spread, and his vengeful words soon came to the ears of Rebekah his mother.

She sent at once for Jacob and warned him of his danger. "Hear me, my son," she said. "Your brother Esau has sworn that he will kill you. Therefore obey my voice and go away from here. Flee to my brother Laban at Haran. Stay with him for a few days, until your brother's fury turns away and he forgets what you have done to him. Then I will send for you and bring you back, for I do not want to lose you."

Then she went to Isaac. Instead of telling him that she was afraid for Jacob's life she brought up a question that she knew was close to Isaac's heart. "I am weary of my life," she said, "because of the daughters of the Hittites. Esau has already married among them, and that is not the way of our people. If Jacob also takes a wife from those Hittite daughters of the land, what good is my life to me?"

Neither did her husband wish their second son to marry one of the women of Canaan. Isaac called Jacob to him and blessed him. "You shall not take a wife of the daughters of Canaan," he told his younger son. "Go to Padan-Aram, to the house of Bethuel from which your mother came, and find a wife among the daughters of your mother's brother Laban. May God Almighty bless you and give to you the blessing of Abraham, so that you will have many children and inherit this land that God has given us."

And thus did Isaac send Jacob away; and Jacob left his home in Beersheba and began his long and lonely journey to Haran. He did not know then that he was to be away for far longer than a few days, and that he would never see his mother again.

When Esau saw that Isaac had again blessed Jacob and sent him away to Padan-Aram to find a wife instead of marrying one of the daughters of the Hittites, he realized that his marriages to the women of Canaan did not please his father. He therefore took another wife; and this time he chose a daughter of his father's half-brother Ishmael, son of Abraham and Hagar.

In the meantime, Jacob was making his way across the hills and plains of Canaan, feeling unhappy and afraid. At last he came to a certain place where there were rocks for shelter, and because the sun had set he decided to stay there for the night. He took one of the stones of the place for a pillow, and lay down to sleep on his hard bed. As he slept, he dreamed.

In his dream he saw a ladder with its feet set upon the earth and the top of it reaching to the heavens, and the angels of God were going up and down upon it. And he saw the Lord God standing there above it, and the Lord spoke to him and said: "I am the Lord God of Abraham, and the God of Isaac. The land on which you are lying, this will I give to you and to your children. Your descendants shall be as many as there is dust upon the earth; and they will spread to the west, to the east, to the north, and to the south, and through them shall all the families of the earth be blessed. Behold, I am with you, and I will be with you wherever you may go, and I will bring you back again into this land. For I will not leave you until I have done what I have promised."

Jacob awoke from his sleep. He looked about him in the starlit night and he saw that he was alone; but he did not feel alone. And he said, "Surely the Lord is with me in this place, and I did not know it."

And he felt great awe. "How wonderful is this place!" he said reverently. "It is none other than the House of God, and this is the gate of heaven."

He rose early the following morning and took the stone he had used for a pillow and set it upright as if it were a pillar in monument to something holy. Then he anointed it with oil as an offering to God, and now indeed it was a holy monument. Though the name of the place was Luz, he renamed it Bethel, or "The House of God." And he made a vow, saying, "If God will be with me and watch over me as I go, and give me bread to eat and clothes to wear, and let me come again to my father's house in peace, then I shall know that the Lord is truly my God. And this stone, which I have set here for a pillar of worship, shall be God's house. And of all that God gives me I will surely give back to him a tenth."

Then Jacob left the place that he had dedicated to the Lord, and went on with his journey to Haran.

RACHEL AND LEAH

Though Jacob traveled alone he was not lonely, for the Lord watched over him as he went along his way. After several days in the desert he came into the land of the people of the east, where Rebekah's family dwelled, and he saw a sight that was a welcome change from the miles of rugged rock and desert sand that he had covered on his journey. It was a fertile field, such as herds and flocks use for their grazing; and Jacob knew that he had come again into the company of men.

He looked about him and saw a well in the field, and there were three flocks of sheep lying near it while their shepherds talked idly among themselves. This was the well out of which all the flocks in the neighborhood were watered, and a great stone covered its mouth while it was not in use. The stone was very heavy, so that it was only when all the flocks were gathered together that the shepherds would roll the stone from the well's mouth, give water to their sheep, and then put the stone back into place over the mouth of the well.

Jacob greeted the men. "Where are you from, my brothers?" he asked of them.

"We are from Haran," they answered, "and this is Haran's well."

Jacob's heart was full of joy, for he was at his journey's end and soon he would see his mother's family.

"Do you know Laban, of the family of Nahor?" he asked.

And they said, "We know him."

"Is he well?" asked Jacob.

"He is well," replied the shepherds. "Look yonder; there comes his daughter Rachel with the sheep."

Jacob looked and saw her coming, and he noticed again that the well was covered even though the flocks were lying nearby.

"What are you waiting for?" he asked. "It is high noon. Why do you not give water to your sheep, and then take them to the field and let them feed?"

"We cannot," they answered, "until all the flocks are gathered together and the stone is rolled away from the mouth of the well. Then we water the sheep. But they are not all here yet."

And while Jacob was still talking to them, Rachel came to the well with her father's sheep, for it was she who tended them. When Jacob looked at Rachel, the daughter of his mother's brother Laban, he decided that so comely a girl should not be kept waiting until all the flocks were there. He went quickly to the mouth of the well and rolled the heavy stone away without the help of any other man, and afterward he himself watered the flock of Laban his mother's brother. Then he turned to the lovely girl and saw that she was looking at him with surprise, for she was not used to such special treatment from her neighboring shepherds.

"You are my cousin Rachel," he told her, "for I am Jacob, the son of Rebekah, who is your father's sister." And then Jacob kissed Rachel and wept tears of joy, so glad was he to see a member of his family after his long journey. He was glad, too, to meet such a lovely relative so soon after arriving at Haran.

Rachel hurried home to tell her father of the meeting at the well. And when Laban heard that Jacob, his own sister's son, had come to visit them, he ran to meet him. The two men embraced warmly, and Laban welcomed Jacob into his house. Jacob told him again what he had told Rachel, and gave his uncle news of Rebekah and her home in Canaan. "Surely you are my flesh and bone," said Laban, "and you shall stay with us and welcome."

Jacob stayed with him, working in the fields and helping Laban with his flocks and cattle. During his youth in Canaan among his father's flocks Jacob had become a skillful shepherd farmer and his knowledge of farming with animals was much greater than that of his uncle Laban. And Laban saw that he was very useful to him in the fields. He said to Jacob, "Because you are my sister's son, should you therefore work for me for nothing? No, you shall be paid for your services. Tell me, what should your wages be?"

Now Laban had two daughters. Leah, the older of the two, was plain-looking and undesirable in Jacob's eyes. But Rachel, the younger, was beautiful and pleasing to look upon. And Jacob had loved her from the start. He said to Laban, "I will serve seven years for your younger daughter Rachel."

Laban nodded agreeably. "It is better that I give her to you than to any other man. It is agreed, then. Stay with me, and my daughter shall be yours."

At the end of his term of service Jacob approached his uncle Laban. "Give me my wife," he said, "because I have fulfilled our agreement and the days are ended."

Again, Laban agreed. He gathered together all the men of the place and prepared a wedding feast. The men feasted long and heartily, and when it was late evening Laban called his daughter to him with her handmaid Zilpah. But the daughter whom he called to him was Leah, not Rachel, and it was Leah in a thick wedding veil that he took to Jacob in the darkness of the night.

And thus did Jacob marry Laban's daughter after seven years of service.

In the light of morning Jacob looked and saw the face of his bride; and he saw that instead of his beloved Rachel, it was Leah.

He did not love her and he had not wanted her, and he was out-raged at Laban's trick.

"What have you done to me?" he said to Laban angrily. "Did I not serve seven years with you so that I might marry Rachel? Why have you deceived me?"

Laban managed to look surprised, and came out with the ex-cuse that he had prepared years before when he had made his promise to Jacob. "It is not the custom in our country," he said smoothly, "to give the younger in marriage before the firstborn. Surely you knew that?" He might have added that he had taken the only course he could think of to find a husband for his homely elder daughter, and that he wanted Jacob to stay there because he needed him; but it was not his way to say the honest thing and deal fairly with a man when he could gain by tricking him. "But you have no reason to be angry," he went on. "Spend a week with Leah, then marry Rachel also as soon as the week is out. Many men have more than one wife; so shall you have Leah and Rachel. Or you shall if you agree to serve me yet another seven years."

Laban drove a hard bargain. Fourteen years of work for Jacob for the sake of one woman whom he loved, and one woman whom he loved not! But Jacob agreed, for he loved Rachel very deeply and wanted more than anything in the world that she should be his wife. He spent his week with Leah, as required by custom, and then he married Rachel. Laban gave Rachel his handmaid Bilhah to wait upon her and obey her; and thus did Jacob's household increase.

It increased a great deal more as the years went by and Jacob continued to work hard and well for his scheming uncle Laban, but the increase was largely through the woman he had not in-tended to marry rather than through the woman that he loved more than any other.

He was husband to them both, but he loved Rachel far more than he could ever think of loving plain Leah; and Leah could not help knowing that she had not been wanted. She felt as though both Rachel and Jacob hated her, and her life was exceedingly unhappy.

But when the Lord saw that Leah was sorrowful, he gave her his own love and mercy so that she had children by Jacob while Rachel could not and did not have a child.

In a short space of time Leah had four sons, whom she named Reuben, Simeon, Levi, and Judah. And then, for a while, she had no more children.

But her younger sister Rachel had no children at all, beautiful and beloved though she was. And envy ate into her heart.

JACOB AND LABAN

*I*t was a shame and a disgrace for a Hebrew woman not to have a child, or so Rachel thought. Childless Sarah had felt bitter and ashamed for many years; Rebekah had been unhappy for a long time before her twins were born; and now Rachel was suffering in the same way. She envied her sister Leah with a bitterness that was close to hatred, and she turned to Jacob with her reproaches.

"Give me children, or else I die!" she begged.

Jacob's anger roused against her, because it was not his fault that she had no children. "Do you think that I am God, to have withheld a child from you?" he said wrathfully.

And Rachel knew that he was not to blame. But, like Sarah, she was almost desperate to give her husband a child that she could call her own, whether she herself bore it or not, so she thought of a way to do it. "Take my handmaid then," she said to Jacob. "Go to Bilhah, that I may also have children by her."

Jacob did as his wife asked him, and Bilhah had first one son and then another. Rachel was pleased and grateful to the Lord, for at least it was her own handmaid who had had the children and not the envied Leah. And then Leah, who had stopped bearing children for a while, decided to follow Rachel's course and give her own handmaid to her husband. So she gave Zilpah to Jacob; and in time Zilpah had two sons on behalf of Leah. Thereupon Leah herself had two more sons, followed by a daughter. Rachel's offspring by this time were hopelessly outnumbered, and she still did not have a child whom she could truly say was her very own.

And then at long last Rachel bore a son, and she felt that she must surely be the happiest mother alive. "God has taken away my shame and given me a child!" she said joyfully, and she called him Joseph. Jacob was just as pleased as Rachel, for he still loved her more than Leah; and so he loved his youngest baby Joseph more than all the rest. Now he had twelve children altogether: one girl, whose name was Dinah, and eleven boys.

It was not long after Joseph was born that the fourteen years of Jacob's promised service to Laban came to an end. During all that time Jacob had had no news of his parents, and he wanted to go home again. He went to Laban and said to him, "Send me away, so that I may go back to my own country. Give me my wives and my children, for whom I have served you through all these years, and let me take them with me; for you know that I have given you the service that I promised."

Laban knew it very well. He also knew that Jacob was a very skilled shepherd and herdsman who had added much to Laban's wealth by his knowledge of animal farming. What was more, Jacob's expert services had cost Laban nothing but two daughters for whom he would have had to find husbands anyway. He had given low wages indeed for the work of fourteen years.

"I pray you," Laban said earnestly, "if I have found favor in your eyes, then do not leave me. While you have been with me I have done well, so I beg you to stay. I have learned by experience that the Lord has blessed me because of you. Stay here; tell me what wage you want, and I will give it to you."

Jacob answered carefully, for he had realized in the course of the years that Laban was cunning enough to cheat him again if he should have the chance. And Jacob himself still had some of the craftiness he had used on his brother Esau. "You know how I have served you," he began, "and how your flocks and cattle have improved under my care. For what you had was little when I came, and now it has increased into a multitude. It is true that the Lord has blessed you since my coming. But what do I have? All these possessions are yours and I have nothing. When shall I provide for my own home?"

"What shall I give you, then?" Laban asked again.

Jacob's answer was a surprise to him. "You shall not give me anything," he answered. "If you will do one thing for me, then I will stay to tend your sheep and cattle and make my wage in my own way. I will go through your flocks and herds today and remove all the sheep and cattle that are speckled and spotted, and all the brown sheep as well; and also the spotted and speckled and striped among the goats. Whatever flocks and herds I may build up from these will be my price of hire. And when the time comes for me to receive my wage from you, you will be able to tell at once that I have taken no animal into my flock that does not belong to me. For I will have nothing in my flocks or herds that is not marked as I have said, nor any sheep that is not brown, or you will know that I have stolen from you. And I will not steal."

Laban quickly agreed to Jacob's proposition. There were not, he knew, more than one or two brown sheep, nor more than a very few animals that were spotted or speckled or striped. "It will be as you say," he said, with a friendly smile.

But just to make sure that he had the better end of the bargain, Laban went to the flocks and herds before Jacob could get to them and removed every animal that was spotted or speckled or striped, every one that had the smallest patch of white in it, and all the brown among the sheep. Then he turned them over to his own sons and sent them all to a far-off pasture three days' journey away from the flock that Jacob was to tend for him.

Jacob looked at what was left of Laban's flock and saw that he had again been cheated, but he had been expecting it and his

plans were ready. He was a far better farmer than Laban or any of
his uncle's sons, and it was not long before he succeeded in breed-
ing several healthy animals that were brown or otherwise marked
in the unusual manner he had specified. From these first few he
bred others; and then he separated them from Laban's flock and
kept them apart from all the other animals. Carefully, and with
great skill, he fed and watered his own flock so that his animals
thrived and became strong, and then he bred the strongest ones
together until his own flock of oddly colored but healthy beasts
was far bigger than Laban's.

So cleverly did he work among the animals that eventually
Laban's flock was not only reduced in size but contained only the
weaker of the cattle and sheep, while Jacob himself continued increasing his possessions and his riches. In time he became very
rich in flocks and herds, maidservants and menservants, camels
and asses, and all manner of household goods.

By this time he had worked for Laban for twenty years, and he
had earned his riches through his hard work and his skill. But
Laban's own sons were jealous, for now they had much less than
Jacob. They began to mutter among themselves about this foreign
relative of theirs.

Jacob heard the things that they were saying about him. "Jacob
has taken away all that was our father's," they said angrily. "From
what was once our father's he has made all these riches for himself. By trickery, he has obtained what should have been ours."
He had, it was true, outwitted them, but in whatever he had done
he had stayed strictly within the terms of his bargain with Laban.
But they were no longer interested in bargains. They had lost
their wealth to Jacob, and that was all they cared about.

Then Jacob saw how Laban himself was beginning to look at
him; and the look was nowhere near as friendly as it had been in
the earlier years when Jacob was working only to make Laban
rich. Indeed, Laban's face was very far from friendly.

It was time, thought Jacob, for him to be on his way. And the
Lord said to him: "I am the God of Bethel, where you anointed

the pillar and made a vow to me, and I have seen all that Laban has done to you. Arise, now, from this place. Return to the land of your fathers and to your kindred, and I will be with you."

Jacob called Rachel and Leah to him secretly and told them how God had helped him in his dealings with Laban, and how it was that he had managed to obtain so many sheep and cattle. "And now I see that your father does not feel toward me as before," he said, "because he no longer has all the riches that he had before. But the God of my father has been with me, and it was God who took away the cattle of your father and gave them to me. You know that I have done everything in my power to serve your father, while he has done nothing but deceive me. He has changed my wages ten times, always saying one thing and then doing the other, and promising me falsely; but God did not permit him to hurt me. The riches that I now have and share with you are ours by right, and God has said to me that I must arise and go. I did deal honestly with Laban, yet he is angry with me. Therefore let us leave, for the Lord my God has told me that I must return to the land of my own kindred."

Rachel and Leah listened to him and both answered, saying, "There is nothing left for us in our father's house. You must do whatever God has said to you, and we will go with you."

Jacob went about his arrangements very quietly, for he was sure that Laban would again try to delay him or even prevent him altogether from leaving with his family and possessions. He chose a time for his departure when Laban was in his distant pastures shearing sheep, and then he quickly gathered together everything he had. He did not know that Rachel was taking something that did not belong to her; for while he organized his servants and his flocks, Rachel stole from her father's household certain gods, or images of gods, that Laban valued highly.

So Jacob set his wives and children upon camels and left Padan-Aram without Laban knowing anything about it. He took with him all his flocks and cattle and possessions, and the servants he had gained, and made for his home in the land of Canaan. He and his caravan crossed the river Euphrates and turned toward Mount Gilead.

It was not until three days later that Laban heard that they had gone. Rapidly he took stock of what was left and what had been taken, and he was very angry. With his sons and a band of fighting men, he hurried in pursuit. After seven days' journey they saw signs of their quarry ahead, for Jacob had stopped on the slopes of Mount Gilead to make camp and let his great flocks and herds out to pasture.

Laban himself pitched his camp before going on to Gilead. And he had a dream by night in which God came to him and warned him that he was neither to harm Jacob nor deceive him with soft words.

In the morning Laban overtook Jacob and pitched his tents near him on the mountain slope. His anger had cooled, but not completely, so he went to Jacob and rebuked him harshly. "What have you done, that you have stolen away without my knowledge and carried off my daughters as if they were captives taken by the sword? Why did you flee away secretly and with such stealth? Why did you not tell me that you were going, so that I might have sent you away with merry-making, and with songs and taborin and harp? You did not even allow me to kiss my daughters and grandsons before taking them away! That was a foolish thing for you to do. It is in my power to do you harm, but the God of your father spoke to me last night, saying: 'Take heed that you do not speak to Jacob, either good or bad.' And yet you have done wrong, and you have angered me. Even though you wanted to be gone because you were longing to return to your father's house, why did you have to steal my household gods?"

"What gods?" said Jacob. "I left secretly because I was afraid, for I said to myself, 'Perhaps Laban will take his daughters away from me by force.' But as for your images, your gods, I know nothing of them. Search my tents yourself; take anything you find that belongs to you. And if anyone has taken your gods, let him not live." For Jacob had no idea that Rachel had taken them.

Laban went into the tents and searched them one after the other, but he did not find the missing gods. They were not in Jacob's tent, not in the maidservants', not in Leah's. Then he went to Rachel's tent. Rachel was resting, and she watched her father as he searched. "Do not be displeased, my father," she said to him, "that I cannot rise in your presence, for I am not feeling well."

And Laban allowed her to remain seated, and he did not find the images. For Rachel had hidden the images in her camel's saddle, and she was sitting on them.

When Laban left the tents with empty hands, Jacob was angry for having been accused falsely of stealing. "What have I done wrong?" he chided Laban. "What is my sin, that you have so hotly pursued me? Now that you have searched through all my possessions, what have you found of your household gods? Set it here, whatever you have found, in front of your brothers and my brothers, so that they may judge between us." And there was nothing for Laban to set down, for Rachel still sat in her tent upon the stolen images.

"These twenty years I have been with you," Jacob went on angrily, "and in all that time I have stolen nothing from you of your flocks or household goods. Your ewes and she-goats have been well and healthy, for I tended them with care, and of the rams of your flock I have not eaten. When wild beasts took any of your flock either by night or day I bore the loss of it. I worked long and hard; in the day I endured the heat and drought, and at night the chilling frost, and I did not sleep for taking care of what was yours. I served you fourteen years for your two daughters and six years for your cattle, and during those years you have changed my wages ten times. If the God of my father, the God of Abraham, had not been with me, then surely you would have sent me away now empty-handed. But God has seen my suffering and the labor of my hands, and when he spoke to you last night he was rebuking you."

Laban answered and said to Jacob, "These daughters are my

daughters, and these children are my children, and these cattle are my cattle, and all that you see is mine. And what can I do this day to my own daughters, or to the children they have borne? Come, therefore, and let us make a covenant, and let it be as a witness between you and me."

So Jacob took a stone and set it up for a pillar, and his men gathered stones into a heap. "This heap is a witness between us," Laban said. "May the Lord watch over us when we are absent from each other, so that you will not harm my daughters. God is witness between you and me. Behold, this heap and this pillar shall be witness that I will not pass beyond this point to come after you, and you shall not pass beyond this heap and pillar toward me to do me harm. May the God of Abraham and Nahor judge between us."

Thus did they make their vows to one another. They called the heap of stones Mizpah, meaning "watchtower," because the Lord himself would be watching over Laban and Jacob to see that each man would fulfill his vow.

Jacob offered up a sacrifice upon the mountain, and called his family and his men together to break bread and eat with him; and after they had eaten they spent all night on the mountain.

Early in the morning Laban rose, kissed his grandsons and his daughters and gave his blessing to them, and departed on the return journey to his own land. Jacob also went his way.

And this was the final parting between the family of Abraham, the Hebrews of Canaan, and the people of the old country. For neither Jacob nor Laban nor their sons would pass that pillar or the heap of stones and meet again. By the vow of Jacob and Laban, the descendants of Abraham were freed of their ties with their forefathers in the land of Babylonia; and from that time on they were a nation in themselves.

THE MEETING OF JACOB AND ESAU

*W*hile Laban traveled north to his home in Haran, Jacob journeyed west and south with his huge company of flocks and family and menservants. He was not entirely easy in his mind as he led his caravan toward the fields of home, for though it was twenty years since he had last seen Esau he was still afraid of his brother's temper. Esau had promised revenge; would he still take it? Or would he have mellowed with the passing of the years and forgive Jacob for his deceptions?

Jacob wanted to see his brother, and yet he did not want to. By this time Esau had left Canaan and made his home in the land of Edom, south of the Dead Sea and some distance from Jacob's destination, yet Jacob realized that a meeting, some time, would be inevitable. And so he felt worried and uncertain, even though he had trained serving men to defend him in case of trouble. But even as he worried a band of angels met him on his way, and Jacob drew courage from his meeting with these messengers of God. He himself sent messengers then, to go ahead of his party and tell Esau of his coming.

"Go to my brother in the country of Edom," he commanded them. "And when you speak to my lord Esau, tell him this: 'Your servant Jacob says that he has been these many years with his uncle Laban, and that he now has oxen, asses, flocks, menservants and womenservants of his own.' Say also that I am sending word of my coming so that I may find grace in his sight."

The messengers hurried off, and Jacob waited for them on the north bank of the river Jabbok. His men came back quickly with alarming news. First, Esau was coming to meet Jacob. That in itself was good; but there was more. "We saw your brother Esau," the messengers said, "and he is coming to meet you—and four hundred men with him."

Then Jacob was greatly afraid and distressed. A company of four hundred men sounded ominous. It surely looked as though Esau planned to attack him with his fighting force. Jacob therefore called all his followers together and divided them, with the flocks and herds and camels, into two groups. "If Esau should attack one company, then at least the other will escape," he explained to them.

And then he prayed. "O God of Abraham and Isaac, the Lord who said to me, 'Return to your country and your kindred, and I will deal well with you.' Lord, deliver me, I pray you, from the hand of my brother, from the hand of Esau. For I fear him, that he will come and kill me, and the mothers with the children. Yet you did say to me that you would surely be good to me, and make my descendants as many as the sands of the sea, which cannot be counted, so great is their number. Help me, God; I pray you."

Jacob spent the night by the river. In the morning he took from his vast possessions a lavish present for his brother Esau: two hundred she-goats and twenty he-goats; two hundred ewes and twenty rams; thirty milk-giving camels with their colts; forty cows and ten bulls; twenty she-asses and ten foals. He divided these into droves and gave each drove to a servant, with instructions to keep the droves separate and drive them one ahead of the other. "Put a space between drove and drove," he told them. "Cross the river before me and travel on ahead." Then, to each of the servants in turn, he said: "When my brother Esau meets you and asks, 'Whom do you serve? Where are you going? And who owns these beasts that you are driving?' you shall say, 'They are your servant Jacob's. It is a present sent to my lord Esau, and Jacob himself follows behind us.'"

He sent them off, hoping that his gifts could appease his brother's anger. "This present that goes ahead of me shall be my peace-offering," he said to himself. "After Esau receives it I will meet him face to face and see what his feelings are toward me. Perhaps he will have forgiven me; perhaps he will accept me."

With the present on its way, Jacob rested in the camp with the remaining company, wondering if he would receive an answering message from Esau or a sign from God that he had not been abandoned. During the night he rose up restlessly and sent his two wives, his two womenservants, and his children across the river Jabbok by the ford. When they were safely across the river he sent after them everything he owned and had with him; and then he was left on the north bank of the river.

Yet, as before at Bethel, he was not really alone. An odd thing happened to him, and yet he was not frightened. In the darkness a strange and shadowy figure appeared in front of him and without a word laid hands on Jacob and fought with all his strength. All night long Jacob wrestled with the stranger, and neither of them said a single word. It was only when the first light of dawn gently touched the sky that the stranger finally spoke. "Let me go, for it is daybreak," he said.

And then Jacob was sure of what he had already half-believed: that this man was no ordinary mortal but a heavenly visitor, the hope and help that he had asked of God.

"I will not let you go unless you bless me," Jacob said.

"What is your name?" asked the other man.

"Jacob."

"You shall no longer be called Jacob," said the stranger. "You shall be called Israel, for you are a prince of power with God and men." And in the language of those days the name 'Israel' meant 'soldier of God' or 'a prince of God.' "You are God's soldier, and you have won your battle," the stranger finished, and tried again to leave.

Jacob held him back. "Tell me your name, I pray you," he asked the wrestler of the night.

"Why should you want to know my name?" the other answered. "You have the blessing that you asked." And the stranger blessed him there beside the river, and then was gone.

And Jacob felt that the blessing had come to him from God. He named the place Peniel, which means 'the face of God'; for, as he said to himself, "I have seen God face to face, and my life is saved." He crossed the river Jabbok by the ford, leaving his fears behind him at Peniel as the sun rose and shone down upon him. On the other side he halted and lifted up his eyes and looked into the distance. In a cloud of dust he saw Esau coming toward him with four hundred men as rough and hairy as Esau himself. But Jacob was no longer afraid. He felt as though he had already won the hardest of his battles. Calmly, he arranged his band of people so that, if there should be a fight against the forces of his brother, he would be ready. He divided the children between Leah, Rachel, and the handmaids; and then he put the handmaids and their children in front, Leah and her children next, and Rachel and Joseph last. He himself strode to the head of the column and watched his brother Esau advancing toward him with his rough four hundred.

Jacob bowed as he walked forward, seven times with his head low toward the ground, until he came near to his brother. Esau ran to meet him with open arms that held no weapons in them, for all thoughts of vengeance had long since passed away, and he embraced Jacob with a heart full of warmth and friendship. Each man fell on the other's neck and wept tears of happiness and welcome after the long years of parting. From one side Jacob's people stood back and looked on; and from the other, Esau's men saw their master greet a beloved brother. No one had come to fight.

At last Esau looked up and saw all the women and children

behind his brother. "But who are all those people with you?" he asked.

"The family and children which God has graciously given to your servant Jacob," answered the younger brother. And Jacob made them all draw close, his handmaids and his wives and children, and lovingly presented them to his rough-looking but forgiving brother. They bowed, all of them, and greeted the gruff and hairy man whom Jacob had feared so needlessly throughout the years. Then Esau had another question.

"And what did you mean by those droves of beasts which I met along the way?" he asked.

"They were a present for you," Jacob answered, "so that I might find favor in your sight."

Esau shook his head. "There is no need for that, my brother. I have enough. Keep what you have for yourself."

"No, I beg you; if I have found grace in your sight, then accept the present that I offer you. I have seen your face at last and my pleasure is great, and I know that you are not displeased with me. I pray you, take the blessing I have brought to you, because God has dealt graciously with me and I have enough."

Jacob went on urging him until Esau finally took his gift and said: "Let us start upon our journey. I will go ahead of you."

"I cannot leave here yet," said Jacob. "You know that the children are young and tender and cannot travel without rest, and that I also have with me flocks and herds with young of their own. If they should be overdriven for only one day all the flock will die. Go on ahead, I pray you, and I will follow at a slower pace, according to what the children and the cattle are able to endure."

"Then let me leave some of my men with you," Esau said.

"Why? There is no need of that," said Jacob. "As long as I have found grace in your sight, that is all I want."

They made their farewells, then, and Esau started back to his home in Edom. Jacob slowly made his way into the land of Canaan, halting whenever it was needed to rest his family and pasture his flocks. He stopped for some time at Shechem to spread

his tents and worship God, and there God said to him: "Arise, go
up to Bethel and dwell there, and make an altar there unto the
God who appeared to you when you were fleeing from your
brother Esau."

So Jacob gathered his household together and traveled south to
Bethel. There he built an altar, and God appeared to him again to
repeat the promise made to Abraham and Isaac that from them
and from Jacob would come a race to whom the land of Canaan
would belong. And he said again the words that Jacob had heard
beside the river Jabbok: "Your name is Jacob, but that is no
longer your only name, for your name shall be called Israel."

And in later years the descendants of Jacob came to be known
as the children of Israel.

At last Jacob felt it was time to move on. But they had not
traveled long when Rachel became ill, for she was about to have a
child and the heavy traveling sapped her strength. Jacob called a
halt again so that she could rest and be cared for. It was too late.
The baby was born, and Jacob called him Benjamin; but Rachel
his beloved wife died in giving birth. Jacob buried her in
Bethlehem and set a pillar upon her grave so that it would always
be remembered. Grieving, he turned south to Hebron and his
home, to find that his mother Rebekah was long dead and that his
father Isaac was a tired and feeble old man of one hundred and
eighty years. He died not long after welcoming his son and all the
new grandchildren; and Esau came from Edom to help Jacob
bury him in the family cave of Machpelah.

Jacob and his family settled down in the land of Canaan, sure
that it would be his home and his family's home for many years to
come. He now had thirteen children; one daughter Dinah, and
twelve sons from whom the tribes of Israel were to spring:
Reuben, Simeon, Levi, Judah, Issachar, and Zebulun by Leah;
Gad, Asher, Dan, and Naphtali by the two handmaids; and
Joseph and Benjamin by Rachel. Of them all, Joseph was still his
favorite. And because Joseph was loved more than the rest, his
brothers came to hate him.

THE COAT OF MANY COLORS

*O*ld Israel, still known as Jacob to his family, made much of Rachel's firstborn. Benjamin was still far too young to be a companion to him, especially since he did not even remember his own mother, and the ten older brothers were rough and ready men who did many thoughtless and sometimes evil things without regret. Joseph, on the other hand, was a good and faithful boy, although a little too anxious to tell his father about the wrongdoings of his brothers. Jacob was so fond of the lad that he made for him a wonderful coat of many colors as a special token of his favor. The older brothers had no such fine robes to wear, and they muttered sourly among themselves. The very sight of the coat enraged them, for they saw it as a sign of Jacob's great love for the boy and his lesser love for them. In their jealousy they hated Joseph, so much that they could not even speak to him without being rude and angry.

One night, when Joseph was about seventeen, he had a dream; and in the morning he told it to his brothers, little realizing how they would feel about it. "Listen to my dream," he said eagerly, quite sure that they would be as interested as he. "In this dream we were binding sheaves in the field, and all at once my sheaf stood upright in the center. And then all your sheaves stood round about and bowed down to my sheaf!"

"Ah, is that the way of it!" his brothers sneered, for they could sense the meaning of the dream. "Will you indeed reign over us, and we bow down to you? Do you really think that you will be our ruler?" And they hated him even more for his dreams and for his words. Yet when he dreamed another dream he told that one of them, too, and said; "I have dreamed again; and in my dream I saw the sun, the moon, and the eleven stars bowing down to me." This time even his father showed a trace of anger, and rebuked him. "What is this that you have dreamed?" he said. "Shall I and your mother and your brothers indeed bow down to the earth before you, as if you were a king?"

Yet Jacob thought about the dream and wondered if it could really mean that some day Joseph would be greater than all his family. The same thought came to the brothers, and it made their hate and envy grow.

The pastures around the family home were not large enough to feed Jacob's growing flocks, and when the fields were grazed clean of grass he would send his sons off to drive the animals as far away as they needed to find fresh pasturage and water. On one occasion Jacob sent his ten older sons to Shechem with the flocks, for he needed Joseph's help at home, and the men stayed away for such a long time that Jacob began to worry and wonder about their welfare.

He called Joseph to him and said, "Your brothers are in Shechem with the flocks, and I wish to send you to them."

"I am here to do as you say, and will gladly go," said Joseph, although it was quite a distance for a young man to travel alone.

"Go, then," said Jacob, "and see if all is well with your brothers and the flocks, and bring back news of them."

Joseph put on his fine coat and set forth on his journey from the vale of Hebron, and he came at last to Shechem. But when he got there, there was no sign of his brothers or their flocks. A man of

Shechem saw him wandering in the fields and asked him, "What are you looking for?"

"I am looking for my brothers from Hebron," Joseph said. "Can you tell me where they might be feeding their flocks?"

"Oh, they have left here," the man replied. "I heard them say, 'Let us go to Dothan.' So at Dothan you should find them."

So Joseph headed north through the hills toward Dothan with the message from his father. After many hours of hard travel he could see the flocks with their shepherds, his brothers, in the distance, and they themselves saw him coming from afar wearing the hated coat of many colors. At the sight of him and his fine clothes, their old dislike and envy burned within them. They watched him approach with his youthful, light-hearted step, and they began to plot against him.

"Behold, here comes the dreamer," they said to one another. "Let us kill him and cast him into some pit, and we can say to our father that some wild beast must have eaten him. Then we shall see what becomes of his dreams!"

But Reuben, the oldest of the brothers, had more mercy than the rest. "Let us not kill him ourselves," he said. "There is no need to shed his blood. Instead, let us throw him into this pit in the wilderness and leave him there, and lay no hand upon him." For Reuben wanted to save the boy from them, and planned to come back later to free him from the pit and return him to their father.

Joseph came to them without any thought but that they would welcome him and gladly give him a return message for their father in Hebron. To his great surprise, they seized him roughly and ripped off his coat of many colors and threw him into a pit. The pit was deep and empty, without even a drop of water in it to quench his thirst or attract other desert wanderers who might come in search of water. And there they let him stay and cry for help while they sat down on the nearby grass to eat.

When they had finished their meal, some of the brothers went back to the pastures to care for the flocks, and Reuben went farther off than any of them to make his plans and wait for an oppor-

tunity to help his brother Joseph. The others stayed near the pit
and talked. As they idled at the pit they saw a caravan of
merchants and their camels approaching across the wilderness.
They knew the men to be Ishmaelites, those who were descended
from Ishmael of the wild lands; and they were coming from Gilead
with their camels laden with spices and balm and myrrh to
take to the markets of Egypt. And brother Judah was struck with
a new and interesting thought.

"What profit is it to us if we kill our brother?" he said. "Would
it not be better to sell him to these Ishmaelites for money? We
should not let him die, for after all he is our brother and our
flesh."

The others agreed to Judah's suggestion. In this way they
would be rid of Joseph at a profit to themselves.

When the caravan of Ishmaelite merchantmen drew close
enough so that the brothers could hail them to come closer yet,
Judah and his brothers pulled the struggling Joseph from the pit
and sold him to the merchants for twenty pieces of silver. The
Ishmaelites took him willingly, for they knew they could easily
sell a strong young man to some wealthy householder in Egypt for
much more than he had cost them. And the Ishmaelites went off
with him, toward the land of Egypt.

Shortly afterward Reuben came back, hoping to find that his
brothers were no longer near the pit so that he could rescue
Joseph. His brothers were indeed out of sight, but when he
looked into the pit he saw that Joseph was no longer there. He
stared down into the empty pit and called out hopelessly, but he
could see that there would be no answer. The boy had gone. And
he could not have climbed out by himself. Reuben tore his clothes
with fright and grief. He ran into the pastures and cried out to his
brothers: "The child has gone! And I, what shall I do, where shall
I go?" For as the oldest son he felt the blame on his own
shoulders, and he could not bear to think what he would have to
tell his father.

The brothers told him what they had done, and he listened in horror. There was no undoing it; even Reuben could see that. So then they took the coat of many colors, which they had stripped from Joseph when he came to them, and killed one of the young goats of their flock. While Reuben looked on in shame they dipped the lovely coat into the blood, and they took it back with them to their father in Hebron.

They handed Jacob the once-beautiful coat, now so horribly stained. "This we found in the wilderness," they said. "It is torn and bloodied, but we think we recognize it. See, Father! Do you know whether this is your son's coat?"

Jacob took it from them and knew it at once. "It is my son's coat!" he cried out bitterly. "Some wild beast has devoured him. Without doubt my son Joseph has been torn to pieces!"

And Jacob tore his clothes in the agony of his grief, and dressed himself in mourning sackcloth. All his family tried to comfort him, even those who had caused his terrible sorrow, but Jacob could not be comforted. Only little Benjamin could ease his pain; yet he was not his brother, and could not make up for the loss of Joseph. Jacob's heart was broken. "I will go down into my grave mourning for my son," he moaned sorrowfully.

Thus did Jacob mourn for his lost son. He had no reason to believe that his beloved Joseph had not been torn apart by some wild animal on his lonely journey. Ten brothers knew that no animal had taken him, but they dared not to say what they had done. In fact, they did not know what had become of the brother they had sold.

Joseph was on a slave block in the land of Egypt.

JOSEPH A CAPTIVE IN EGYPT

The slave buyers of the Egyptian market place prodded and peered at Joseph with critical interest. He was a strong and handsome lad and would surely make a useful servant. Joseph in his turn looked around and saw wonders he had never seen before in his short life on the plains of Canaan: splendid temples to strange gods; odd, massive structures he had heard called pyramids; busy city streets thronged with swarthy men, some important in their rich robes and some surly in the rags of beggars; and goods of all kinds up for auction in the market.

And he himself was one of the goods, an object sold for silver by the brothers who hated him, and brought to this foreign place to be sold again.

The Ishmaelite merchants quickly found a buyer for their captive. A man named Potiphar, himself an Egyptian and captain of the Pharaoh's guard, bought Joseph to be his slave and took him into his own house. And the Lord was with Joseph, for Potiphar was not only a wealthy man but upright, a man of honor as well as rank. He soon saw that Joseph was no ordinary slave. The boy learned quickly, and he was honest. Everything he did seemed to prosper at his hands. In a very short time he became a favored servant, and after a while Potiphar made him overseer over his house and all his wealth. So thoroughly did the captain of the guard trust Joseph that he put all his business and household affairs into the young man's hands, no longer troubling himself about any of his possessions except the food he ate. Potiphar needed a man like Joseph to take charge of such matters for him, because as a high-ranking military officer he was often away from home and unable to attend personally to his business.

The years went by; Joseph worked hard and Potiphar's wealth increased. Even though he was a slave, Joseph was treated well in the Egyptian's household, almost as though he were a free man and an equal; and he was not unhappy. But his comfortable state could not last forever. Joseph was a good-looking young man, and as he added years he became even more handsome and good to look upon. His master's wife began to cast her eyes upon him in a way that was a great embarrassment to Joseph. Time after time she tried to make him love her, but Joseph would not be persuaded.

"My master trusts me with everything he has," he told her, "I am responsible for everything in this house, so that he does not even question what I may be doing. He has been kind and generous, keeping back nothing from me but yourself, because you are his wife. How, then, can I betray him? How can I do this great wickedness to him, and also sin against God?"

Nevertheless, Potiphar's wife kept on trying to win Joseph's love. And still he would not let her have her way. She grew more and more determined. One day, when Potiphar was away and all the other people of the house were about their business, she tricked Joseph into coming into her room. Still he refused to love her, and ran from her in great dismay. This time she became so angry that she screamed for help and pretended that Joseph had tried to do her wrong. To her husband, when he came home, she told a wicked lie. "That Hebrew servant of yours!" she cried, full of false rage. "While you were gone he tried to force himself upon me, and only when I lifted up my voice and cried out for help did he run away."

When Joseph's master heard his wife's words he was surprised and angry. He took Joseph from his house and thrust him into the prison where the king's own prisoners were kept. There Joseph stayed, innocent of any crime.

But the Lord was still with him. Even in prison Joseph did well, because he remained as cheerful and intelligent and honest as he had always been in Potiphar's house. The Lord was merciful to him and gave him favor in the eyes of the keeper of the prison. After a time, the keeper placed so much reliance upon Joseph that he felt safe in putting all the prisoners in Joseph's care. The keeper himself, like Potiphar before him, questioned nothing that Joseph did. As far as he was concerned, Joseph was in charge, and Joseph could be trusted.

A while later it happened that the chief butler and chief baker of the king's household offended their lord the Pharaoh, king of Egypt, and Pharaoh angrily threw them into the prison where Joseph was held. They, too, came under Joseph's charge, and he looked after them. They were exceedingly unhappy, for their ranks in the king's household had been high, and now they were prisoners with no idea of what the future held for them.

One night these two men dreamed a dream, each a sightly different one, and the strange dreams puzzled them. The next morning Joseph came to them and saw that they were sad. And he asked these one-time officers of the Pharaoh: "Why do you look so sad today?"

And they said to him, "We each have dreamed a dream, and we have no one here to tell us what they mean." For they took dreams very seriously, believing that they were prophecies. In Pharoah's court there were wise men who were supposed to be able to interpret dreams, but in prison there was no one to explain the meaning. Or so they thought.

But Joseph was an experienced dreamer himself; and also he believed in God.

"Do not interpretations come from God?" said Joseph. "I am God's servant. Surely he will reveal his meaning through me. Tell me your dreams."

The chief butler, whose duty it had been to serve Pharaoh with wine, spoke first. "In my dream," he said to Joseph, "there was a grapevine in front of me, and on the vine there were three branches. Before my eyes the branches seemed to bud; then the blossoms opened and became clusters of ripe grapes. Pharaoh's wine cup was in my hand; and I took the grapes and squeezed them into Pharaoh's cup. And then I took the cup and gave it into Pharaoh's hand, even as I used to do when I served wine at my master's table."

And Joseph said to him, "This is the interpretation of your dream. The three branches are three days. Within three days Pharaoh will raise your head high and restore you to your place. You will serve him just as you used to when you were his butler. All shall go well with you. But think of me, I beg you, when you leave here and prosper once again. Show kindness to me and mention me to Pharaoh that I may be released, for I have been imprisoned unjustly. Indeed, I was stolen away out of the land of the Hebrews; and here also I have done nothing to deserve being put into this dungeon."

The butler was pleased with Joseph's explanation of his dream and readily promised to speak to Pharaoh about Joseph. And when the chief baker saw that the first interpretation was good he was encouraged, and he said to Joseph: "I also dreamed, and in my dream there were three white baskets on my head, one above the other, and in the topmost basket there were all manner of baked foods for Pharaoh. And the birds flew down and ate the food out of the basket on my head. What does this dream mean?"

Joseph did not like what he had to say, but he answered the baker: "This is the meaning of your dream. The three baskets are three days. Within three days Pharaoh will raise your head high— and hang you from a tree. And the birds will eat your flesh."

On the third day, which was Pharaoh's birthday, the king held a great feast for all who served him. It was the custom on such festive occasions for Pharaoh to review the sentences of those he had cast into the royal prison. Some would be pardoned; others would not. Pharaoh therefore sent his men to take his chief butler and chief baker from the prison. And he restored the chief butler to his old place beside the king's table; and once again the man offered the wine cup to his Pharaoh. But Pharaoh hanged his chief baker from a tree, as Joseph had said he would.

The butler was impressed with Joseph's interpretations, but he was so overjoyed with his good fortune at being restored to his former place that he did not remember his promise to Joseph. He forgot all about him. Joseph remained a captive in Pharaoh's prison while the weeks and months dragged into years.

JOSEPH'S BROTHERS BOW

*I*f Pharaoh had not dreamed of cows and corn, Joseph might have been a captive even longer than he was. As it was, two full years passed while he waited for release; and then Pharaoh dreamed first one strange dream, then another. While the king of Egypt slept he saw fat cows and lean ones at the riverside; and after this he saw full, luxuriant ears of corn and thin ones in a field of grain.

In the morning he was greatly troubled. He sent for all the wise men and magicians of Egypt and told them what he had dreamed. But none of them could explain the dreams to Pharaoh. And then, all at once, the chief butler thought of the dream he had had while in prison.

"I do remember my faults this day!" he told his king. "Pharaoh once was angry with his servants, both the chief baker and me, and put us into prison. Each of us dreamed a dream one night, which we could not understand. There was a young man in the prison, a Hebrew, who was servant to the captain of the guard. We told him our dreams and he told us what they meant; and within three days we saw that he was right. I was restored to office, and the other hanged."

In haste, then, Pharaoh sent for Joseph. The young Hebrew

shaved quickly and changed his clothes; and the king's men took him out of his dungeon and led him into the presence of Pharaoh.

The king of Egypt looked at him, this foreigner from Canaan, and wondered how he could help where all the old wise men had failed. Nevertheless, the Hebrew had been right before. Perhaps he would be right again.

"I have dreamed a dream," he said to Joseph, "and there is no one here who can tell me what it means. I have heard it said of you that you can understand dreams and explain their meanings. Is it indeed so?"

"The understanding is not in me," said Joseph. "But God will give Pharaoh an answer through me so that your mind shall be at peace."

"In my dream, then," Pharaoh said, "I stood upon the river bank. And as I watched, there came out of the river seven cows that were fat and healthy, and they went to graze in the meadow grass. Then seven other cows came up after them; and these were poor, bony, and very lean, such meager and unsightly cattle as I have never seen in the land of Egypt. And the lean, ill-favored cows ate up the first seven cows, those that were good and fat; but the thin ones were still as thin as ever! Then I awoke, and some time later slept again."

Joseph listened carefully to the troubled man in the regal robes. Whether he would be rewarded for his help, he did not even think. But he did know that God would give him understanding.

"And now I dreamed," Pharaoh went on, "that I saw a stalk of corn with seven rich, good ears upon it. Then seven other ears sprang up after the good ones, and they were withered, thin, and blasted by the east wind. As I watched, the thin ears ate the seven good ears; and again I woke. But when I told these dreams to my magicians, they could not explain them to me."

"It is but one dream," Joseph said. "God has shown to Pharaoh what he is about to do. The seven fat cows are seven good years, and the seven good ears of corn are also seven years: the dream is one. The seven thin and ill-favored cows that followed the first

are seven poor years; and the seven empty ears blasted by the
east wind shall be seven lean years of famine. In this way God is
showing to Pharaoh that there will be seven years of great plenty
throughout all the land of Egypt, which will be followed by seven
years of famine."

All Pharaoh's court was silent as Joseph explained the dream,
dismayed by his interpretation but believing in it.

Joseph went on to tell them more. "The famine shall consume
the land," he said, "and cause such desolation that the years of
plenty will soon be forgotten, and there will be no food at all to
eat. God sent Pharaoh a double dream to show that these things
are certain to come to pass and that they will happen soon. It is a
warning, so that Pharaoh may prepare for the bad years that will
follow the good. Therefore, let Pharaoh find a man both discreet
and wise and put him in charge of preparing for the years of need.
And let that man appoint officers to make sure that a fifth part of
the harvest is gathered up and set aside during the seven good
years; and let them lay up corn and keep supplies of food in all
the cities. Have them see that the food is stored as a supply for
the people to draw against when the seven years of famine shall
be in the land of Egypt. If this is done, then the people and the
land will not perish from the famine."

The plan was good in the eyes of Pharaoh, and in the eyes of
his men at court. "Can we find such a man as this?" he said to his
attendants. "A man with the Spirit of God in him? Surely there
can be no man more wise, more suitable, than the very man to
whom God has shown all this." And the king of Egypt turned to
Joseph. "You yourself shall be put in charge," he said. "My people
shall be ruled according to your word. Only on the throne shall I
be greater than you. In everything else, I am setting you over all
the land of Egypt to do as you have said."

And Pharaoh took from his own hand the ring with his kingly
seal upon it, and himself put it onto Joseph's finger. Then he
dressed Joseph in royal robes of the finest linen, and put a gold
chain about his neck, and gave Joseph a chariot to ride in that

was second only to his own. "Without you," Pharaoh said to Joseph, "no man shall lift his hand or foot in all the land of Egypt."

Thus did Joseph of Canaan, he that was sold at seventeen by his ten older brothers, become ruler over all of Egypt at the age of thirty. In his royal robes he rode in his glorious chariot, in front of which the people cried: "Bow down! Bow low the knee!" and he was a mighty man in the eyes of all Egyptians. In time he married an Egyptian girl, daughter of an honored priest, a girl given to him as his wife by Pharaoh himself.

In the seven plentiful years that followed, the earth brought forth abundant food. Joseph traveled throughout the land of Egypt, showing the people how to make the best use of their soil and how to conserve what they grew. He and his officers gathered up corn wherever they went, until it seemed as though they had saved as much corn as there were sands of the sea. Joseph gave up counting his supplies, for they were well past counting. From the grainfields around each city he gathered corn for that city's storehouses, so that throughout the land the cities were supplied with stocks of grain from their own nearby fields. Wherever he went he made sure that every fifth part of every harvest was taken from the whole and stored against the day when there would be no harvest. And when that happened, he himself would give out food as needed. Those seven years were good and happy years for the people of Egypt; and they were happy, too, for Joseph. His wife bore him two sons, Manasseh and Ephraim; and Joseph was grateful to the Lord for having caused so much good to come out of his earlier afflictions.

Then the drought fell upon the land. The soil no longer yielded fat corn nor even empty ears; the cattle became lean and miserable for want of food and water. At first the famine was less severe in Egypt than in the neighboring lands, for the waters of the Nile still trickled through the fields. But it was very bad in other countries that had never been well-watered, and their fields dried up and their cattle slowly died. After a while even the people of

Egypt used up the small stocks they had kept in their own homes. And when all the land of Egypt was famished, the people cried out to their king for food.

Pharaoh said to them: "Go to Joseph. Do what he tells you to do." They went to Joseph. He opened all the storehouses and supplied the Egyptians from the stores gathered in the years of plenty. Soon the people of the neighboring countries came into Egypt to buy corn from Joseph, for he had conserved so well that there was food to spare.

And the famine was over all the face of the land. Soon it reached the land of Canaan, even as it had during the time of Abraham when it had driven him into Egypt with his flocks. Joseph's own family began to suffer badly in their parched and sunburnt land.

Now when Jacob heard that there was corn in Egypt, he called his sons to him and said: "Why do you look at one another, asking where you may find food to eat? I have heard that there is corn in Egypt. Go down there and buy food for us so that we may eat and live."

So the ten older brothers gathered up their empty grain sacks, saddled their donkeys, and departed to buy corn in the land of Egypt. But Benjamin, the youngest brother, stayed home with his father, for Jacob had never given up sorrowing for his one lost son and was afraid that some mishap would take Benjamin from him as well.

The ten men traveled through the starving land of Canaan and other lands that were as dry and famished as their own. At last they came to Egypt, not knowing that their own brother Joseph was the governor of the land and that it was he who sold the grain to all the people that came from the hungry lands.

Even when they saw him they did not realize who he was, for it was more than twenty years since they had seen him last. Then he had been a lad, and now he was a man; then he had been stripped of his coat of many colors and sold from a pit in Canaan to a group of passing merchants, and now he wore fine robes and sat upon a throne in Egypt.

They went toward his throne and bowed low.

But Joseph knew them at once. And as he saw them bow down to the earth in front of him, he remembered his old dreams. His brothers were indeed bowing down to him; the same brothers who had sold him into slavery. There was no thought of vengeance in his heart, but he did wonder if his brothers were as harsh and cruel as they had been in the old days. He spoke to them in the language of Egypt through an interpreter, and he pretended that he did not know or trust them.

"Who are you?" he asked roughly. "Where do you come from?"

"We are from the land of Canaan," they replied, "and we have come here to buy food."

"You are spies!" Joseph said sharply. "You have come to see the famine and weakness of the land, and then you will send an army to make war against us."

"No, no, my lord," they protested. "We are not spies. It is only to buy food that we, your servants, have come. We are twelve brothers, sons of one man in the land of Canaan. Our youngest brother is with our father, and one brother has been lost to us."

"You are spies," Joseph said firmly, determined to test them to the limit. "And you will not leave here until I see this younger brother that you talk about. When he comes here, only then will I know that you are telling me the truth." For he wanted very much to see his brother Benjamin, and yet he also hoped that they would not forfeit the youth to save themselves.

They gave him no further answer, except to repeat that they were honest men in search of food. Joseph hardened his heart, although he was a kindly man and wished no harm to them, and put them all into prison for three days. Only by their words and actions under hardship would he know if they had changed.

On the third day he released them from the prison.

"Do as I say and you shall live," he said, "for I am a God-fearing man and will not hurt you if you are what you say. If you are honest men, nine of you shall return home with corn for the famine of your houses, and one shall stay here, bound in the place where you have been imprisoned. And he shall stay here until you return with your youngest brother, for only by bringing him back to me will you prove your words. Then none of you shall die. But if you do not do what I ask, then I will know that you are spies."

Deeply disturbed and very much afraid, they talked among themselves in their own language. They did not know that Joseph could understand their every word.

"This has come upon us because of our own guilt," they whispered to each other. "We saw the anguish of our brother Joseph, and when he pleaded with us we would not hear his cries. That is why we suffer now, and it is right that we should suffer."

"Did I not beg you then not to harm the boy?" said Reuben. "And you would not listen to me! God requires us to answer for the shedding of our brother Joseph's blood. We did wrong, my brothers, and that is why this punishment is on us."

Joseph heard them and his heart was touched by their repentance. He turned away from them and wept. But he was still not sure that they had fully learned their lesson, nor did he yet know what they would do about his brother Benjamin.

He turned back to them and spoke again through his interpreter, and in front of their eyes he took their brother Simeon and had him bound for his return to prison. Then he ordered the other nine to go.

They left for Canaan with their grain sacks full of corn, not knowing that he had commanded his steward to put each man's money back into his sack. Their donkeys were laden with corn and they had good provisions for their journey, yet they were sad and troubled as they traveled home. Joseph had been lost to Jacob many years before; now their brother Simeon was a prisoner in Egypt and must stay there until they came back with Benjamin. If they did not return with their youngest brother, then Simeon would surely die.

But worse fears were still to come. When at last they reached home and their waiting father, they emptied their grain sacks and found that each man's bundle of money—the money they thought they had paid to the cruel governor of Egypt—was still there in each sack. Haltingly, they told their story to their father, and all were much afraid. Now the Egyptian would not only think that they were spies, but thieves as well!

"I will go back!" said Reuben. "If the man sees Benjamin, he will know we did not lie. And I will take the money back with me."

"No, you shall not!" cried Jacob. "I have already lost both Joseph and Simeon. You will not take Benjamin away from me. All these things are against me!"

"I must go back with the money," said Reuben. "And I must take Benjamin. I swear that if you let me take him, I will bring him back to you. I swear it by my own two sons."

"I will never let you take him," Jacob said. "His brother is already dead; must I lose him as well? No, if any harm should come to Benjamin through what you do, then you will bring my gray hairs down into the grave with sorrow."

And there the matter stayed.

But the corn brought from Egypt did not last long, and the famine lasted for as many years as Joseph had predicted. Still there was no rain in Canaan. Still there was no fodder for the starving flocks. Still the fields were bare of corn to feed the family of Jacob, who was also Israel.

It was impossible for the brothers to go back to Egypt. Surely they would lose their brother Benjamin. And yet—what else was there to do?

JOSEPH'S FAMILY IN EGYPT

𝒯he children and grandchildren of Israel who lived in Canaan numbered sixty-six, and with them in their home were many workers of the fields. The food from Egypt was soon gone. The bare land could not feed them all, and all of them were hungry. When the time came that they had eaten up the corn from Egypt they knew they had, somehow, to find more food, or die.

Jacob called his sons together. "You will have to go again," he said. "Go back to Egypt, and buy more food for us."

"We can only go if we take Benjamin," Judah reminded him. "The man who rules there told us that he would not see us again unless we take our youngest brother with us. If you let us take him, we will go. Otherwise, there is no use in going."

Jacob groaned bitterly, remembering. "Why did you tell the man you had another brother?" he asked reproachfully.

"Because he asked us," Judah answered. "He asked about our family, and wanted to know if our father was still alive and if we had another brother. There seemed no reason not to answer him. How could we know that he would say, 'Bring your brother to me'? But we *must* go, my father. Send the lad with me, so that we may see the man and buy the food. Or else all of us shall die of hunger—you, we, and all the little ones. I myself will be the guarantee for Benjamin. If I do not bring him back to you, then all blame shall be on me forever."

They argued more, the brothers and the old man, and at last Jacob agreed to let them go with his beloved Benjamin. "If it must be so," he sighed, "then it must be. Take your brother and go. But do this, too: take with you the best fruits of the land. Carry a good present to the man; a little balm, some wild honey, rich spices and perfumes, nuts and almonds, the best of everything we have. And take double money with you also, so that you may pay for what you buy and return what you found in your sacks. Perhaps it was an oversight, that it was given back to you. Go now, and look after Benjamin, and may that man be kind. Pray that God Almighty will show you mercy before the man in Egypt so that he will send back both Simeon and Benjamin. But if it is God's will that I should lose my children, then . . . it is God's will."

The brothers took the presents and the double money, and young Benjamin journeyed with them to the land of Egypt. Once again, ten brothers stood before Joseph, ruler in a foreign land. But this time Rachel's younger son stood with them.

When Joseph saw Benjamin he was deeply moved. "Take the men from Canaan to my house," he told his steward, "and prepare a feast, for these men shall dine with me at noon."

Joseph's servant led the brothers away. And the brothers were very much afraid when they saw that they were being taken to the ruler's house, for they thought that some terrible punishment was in store for them. "It is because of the money put back in our sacks," they told each other. "He thinks we stole it, and now he will throw us into prison with Simeon and we shall all be slaves." When they reached the door of Joseph's house they could contain their fears no longer.

"About the money in our sacks," they said to Joseph's steward. "We did not steal it; we do not know how it came to be put back in the sacks. But we have brought other money to replace it if you think we stole it."

"Why, no," the steward said, as he showed them into Joseph's home. "Peace be to you; do not be afraid. It must have been your God that gave you treasure in your sacks. I received your money, and you owe us nothing." So saying, he left them and came back with Simeon. Then he made all of them comfortable in Joseph's house, washing their feet according to the custom and providing fodder for their donkeys. "My master will be here at noon," he explained to Joseph's brothers, "and he has asked that you should eat with him."

Joseph came home at noon and welcomed them kindly to his house. They bowed low in front of him, grateful for his kindness and for Simeon's release, and they gave him the presents they had brought from Canaan. Joseph accepted their gifts cordially and inquired about their welfare. "And is your father well?" he asked, with far more interest than they could know. "The old man of whom you spoke, is he still alive?"

"He is alive and well," they answered, bowing low again.

Then Joseph looked at his brother Benjamin, son of Rachel his own mother. "Is this your younger brother, of whom you spoke to me?" They nodded. "That is he," they said.

"God be gracious to you, my son," said Joseph, scarcely able to hide his powerful emotions, for he yearned to greet the youth and show his love. Yet he was not ready to reveal himself. Alone for a moment, he wept, then washed away his tears and went back to his brothers.

They all sat down to dine. Joseph, as ruler, had a table to himself, and his Egyptian officers sat apart. And the eleven men from Canaan sat at the table by themselves, marveling and wondering how Joseph could possibly have known their ages—for he had seated them himself, in order, from the firstborn to the youngest. And Joseph sent dishes from his own royal table to his honored visitors, offering Benjamin five times as much as all the others.

They dined and drank, and all were merry. The strange man

who was ruler seemed to be their friend, and he had brought
them all together again. Simeon was free, and Benjamin had not
been taken in his place. All fears were forgotten.

The brothers set forth again on the following morning, their
hearts full of relief and their sacks full of the grain so badly
needed by Jacob and his family. But again they did not know that
Joseph had given his steward special instructions that would put
them to a further test.

"Fill the men's sacks with food," Joseph had said, "as much as
they can carry and put each man's money back into his sack. But
to the youngest one you shall not only return the corn money, but
also take my silver drinking cup and put it into his sack."

The steward did as Joseph had commanded him. And the
brothers traveled cheerfully toward the land of Canaan.

They had not gone far when Joseph gave his steward fresh instructions. "Hurry, now!" he said. "Go after those men, and when
you overtake them, you must say: 'Why have you returned evil for
good? You have stolen my lord's drinking cup, and in this you
have done evil!'"

The steward hurried off. Soon he overtook the brothers, and he
said to them what Joseph had commanded him to say.

"We did steal a silver cup?" The brothers were shocked. "How
can you say such a thing? God forbid that your servants should
have stolen anything. Did we not bring back the money we found
in our sacks when we last traveled up to Canaan? Is it likely that
we should steal from your lord's house either gold or silver?
Search us, if you like. If the cup is found with any of us, then let
that man die, and the rest of us will be slaves to your lord of
Egypt."

"I will look," said Joseph's steward. "And he with whom the
cup is found shall be my servant, but only he. The rest of you
shall not be blamed."

The brothers took their sacks down from their donkeys and
confidently opened them. They were very sure that the cup

would not be found, for each man knew that he had not been the one who had taken it.

The steward searched each sack, beginning with that of the oldest son Reuben and ending with the sack of Benjamin, the youngest. And there, in Benjamin's sack, the steward found the silver cup that he had put there himself.

The brothers were astounded and dismayed. They tore their clothes in fear and sorrow, but they loaded up their donkeys once again and returned to the city where Joseph awaited them with a stern, accusing face.

Joseph saw that they had all come back; not only Benjamin, but all of them. His heart rejoiced that the younger brother had not been abandoned. "What deed is this that you have done?" Joseph demanded, pretending an anger that he did not feel. "Did you think that I would not find you out?"

And then Judah, the one who had been most responsible for selling Joseph into slavery, showed that he was a changed man indeed. He said: "What can we say to you? How shall we clear ourselves? We know not how the cup came into our brother's sack, but we do know that God has seen the sins of our younger years and is punishing us. If one of us is guilty, then all of us are guilty, and all of us shall be your slaves."

"God forbid that I should keep you all as slaves," Joseph replied. "Only one of you is guilty. The man who took my silver cup shall be my slave, and only he. The rest of you shall go in peace to your father's land."

Here was their opportunity to escape and leave Benjamin behind in slavery. But the brothers would not take their chance to go. Judah, once so hard of heart and selfish, came forward once again and spoke to Egypt's ruler.

"Oh, my lord, let me speak, I beg you," he said, "and do not let your anger burn against us. You remember that you asked us once before about our father, and if we had another brother. And we answered you. Then you wanted us to bring our brother to you, but we knew it would break our father's heart if we did so. If our father loses Benjamin, he will die of sorrow. Yet all of us would have died of famine if we had not come to you again; so we came again to Egypt and brought with us our younger brother as you said we must. And now, if we return without this lad who is everything to Jacob since the loss of his son Joseph, our father will surely die of sorrow. My lord, I promised my father that no harm would come to Benjamin, that he would return in safety. Therefore, my lord, I pray you, let me stay here in his place to be your slave, and let my brothers take the lad home to his father. For I could not bear the sadness that would come upon my father if his beloved youngest son were taken from him."

Now Joseph could not restrain himself, for he could see that his brothers were no longer the cruel men they had been.

"I am your brother Joseph!" he cried out. "Tell me again that my father is still alive!"

His brothers were thunderstruck, and could not answer him. For the first time this hard Egyptian ruler had spoken in their own language, and he had said this incredible thing! In their astonishment and fear they hung back, and said nothing.

"Come near me, I beg you!" Joseph said, and held his arms out to them.

At last, and slowly, they went close to him.

"I am Joseph, your brother, whom you sold into Egypt," this powerful ruler said; and now they shook and trembled. "But do not be grieved or angry with yourselves because you sold me, for it was God who sent me here ahead of you to save our people's lives. God brought me here and made me ruler throughout the land of Egypt; God, not you; so that you might be preserved upon this earth. For two years now there has been famine in the land, and there will be five years more without a harvest. Therefore hurry to your home, and speak to our father. Tell him: 'God has made your son Joseph lord of all Egypt.' Tell him that he is to come at once with all his family and live near me in the part of Egypt called the land of Goshen. Say that he must bring his children, and all his children's children, and all his flocks and herds and everything he has, for I will look after all of you in this time of poverty. Make haste, tell my father, and bring him here to me!"

And then Joseph took his brother Benjamin into his arms and wept tears of joy after the many years of parting. Afterward he embraced his other brothers, too, as proof that all had been forgiven and that he loved them also; and then they talked together as they had never talked before.

Pharaoh soon heard that Joseph's brothers had come, and he himself insisted that their father and all their family should come to live in Egypt where there was food in plenty.

Eleven brothers, guilt-free and happy at last, took the rich gifts given to them by Pharaoh and his governor Joseph, and went back into the land of Canaan to tell the good news to their father. With the gifts they took provisions for their journey, and wagons from the king so that they might bring back to Egypt all their family and their goods.

When Jacob saw that not only Benjamin but Simeon as well had come back with all the others, his relief and joy were great. But greater still was happiness when they told him: "Joseph is alive! Your son is governor over the land of Egypt! And we have come to take you and all our family back with us to be near him."

At first the old man could not believe his ears, and his heart was faint because of what he heard. But when they told him everything his son had said, he believed them and rejoiced. Yet he was not sure that God meant him to go into the land of Egypt, for Canaan was his promised land. Then the Lord God spoke to him and said: "I am God, the God of your fathers. Do not be afraid to go to Egypt, for I will be with you and make of you a mighty nation. You shall see your son Joseph again, and in time I will bring your family out of Egypt back into the land of Canaan."

Then Jacob, father of all the people whom the Egyptians called the Israelites, took his family into Egypt and once again saw his beloved, long-lost son. Joseph greeted him with tears of joy, and

Pharaoh himself accepted the children of Israel as honored friends.

Thus did the children of Israel settle in the land of Goshen, a rich and fertile district that was part of Egypt, and there they lived for many years. Pharaoh was kind to them, and the people of Egypt loved and respected the children of Israel because they were the family of Joseph who had saved them all from famine and starvation.

No more than seventy Israelites, including Joseph and his children, settled in the land of Goshen. But in time the family grew, became great in numbers, and prospered among their Egyptian friends. For several hundreds of years the children of Israel were happy in the alien land.

MOSES IN THE BULRUSHES

*T*he Hebrews in the land of Goshen grew rich and multiplied exceedingly. Each of Jacob's twelve sons became the father of a tribe of Israel, and all the tribes but one were named after Joseph's brothers. Joseph's own tribe became two, which were named after Joseph's two sons, Manasseh and Ephraim.

Old Jacob, father of all Israel, died, and was mourned by Egyptians and Israelites alike. Then Joseph died, and those of his generation. But still the children of Israel were fruitful, and increased to hundreds of thousands. The land was filled with them, and they were mighty.

Then there arose a new king over Egypt, one who had not known Joseph and his brothers. And this Pharaoh was afraid of all these foreign people in his land, for it seemed to him that soon there would be more Israelites than Egyptians in the land of Egypt. They worked hard and he needed them, but he did not want their numbers to increase. He said to his people: "Behold, the people of the children of Israel are more and mightier than we. Come, let us deal wisely with them so that they no longer multiply. For what if there is war, and they should join our enemies and fight against us, and then leave this land? They must not go from Goshen, nor become too powerful. I shall make their lives a burden to them; I shall make them slaves."

Therefore the Egyptians set taskmasters over the children of Israel to make them work as hard as men can work. Pharaoh wanted treasure cities built; the slave drivers made the Hebrews build them. But the harder they worked and the more rigorous their lives, the stronger the Israelites grew and the more they multiplied.

"Work them harder yet!" Pharaoh commanded. "Increase their burdens, double their labors. Make each man work until he drops and then flog him until he works again."

The Egyptian overseers did as they were ordered. In every way they made life bitter for the children of Israel, driving each man to work to the very limit of his strength. The Hebrews carried great loads of bricks and mortar, and they built from morn to night; they slaved in the fields with the crops and the cattle; they dug and they dragged and they carried to the sound of the whip and the shout; and they were beaten savagely if their masters thought they were not working hard or fast enough. And yet, in spite of the misery of their lives, the Israelites continued to thrive.

Then the king of Egypt spoke to the Hebrew midwives and ordered them to destroy all boy babies when they were born to the women of Israel. But the midwives believed in the God of Israel and could not bring themselves to obey the king. Instead, they saved the boy children, and told Pharaoh that Hebrew women were not in the habit of waiting for midwives before having their babies, and that therefore they had been unable to follow his orders.

Pharaoh thereupon devised another plan. He gave his people a cruel command: "Every son that is born to the Israelites from this day on, you shall cast into the river. Only the daughters shall you save alive."

Now there was a man of the house of Levi who had married a woman of his tribe. They already had a three-year-old son named Aaron and a daughter, Miriam. And now the woman bore another boy. When she saw what a lovely, sturdy child he was she could not bear to part with him, least of all in the terrible way commanded by the king, and she kept him hidden so that the king's men would not find him. For three months she managed to keep his birth a secret, but then she found that she could no longer hide him. Pharaoh's men were coming too close to her home in their search for Hebrew babies. So she wove for him a basket out of bulrushes, shaping it like a tiny, covered ark and plastering it with pitch and clay to keep the water out. She laid the child inside it and set the basket down among the tall reeds at the river's edge. Sadly, she turned away and went back to her house. But her little daughter Miriam stayed hidden among the reeds a short distance away to see what would become of her baby brother.

A group of women in fine clothes came into view. They were maidens of Pharaoh's household, come down to the river with the daughter of Pharaoh; for Pharaoh's daughter meant to bathe in this quiet stream with its concealing bulrushes. The women walked together along the river bank while Miriam watched. And then Pharaoh's daughter saw the strange little woven boat lying among the reeds. At once, she sent a maid to bring it to her.

And she opened it and saw the child, and the baby began to cry. Pharaoh's daughter picked him up tenderly and with compassion in her heart, for she knew about her father's cruel decree. "This is one of the Hebrew children," she said gently. And she could not think of letting the lovely, innocent baby die.

Sister Miriam watched from the tall reeds and saw the look of love and pity on the princess' face. She left her hiding place and went to Pharaoh's daughter, who was holding the child as if he were her own.

"Shall I go and bring you a nurse from among the Hebrew women?" the girl asked eagerly. "So that she may nurse the child for you?"

"Yes, go," Pharaoh's daughter said to her.

And the baby's sister ran off to find her mother. The woman of Levi came quickly and saw the princess holding the tiny baby she herself had placed so lovingly in the bulrush basket.

"Take this child away," Pharaoh's daughter said softly to its mother, "and nurse him for me. I will give you wages for your work."

Then the woman, with a happy heart, took back her own child and nursed him with a mother's love and care. No longer was she afraid that harm would come to him, for Pharaoh's daughter was the boy's protection.

When the child was old enough to leave his mother she took him to the palace and gave him to Pharaoh's daughter, knowing that he would be well looked after. Pharaoh's daughter called him Moses, "because," she said, "I drew him out of the water." And the boy became her son.

Moses, the Hebrew boy, grew up in the palace of the Pharaoh who feared and hated Hebrews, but Pharaoh's daughter cherished him and saw to it that he was educated as if he were a royal prince. From the Egyptians he learned much of the arts and sciences unknown to his own people; and from his mother's early training he learned that he was one of the children of Israel, whose God was the one true God.

As he grew to manhood he would often leave the royal palace and go out among his own people. He would see their sufferings and their heavy burdens, and the taskmasters who drove and struck them. And it happened, on one of those days that he walked among his fellow men, that he saw an Egyptian overseer reach out his hand against a Hebrew slave and strike the man unmercifully. Moses suddenly forgot himself, forgot that he was a noble in the court of Pharaoh. All he could think was that a brutal slave driver had struck a brother Hebrew. He swiftly looked this way and that, and when he saw that there was no one watching him he hit out savagely and killed the Egyptian. Carefully, he hid the body in the sand and quietly went away. He knew that he had been wrong to kill the man, but he had seen much oppression and his anger had been great.

The next day he went out again. This time he saw two men of the Hebrews fighting one another, and he said to the one who was in the wrong: "Why do you strike your fellow Hebrew?"

The man stared back at him with hatred in his eyes, not knowing that Moses loved his people and only wished them well.

"Who made you a prince and a judge over us?" the man said bitterly. "Do you intend to kill me, as you killed the Egyptian yesterday?"

Fear struck at Moses' heart. So the deed was known; it was being talked about! Word of his crime would surely come to Pharaoh, and the punishment would be terrible. He turned away from the two men and walked off rapidly. He would have to flee at once.

It was not long before the king heard about the murder of his overseer and gave commands that Moses be found and put to death. But Moses had already gone. He left the land of Egypt and traveled deep into the wilderness, looking for a place where he might be safe from Pharaoh's wrath and live in peace. Somewhere he would find a new home and forget the past and the riches and the tyranny of Egypt.

He came eventually, tired and footsore, to the land of Midian. And he sat down by a well.

Now Jethro, the priest of Midian, had seven daughters. While Moses was resting at the well they came there with their father's flock to draw water and fill the troughs so that the sheep might drink. But as they tried to water their flocks, other shepherds came with flocks and tried to drive the women away. It was not the first time this had happened, for there were few wells in the wilderness; the flocks were many, and the daughters of Jethro were no match for the rough, discourteous men. But this time there was a stranger at the well, a man who looked like an Egyptian, and for once the women had a man to help them. Moses stood up and firmly held the shepherds back while he helped the seven sisters draw their water, and he filled the troughs until the thirsty sheep had drunk their fill.

When the women came home their father was surprised to see them, for they were earlier than usual. "How is it that you have come so soon today?" he asked.

"There was an Egyptian at the well," they said. "He defended us from the rough shepherds, and he drew water for us, and he watered our flock himself."

"Well, where is he?" demanded Jethro. "Why did you not bring the stranger with you? Go and call him, that he may eat with us."

And so they did. The family of Jethro welcomed Moses to their home, and a friendship quickly grew between them.

Moses was happy with his new friends. When Jethro asked him to stay with them, Moses was grateful and content to live in Midian. He soon took charge of the family flocks and spared the women from their work.

In time, Jethro gave his daughter Zipporah to Moses for his wife. She bore him two sons, and they all lived a peaceful life together in the land of Midian. The man who had learned so much from the wise teachers of Egypt had now become a simple shepherd in a wilderness far from the land of Pharaoh and the captive Hebrews. He could not forget the sadness and slavery of his own people; but he was an outcast and a murderer who could find no way to help them.

And then the king of Egypt died. At first there was rejoicing among the Israelites, for they thought his cruelty might die with him and that their lot would change.

Their hopes were quickly shattered. The new Pharaoh was even more cruel than the old, and the children of Israel were forced into a state of slavery and misery worse than they had ever known. They cried to heaven with the anguish of their bondage; and their cries went up to God.

The Lord heard the agony of their voices and saw their dreadful burden. In his great pity he remembered his covenant with Abraham, with Isaac, and with Jacob, and he resolved to set their children free.

A man would have to be found who was capable of leading the Israelites to freedom. Moses, a man of the tribe of Levi and a man who knew both Hebrews and Egyptians well, might be such a leader. Yet he was far away in exile, hiding from a king, knowing nothing of recent happenings in Egypt.

THE BURNING BUSH

*F*or many days and months and years Moses tended the flock of Jethro his father-in-law, priest of Midian. As time went by he thought less and less of faraway Egypt, although he never quite forgot. So far as he knew he would be nothing but a shepherd all his life, caring for another man's sheep.

One day he led the flock to the far side of the desert in search of greener pastures, and he came to the foot of Mount Horeb, also known as Sinai, which was the mountain of God. As he grazed his flock he saw, some distance from him, a most unusual sight. A flame sprang suddenly from the middle of a bush, and as he watched the bush kept burning brightly with the fire until it seemed that it would surely turn to ashes and die. But the flames kept on blazing through the dry desert shrub and yet the bush was not destroyed.

"This is strange indeed!" said Moses to himself. "I must turn aside and look more closely at this great sight, to see why the bush does not burn through and die."

It was the angel of the Lord in the flame of fire, though Moses did not know it yet. He left his flock and slowly came toward the burning bush. When the Lord saw that he had turned aside to

see, he called out to Moses from the midst of the miraculous fire
and said: "Moses, Moses!"

Moses looked about him in astonishment. "Here I am," he
answered.

God's voice came again from the burning bush. "Do not come
closer. Take off your shoes, for this is holy ground. I am the God
of your father, the God of Abraham, the God of Isaac, and the
God of Jacob; the God of all your people."

Moses took off his shoes as he was bidden and hid his face, for
now he knew why the bush was not consumed by the fire and he
was afraid to look upon his God.

The heavenly voice went on. "I have seen the sufferings of my
people in Egypt and I have heard the cries wrought from them by
their Egyptian taskmasters; I do know their oppressions and their
sorrows. And I have come down to deliver them from the Egyptians. I will bring them out of that land into another, a good land
and large, flowing with milk and honey; the land of Canaan.
Come now, therefore, and I will send you to Pharaoh, so that you
may lead forth my people the children of Israel out of Egypt to
the promised land."

Moses was astounded by these words. "I, lead them out of
Egypt?" he thought to himself in wonderment; for he had no no-
tion of how he would set about such a difficult task.

He said to God: "Who am I, that I should go to Pharaoh, and
lead the children of Israel out of Egypt? I do not know how I
shall do it."

"Fear not," said the Lord. "I will be with you, and this shall be
a token to show that I have sent you: I tell you now that when
you have brought my people out of Egypt, you will worship me
upon this mountain of Sinai."

"But when I go to the children of Israel and say to them that
the God of their fathers has sent me to them, what if they no
longer know their God?" Moses protested, for he knew how easy
it was for people to turn to idols and forget the one true God. "If
they say to me, 'What is his name?' what shall I say to them?"

And God said to Moses, "You shall tell them that I am Jehovah, he who exists that you may exist. You shall say that you have been sent by God who made all mankind. And this also shall you say to the children of Israel: 'The Lord God of your fathers, the God of Abraham, the God of Isaac, and the God of Jacob, has sent me to you.' This is my name forever, and by it shall I be remembered through all generations."

And then God described to Moses how he should free the Israelites.

"Go and gather the elders of Israel together, and say to them that I, the Lord God of your fathers, have appeared to you. Tell them that I have seen what is being done to my people in Egypt and that I will lead them out of their bondage into a land flowing with milk and honey. They will listen to your voice. And then you and the elders of Israel shall go to the king of Egypt and say to him: 'The Lord God of the Hebrews has appeared to us. Now let us go, we beg you, three days' journey into the wilderness, so that we may make offerings to the Lord our God.' And I am sure that the king of Egypt will not let you go even for these three days; no, he shall refuse completely. And then I will stretch out and strike Egypt with the wonders I will do in the midst of them. After that, the king will let you go. And you shall not go empty-handed, for the Egyptians will give your people fine clothes, and jewels of gold and silver, and you will take these things with you."

"But they will not believe me or listen to my voice," Moses protested. "They will say, 'The Lord has not appeared to you; who are you to say that he has done so?' How shall I make them believe?"

"They will believe," God answered. "What is that in your hand?"

"It is my shepherd's rod," said Moses.

And God said, "Cast it on the ground."

Moses obeyed. He threw his shepherd's crook down on the ground and started back in horror, for it had turned into a wriggling snake.

"Do not be afraid of it," said God. "Reach out your hand and take it by the tail."

So Moses reached out his hand unwillingly and grasped the tail, and at once the snake became a harmless rod in his hand.

"That is so they may believe that the Lord God of their fathers has appeared to you," God said. "Now reach your hand beneath your cloak and place it against your chest."

Moses did so, and when he drew his hand out from beneath his cloak he saw that it was white as snow and diseased as if with leprosy.

"Again," said God. "Put your hand once more against your chest."

And Moses once again reached beneath his cloak and placed his hand against himself. This time, when he drew it out, it had turned again into healthy flesh.

"If they do not believe these signs," said the Lord, "there will be other signs that they will believe. After these signs you will take water from their river and pour it onto the dry land. And the water from the river will turn at once to blood."

But Moses was still not convinced that he was the man to set his people free.

"O my Lord," he said, "I am not an eloquent speaker. My tongue is slow, my words are halting. I know not how to use my speech so that men may be persuaded."

"Who made man's mouth?" said God. "Was it not I? Who makes the dumb, or deaf, or the seeing, or the blind? Is it not I, the Lord? Therefore, go now, and give no more thought to your halting speech. I will be with your mouth, and I will teach you what to say."

"O my Lord, I pray you," Moses pleaded, "send another man, not me."

Then the Lord was angry with him. "Is not Aaron the Levite your brother?" he said sternly. "I know that he speaks well. I know, too, that he is coming out to meet you, and when he sees you he will be glad of heart. Therefore let him be your spokesman. I will teach you what to do and say; and you will speak to him and put the right words in his mouth. He shall be your mouth, and you will instruct him in what he has to do. And you will take that rod in your hands and do signs with it as I have shown you."

Then Moses had nothing more to say. He left the holy mountain and the bush that would not burn to ash, and he returned to Jethro his father-in-law. The story that he told was strange. But Jethro was a good man and a priest, and he believed that Moses truly had been given a mission. It was right, he said, for Moses to return to Egypt and see if his people were still living.

"Go in peace," said Jethro.

Yet Moses was still uneasy about returning to the place from which he had fled in haste so many years before.

God spoke again to Moses in the land of Midian. "Go, return to Egypt," said the Lord, "for all the men who sought your life are dead."

So Moses saddled up his donkeys and took his wife and sons with him on his journey into Egypt, and all the while he held the rod of God firmly in his hand.

The Lord said to Moses: "When you return to Egypt, see that you do before Pharaoh all the wonders that I have put into your hand. His heart will be hard against you, and at first he shall not let the people go. But the harder his heart, the greater shall be his punishment, and my people shall be freed."

And he said to Moses' brother Aaron in Egypt: "Go out into the wilderness and meet your brother Moses."

So Aaron went out from Egypt and met Moses at the mountain of God, and he greeted his brother with love. Moses told Aaron everything the Lord had said to him, and all about the signs he was to show to the people in the land of Egypt.

Aaron's faith and great enthusiasm gave Moses the extra strength he needed. Together, the two brothers of the tribe of Levi traveled back to Egypt with the woman Zipporah and her two sons riding on the donkeys; and as soon as they arrived they gathered together all the elders of the children of Israel and told them that God had sent Moses to deliver them from the unfriendly land.

Aaron spoke as one inspired. Eloquently, persuasively, he told the elders everything the Lord had said to Moses, and he showed them the signs that proved that Moses had indeed seen God. And when the people heard his words and saw the signs, they believed with all their hearts that the Lord had truly visited them and seen their suffering. For the first time in many years they felt real hope that they would be freed from slavery. And they bowed their heads and worshiped God.

"LET MY PEOPLE GO"

*P*haraoh was not impressed with the two bearded Hebrews who stood before him and told him a strange tale of a voice from a burning bush and its heavenly command.

Moses and Aaron asked little of him to begin with. "These are the words of the Lord God of Israel," they explained to Pharaoh. "He said: 'Let my people go so that they may hold a feast to me in the wilderness.' Therefore we ask that you let the children of Israel go forth to make offerings to their God."

"Who is this Lord, that I should obey his voice to let Israel go?" said Pharaoh haughtily. "I do not know him, nor will I let the people go."

"He is the God of the Hebrews and he has appeared to us," said Aaron. "We ask only that you let us go three days' journey into the desert to make sacrifices, or the Lord our God many punish us with death or pestilence."

"Sacrifices!" Pharaoh said contemptuously. "All you want is to take the people away from their work. Get back to your own work, Aaron and Moses, and interfere no more. I will not have my slaves resting from their burdens."

That same day Pharaoh issued new commands to the taskmasters of the Israelites. "The people are lazy," he complained. "They do not have enough to do. You shall no longer give them straw to make brick, as you have been doing. Let them go and gather the straw for themselves. But at the same time you will make sure that they make as many bricks as before. It is because they are idle that they cry out, saying, 'Let us go and sacrifice to our God.' Give them more work so that they may labor longer and not have time to listen to the empty words of Moses and Aaron."

His taskmasters went out and relayed their new orders. "Go, get straw wherever you can find it," they told the Israelites. "But do not let your work fall behind. No matter how long it takes you to gather the straw, you will still produce your daily number of bricks."

So the people were forced to go all over the land to gather their own material for making bricks. And all the while the taskmasters were hurrying them and driving them relentlessly. If they were slow, or fell behind with their quota of new bricks, the taskmasters would lash at them with harsh words and whips. "Why have you not fulfilled your task of making bricks? Why is the number short, both today and yesterday? You are idle, idle!" And the cruel whiplash sang down against bare backs.

The children of Israel turned their hatred against Moses and Aaron.

"Is this how you help us?" they demanded. "May the Lord judge you! You have caused us to be loathesome in the eyes of Pharaoh and his servants, and given him yet another weapon against us. We will die from this! Why could you not leave us alone?"

Their faith, so easily kindled by their hope, died just as easily in the face of this new torment.

Moses was troubled, too. He returned to the Lord and said: "Lord, why have you dealt so harshly with our people? Why did you send me here? For since I came to Pharaoh to speak in your name, he has been even more cruel than before. Lord, you have not delivered your people at all!"

"I have heard the groaning of the children of Israel," said the Lord, "and I have remembered my covenant. Go to them and tell them that I will surely free them from their slavery and bring my judgments against Egypt. You shall see what I will do to Pharaoh now. He will not let the children of Israel go; he will be glad to drive them out. But first I have signs to show to him that I am God. Go to your people; tell them that I am the Lord and I will save them, for I will take them out of Egypt into the land of Canaan, which will be their land and their heritage."

Moses went to the children of Israel and told them what the Lord had said, believing that they would be encouraged by his words of hope. But they were so disheartened by their sufferings that they would not listen to him.

The Lord spoke again to Moses and to Aaron. "Go to Pharaoh," he commanded. "When he asks you to show him a miracle to prove that I have sent you, tell Aaron to take your rod and cast it down at Pharaoh's feet, and it shall become a serpent. For I will show my wonders in the land of Egypt; and though the Pharaoh's heart may harden, he must some day see that I am the Lord who will bring forth my people and punish the Egyptians who have made them slaves."

The two brothers went to Pharaoh for the second time. Again they asked that their people be allowed to leave the land; and Pharaoh's heart was hard. Aaron cast the rod down in front of Pharaoh and his servants, and the rod became a serpent. But Pharaoh had seen such tricks before, or so he thought, and this was nothing to him. He called in his own wise men, the sorcerers and magicians of his court who could use enchantments of their own to do such things, and ordered them to do the same. Each of them cast down a rod, and each of their rods also turned into a snake. Pharaoh smiled with pleasure. But he no longer smiled when Aaron's rod-snake swallowed up the other rods. Then he was angry, and he refused to listen any more to Aaron.

The Lord instructed Moses to show another sign. "Go to Pharaoh in the morning," he commanded. "You will find him bathing in the waters of the Nile. Take your rod and stretch it over all the waters of the land. Say to him that the Lord God of the Hebrews has empowered you to turn the water to blood because he, Pharaoh, will not listen to you and let my people go."

Moses and Aaron did as the Lord commanded. They went to the river and found Pharaoh bathing; and Aaron, in the sight of Pharaoh, lifted up the rod and held it over the waters of the Nile. At once the river turned to blood. The fish died, the river smelled of blood and death, and all the waters of the land were foul and bloody. Even the water in the drinking vessels was turned to blood, and throughout the land there was only blood in the pools and springs and wells. There was water in the land of Goshen, where the children of Israel lived; but there was no water anywhere for the people of Egypt to drink.

Yet this, too, was a feat the magicians of Egypt could achieve with their enchantments, and Pharaoh was not moved.

After seven days the waters cleared.

God spoke again to Moses. "Tell Aaron to stretch his rod again over the waters of the land, over all the streams and rivers and over all the ponds."

Aaron stretched his rod out over the waters of Egypt and a plague of frogs came up and covered the land. They went into the houses and into the bedchamber of the king; they hopped into his bed and scurried through his kitchen; they jumped into the ovens, into the cooking pots, into the freshly kneaded dough; they swarmed over nobleman and servant, and they were everywhere.

Again Pharaoh's magicians could do the same thing with their enchantments. They did so, and brought even more frogs into the land of Egypt.

Pharaoh could not stand it. He called for Moses and Aaron. "Speak to your Lord!" he begged them. "Make him take the frogs away from me and from my people and I will let your people go so that they may make their offerings to their Lord."

Moses did not believe him, but he said: "When shall this be done? Tell me when, and it shall be done at the time you say."

"Tomorrow!" answered Pharaoh, outraged yet desperate.

"Tomorrow it will be," said Moses, "and then you will know that there is no God like the Lord our God."

The next day the frogs died in the houses, in the villages, and in the fields, until all were gone but those that still lived in the river.

But when Pharaoh saw that the plague was over he hardened his heart again. "Certainly your people shall not go into the desert to make offerings," he said harshly, and drove Moses from his presence.

The Lord gave instructions for another plague.

Aaron raised his rod over the dust of the land, and all the particles of dust became lice that settled on man and beast alike, each and every one. Pharaoh's magicians tried with their enchantments to equal what Aaron had done, but they could not bring forth lice. Neither could they rid the Egyptians of the plague sent by the Lord.

Then the magicians knew that the things wrought by Aaron with his rod were more than magic tricks. "This is the work of God!" they said to Pharaoh. But the king, instead of being humbled, further hardened his heart; and he listened neither to Aaron and Moses nor to his magicians with their small enchantments.

So God sent to him another plague. Great swarms of dirt-bearing flies filled the house of Pharaoh and the houses of his servants, buzzing through the homes and fields and spreading their diseases everywhere except into the land of Goshen, where the Israelites lived. The very land was made filthy by the flying swarms.

"Stop!" screamed Pharaoh, flailing at the buzzing flies around his head. "Make your sacrifices! Make them in the land of Goshen, where your people live." For he thought that he could bargain with Moses; but he could not.

Moses shook his head. "No, we shall not worship our God before the eyes of the Egyptians. Their customs are not the same as ours, and they will surely stone us. We will go three days'

journey into the wilderness and worship there, as we have been
commanded by our Lord."

"Then go into the wilderness," Pharaoh said wearily. "Only do
not go far away. And pray to your God to remove this swarm of
flies!"

"I will pray," said Moses. "The flies will go tomorrow. But you,
Pharaoh, may no longer deal deceitfully by promising and then
not letting the people go to make their sacrifices. This time you
must let them go."

"Yes, yes, they shall go. But make this swarm of flies go first!"

On the next day God removed the plague. All at once the flies
disappeared from Pharaoh's palace, from his servants, from his
people; there remained not a single one to anger Pharaoh.

And Pharaoh broke his promise. As soon as the plague of flies
was over, he refused to let the people go. And he was deaf to
Moses' warnings.

God sent another plague. This time a deadly disease swept
through the Egyptians' herds. Their bulls and cows sickened and
died; horses, asses, camels, oxen fell in the fields and never rose
again; sheep in the pastures died off by the hundreds until the
flocks had dwindled to almost nothing. None of the cattle of the
Israelites was dead; and Pharaoh knew it from his messengers.
Yet he hardened his heart, and he did not let the people go.

And then the Lord said to Moses and Aaron: "Take handfuls of
ashes from the furnace, and sprinkle them toward the heavens in
the sight of Pharaoh."

Moses went to Pharaoh and cast the ashes into the air. They
drifted off in tiny spects of dust and settled over Egypt. And
wherever the fine dust settled on man or animal it caused a
painful sore: open boils broke out on every Egyptian beast and
human being. The magicians could do nothing. Their own boils
were so bad that they could not come to see Moses nor even stand
before their king.

But Pharaoh did not relent. Moses warned him once again; it
was no use. "The people shall not go!"

And the heavens resounded with thunder. Hailstones, of a size and quantity never before seen in the land of Egypt, slammed down from above and ravaged the fields. Unprotected cattle, ripening crops, men hurrying home to safety—all were killed. Lightning flashed across the sky, came down to earth mingled with the heavy rain of hail, and ran along the ground in tongues of fire. Trees fell, their limbs broken and trunks uprooted; flax and barley crops were flattened against the soil, and the fields were devastated. But the children of Israel in the land of Goshen were untouched by the terrible storm.

This was still not enough for Pharaoh. He pleaded for an end of it and made his promises, but when the hailstones ceased to fall his heart was harder than ever.

The Lord spoke to Moses.

Moses stretched forth his rod over the land of Egypt, and there was another plague. An east wind blew across the land and brought with it a cloud of locusts that covered the face of the earth, stripping it of every fruit and blade of grass and every young crop which the hail had left untouched. The land was dark with locusts, and not a green thing lived in all of Egypt. The king's own elders turned on him and said: "How long will you let this man bring suffering to us? Do you not see that Egypt is destroyed?"

In his terror Pharaoh called for Moses. "Forgive my sin once more!" he begged. "Be merciful, and take away this death. Only this I ask you!"

Moses spoke to the Lord. And the Lord sent a mighty west wind to blow across the land and sweep the swarms of locusts from the earth and into the Red Sea. But with the passing of the plague, Pharaoh again went back upon his word and would not let the people go.

And again Moses stretched his rod toward the heavens. A dreadful darkness settled over Egypt for three long days and nights. Sun, moon, and stars all ceased to give their light. The children of Israel had light in their homes, but the Egyptians could not even see each other, much less go about their business.

Pharaoh, desperate, called Moses to him. "Take your people and go!" he said. "All of them, the men and women and children. Only leave your flocks and herds behind."

"No," said Moses. "We will take everything with us, everything we have."

"Then you take nothing!" Pharaoh growled. "You shall not leave at all. Get out of my presence and never let me see your face, for on the day I see you, you shall die."

Moses left him and listened once more to the voice of God.

"I will bring one more plague on Pharaoh," said the Lord, "and he will let you go, he will thrust you out of Egypt altogether. Warn him, and then prepare yourself and your people for the thing I am about to do."

Moses listened. The next, and last, would be the most terrible plague of all, and it would strike at the heart of Pharaoh himself.

It was almost too horrible a thing to think about; but Pharaoh in his cruelty had brought it down upon himself.

THE NIGHT OF PASSOVER

*M*oses called together all the elders of Israel to tell them what was going to happen and what they had to do.

"This time we shall leave," said Moses. "First, every man and woman among us will go to his Egyptian neighbor and ask for jewels of silver and gold so that we are not empty-handed. Then you must prepare yourselves to leave with these gifts, and with your children, and with your cattle and all your goods."

The Egyptians gave freely when they were asked for gifts that would enable the Israelites to trade with merchants while they traveled. Even though their Pharaoh had refused to listen to Moses, they had come to regard the Hebrew leader as a great man in the land. They had seen his prophecies come true, and they had respect for him and the wonders he could do.

"And now," said Moses to the elders, "you must listen to me closely and do exactly as I say. The Lord has spoken to me, and this is what he said: 'At midnight I will go out into the midst of Egypt. And all the first born in the land shall die, from the oldest child of Pharaoh who sits upon the throne to the oldest child of the maidservant working at the mill, and every first born of the cattle. And there shall be a great cry throughout the land of

Egypt because of this, such an outcry as there never was before nor ever will be afterward. But against the children of Israel, not even a dog will so much as bark.' That is what the Lord has told me, and that is what I have said to Pharaoh. And when this thing happens, as it must because Pharaoh's heart is hard against us, then the people of Egypt will come to us and beg us to go quickly from their land. And we will go."

And that was to be God's last and most terrible sign to the cruel king of Egypt.

"What you must do," Moses continued, "is take a lamb, a young male lamb that is strong and perfect, one for every household of the Hebrews. The size of it will depend upon the household, for in the meal that you make of this lamb there must be nothing left over. Therefore, if the family is small, let it share its lamb with a neighboring family that is also small. The head of each of your households must kill the lamb himself and collect its blood in a basin, and then take a bunch of the herbs called hyssop and dip it into the blood. With the hyssop each man is to smear the blood over the lintel and side posts of the door so that every house in which a Hebrew family lives is marked with the blood of the lamb. After marking the doors you shall roast the lamb and eat it with unleavened bread and bitter herbs; but even while you eat you must be dressed and ready for travel, for it is likely that we will have to leave in haste.

"Also," Moses said, "when you have finished sprinkling the blood you are to remain inside your houses until early morning, for during the night the Lord will pass this way to strike his punishment at the Egyptians. When he sees the blood on the lintels and the doorposts of your houses, the Lord will pass over your doors and not permit death to enter in to harm you. And you shall observe this same day as a memorial every year from this day on, and keep it as a feast to the Lord forever in memory of this night of the passover."

The people of Israel bowed their heads and worshiped, for now they fully believed that Moses and the Lord their God would deliver them not only from the dreadful sorrow that was to fall upon the Egyptians but also from their slavery in the land of Egypt. When they had prayed they hurried home and made the preparations commanded of them by the Lord through his spokesmen, Moses and Aaron; and they roasted lamb, prepared their dough, and painted blood around the doorways of their houses.

That night at midnight the Lord passed through the land of Egypt, and death struck at the homes of the Egyptians. In each household the oldest child died suddenly: from Pharaoh's own firstborn to the firstborn of the lowliest captive in the dungeon and the firstborn of the cattle in the fields, all died. There was not a house of the Egyptians that was spared this tragedy. But wherever the blood of the lamb marked the doorway of an Israelite household, the Lord passed over the house and the people within it were spared.

There was a great cry of anguish throughout Egypt on that night. Pharaoh arose from his bed in the dark hours and saw his terrible loss; his servants and his subjects rose and found their eldest dead; and in every house of the Egyptians there was dreadful sorrow.

Pharaoh called for Moses and Aaron. "Leave!" he cried. "Go! Get away from among my people, you and all the children of Israel! Go, serve your Lord as you have said. Take your flocks, your families, your herds, take everything—be gone!"

His people were no less anxious to be rid of the Israelites, for they knew that they were plagued because of them. "We are dead, unless you go from us," they cried. "Go, and go quickly. Take what you want from us, only leave our land."

The Israelites were ready for travel. They had gathered their goods and flocks; they had eaten their passover meal; and they were dressed to leave even though the hour was late and the night still dark. But the dough they had prepared had not yet risen in its pans, so they bound up the pans of unleavened bread in their bundles of clothes and carried them away upon their

shoulders. The Egyptians speeded them on their way with gifts of
fine clothes and jewels of gold and silver, giving them whatever
they required of Egypt's riches. Thus the Israelites did not leave
the land of their slavery with empty hands.

It was a great procession that departed the land of Egypt in the
early dawn. Four hundred and thirty years before, at the time of
Joseph, seventy Hebrews had settled in the land; now six
hundred thousand of them—not even counting the many little
ones—journeyed away from the Egyptians and took their first
steps toward the promised land.

There was war among the people of the north so that it was not
wise to travel there. Instead, God led the children of Israel
through the way of the wilderness of the Red Sea, going before
them by day in a pillar of cloud to show them the way and by
night in a pillar of fire to give them light for their journeying.

They traveled on for several days, putting more and more distance between themselves and the cruel king of Egypt, until it
was time for them to make camp and rest themselves before going
further. Then they pitched their tents beside the Red Sea, which
they would somehow have to cross, and gathered strength for further journeying.

But Pharaoh heard through his messengers that they had
stopped to camp, and he thought to himself that they would
surely be trapped there in the wilderness beside the sea. Now that
there were no more plagues to trouble Egypt, Pharaoh and his
court attendants were sorry that they had let the Israelites go.
Once again their hearts were hardened. "Why did we do it?" they
asked each other angrily. "Why should we have let them go from
serving us? Now we no longer have the Israelites as slaves to
make our bricks and carry them, to build our buildings and work
long hours in the fields. How foolish of us, to have let them go!"

And Pharaoh, cruel and hard as ever, readied his chariot and
took his forces with him. With six hundred other chariots and an
army of men mounted on horseback, he drove his warriors and
their captains in swift pursuit of his one-time slaves. It was not

long before he came close to overtaking them in their encampment by the sea.

The Israelites saw the clouds of whirling sand churned up by the approaching chariots and horses, and they were terrified.

"Were there no graves in Egypt that you had to bring us out here into the wilderness to die?" they cried out to Moses. "Did we not beg you to let us alone so that we might serve the Egyptians as before? It would have been far better for us to go on being slaves than to die here in the desert!"

Their hearts were faint, but Moses still had faith. "Fear not," he said to them. "Stand still and see the salvation of the Lord, which he will show you today. After this day you will never see these Egyptians again, for the Lord will fight for you. Hold your peace, and see what happens."

They waited and they trembled as the thunder of the horses' hooves and chariot wheels grew close.

Now the pillar of cloud that had led them by day to the wilderness moved and went behind them so that it hung heavy in the air like some great screen of smoke between the Israelites and the forces of the Egyptians. On the one side it plunged the army of Egypt into darkness, and on the other it gave light to the camp of Israel. All the night it stayed there so that no one from either camp could cross into the other.

And while the cloud protected the children of Israel, Moses lifted up his rod and stretched his hand out across the waters of the Red Sea as the Lord had bidden him. A wind sprang up from the east and grew strong and wild throughout the night, until its force became so great that the waters of the sea were parted and there was a path of land between them.

"Now cross the sea!" commanded Moses.

The children of Israel saw the path that had opened before them and quickly gathered their possessions. They hurried and stumbled along the path left by the windblown waters, and on each side of them there was a wall of sea held back only by the power of the God-sent wind.

The cloud screen lifted in the early hours before dawn, and

Pharaoh in his camp saw the last of the great band of Israelites reaching the far side of the sea. "After them!" he shouted. He plunged after them with his galloping horses and his speeding chariots until he and his huge army were well along the path leading through the sea. The Lord looked down on them then as the chariot wheels dug deep into the wet sand and lumbered heavily and slowly between the walls of water.

"Stretch out your hand," said the Lord to Moses.

Moses held his rod out over the waters of the sea. Slowly, as early dawn became full morning light, the strong wind softened to a breeze. Water lapped at the horses' legs and chariot wheels. The horses fell, throwing their Egyptian riders, and chariots overturned and spilled out the charioteers. While they struggled to right themselves and turn back across the flooding path, the walls of water broke against them. Men, horses, chariots, and the king himself were plunged deep into the midst of the returning sea. When the waters quieted down into their accustomed tide there was not a live man to be seen among the armies of Egypt.

The Israelites stood on the far side of the Red Sea and watched the closing waters, and they saw the Egyptians dead upon the seashore. They were saved! Moses had said they would be saved; the Lord had given his children their salvation; the Lord had delivered them that day from the hand of the Egyptians!

All fear went from their hearts, and the children of Israel saw the great work of their Lord and they believed in him. Their groans turned into great shouts of gratitude and triumph, and on the safe shore of the Red Sea they joined with Moses in a song of thanksgiving to their God:

> "I will sing unto the Lord, for he has triumphed gloriously,
> The horse and his rider has he thrown into the sea.
> The Lord is my strength and song,
> And he is my salvation:
> He is my God, and I will prepare for him a temple;
> He is my father's God, and I will exalt him!"

And as they sang their song of love and praise, Miriam, the sister of Moses who had watched him from the bulrushes, took a timbrel in her hand and led the women in a rapturous dance of relief and joy. With their own tambourines they danced and followed her, answering the song of Moses with his same words in their own joyous voices:

"Sing unto the Lord, for he has triumphed gloriously,
The horse and his rider has he thrown into the sea. . . ."

Thus did Moses bring his people safely across the Red Sea away from Egypt into another land.

INTO THE WILDERNESS

*M*any generations of slavery in the cities of Egypt had changed the children of Israel from a self-reliant tribe of hardy shepherd-farmers into a timid, downtrodden people accustomed to being told exactly what to do and how to do it. And although they had been able to keep their own flocks and herds in the well-watered land of Goshen, they had long since forgotten what it was like to take care of their flocks or even themselves under the hard conditions of life in the desert. They had hated the cities of Egypt but they were used to them. The world outside was very different.

They journeyed to the south, following Moses into the Wilderness of Shur. It was hot and very dry, and their progress was slow because of their great numbers and the plodding pace of their cattle and sheep. For three long, tiring days they were without water in the wilderness, and their relief was great when they came to a place called Marah. Here at last was water. This, they thought, would save their very lives, for they could go on no longer without drinking.

But when they tasted it they found the water bitter and not fit to drink. Moses was to blame, they told each other; in Egypt they had never had this kind of hardship. They turned on him at once.

"What are we supposed to drink?" they demanded of their leader. Only three days in the wilderness after many years of slavery, and already they were losing heart!

"What shall I do, Lord?" Moses cried. The Lord showed him a tree whose wood was sweet, and told him what to do. Moses cast the young tree into the bitter waters of Marah, and the waters became sweet. The people drank deeply and gave water to their herds.

"If you will believe in me," said the Lord, "and do what is right in my sight, I will always be with you. Listen to my voice and obey the things I ask of you, and I will bring upon you none of the diseases which I brought upon the Egyptians. For I am the Lord who helps and heals you."

When the children of Israel were refreshed they traveled on again, now a little more confident that they would find green oases in the desert where they might rest and draw fresh water. The cloud of the Lord moved on ahead and led them to a lovely place called Elim where there was a large, cool grove of palm trees and twelve wells of fresh, sweet water. Here beside the waters they pitched their camp and stayed for several days. It was so pleasant a place that they would just as soon have stayed there longer.

But the cloud moved on again, and they moved with it.

On the fifteenth day of the second month after leaving Egypt, the children of Israel entered the Wilderness of Sin, a vast desert country which lay between Elim and the mount of Sinai where God had spoken to Moses through the burning bush.

The Israelites looked around them and did not like the land at all. The flat plain stretched out for what seemed endless miles, unbroken anywhere by the shapes of tall green palms. Wells there might be, somewhere in that expanse of wilderness, but clearly no food would be found to eat. The children of Israel looked at Moses doubtfully. He led them on.

They plodded on through the dust and heat, seeing no sign of life other than the low shrubs of the desert and once in a while a lizard basking in the sun, and as the days passed they found no food and the pangs of hunger gnawed inside them.

The whole congregation of the children of Israel began to murmur against Moses and Aaron in the wilderness until their murmurs became loud words of anger. "Far better for us to have died by the hand of the Lord in Egypt instead of in the desert! There at least we had pots full of meat and we could eat our fill of bread. But you made us leave and brought us into this wilderness, and now all of us will die of hunger."

God heard their outcry and spoke to Moses. "They will not die of hunger. You shall see that I will rain bread down from heaven for you, every day from this time forth until you end your journey. The people must go out and gather a certain amount, but only what they need, each morning after it has fallen; in this way shall I test them to see whether they obey my words or not. On the sixth day they are to collect twice as much as on the other days, for there must be no work on the seventh day. This evening I will send them meat, and from tomorrow morning forth I will send them their daily bread."

Moses and Aaron relayed these words to the complaining people. "Now you shall see the glory of the Lord," they said, not without some anger. "He has heard your murmurings, and he will send you meat and bread to eat. But remember this: When you complain, you are murmuring not against us—for what are we?— but against the Lord who sends you all his glories."

That evening a flight of quails flew into the camp. The people caught them easily, great quantities of them, and for the first time in many days they had plenty of meat to eat. And in the morning, when the dew had disappeared from the ground around the camp, a strange substance was left behind on the face of the wilderness. A closer look showed that it was a mass of small round things that looked like beads of frost. "What is it?" the children of Israel asked each other.

Moses answered them. "It is the bread sent by the Lord for you to eat," he said. "Go and gather it, each man for the members of his tent. Take no more than you will need for this day, according to the numbers you must feed."

The children of Israel took their food vessels from their tents and collected the Lord's bread eagerly. Some gathered too much, some too little; but when each man measured out how much he had collected, all found to their surprise that they each had exactly as much as they needed. They ate with pleasure. The new food was white like coriander seed, and the taste of it was like wafers made with honey. They called it Manna, meaning 'what is this?', for they did not know what they were eating except that it was good.

"Do not leave any until morning," Moses said. "Eat what you have, for what you keep will spoil. There will be more tomorrow, and every morning except on the seventh day."

But some of the people did not listen to Moses, and they kept some of the manna from one day to the next. It did them not the slightest good, for it turned bad overnight and smelled foul in the morning. And there was fresh manna outside on the ground for them to gather. After that they made sure to collect only what they needed every day, and they did not try to put a store aside. They filled their pots, and when the sun grew hot the remaining manna melted on the ground.

On the sixth day they gathered twice as much as usual for, as Moses said, "Tomorrow is the day of rest, the holy sabbath of the Lord. Therefore bake what you want to bake today and boil what you want to boil, and keep the rest until tomorrow."

They did so, nearly all of them, and in the morning the manna they had put aside was still fresh and good to eat. But some had disobeyed again, and had failed to gather enough for both the sixth and seventh days. When they went out on the sabbath day to gather manna, there was none to gather.

Thereafter they collected manna in the way the Lord had told them, for six days out of every week that they spent wandering through the wilderness.

The cloud moved on. The great caravan of Israelites, with all their goods and sheep and cattle, continued on their journey south. The pillar of cloud led them out of the Wilderness of Sin toward the distant mountain of the Lord.

Then the cloud stopped. The caravan halted with it, and the children of Israel pitched their camp at Rephidim to rest there and refresh themselves.

Again they found cause for complaint. The Lord had commanded them to stop, and yet there was no water for the people to drink. They were burned brown and dry by the blazing heat, parched for want of water, and filled with new despair. Even though God had led them across the Red Sea, made sweet water for them to drink at Marah, and provided them with their daily bread, they still did not have faith enough to know that God would help them now.

"Moses!" As before, they turned their anger against Moses, and this time they were so enraged that they seemed about to kill him. "Give us water!" they demanded hotly. "Why did you bring us out of Egypt—so that you could kill us and our children and our cattle with thirst? Is the Lord with us, or is he not?"

Moses cried out to the Lord. "What shall I do for these people?" he begged. "They are almost ready to stone me!"

The Lord answered, saying: "Take the elders of Israel and go on before your people with your rod in hand. I will show you a certain rock in Horeb, and you shall strike that rock with the rod. Out of it there will come water so that the people may drink."

Moses and the elders went ahead and came to the place of which the Lord had spoken. There was no stream in sight among the mountains, nor any place that looked as though it might yield a spring of water, but Moses did not waver in his faith. The Lord showed him the rock, and Moses struck it before the eyes of the astonished elders. They saw what happened: a stream of water gushed out from beneath the stone and ran in rivulets down the mountainside.

Then fear and anger were forgotten. The children of Israel ran to the water with their pitchers and drank gratefully, and when their thirst was satisfied they watered their flocks and filled their drinking vessels for their tents. For a little while they would again trust Moses and their Lord, until some new thing made them cry out their regrets at ever having left the land of Egypt.

And something happened very soon. In the land where they had pitched their camp there lived a fierce tribe of people called Amalekites after their leader Amalek, who was descended from Esau. Amalek saw the goods and cattle in the Israelite camp, and he launched a series of raids to secure them for himself. The Israelites were not good fighters and they were easily disheartened by Amalek's swift and daring attacks, but Moses could not permit those wild men of the desert to steal from his people and harass them on their journey. He looked over his ranks and called out a stalwart young man by the name of Joshua.

"Choose the best men you can find," he ordered, "and go out and fight with Amalek. We will attack tomorrow. You shall lead the army, and I will stand on top of the hill with the rod of God in my hand so that victory will be ours."

Joshua went among the men and quickly organized a force of the strongest and most courageous of the children of Israel. The next day he went out with his chosen warriors and clashed against the forces of Amalek. Moses, Aaron, and a trusted friend named Hur went up to the top of the hill to watch the course of battle and inspire their people. The Amalekites were powerful and cunning, practiced in fighting and plundering people less warlike than themselves, and Joshua's men were untrained in the arts of war. It was not an even battle; but Moses, on the hilltop, held the rod in his hand and put his faith in God. Whenever he held up his hands the forces of Joshua gained and drove the Amalekites back; and whenever he lowered his hands to rest them the forces of Amalek surged forward and drove back Joshua's men.

It was plain to Moses that he would have to keep his hands raised all the time or Amalek would win the victory. But his hands were heavy and his shoulders tired, so that he had to rest every once in a while and see the Amalekites cut down the children of Israel. Then Aaron and Hur found a large stone for him to sit on, and they placed themselves at either side. One of them raised his left hand and the other his right, and between the two of them they kept Moses' arms upright and stretched toward the heavens until the end of the day.

The Amalekites no longer advanced. Slowly, steadily, they started their retreat, and as the day grew late they fell back in confusion. As they weakened, the Israelites gained strength, and went after them with swords.

Moses' hands were steady until the sun went down. In the dim light of early evening the Amalekites broke ranks and fled, utterly defeated by Joshua's fighting forces and this man upon the mountain. When Moses saw that his people were victorious he lowered his tired arms and offered up a heartfelt prayer of thanksgiving to God.

Now they could travel on from Rephidim untroubled by marauding tribes, and soon they would reach the mountain of God where great things were to happen to them.

THE TEN COMMANDMENTS

*I*n the third month after the children of Israel had gone forth out of the land of Egypt, they came into the Wilderness of Sinai and pitched their camp near the holy mountain.

It was familiar territory to Moses, for while he had been living with Jethro in the land of Midian he had often come here to the far side of the desert to find green pastures for his flocks. He left his people in their camp at the foot of the mountain and climbed the slope where once he had seen a thorn bush blazing with unearthly fire.

"I will be with you," the Lord had told him then, "and I tell you now that when you have brought my people out of Egypt, you will worship me upon this mountain of Sinai."

And now, here he was, climbing the mountain of God; and God was speaking to him from the mountain:

"You have seen what I did to the Egyptians, and how I carried you on eagles' wings and brought you back to me. Now say this to the house of Jacob, to the children of Israel: 'If you obey the voice of the Lord and keep his covenant, then shall you be a special treasure to him above all other people. And you shall be to him a

kingdom of priests, and a holy nation.' Say this to the children of
Israel, and then return to me."

Moses called his people together and repeated the Lord's
words. They answered as one man. "All that the Lord has asked
us, we will do," they promised. "Surely we will obey and keep his
covenant." And Moses went back to the Lord and told him what
the people had said.

Then the Lord was glad, and said to Moses: "From the top of
the mountain will I come to you in a thick cloud, so that the people may hear for themselves when I speak to you and will forever
believe you. Now go to them; have them wash their clothes and
purify themselves today and tomorrow, and be ready by the third
day. For on that day I will come down in their sight upon Mount
Sinai. Only be sure that none of them sets foot upon the mountain, for it is holy ground. When the voice of the trumpet sounds
long and loud, they shall approach the mountain and I will come
near."

Moses went back to the camp and prepared his people.

Dawn of the third day broke with thunder and lightning, and a
thick cloud covered the peak of the mount. The blare of a trumpet
resounded across the camp, and the people trembled with fear.
And Moses brought them out of the camp to meet with God.
They stood at the foot of the mountain watching it quake and
shake in a terrifying manner. It seemed to be covered with smoke,
for the Lord had descended upon it in a great flame and the
smoke from the flame reached into the heavens like the fiery red
smoke of a gigantic furnace.

Then the voice of the trumpet sounded again, and its blasts
grew louder and louder. Moses called out to the Lord, and the
Lord answered in a voice that could be heard by all the people.
And they all heard the thunder rolling across the valley, and saw
the shaking, smoking mountain. They stared at it in awe and fear
and stumbled back away from it. "Speak to us!" they said to
Moses. "Speak, and we will hear. But do not let God speak to us
or we will surely die."

"Do not be afraid," Moses answered them, "for God has come to show his greatness to you so that you will believe in him and will not sin."

And the people stood as far back as they could from the frightening scene as the Lord came down upon the mountain in his cloud and called to Moses.

Moses went up to the top of the mountain into the thick cloud of darkness where the Lord was, and he listened to the words of God. "This shall you say to my people," said the Lord.

"I am the Lord your God, who brought you out of the land of Egypt, out of the house of bondage.

"You shall have no other gods before me.

"You shall make no graven images nor any likeness of anything that is in heaven above, or that is in the earth beneath, or that is in the water under the earth. You shall not bow down yourself to them or worship them, for I the Lord your God am a jealous God.

"You shall not take the name of the Lord your God in vain.

"Remember the sabbath day, to keep it holy. Six days shall you labor and do all your work. But on the seventh day is the sabbath of the Lord your God, and on it you shall not do any work, neither you nor those who are with you. For in six days the Lord made heaven and earth and sea, and all that is in them, and rested the seventh day. Therefore the Lord has blessed the sabbath day and made it holy.

"Honor your father and your mother, that your days may be long upon the land which the Lord your God has given you.

"You shall not kill.

"You shall not commit adultery.

"You shall not steal.

"You shall not bear false witness against your neighbor.

"You shall not covet your neighbor's house, nor your neighbor's wife, nor his servants, nor his cattle, nor anything that is his.

"All this," said the Lord, "shall you tell the children of Israel. Yet there is more to tell. Now these are the judgments you shall set before them." And God spoke further to Moses, giving him a code of justice by which his people might live and describing the rules and laws that would govern their conduct in the course of their daily lives and in the observance of religious ceremonies. "These things shall you tell them," said the Lord, "so that they will know what is right and what is wrong in everything they do. Say also that I will lead them into Canaan and make their enemies flee before them; not all at once, but little by little, until you inherit the land. Now return to the people and tell them what I have said. Tomorrow I will call you back to speak more upon the mountain."

Moses went back to his awe-struck followers. He told them everything the Lord had said, all his words and all his laws. "And these you must obey," he finished.

The people answered with one voice: "We will do everything the Lord has said!"

Early the next morning Moses arose and built an altar at the foot of the mountain of God, with the twelve pillars for the twelve tribes of Israel, and sent the young men of the camp to bring oxen to place as burnt offerings on the altar. Together, all the children of Israel worshiped the Lord, and Moses once again told them the words of God. When the service was over he feasted with his elders on the mountainside, until the Lord called to him and said: "Come up to me on top of the mountain, and I will give you tablets of stone upon which I will write my law and the commandments with my own hand, so that you may teach them to the people."

Moses rose from the feast, bidding Joshua to join him. "Wait here for us, until we return again," he told the elders. "Aaron and Hur are with you; if any man has any matters to decide, let him go to them."

And Moses went up into the mountain, taking Joshua with him almost to the summit, and then he climbed onto the cloud-capped peak alone.

To the children of Israel, watching from below, the glowing

cloud looked like a blaze of glorious, heavenly fire; and they knew that their leader Moses was within it communing with the Lord.

This time the Lord spoke to him about the building of a tabernacle, a tent sanctuary which the Israelites could take with them on their journey. In it, the Lord would meet with Moses, and the children of Israel would hold services in worship to their God. It was to have several rooms, and the innermost chamber would be the most sacred of all. For this room the people must make an ark, or chest, of acacia wood and gold, and the two stone tablets bearing God's commandments were to be placed in this ark and revered forever. To build and furnish this tabernacle the people must bring offerings, with willing hearts; and many such offerings would be required.

"Gold, silver, and brass shall they bring," said the Lord, "and fine linens in blue, purple, and scarlet; goat's hair, and ram skins dyed red, and acacia wood; oil for the light, spices and incense; onyx stones and other jewels. And the goat's hair shall be used as curtains in the tabernacle; and the acacia wood will support the covering of the tent which must be made of the dyed ram skins. . . ."

Moses listened intently to the detailed instructions given to him by the Lord. The hours and days passed into weeks while he remained within the cloud, but he was not aware of time.

"From the fine linens and jewels," said the Lord, "you shall make ornaments for the tabernacle and holy garments for the priests; and your brother Aaron the Levite and his sons shall be the first of the priests."

There was more, much more, and even while Aaron was being mentioned as a holy priest by the speakers in the cloud, he was performing priestly duties down below. But, although he was a good man, there was wickedness in what he did now.

For forty days and forty nights Moses spoke with God on the cloud-topped mountain. And the people began to be afraid that he would never come back. "We are lost!" they cried to Aaron. "What has happened to Moses, the man who brought us out of the land of Egypt? Make us gods to go before us, so that we shall not be deserted."

Aaron was deeply distressed, but he did not have the courage to refuse in the face of their rising restlessness. "Bring me all your golden ornaments and earrings," he said sadly.

They brought him what they had, all the earrings that they wore, and he took them for his work. He melted them down and fashioned the molten gold into the figure of a calf. It was a shape the people knew and secretly admired, for the Egyptians and other pagan peoples often worshiped such things as bulls and calves.

"This is our god!" the Israelites shouted joyfully. "These are the gods, O Israel, that brought you out of the land of Egypt!"

Aaron saw their great delight and, having already broken the commandment against making graven images, committed an even greater blasphemy. He built an altar before the golden idol so that a ceremony of worship might be held, and he made a proclamation.

"Tomorrow is the feast of the Lord!" he shouted, though the Lord's feast it certainly was not. "Bring offerings, and food, and let us feast!"

Early next morning the children of Israel, happy and excited as they had not been for many days of fear, brought offerings to the altar. They worshiped the false idol, ate and drank until they could fill themselves no more, and then rose up to play. Soon they were in a frenzy of singing and abandoned dancing.

The Lord God on the mountaintop knew at once what they were doing.

"Go!" he said to Moses. "Get down to your people that you led from Egypt, for they have already disobeyed me and made a molten calf to worship. 'These be your gods, O Israel,' they are saying to each other! They are a stiff-necked, stubborn people. Leave me now, for my anger has grown hot against them for their wickedness. Of you, I shall make a great nation; but those people, I shall destroy."

"Lord, do not destroy them," Moses pleaded. "Why be angry against the people you brought out of Egypt with your own mighty hand? Then will the Egyptians say 'It was for an evil trick that their Lord led them out, so that he might kill them in the mountains and destroy them from the face of the earth.' I pray you, Lord, have mercy on your people and remember your vow to Abraham, to Isaac, and to Israel, that their race would be great upon this earth and inherit the land."

The Lord heard him, and repented of his wrath. Whatever he would do, he would not destroy them.

Moses hurried down the mountainside, taking with him the two precious tablets of stone on which the Lord had inscribed his commandments with his own hand. Joshua met Moses on the way, for he was waiting for him still.

"There is a noise of war in the camp!" Joshua said urgently.

"No, that is not the noise of war," Moses answered grimly. "That is the sound of revelry and singing."

When he came to the camp the sight that met his eyes was even worse than he had imagined. He saw the calf with Aaron standing by it; he saw the meat, the drink, the worshipers, and the wild, abandoned dancing, and he was hot with anger. There was scarcely a commandment that had not already been broken. Then they might as well be truly broken! In the white heat of his rage Moses raised the sacred tablets of stone high above his head and flung them down with all his strength against a rock at the foot of the mountain. They shattered noisily into tiny pieces; and with the shattering sound the children of Israel suddenly grew silent. Aaron turned pale and trembled. The whole assembly looked at Moses, and he stared back at them.

After many months of guidance through the desert, after coming to a holy place and hearing God, after receiving his commandments and his laws of conduct and of justice, they had brought themselves to this.

The precious tablets lay like dust upon the ground.

THE CLOUD MOVES ON FROM SINAI

*T*he godless image of a calf stood upon its pedestal amongst the people, unseeing and unsightly. But many of the Israelites were still defiant of Moses and would rather keep their useless idol than follow their stern leader.

Moses turned with fury upon the golden calf that Aaron had made and flung it into the fire. When it had melted into a shapeless mass and cooled into an ugly lump, he ground it into powder and put the fine gold dust into the drinking water. It tasted bitter and poisonous, but Moses forced each man and woman to drink it.

Then he sought out Aaron, who stood aside, shamefaced and silent.

"What did the people do to you, that you have brought so great a sin upon them?" he demanded.

"Do not be angry with me," Aaron begged him humbly. "You know the people, and the wickedness of their hearts. For they said to me, 'Make us gods to go before us, for we do not know what has become of Moses who led us out of Egypt.' I told them, then, to bring me gold. So they gave it to me, then I cast it into the fire, and there came out this calf."

Moses' anger still burned hotly. These rebellious people must be made to realize that they could not sin without being swiftly punished! And although he did not want them to be destroyed by the wrath of God, examples must be made among them or mutiny would wreck the expedition. He therefore stood at the gate of the camp and called out: "Who is on the Lord's side? Let him come to me!"

The idol worshipers hung back, muttering among themselves against God and their leader. But all of the tribe of Levi, those destined to be priests, gathered by his side.

Moses gave his orders. And there fell by the sword that day many men who were not on the side of the Lord.

On the following day Moses said to his people: "You have sinned a great sin, and the anger of God is mighty. But I will go up to the Lord now, and perhaps I may obtain forgiveness for your sin."

With heavy heart he climbed the mountain once again and returned to the Lord to beg forgiveness for his people.

"O Lord, these people have sinned terribly," he said. "They made for themselves gods out of gold. Yet I beg your mercy. And if you cannot forgive their sin, let me die, I pray you, to atone for them."

"No, you shall not die for them," said the Lord. "Whoever has sinned against me shall suffer for his own sins. Now return to your people, and tell them that I will plague them for their wickedness. And say also that you shall still lead them into the land flowing with milk and honey; but my angel shall go before them, and not I. I will not be with them, for they are such a stubborn and sinful people that I might destroy them on the way."

And the Lord did plague the people, because they had made the calf; but they were more troubled by the Lord's words than the plague. When they heard that God would no longer lead them himself they mourned with all their hearts and cried with sorrow.

Their penitence was so sincere and their sorrow so deep that the Lord felt pity for them. Moses saw them praying, and he saw

the honesty with which they worshiped, and once again he spoke
for them with his Lord.

Then God relented. "I will be with you on your way," he said,
"so that it shall be known that you and your people have found
grace in my sight. For this nation is my chosen people. Now cut
two more tablets of stone, like the first, and I will write upon
those tablets the words that were on the first tablets that you
broke. Be ready with them in the morning, and come to me alone
on the top of the mountain."

Moses cut the two new tablets of stone, and in the morning he
went up the mountain with them as the Lord had commanded
him.

The Lord descended in the cloud and stood with Moses as
before. Again, it was many days before the leader of the Israelites
left the presence of his God, but this time there was no murmur of
rebellion from his people.

When Moses came down from Mount Sinai he carried with him
a new set of written laws, for upon the second pair of stone tablets
were written the words of the Lord's covenant, the ten commandments of the Lord. He did not know that his very being shone
from talking to God; and when Aaron and all the children of
Israel saw Moses and the strange light that glowed from his face
they were afraid to come near him.

Moses called to them, for he had much to say to Aaron and all
the rulers of the congregation; and he put a veil over his face to
shield them from the light that frightened them so much. Afterward he gathered to him all the children of Israel and told them
what God had taught him on the mountain: all about the laws
they were to follow, about their duties, their offerings, and the
building of the ark and tabernacle.

Then every man and woman with a willing heart went to their
tents and came back with offerings of materials for the tabernacle.
Lovingly, and with the greatest skill, they built the holy tabernacle and all the furnishings within. And when it was complete they

placed in it the ark containing the stone tablets on which the
Lord had written his commandments.

There in the wilderness they celebrated the first anniversary of
the passover, and Aaron and his sons began their priestly duties.
On the day that the sanctuary of the Lord was made ready for
worship—one year after the children of Israel had made their
camp at the foot of Mount Sinai—the cloud of the Lord settled
upon the tabernacle. That meant that Moses would no longer
have to go up into the mountain to commune with God; and also
that they had an unmistakable sign to follow as a guide. The
cloud was with them always, a smoky covering by day and a pillar
of fire by night.

When the cloud lifted from the tabernacle and moved on
ahead, the children of Israel continued on their journey. But
when the cloud stopped and covered the tabernacle, they pitched
their tents and rested. And so it was, throughout the remainder of
their journey, that at the commandment of the Lord they rested
in their tents, and at the commandment of the Lord they journeyed on. As the cloud traveled, so did they.

On the twentieth day of the second month of the second year of
their wanderings, the children of Israel followed the cloud of the
tabernacle out of the Wilderness of Sinai toward the Wilderness
of Paran. After three days' journey the cloud searched out a
resting place for them, and there they stopped.

During all this time the Lord had sent them manna for their
daily bread. Every day the people gathered it: they ground it to
fine flour in their mills, and they beat it in their mortars; they
baked it in pans and made bread or cakes of it; they boiled it, and
they sliced it and roasted it, and they ate it in as many ways as
they could think of, and it tasted like fresh oil and honey. And
always when the dew fell upon their camp toward morning, the
manna fell upon it.

Manna! Every meal was manna. The children of Israel began to
long for other food; they hungered for the taste of meat and the
fresh fruits they had known before. Again they complained and

wept as though they were the most miserable and neglected of all people. "Who shall give us meat to eat?" they cried. "Where is the other food we used to eat? We remember the fish, which we did eat in Egypt freely; the cucumbers, and the melons, and the leeks, and the onions, and the garlic. But now there is nothing at all before our eyes except this never-ending manna!"

From every tent door came the sound of their weeping and their moaning. The Lord heard them, and was angered by their complaints; Moses also was displeased. He went to the Lord with shame and sadness in his heart.

"Why do you punish me, O Lord?" he begged. "Why have I not found favor in your sight, that you should lay the burden of these people upon me? They are not my children, that I should carry them like a father carrying babies to the land you promised them! Where in this wilderness shall I find meat to give to all of them? For they groan to me, and weep, crying for meat to eat. I cannot bear the burden of these people all alone; it is too heavy for me."

The Lord took pity on him, for he could see that Moses' burden was heavy indeed and that he needed help. "Gather seventy men of the elders of Israel, those you know to be the leaders among them, and bring them into the tabernacle," he commanded. "I will come down and talk with you there, and my spirit shall be upon the elders so that they shall share the burden of the people with you and you will no longer have to bear it alone. As for the people who are crying out for food, call them together and say this: 'You shall eat meat—not only for one day, nor two days, nor five days, nor ten days, nor even twenty days, but for a whole month, until it comes out of your nostrils and is loathsome to you!' So shall it be because they have despised the Lord with their weeping and complaints."

"But there are six hundred thousand people with me!" Moses objected. "And you say that you will give them meat to eat for a whole month! Shall the flocks and herds be killed for them? Or shall the fish of the sea be gathered together so that they might eat? How else will they have enough?"

"Is my power less than before?" said the Lord. "You shall see now whether my words come true or not."

Moses went out and told the people what the Lord had said, and chose seventy of the elders to take with him to the tabernacle. There, as the Lord had promised, a new spirit came upon them and brought with it new strength and wisdom so that they might help Moses in his difficult task of leading six hundred thousand wayward people.

Then a wind from the sea blew masses of quail toward the camp of the Israelites. Great flocks of them flew near the ground on either side of the camp. At once the people stopped everything else they were doing and rushed out to gather the meat they had longed for. They gathered the birds all that day, all that night, and all the following day, and by the time they had finished the man who had gathered least had about a hundred bushels. With great joy the children of Israel brought the food back to the camp and spread it about for everyone to eat. It was indeed enough food to last them all for at least a month.

But even while they were eating, the Lord, who was angered by their greed and their everlasting complaints, sent a plague upon them. Many became sick, and many died, and even before the meat was finished there were burials in that land. It was another lesson to those who still lived when the plague was over, if they could only learn.

And it was time they learned, because now that they were in the Wilderness of Paran they stood very close to the borders of the promised land. Only if they were worthy could they cross into the land of Canaan.

LAND OF MILK AND HONEY

*T*he cloud over the tabernacle rose up and drifted through the wilderness to a place very close to the southern border of Canaan. Here at Kadesh, as the site was called, the children of Israel stopped to water their cattle and make plans for their final march. While they pitched their tents and settled into camp, Moses sought counsel from the Lord.

"Send out men to search the land of Canaan, which I am giving to the children of Israel," said the Lord. "Choose one man from every tribe, each one a ruler among his people."

So Moses by the commandment of the Lord chose twelve men, all of them headmen of their various tribes, and instructed them to spy out the land of Canaan to see what lay ahead. Joshua, of the tribe of Ephraim and already Moses' chief military leader, was to lead the scouting expedition; and Caleb, a valiant young captain of the tribe of Judah, would act as his second-in-command.

"Go up into the mountains of the south," said Moses, "and see what the land is like. Find out what kind of people live there; whether they are weak or strong, or few or many. Make note of the cities that they live in, whether they are tents or strongholds. See if the land itself is good or bad, rich or poor; and whether it has wood or not. Go now, and be of good courage. Bring back some of the fruit of the land so that we all may see."

This was the time for the first ripe grapes, and therefore there should be no difficulty in bringing back some sample of the riches of Canaan. So the twelve spies went on their way. From the heights of Hebron, once so well-known to Abraham, they viewed the valleys below. There, they saw, were small, pleasant villages and great walled cities, and fields that were carpets of fresh young corn.

The spies went down from the mountains and went carefully through the land. The soil was rich and prosperous, and trees grew up the slopes toward the hilltops. Sheep grazed in green, well-watered pastures; people lived in well-fortified towns. And those people looked very strong and vigorous, especially those of the tribe of Anak.

Joshua led his scouts through the land for forty days, until they had seen hills, plains, valleys, and the coast, and they knew they had indeed come upon a fertile land. They also knew that it was already occupied by various tribes, each of which no doubt intended to keep occupying it.

They went on, and they came to a gently flowing brook with lush vineyards on either side. From a great vine they cut a branch bearing one huge cluster of grapes, and so marvelous was this cluster that two men had to carry it between them hung upon a staff. The place they called Eshcol, meaning "cluster," because of the grapes they had found. They found ripe pomegranates, too, and figs; and saw all manner of flocks and herds and fruits of the field. Many of the fruits and crops were the same as they had known in Egypt, and there were even some that they had never seen before.

After the forty days they returned to their camp at Kadesh in the Wilderness of Paran, taking with them the huge cluster of grapes, the pomegranates, the figs, and many a tale of the wonders they had seen. They reported at once to Moses and to Aaron, and all the children of Israel crowded around to listen.

"We went into the land to which you sent us," Joshua began. "It surely is flowing with milk and honey, and this is the fruit of it." He showed the people what his spies had brought back, and they delighted in the sight.

"But the people are strong who live in that land," said another of the spies, "and the cities are walled and very great. And moreover, we saw the children of Anak there. The Amalekites live in the south, and the Hittites and other strong tribes live in the mountains, and the Canaanites live by the sea. Altogether there are many powerful and warlike people in that land." Nine other spies nodded agreement as he spoke, and added their own words of alarm about the dangers of the land.

Their listeners murmured unhappily. Caleb silenced them and turned to Moses. "It is a good land, well worth having. Let us go up at once and take possession," he said boldly. "We are well able to overcome it."

But all the other spies who had been with him, except Joshua, shook their heads in gloom and said: "No, we cannot go against those people. They are much stronger than we. We shall have no chance at all."

And the spies gave an evil report to the children of Israel about the lovely land which they had searched. The more they talked, the less they said about its riches and the more they said about its dangers. What they had seen, they exaggerated; and what they had not seen, they imagined. "There are giants in that land!" they said. "All the people that we saw in it are men of great stature, but especially the sons of Anak who are descended from the giants. Beside them, we were no more than grasshoppers; and to them, we were no more than grasshoppers that they could easily crush beneath their feet."

The children of Israel were terrified, and deeply disappointed. All this way through the wilderness, only to come to a land they dare not enter! There was weeping in the camp that night; and a murmuring against Moses and Aaron.

"Would God that we had died in the land of Egypt!" they cried out to their leaders. "Or that we had died in the wilderness! Why has the Lord brought us to this land? Are we to fall by the sword of these giants in Canaan, and have our wives and children taken as prisoners? Would it not be better for us to return to Egypt?"

The suggestion caught fire and ran through the camp. They said to one another, "Let us choose a captain for ourselves, and let us return to Egypt. Moses shall not lead us any longer, for see where he has brought us."

The sounds of their rebellion came to their leader's ears. Both Moses and Aaron fell on their faces in front of all the people, praying God that the children of Israel should overcome their cowardice. And to the people themselves Moses cried out: "Why can you not obey and trust the God who has helped you so many times before when you have thought that all was lost?"

Joshua and Caleb tore their clothes in great dismay. Out of all the twelve spies, they were the only two who tried to reason with the people; for they were brave men, and they had faith in God. "It is a good land, and a fertile one!" they said. "It truly flows with milk and honey. Why do you have doubts, when you know that if the Lord is pleased with us he will lead us there and give it to us? It is promised to us! Only you must not rebel against the Lord, nor be afraid of the people of the land. We can crush them easily, for they have no defense when the Lord is with us. Fear them not!"

But the Israelites were too afraid to listen to words of reason, and their fear showed itself in anger against Caleb and Joshua. They reached for stones to fling at them, and would have stoned not only the two brave spies but Moses and Aaron as well if a strange and wonderful distraction had not suddenly occurred.

The glory of the Lord appeared in the form of a brightly glowing light from the tabernacle, in front of all the children of Israel. And the voice of the Lord came from the brightness.

"Moses! How long will these people provoke and disobey me? How long will it be before they believe in me, after all the signs that I have shown them? I will send a plague to wipe them out; I

will disinherit them. Of you, and you alone, shall I make a great
and mighty nation."

But Moses pleaded for them, as he had done countless times
before. "Do not destroy them, Lord, I beg you; not after having
brought them all this way and becoming famed as the Lord who
leads by cloud and fire and talks to his people face to face. If you
should kill them here, then the nations which have heard of your
fame will say that you were not able to bring your people into the
land you promised them, and that you therefore destroyed them
in the wilderness. You are long-suffering, O Lord, and of great
mercy. Pardon, I pray you, the wickedness of the people in accordance with the greatness of your mercy, as you have forgiven
them since leaving Egypt even until now."

The Lord listened, and relented; but not altogether. "I will
pardon them, as you ask," he said. "They shall not be destroyed,
nor will I disinherit them. But because all these men, who have
seen my glory and my miracles which I did in Egypt and in the
wilderness, have not listened to my voice and have tempted me
now ten times, they shall none of them see the land which I
promised to their fathers. Tell them this: 'Not one of you who is
twenty years or older, and has murmured against me, shall ever
go into that land. Only Joshua and Caleb, who have been faithful
to me, shall be allowed to live in Canaan. And the little ones,
whom you feared would be made prisoners, shall grow up to inherit the land which you have despised. But as for the rest of you,
you shall stay in the wilderness and wander there until you die.
And your children shall wander in the wilderness for forty years,
one year for each of the days in which you searched the land,
until they are grown and you are gone.'"

The children of Israel were overcome with grief. The thought
of wandering in the desert for a lifetime was more than they could
bear, and they quickly changed their minds about the dangers of
entering into Canaan. "Caleb and Joshua have said that we are
well able to take that land," they told each other. "Let us go and
do so. It was wrong of us not to trust the Lord."

It did not even occur to them that they had lost their chance, and that what they were planning now was fresh disobedience. Even when all the spies except Caleb and Joshua died by the plague as punishment for bringing back an evil report and causing the murmurings among the congregation, they would not realize that there was no escape from the wrath of God except through absolute obedience.

They rose up early in the morning and gathered on the mountain that overlooked their camp. "See, we are here," they said to Moses. "We will go now to the place which the Lord has promised us, for in our fear we sinned. Now we are not afraid."

"But you are sinning again!" said Moses. "Why do you go now against the commandment of the Lord? Do not go, for you will surely fall by the sword. The Lord will not be with you because you turned away from him, and the Amalekites and the Canaanites will strike you down."

But they would not listen to him, and they rushed upon a hilltop that was occupied by the people of Canaan. Without Moses, without the ark and tabernacle, without the cloud that guided them and without the Lord, they had no chance. The Amalekites and Canaanites fell upon them from the hill. The battle was quick and bloody. Many of the Israelites were killed outright, and all the rest were driven away with their enemy at their heels.

Defeated and despairing, they gathered in their camp and made ready to go once more into the wilderness.

"Now turn you," said the Lord. "Leave this land and get you into the wilderness near the Red Sea."

They turned sorrowfully away from the borders of Canaan and went back to their wanderings. The promised land was still their goal, but their route would be long and devious and the journey was to last them many years because they had not trusted God.

The miles and the years dragged slowly by. They moved on, made camp, moved on again. And the Israelites found many causes for complaint. Again they were thirsty, again they were hungry, again they rebelled, and again they fought with hostile tribes. And each time they were in need, the patient Moses called on God to help them. His own faith never wavered.

At long last, after what seemed like endless hardships and setbacks, the children of Israel once again came within sight of the land of Canaan. This time they approached it from the country of Moab, near the river Jordan and the valley of Jericho. The forty years were drawing to a close, and all the people who had murmured against God had died and had been buried in the wilderness. The new generation of Israelites were seasoned shepherd-farmers of the desert, skillful in battle against enemy tribes, hardened by their wanderings, and strong in their faith. Aaron had died, and Miriam was gone; of those who had made their camp at Kadesh and hoped to enter Canaan through the southern hills, only Moses, Caleb, and Joshua still lived.

And Moses was a very old man, and his days were coming to an end. He gathered the children of Israel together, the new generation, and once again taught them all the judgments and commandments of God. To each of the tribes he gave a special blessing, and to all he renewed God's promise that Canaan would be theirs. "You will cross the Jordan into Jericho," he said, "and although the Lord has told me that I will not be with you, Joshua shall lead you and you will put your trust in God. For the Lord our God is one Lord, and you shall love the Lord your God with all your heart and with all your soul and with all your might."

Then he spoke these words to all the people of Israel:

"I am a hundred and twenty years old this day. I can no longer lead you. But God will go with you and you shall possess the promised land. And Joshua shall be your leader; he will take you over Jordan." To Joshua he said, in the sight of all Israel: "Be strong and of good courage. For the Lord has given you the task of taking these people into the land which he promised their fathers, and you shall cause them to inherit it."

Then the Lord spoke to Moses, saying: "Go up to the top of Mount Nebo, which is in the land of Moab near the Canaanite city of Jericho. And behold the land of Canaan which I give to the children of Israel for a possession. You shall see the land before you, though you shall not enter it."

So Moses went up from the plains of Moab onto the mountain of Nebo, to the peak of Pisgah near the city of Jericho. And the Lord showed him all the promised land that he was giving to each of the tribes of Israel. Moses looked down and across the valleys; he gazed at the plain of Jericho, and raised his eyes to scan the farthest sea. He looked to the south and saw its beauty, and he looked at Zoar, city of the palm trees; and he saw all the green hills and fertile valleys that his people would soon be seeing for themselves.

"This is the land that I promised to the children of Abraham, of Isaac, and of Jacob," said the Lord. "I have caused you to see it with your own eyes, though you shall not go there. For the end of your days has come."

So Moses, the servant of the Lord, took one last, long look at the land of milk and honey, and died there in the land of Moab. He was buried in the valley; and to this day no man knows where his grave may be.

And the children of Israel wept for Moses in the plains of Moab for thirty days.

When the days of mourning were over they turned to Joshua for leadership, for the spirit of God was upon him. But never again in all Israel was there a prophet like Moses, whom the Lord knew face to face.

JOSHUA FIGHTS THE BATTLE OF JERICHO

On one side of the river Jordan was the camp of the Israelites; on the other, the Canaanite city of Jericho. If the children of Israel were to enter Canaan by this route then they would have to capture that great walled city first. They knew this, and they felt confident of success. The people of Jericho, for their part, were growing increasingly alarmed by the presence of the armed camp across the river. They had heard about the wonders of the God of Israel and the many victories the Israelites had won against the wilderness tribes, and even behind the great walls of their fortified city they trembled with fear.

Now after the death of Moses the Lord said to Joshua: "Arise, go over the river Jordan with the children of Israel. All the land that your feet shall tread upon, from the wilderness to the great river Euphrates and to the edges of the great sea toward the west, shall be yours to divide among your people for their inheritance. As I was with Moses, so will I be with you. I will not fail you or forsake you. Therefore be strong and of good courage, and obey me always. Then shall you succeed in whatever you do, for the Lord your God will be with you wherever you go."

Joshua called his officers to him and gave them the first command of his campaign against the Canaanites. "Go through the

camp and tell the people to prepare food and gather their possessions, for within three days we will cross the Jordan and possess
the land." And while the people were making their preparations,
Joshua sent two men across the river to spy out the territory
beyond. "Go view the land and the city of Jericho," he told them,
"so that we may know the weaknesses of the place and what
manner of men we shall have to fight."

The two spies stole quietly across the river and scouted the
land around the city. Then, seeing that the gates of the city were
still open for the daylight hours, they slipped stealthily into
Jericho to mingle with the people and study the fortifications.
When evening came they went into the house of a woman named
Rahab to find lodgings for the night. So far as they knew, Rahab
did not recognize them for what they were, nor had their movements been noticed by anyone else; but even while they talked to
Rahab someone was hurrying to the king of Jericho to tell him
that two scouts from the camp were in the city to spy out the land
for the forces of Israel.

The king at once sent soldiers to Rahab's house to find the
strangers.

"Bring out the men who came here tonight!" the soldiers told
her roughly. "They are spies come here to search out our land so
that they might conquer us."

But Rahab, from her house on the city wall, had seen the vast
camp of the Israelites across the river and come to certain
conclusions of her own. And she had also seen the king's men
coming to her house.

"Why, there were two men here earlier," she said thoughtfully,
"but I did not know where they had come from. They left here
not long ago, at about the time of the shutting of the gate when it
was getting dark. Where they went I do not know, but if you go
after them quickly you will surely overtake them."

They took a swift look over her house in case she had been
lying to them, for she was not known to be a very honest woman,
but they did not find the spies. Rahab had taken them up to the

flat roof of her house and hidden them beneath the stalks of flax that she had been drying in the open air, and the searchers did not think to look there for the spying Israelites.

Rahab watched the searchers running out through the city gates and saw the gates being firmly shut behind them. Then she went up to the roof. "They have gone," she said, and removed the flax that covered the spies. "The gates are locked, but I will see that you leave the city safely."

The two men looked at her and wondered why she had not betrayed them.

As if in answer to the question that they did not ask, she said: "I know that the Lord has given you this land. All the people here have heard it, and they faint with terror because of you. For we know how the Lord dried up the water of the Red Sea for you, and how you have destroyed your enemies as you came this way. As soon as we heard these things our hearts did melt, and there is not a man among us who has any courage left. We can see that the Lord your God is God in heaven above and here on the earth beneath; I know that we cannot win against you."

Joshua's spies were greatly encouraged by these words, for surely people of such faint heart would easily be defeated. Yet, with the city gates closed upon them and the people of Jericho alerted to their coming, they could see no way of getting back to camp with their heartening news.

But Rahab knew a way. Her house was built into the very walls of the city and it was possible for agile men to come and go without using the heavily guarded gate.

"I pray you," she went on, "swear to me by the Lord that you will show kindness to me and to my father's house, since I have shown kindness to you. Promise me that you will spare my life when you take the city, and that you will save the lives of my father and my mother, and my brothers and my sisters."

They gave their promise readily. "If you save our lives," they said, "we will save yours. But you must not say a word about this to any other soul. And when the Lord has given us this land, we will deal kindly with you and return your kindness."

She led them, then, to a high window and hung a strong cord down the outside of the city wall upon which she lived. "Let yourselves down upon this rope and go into the mountains instead of toward the river, so that your pursuers will not find you," she told the Israelites. "Stay there for three days until they give up the search and return here to the city. After that, you may go upon your way toward the camp."

They thanked her and made sure that their escape rope was secure. "We will keep our oath," they promised again. "When you see our forces coming into this land, take a piece of scarlet line and tie it in this window so that we may see it from outside. As soon as we are gone you must send secretly for your father and your mother, your sisters and your brothers, and all your father's household. Once they are here you must make sure that they do not go out of the doors of your house into the street. If they do, it will be their own fault if they die. But as long as they remain in your house we will be responsible for them."

"So be it," she agreed, and sent them on their way. They let themselves down on the rope that dangled from her window, and vanished into the darkness outside the city wall. When they had gone she bound the scarlet line in the window and sent urgent messages to the members of her family.

The two spies hurried into the mountains and hid there for three days while their pursuers searched vainly for them in the vicinity of the river Jordan. Then they came down from their hiding place, crossed the river, and took their story back to Joshua.

"Truly the Lord has delivered the land into our hands," they reported. "The inhabitants are faint with fear because of us! They themselves believe that we will conquer them, for they know the Lord is with us."

This was welcome news indeed for Joshua.

Early the next morning he arose and struck camp, moving all the children of Israel to the very banks of the river Jordan. For the next three days he let the citizens of Jericho see his vast forces, and then he said to his people: "Sanctify yourselves, for to-morrow the Lord will do wonders among you."

And it happened the next day that the priests carrying the ark of the covenant went ahead of the people; and as they dipped their feet into the brim of the river the waters of the Jordan rolled back to leave a path between the waters. All the Israelites crossed over on dry land while the waters held back, and they made camp in Gilgal on the eastern border of Jericho.

Forty thousand fighting men prepared themselves for battle in full view of the frightened people behind the city walls. Again they camped for several days before making their final move. On the first day they celebrated the passover. On the next day they ate parched corn and unleavened cakes. And on the day after that, the manna that had fallen on them for six days out of every week during their more than forty years of wandering after leaving Egypt ceased forever to fall. At last the children of Israel were truly in the promised land. From that day on they ate of the fruits of Canaan and never again saw the desert food they had called manna.

Now the great walled city of Jericho was shut up tightly and its gates were sealed. No one stirred through the gates for fear of the Israelites. Joshua, from the camp at Gilgal, surveyed the walls and saw how solid they were. Behind the fortified stone barriers the people of Jericho were armed and ready to fight. It seemed that only the mightiest of weapons could prevail against them. And yet the children of Israel, armed though they were, had only the most simple of weapons to use against those sturdy walls.

Then the Lord spoke to Joshua, saying, "See, I have given into your hands the city of Jericho, and its king, and all its mighty men of valor. And you shall march around the city, all you men of war, with the ark among you. And before the ark shall go seven priests with seven trumpets of rams' horns, and before them shall go your armed men. . . ."

Joshua listened closely as the Lord described how the city was to be taken. It was unusual strategy for war, but Joshua had no doubt that it would succeed according to the words of the Lord.

Then Joshua called the priests and all the people together to give them their instructions. "And you must not shout," he told them, as God had commanded, "nor make any noise with your voices, not even a single word, until the day I order you to shout. Then cry out with a great and mighty shout! Now go, and march once around the city, and let those of you who are armed march in front of the ark of the Lord."

And it did happen, after Joshua had spoken to the people, that the seven priests bearing the seven trumpets of rams' horns marched ahead of the ark of the Lord and blew upon their trumpets. Half of the armed men went before them, and the other half formed the rear guard that followed behind the ark.

From behind the walls of Jericho the city dwellers watched a strange and unexpected sight. The forces of Israel were marching around their city, making no attempt to scale the walls or batter down the gates; the priests among the Israelites did nothing but blow on trumpets, and the rest of the procession made no sound at all except with their steadily marching feet. When the marchers had gone once around the city, they turned and went back to their camp in silence. It was extraordinary, and it was disturbing. Only Rahab, watching with her family from her house, was not afraid.

On the second day the Israelites, with their ark, their silent marching men, and the trumpet-blowing priests, again circled the great city just once and then returned to camp.

For six days they marched around the city, once each day, and departed silently.

On the seventh day the Israelites rose early, at the dawning of the day, for this time they would have a very much longer march. Trumpets blasting, armed men silent, they marched around the city not once but seven times. On the seventh round the priests gave a great long blast on their trumpets and Joshua turned to face his forces.

"Now!" he ordered. "Shout, for the Lord has given you the city. The whole city and everyone within it shall be accursed; every living thing shall die but Rahab and the people that are with her in her house, because she hid the messengers we sent. Shout, O Israel!"

So the people shouted together in a mighty shout while the priests blew hard upon their trumpets. The walls began to tremble, to shake, and then to totter; and suddenly they all came tumbling down to lie flat upon the earth. The children of Israel turned where they stood and swarmed straight into the city. They took it easily, falling upon the terrified inhabitants and destroying with their swords every living thing they found.

But the two young men who had spied out the land were keeping their promise to the woman who had hung a scarlet line in her window for all of them to see. "Go to Rahab's house," Joshua had said, "and bring her out in safety as you promised."

So the two spies went into her house for the second time and brought her out, with her father and her mother, and her sisters, and her brothers, and everything they had. After escorting them safely to the outskirts of the Israelite camp, the spies went back to the broken city of Jericho to help their fellow soldiers finish their task. Between the lot of them they retrieved the city's silver and gold, and vessels of iron and brass, for the tabernacle of the Lord; and then the Israelites burned the city to the ground. Only Rahab and her father's household were spared; because she had given aid to Joshua's messengers, she and her family lived with the people of Israel all the days of their lives, and no harm came to them.

So the Lord was with Joshua in his onslaught against the first stronghold in Canaan. And the fame of Joshua and his God spread throughout the land.

In the course of the next few years the Israelites fought many times against the kings and tribes of Canaan. In time, Joshua took the whole land in accordance with God's promise to Moses, and divided it among the children of Israel according to their tribes.

The Israelites settled down in the promised land after many years of hardship and of battle. And the land rested at last from war.

GIDEON'S THREE HUNDRED

*J*oshua died peacefully at a good old age, his task well done. The children of Israel spread throughout the land of Canaan to live contentedly in their allotted portions. Many of them became prosperous, and many of them married into the heathen tribes that were their neighbors. No longer did they need a prophet like Moses or a warrior like Joshua to lead them, for it seemed that they were finished with war.

But in their prosperity and contentment they gradually forgot the goodness of the God who had brought them out of the land of Egypt, and turned away from him to bow down to the gods of the people who lived round about them. These were the false gods called Baal and Ashtoreth, and in worshiping them the children of Israel did evil in the sight of the Lord.

Then the anger of the Lord was hot against them, and for their sins he punished them by allowing their enemies to come down upon them and enslave them. Yet even then he would raise up judges, or deliverers, to help them in their time of need. For a while they would repent, but when the judge was dead they would go back to their evil ways. And then a new enemy would come upon them to oppress them.

Their enemies were many. Within the borders of their land

there still lived many Canaanites; and there were also Philistines, people from a far-off land who now lived along the coast and tried again and again to extend their power inland and capture Israelite territory. Outside their borders were the warlike Ammonites and Midianites, as well as Moabites and Amalekites, and even the tremendous forces of the Babylonians. All these people were ready to fall upon them when they found the Israelites in a state of weakness. But the children of Israel would not learn that whenever they deserted their God he punished them by letting them fall prey to one of these great enemies. Wise judges came and went—Othniel, Ehud, Shamgar, Deborah—and used their courage and wisdom to raise their people from oppression; but when they were gone the Israelites went back to their idol worshiping.

And because the children of Israel again did evil in the sight of God, the Lord delivered them into the hands of the Midianites for seven years. Their trials began one season after they had sown and their valleys were thick with ripening corn. Like a sudden swarm of starving grasshoppers, the Midianites and their allies the Amalekites descended on the tribes of Israel to ravage their lands and strip their homes. Year after year, for seven years, they became increasingly bold. At first they attacked from the borders of their own land. Then they invaded Israel and camped on Israelite soil, bringing in their own herds and flocks to graze upon other people's land and swooping down upon the grainfields whenever the crops were ripe. And finally they spread themselves throughout the land with their cattle and their tents and camels, plundering savagely as they went. There came a time when there was no food left for Israel, nor sheep nor ox nor ass, and even the people's homes had been taken from them. Terrified and helpless, they fled into the hills to make new homes for themselves in the mountain caves and dens. From these strongholds they crept out timidly to tend their tiny patches of corn and pray that the Midianites would not discover them.

So it was in the land of Israel when the angel of the Lord came down in the seventh year. Gideon, the son of Joash and descendant of Manasseh, was threshing his small crop of wheat in a hidden wine press to keep it from the Midianites; and while he worked the angel appeared before him and sat down beneath an oak.

"The Lord is with you, O mighty man of valor," the angel greeted him.

Gideon looked up, startled. He was no mighty man, nor did he believe that the Lord was any longer with the Israelites.

"My lord," he answered, "if the Lord is with us, then why have all these things happened to us? And where are all the miracles of which our fathers told us? No, we are forsaken. The Lord has delivered us into the hands of the Midianites and he has not been with us for these many years."

"You shall save Israel," said the angel. "Go out with all your might and you will overthrow the Midianites, for it is the Lord himself who sends you."

"I, save Israel?" Gideon was doubtful, for he was not only a humble man but a simple farmer who knew scarcely anything of war. "My lord, how shall I save Israel? My family is poor in the tribe of Manasseh, and I am the least in my father's house."

"The Lord will be with you," promised the angel. "You shall strike down the Midianites as one man."

"Then if I have found favor in your sight," said Gideon, "show me a sign that I am indeed talking to the angel of the Lord. Stay here, I beg you, until I come back and bring a gift of food to set before you."

"I will wait," the angel said.

Gideon went into his home and came back with meat, unleavened cakes, and a pot of broth. These he set before the stranger underneath the oak.

"Take the meat and the unleavened cakes," said the angel of God, "and lay them upon this rock, and pour out the broth."

Gideon did so.

The angel of the Lord reached out his staff, and with the end of

it he lightly touched the offering of food. Miraculously, fire
flamed from the rock and burned the food to ashes. Then the
angel of the Lord vanished from Gideon's sight.

When Gideon saw that he had, beyond a doubt, been talking to
the angel of the Lord, he cried out with fear. "Alas, O God! I am
afraid, for I have seen an angel of the Lord face to face and I shall
surely die!"

"Peace be to you," answered the Lord. "Do not be afraid, you
shall not die."

Then Gideon built an altar in that place, and called it by a
name which means "The Lord is Peace." With the building of this
altar, the first one built in honor of the true God for many years,
the spirit of the Lord began once again to reach out to the
children of Israel.

That night God spoke to Gideon again. "Take one of your father's young bulls," he said, "and tear down the altar that your father built to Baal. Cut down the grove of trees around it; build a
new altar to the Lord in place of the heathen altar, and offer the
young bull as a burnt sacrifice with the wood that you cut down."

Later that same night Gideon gathered together ten men.
Under cover of the darkness and with their help, he did as the
Lord had told him. When they had utterly destroyed the altar of
Baal and cut down the grove of trees, the men built a great fire
from the fresh-cut wood and sacrificed the young bull upon the
new, and holy, altar.

When the men of the city arose early the next morning and
came to worship Baal, they saw what had happened and grew hot
with rage. "Who has done this thing?" they asked furiously. And
as they inquired among the people they found one man who said:
"It was Gideon, the son of Joash."

In their anger they went to Joash and told him what his son
had done. "Bring him out!" they demanded. "He has thrown
down the altar of Baal, and for that he will die."

But Joash, who himself had built the heathen altar, was loyal to
his son. "Does Baal need you to plead for him?" he asked. "Why

should you help Baal? If he is a god, let him help himself. Let him punish Gideon."

But Baal was a god in their imagination only. Such a god could not harm the man who had broken down his altar. After that the people had respect for Gideon. And when the Midianites and Amalekites banded together to launch another murderous drive from their war tents in the valley of Jezreel, it was to Gideon that the people of Israel turned for leadership. The spirit of the Lord came upon Gideon, and he felt inspired. At once he sent messengers throughout the land to sound a call to arms among his own tribe and among others; and more than thirty thousand men gathered by his side.

As his people came together Gideon called upon God to give him a sign that his attack against the Midianites would indeed have the help and blessing of the Lord. "O Lord God," he said, "let me have some token that you will help me save Israel. I will put this fleece of wool upon the ground. If, by morning, the fleece is wet with dew and all the earth nearby is dry, then I shall know that you are with me and will give to us the victory."

And it was so. When morning came Gideon arose and saw that the earth was dry, but the fleece was so heavy with dew that Gideon was able to wring a bowlful of water from it.

Again he prayed to God, saying: "O Lord, do not be angry with me, but give me one more sign and I shall not speak again. This time, let the fleece alone be dry, and let all the ground around it be wet with the dew."

And again it was so. When morning came there was dew on all the ground, but none upon the fleece. Then Gideon no longer had any doubts about his victory. He swiftly assembled his army and pitched camp beside the well of Harod, across the valley of Moreh from the army of the Midianites.

But then the Lord said to Gideon: "You have too many people with you for me to let you have the victory. The men of Israel will boast that they have won by their own might. They must know that it is the Lord who has saved them. Therefore go to the people and say: 'Whoever is afraid and fearful, let him leave this place at once.'"

Twenty-two thousand men left Gideon's camp, and ten thousand stayed. But the Lord told Gideon that there were still too many, for only the bravest and most alert of men would be needed in the coming battle. "Bring all the men to the river," said the Lord, "and I will test them for you there. When you see how they drink, divide them into two groups according to the manner of their drinking."

So Gideon took his ten thousand men down to the water's edge and watched them as they drank. Most of the men laid aside their weapons and bent down low to drink. But three hundred men held their weapons ready, and each one of these scooped up the water and lapped it from one hand so that he could still keep watch while drinking.

Gideon arranged each group into a company, with those who bent down low to drink in one company, and those who lapped the water in the other. The second group looked very small beside the first.

"With these three hundred men who lapped the water with their hands shall I save you from the Midianites," the Lord told Gideon. "Keep them, and send the rest away."

Gideon did so. With his small company of three hundred men on the mountainside, he looked down upon the vast forces of Midian in the valley. That night, instructed by the Lord, Gideon and his servant Phurah stole quietly down to the enemy camp to find out what the people there were saying.

The enemy forces looked even more formidable at close range: Midianites, Amalekites, and all the soldiers of the eastern lands were stretched out across the valley like a massive swarm of grasshoppers, and their camels were as many as the sands beside the sea. Gideon and his man approached cautiously and stopped in the deep shadows behind the tents on the outskirts of the camp. And here they overheard a soldier talking.

"I had a dream," said a voice from the tent, "and in my dream a cake of barley bread came tumbling into our camp. It rolled against a tent and struck it hard, so that the tent fell over and lay flat upon the ground."

"Oh! That can only mean that Gideon and the forces of Israel will defeat us by the sword!" said another voice. "Truly, the Lord has delivered us into their hands."

Then Gideon knew why God had told him: "When you have heard them talking, your hands will be strengthened to meet the enemy in battle." He offered up a prayer of thanks to God and then returned with Phurah to his waiting army. "The Lord is with us!" he said, as one inspired. "He has delivered the armies of Midian into our hands!"

He divided his three hundred men into three companies, and swiftly outlined his strategy. When they all understood exactly what they were to do, he gave them each a trumpet, and a deep pitcher with a burning flare inside. Armed with these unusual weapons, Gideon's men crept toward the enemy camp. No sound came from their stealthily moving feet, and no light showed from beneath the blazing torches hidden within the pitchers. The Midianite watchmen at their posts noticed nothing strange about the gentle rustlings of the night.

In silence the three companies took their places around the camp of the sleeping Midianites and waited for Gideon to give the signal.

Suddenly the shrill blast of a war trumpet pierced the stillness. It was Gideon's call to action: all at once, three hundred other trumpets blew their shattering sounds, and three hundred empty pitchers smashed against the rocks of the valley with one great echoing crash. Flaming torches, now held high in each man's left hand, flared around the outside of the camp. Trumpets blared again in a mighty chorus of sound. "The sword of the Lord and of Gideon!" the three hundred cried out in one tremendous voice.

The Midianites, shaken abruptly from sleep, rose from their tents and saw flashes of bright flame in all directions. Noise— triumphant shouts and trumpet blasts—came at them from every side. In their terrible confusion they were convinced that they were hopelessly outnumbered by those bellowing, blaring forces, and their one thought was to escape. They picked up their swords and ran in panic through the camp.

But in the darkness of the camp, made worse by the dazzling flares encircling it, they could not see where they were going nor could they tell friend from foe. The Lord turned each man's sword against each other, and Midianite killed Midianite as they stumbled blindly toward the outermost ring of tents. But neither was there safety for them there; wherever any man came through the chaos of screaming, frightened soldiers and falling tents, he met a warrior with drawn sword and flaming torch.

The rush to get away became a stampede, and the stampede became a total rout. Gideon's three hundred fell upon the men of Midian and pursued them to the borders of their land. Other men of Israel followed Gideon now, joining in to chase their oppressors out of the land of Canaan altogether; and they killed both kings and princes of the enemy on the far side of the Jordan.

Thus were the forces of Midian driven out by the children of Israel. A grateful people begged Gideon to be their king, but he did not want the trappings of royalty or believe that a king was right for Israel. Instead, he promised to rule them as their judge and use all his strength and wisdom to lead them in the way of the Lord.

And the country lived in peace for forty years, all the rest of the days of Gideon.

But peace did not last long after Gideon's death, for even while he still lived another powerful enemy was quietly building up its forces.

SAMSON AND DELILAH

*Y*ears and rulers passed away. The Philistines along the coast grew mightier and mightier. But the children of Israel too easily forgot the lessons of their past, and turned away from the Lord to worship their neighbors' heathen gods. And because they were again doing evil in the sight of the Lord, they again fell into the power of their enemies.

For forty years the warlike Philistines, who themselves worshiped a strange, fishlike idol they called Dagon, oppressed the people of Israel. And among the loosely scattered tribes there was no leader close enough to God to find the strength to free the Israelites from their new enemy.

Yet there was a certain man named Manoah, of the tribe of Dan, who still loved and served the Lord. His wife had borne no children, and it seemed she never would. But one day an angel of the Lord appeared to Manoah's wife and told her that she would have a son. "Take care that you drink no wine or strong drink," the angel said to her, "nor eat food that is not clean. For you shall bear a son who will be a Nazarite, a man who belongs to God, and he shall begin to deliver Israel out of the hands of the Philistines. And he shall not cut his hair for as long as he lives, for if his hair is cut he breaks his vow with God and the Lord will no longer be with him."

It happened as the angel said. The woman bore a son, and called him Samson. The child grew into a youth of extraordinary strength, and the long hair that was a symbol of his covenant with God fell about his shoulders. By the time he had reached manhood he was the strongest man in all the land, blessed by God and destined for great things. Yet though he felt the spirit of the Lord moving in him at times, he was not always wise. His hatred for the enemy Philistines did not prevent him from admiring their women. This, in time, caused great trouble for him; and yet it also was the cause of eventual disaster for the Philistines.

His feats of strength were many and marvelous. One day, while he was on his way to meet a Philistine woman whom he wished to marry against his parents' wishes, a young mountain lion leaped down from its lair and roared menacingly in Samson's path. The spirit of the Lord came upon him, and Samson seized the lion with his bare hands and tore it apart as easily as if the wild and clawing creature had been a timid young goat.

After that he went along his way to make the Philistine woman his bride. But the Philistines did not like this Israelite, and even at the wedding feast they persuaded the woman to help them deceive Samson with a trick. In his terrible rage at being deceived, Samson used his great strength to kill thirty of their countrymen. And one awful incident led to another.

Again the Philistines cheated the young man with the flowing hair, and again Samson swore vengeance.

This time he went out and caught three hundred wild foxes and tied their tails together two by two. Then, between each pair of foxes, he tied a piece of dry wood to the knotted tails and set the wood on fire. When the firebrands were blazing hotly with great tongues of flame, he set the foxes loose to run through the tall ripe corn in the Philistines' fields.

In their agony and terror the foxes ran wildly from one field to another, and the blazing firebrands burned up the sheaves of harvested grain, the growing corn, the olive groves, and the vineyards of the Philistines.

Now the Philistines, in their turn, took their own terrible revenge. They went to the home of Samson's Philistine wife and burned it to the ground. Both the woman and her father died by fire.

Then Samson's anger blazed again. He leaped upon the Philistines with all his strength and slaughtered them in great numbers. "I will have vengeance!" he roared. "I will not cease until I am avenged of you!" When the dead lay thick in front of him he turned away and made a new home for himself in the land of the tribe of Judah.

The Philistines were not finished with him yet. An army of them went into the land of Judah and pitched their war tents in Lehi, hoping to find Samson and have done with him.

The men of Judah had been trying to keep peace with these savage Philistines, and when they saw the army their alarm was great. "Why have you come here?" they asked. "Why do you bring your forces here against us?"

"We have come to find Samson," they replied. "To capture him and bind him as a captive so that we can do to him as he has done to us."

The men of Judah knew where Samson could be found. They had no wish to betray him, but neither did they want the anger of the Philistines to be turned against themselves. So they went to Samson's home among the rocks and called him out.

"Do you not know that the Philistines are rulers over us?" they said to him. "Would you have us suffer for what you have done to them?"

"I did nothing more to them than they have done to me," said Samson.

"Yet we will have to bind you as a captive and take you to them," the men of Judah told him, "or their anger will descend on us."

"Take me, then, and bind me," Samson said. "Only swear to me that you will not kill me yourselves while I am bound."

They gave their promise and bound him tightly with two new

cords, then took him from his sheltering rock down to the waiting Philistines. When his enemies saw him coming, bound and apparently helpless, they shouted with triumph and bloodlust.

But Samson was far from helpless. Power surged through his mighty body, and strength poured into his limbs. He flexed his muscles and strained against his bonds; they burst from his arms and fell off in broken strands as if they had been flax burnt through by fire. When his hands were free he searched upon the ground and picked up the sun-dried jawbone of a long-dead ass, and with it he lashed out at the men who had come to take him. Again and again he struck his furious blows with the sharp side of the bone, until a thousand Philistines lay dead upon the earth around him.

"With the jawbone of an ass have I killed a thousand men!" his great voice bellowed out victoriously. And when he had done with killing he threw the bone away.

After that he was recognized as a powerful judge among the people of Israel.

But then, instead of staying away from the people who hated him, Samson went to Gaza. This was a great stronghold of the Philistines, and a dangerous place for any Israelite to visit, and dangerous especially for Samson.

Word flew around the city that he was there. "Samson is in Gaza!" so the people said. And the Philistines rejoiced at this unexpected chance to trap him. When evening came they arranged themselves around the great stone walls of the city and secured the heavy gates. All night they lay quietly in wait for him, planning to ambush him when he came out in the morning. But again Samson was too much for them. He did not wait for morning but approached the gates at midnight. His huge arms reached for the barred gates and tore them from the walls—posts, crossbar and all—and carried them away upon his shoulders to drop them on a hilltop looking down on Hebron.

Some time afterward he came to love a woman in the valley of Sorek, a Philistine whose name was Delilah.

It was not long before his enemies discovered that Samson was bewitched with love for Delilah and that he was often to be found with her in her home. The lords of the Philistines went to her and proposed a bargain.

"Entice him," they said. "Use your wiles upon him to find out where his great strength lies and how we may defeat him. If you discover his secret we will each give you eleven hundred pieces of silver."

It was a large sum of money, an alluring offer. Delilah agreed.

The next time Samson came she began at once to coax his secret out of him. "Tell me," she said seductively, "what it is that makes you so wonderfully strong, and what manner of cords can possibly tame your marvelous strength."

Samson was not quite so easily enticed as she had hoped.

"If I were bound with seven green willow switches that have not been dried," he answered, "I should be as weak as any other man."

Delilah passed her report on to the rulers of the Philistines. They came to her house with the seven green willow switches and lay in wait while Delilah soothed Samson into sleep. Then she bound Samson with the supple green stems and called out: "Samson! Awake! The Philistines are upon you!"

Samson woke up and stretched. The willow bindings broke as easily as a strand of rope is broken when it touches fire.

"You have mocked me," said Delilah sadly. "Why do you tell me lies, when you know I would not harm you? Now tell me truly: With what may your great strength be bound?"

"Only with new ropes that have never been used before," said Samson. "Then I shall be as weak as any other man."

Delilah therefore took new ropes and bound him while he slept. "Awake, Samson!" she called out. "The Philistines are upon you!" Samson got up lazily, and the ropes around him snapped like threads.

"You have mocked me again!" Delilah cried reproachfully.

"You have told me lies. Now tell me truly how you may be bound!"

"If you weave my hair into the web of cloth you are weaving on your loom," he said, "then I shall be as weak as any other man."

Later, Samson slept again and Delilah quickly went to work at her weaving loom. She parted Samson's long, thick hair into seven strands and wove each one into the fabric on her weaving frame, then fastened the fabric securely with the sturdy pin of the loom to make doubly sure of subduing Samson.

"The Philistines are upon you, Samson!"

But the Philistines, still hiding, had no chance to fall upon him, for Samson was as strong as ever. He rose up without effort and walked away, dragging with him the weaving frame, the pin, and the web of cloth in which his long hair was entangled. Delilah was left with a broken loom and a growing fear that she would never see the silver promised her by the Philistine rulers.

Yet Samson kept coming back to her, and Delilah kept on trying to lure his secret out of him. "You have mocked me now three times," she rebuked him sorrowfully, "and still you have not told me where your great strength lies. How can you say, 'I love you,' when your heart is not truly with me?"

And she pressed him daily, pleading and coaxing until Samson became harassed beyond endurance. Tired of her constant badgering, he at last gave up the secret that had been locked so long in his heart.

"There has never been a razor on my head," he said, "for I am a Nazarite, given to the Lord from birth. If I should let my hair be shaved, then my strength would go from me and I would truly be as weak as any other man."

Delilah saw that he was telling the truth at last. As soon as Samson's back was turned she sent for the Philistine lords. "Come up this one last time," she said urgently. "He has told me the secret of his heart."

The Philistine leaders went to her with the money in their hands. Delilah hid them and greeted Samson with smiles and words of love. When the big man was asleep she called out softly for a Philistine to come quickly with a razor. "Shave off the seven locks of his head," she ordered.

The man raised the razor and deftly slashed it through the thick tangle of hair. One after the other, the seven locks came off and dropped like dead leaves to the floor.

Delilah shook Samson roughly. "The Philistines are upon you, Samson!" she cried harshly, and struck him with her hand. He awoke out of his sleep, thinking that this time would be the same as other times. "I will shake myself," he said, "and go out as before." He did not know that his long hair was cut short, that his vow to the Lord had been broken for him, and that his heaven-sent strength had left him.

When the Philistines sprang from their hiding places he swung out to strike them down. To Samson's great alarm he suddenly felt as weak as any ordinary man and his blows were useless. His gloating enemies captured him with ease and cruelly thrust out his eyes to make certain that he never again could do them any harm. They took him back to Gaza, where they bound him with brass chains and thrust him into prison.

Day after day he labored in the prison house, turning a heavy millstone and grinding corn to make bread for his enemies.

Meanwhile the rulers of the Philistines were gathering together from all corners of their land to prepare a great sacrificial offering to Dagon, their fishlike god, and to rejoice in their triumph over Samson. "Our god has delivered our enemy into our hands!" they said joyfully. "Samson, the destroyer of our country, who killed so many of us, will never again do any harm!" When the long preparations were complete and all the prayers had been offered up to Dagon, the Philistines thronged in even greater numbers than before into the huge stone temple of their false god, to feast and drink and celebrate their deliverance from the strong man whom they had managed to imprison several weeks before.

At the height of the merrymaking someone, one of the Philistine lords, shouted out drunkenly: "Call for Samson, so that we may have sport with him!" Others picked up the cry, and soon they called for Samson to be brought out of the prison house so that they might make fun of him. A young lad led him to the temple, in his rags and chains, and he was made to stand between the pillars of the temple where all could see and throw their taunts at him. There were three thousand men and women who stood there laughing at him for his helplessness, among them all the lords and rulers of the Philistines, and they gloated at the sight of a giant made blind and powerless by their cunning.

They did not notice how long his hair had grown during his time in prison.

As he stood between the pillars and heard their mocking shouts, Samson said to the lad who held him by the hand: "Let me feel the pillars that support this house, so that I may lean upon them."

He leaned upon them, as if weak and tired, and the people jeered.

"O Lord God," he prayed, "remember me, I pray you! Strengthen me only this once, O God, so that I may be avenged of the Philistines for my two eyes."

He took hold of the two middle pillars that supported the temple, and braced himself. "Let me die with the Philistines!" he cried.

Then Samson tightened his grip upon the pillars and bowed forward with all his might. The pillars crashed to the floor in a terrible rumble of sound; the temple shattered down and crumbled into ruins on top of all the people in it—all the merrymakers, all the priests of Dagon, and all the rulers of the Philistines.

Thus, in his death, Samson destroyed more Philistines than he had killed in all his life. And the power of the Philistines was broken with the temple. It was to be many years before they regained sufficient strength to again threaten the peace and freedom of the children of Israel.

THE STORY OF RUTH

*N*ow it happened, in the days when the judges ruled, that there was a famine in the land. And a certain man of Bethlehem in the tribe lands of Judah took his wife and two sons into the country of Moab where the grass was green and food was plentiful.

The name of the man was Elimelech, and the name of his wife, Naomi. The two sons were named Mahlon and Chilion.

It was not a very long journey, for Moab lay directly across the Salt Sea from the land of Judah. Nor was the land itself unknown to the people of Israel, for it was from a mountain peak in Moab that Moses had seen the promised land for the first and only time. Yet it was a strange land, and it was no small venture for a family of Israelites to leave their home and friends to start a new life among strangers.

The Moabites were Gentiles and worshiped strange gods. At times there was bitter warfare between them and the people of Israel. But this was a time of peace, and the family of Elimelech settled quietly in the country of Moab. They brought their own faith with them, and prospered in the land. Their new neighbors welcomed them with kindness; and the land was fertile so that there was always bread to eat.

Yet life was not always easy, and the woman Naomi suffered many tragedies. Elimelech, her husband, died, and she was left with her two sons to care for her. In the course of time her sons took wives from among the women of Moab; the name of Chilion's wife was Orpah, and the name of Mahlon's wife was Ruth.

For about ten years all was well. Ruth and Orpah became devoted to their mother-in-law, and she to them, and though they were Moabite women they gave up the gods of their people to worship the God of Israel. Then Mahlon and Chilion both died, leaving Naomi without either husband or sons. She wanted to return to her own country, for she was lonely among the Moabites without her family around her. Also, she had heard that the Lord had ended the famine in Judah and given his people bread, so that it was no longer necessary for her to stay away from home. So she left the place where she was living and started on her way back to the land of Judah. Her two loving daughters-in-law left with her, for with their own husbands gone it seemed to them at first that they had no one left but Naomi. They did not want to lose her, too, and they did not want her to be alone and sad.

But Naomi, for her part, had no wish for Ruth and Orpah to be lonely in the land of Judah as she herself was, now, in the country of Moab. When the three women had gone some little distance together she stopped, and they stopped with her.

"Go, now," she said. "Go back, each of you, to your mother's house. May the Lord deal kindly with you, as you have been kind to my sons and to me. And may he grant that each of you marry again, so that you may find rest and happiness, each in the house of her husband."

Then she kissed them and the young women wept.

"We cannot leave you," they sobbed. "Let us go with you and live among your people."

But Naomi answered: "No, turn back, my daughters. Why should you go with me? Turn again, my daughters; go your way. I am old, too old to have another husband. And even if I should marry again and have more sons, would you wait for them until they were grown? Would you do that, instead of marrying other husbands here? No, you must stay, for I am grieved for your sakes and wish you to remain in your own land and be happy with your people."

Ruth and Orpah wept again, and Orpah said a sad farewell. She kissed her mother-in-law as the tears trickled down her cheeks. Slowly and sadly she turned away. But Ruth clung to Naomi and held her close.

"Look, your sister-in-law has gone back to her people and her gods," Naomi said gently. "You must go after her and do what she does."

"Do not make me leave you," pleaded Ruth. "Do not ask me to turn away from following you. For wherever you go, there will I go, too; and wherever you stay, there will I stay with you. Your people shall be my people, and your God shall be my God. Where you die, there will I die, and there will I be buried. May the anger of the Lord be upon me if anything but death parts you from me."

Naomi said no more. She could see that Ruth was steadfast in her purpose and would not be turned away. In silence she walked on. Ruth followed her. And in her heart Naomi was glad that Ruth was with her.

So the two women traveled together to the town of Bethlehem, arriving there at the beginning of the barley harvest when the fields were rich with grain and the people of Israel were rejoicing because the Lord had sent them plentiful crops. "Is this Naomi?" they cried out in welcome when they saw the women. Yet in spite of all their greetings it was a sad return for Naomi, who had left her home ten years before with a husband and two fine sons only to come back poor, empty-handed, and alone but for the Moabite girl Ruth.

Their first concern was to find food. In Moab they owned land, but here in Bethlehem they had nothing of their own and no means of earning silver even to buy bread. Now it was the custom among the people of Israel that every farmer, when he and his laborers reaped the grain and gathered it into bundles, would permit the poor and hungry to follow behind the reapers and gather all the loose stalks that had fallen by the way. And it so happened that one of the richest farmers in Bethlehem was a man named Boaz, who was not only a mighty man of wealth but a kinsman of Elimelech, Naomi's husband. Naomi did not know how rich he had become, nor did she give the matter any thought. But Boaz, too, was reaping at this time.

Ruth looked around the strange new land, saw the great harvest of barley being reaped on all sides of the town, and took note of the custom that permitted the poor to glean the fields for whatever the reapers might have left.

"Let me go now to the fields," she said to Naomi, "and gather grain from whoever allows me to glean."

And Naomi answered, "Go, my daughter."

So Ruth went into the fields and gathered the fallen stalks of grain left by the reapers. And it was her good fortune to chance upon a part of the great field belonging to the wealthy Boaz.

As the day passed Boaz came out of the city to watch his reapers at harvest. He walked slowly through the tall grain, looking about him at the workers and the growing piles of sheaves. Suddenly he saw a young woman who was a stranger to him. He saw, too, that she was fair of face and working diligently. "Who is she?" he asked his overseer. "She is the Moabite maiden who came back with Naomi out of the country of Moab," the overseer answered, for he knew her story. "She asked leave to glean and gather behind the reapers among the sheaves. I gave permission, and she has worked hard since morning with scarcely any rest."

Boaz looked at her with even greater interest. So this was the young woman who had come back with Naomi! He, too, had heard the tale of her departure from Moab and her devotion to his kinswoman. He watched her for a while, and then made his way between the sheaves to where she worked.

"Hear me, my daughter," Boaz said to her, and she raised her head to look at him. "Do not go to any other field to glean. Stay here with my maidens and follow after them. My young men will not disturb you; I will see to that. And when you are thirsty, go to the drinking vessels and drink the cool water which the men have drawn. Gather whatever you wish until the harvest is over."

Ruth bowed low to Boaz in her gratitude. "I thank you, my lord," she said. "But tell why I have found favor in your sight, so that you take notice of me? For I am a stranger, and did not expect such kindness."

"I have heard all that you have done for your mother-in-law Naomi since the death of your husband," Boaz answered. "I know how you left your father and your mother and the land of your birth to come here to live among strangers, so that you could be with Naomi and care for her. May the Lord God of Israel, under whose wings you have come for protection, reward you in full for the good you have done!"

She thanked him for his kindness; yet there was more to come.

"Go and glean," he said, "but at mealtime come back here to eat bread with the reapers."

And so she did; she sat beside the reapers and they passed her parched corn until she had had enough. Then she arose, taking with her what she had not been able to eat, and went back into the field to glean. When she was out of earshot Boaz gave more orders to his men. "Let her glean all she needs," he commanded, "even among the sheaves you have already gathered. Also, as you reap, let some handfuls fall on purpose and leave them there for her. Do not reproach her no matter what she takes; it is my wish that she should have all that she can carry."

So she gleaned in the field until evening, gathering many more stalks than she had been able to find in the morning. When she beat out what she had gleaned she found she had about a bushel of barley, an unusual amount for one day's work. She took her barley and went into the city, and there she gave it to her mother-in-law with the food she had saved from her meal with Boaz and the reapers. Naomi was amazed.

"Where did you glean today?" she asked. "And how did you gather so much? Blessed be the man who took notice of you!"

"It was a man named Boaz with whom I gleaned today," Ruth answered.

"Boaz!" said Naomi, greatly pleased that Ruth should have been noticed by this man of all men. "May the Lord bless him for his kindness! The man is near of kin to us, one of our closest kinsmen. It is good that you are gleaning in his fields."

"He also said to me that I should stay with his reapers and his maidens in the fields until the end of harvest," Ruth told her.

"That is good, my daughter," said Naomi. "Then you will not need to look for any other field to glean in, and Boaz surely will protect you."

So Naomi was glad; and Ruth stayed with the maidens of Boaz, gleaning in his fields until the end of barley harvest and of wheat harvest. During all that time she lived with her mother-in-law and gave her comfort.

Naomi in her turn was concerned more for Ruth than for herself. Ruth was young and fair to look at, and it was right that she should marry again and find happiness in a home of her own. To live as Ruth was living now was not what Naomi wanted for her loyal daughter-in-law.

Therefore she said to Ruth at the end of harvest: "My daughter, shall I not seek rest for you, that you may have a home and be provided for? And Boaz, with whose maidens you have been working—is he not our kinsman? And you know that he is winnowing barley tonight upon the threshing floor. Bathe and anoint yourself with fine perfumes and put on your loveliest robes, and then go down there to him. Let him first eat and drink with his men, and afterward approach him. He will tell you what to do."

"All you tell me to do, I will do," said Ruth.

That night, when Boaz had done with eating and drinking and his heart was merry, he lay down on the threshing floor with his head on a soft heap of grain. At midnight he awoke suddenly and knew that someone was with him. "Who is it?" he called out, startled.

"It is Ruth, your handmaid," she answered. "I have come to you for help, for you are a near kinsman of mine through Elimelech."

"The Lord bless you, my daughter," Boaz said. "You have shown kindness again, for you have not followed the young men, either rich or poor, but have come to me. And now, my daughter, do not be afraid. I will do whatever you ask, and provide whatever you need. The people of this city know that you are a good and virtuous woman, and all will be well with you. Now it is true that I am your near kinsman, for I was related to your husband who died. But there is a man who is more closely related than I. Tomorrow we will find him out if he will do his part as the closest kinsman. If he does, then let him do it. But if he is not able to, then I shall do it in his place."

He did not say that he had come to love Ruth and had secret hopes that the closer kinsman would not be able to perform his family duty in caring for the daughter-in-law of the late Elimelech; and Ruth did not say that she had come to love Boaz and had no real interest in any closer kin.

Both she and Boaz would abide by the custom that the closest relative of a man who had died had first right to buy his property and marry the widow. He was also expected to take responsibility for the dead man's mother, if she was not still married herself. What Boaz must do before declaring his love for Ruth was to find out if the nearest male relative would claim his rights and duties.

The next day Boaz went to the city gate where the elders of the city were usually to be found and where, sooner or later, his kinsman would be sure to pass. Boaz sat down and waited.

Meanwhile Ruth had gone back to Naomi with six measures of barley as a gift from Boaz. "Do not go empty-handed to your mother-in-law," Boaz had said, and Ruth gave Naomi his present of food while she told the older woman every word that Boaz had said to her.

Naomi listened and nodded. "That is good," she said. "Now sit down and wait until you know how this matter will end. For the man will not rest until he has finished the thing this day."

Ruth waited with Naomi and Boaz waited at the gate until the kinsman of whom he had spoken came by.

"Ho!" Boaz called. "Turn aside, sit down here with me." The kinsman turned aside and sat down. Then Boaz sent for ten men of the elders to sit down with him and his kinsman to witness the discussion, and he spoke thus to the kinsman: "Naomi, who has returned from the country of Moab, has land to sell which was our relative Elimelech's. I ask you now, in the presence of these elders, if you wish to redeem it in accordance with your right. If you wish, then do so. If not, then I shall do so."

"I will redeem it," said the kinsman, glad of such an opportunity.

"But you know," Boaz reminded him, "that on the day you buy the land, you must take Ruth the Moabite woman, Mahlon's widow, to be your wife, so that she may have children and her family will not end with her. And you shall also care for Naomi, the woman's mother-in-law."

"That I cannot do," the man declared, "or I shall lose my own inheritance. For I have a family already. Take my right as your own; I cannot use it myself."

Boaz had heard all that he needed. In front of his kinsman and the ten elders, he announced what he would do: "You are witnesses this day that I am buying from Naomi all that was Elimelech's, all that was Chilion's, and all that was Mahlon's. Moreover, I am taking Ruth, the Moabite woman who was Mahlon's wife, to be my wife so that the family of Elimelech continues on this earth. Naomi, also, shall I care for until the end of her days. You are witnesses?"

"We are witnesses," the elders said. "May your house prosper!"

Then Boaz went back to Ruth where she awaited him, and took her for his wife. In happiness, they married; and soon the Lord gave Ruth a child.

The women of the city rejoiced with their friend Naomi. "Blessed be the Lord who has not left you without a kinsman!" they said joyfully. "May his family name be famous throughout Israel. And he shall be to you a restorer of your life and a comfort in your old age. You are blessed indeed, for the daughter-in-law who loves you and is better to you than seven sons has borne a son to the family of Elimelech!"

Naomi laid the child on her bosom and was comforted. She nursed him lovingly through his babyhood, and the women said: "It is as if Naomi had a son herself." And it was so, for she loved him as her own.

Ruth and Boaz named their boy Obed, and in great happiness they watched him becoming a sturdy lad who walked in the ways of the Lord.

Obed grew to manhood and had a son named Jesse. Jesse, when he became a man, married and had several sons. One of them was David, the singing shepherd boy, who was to be a mighty king of Israel. And from David's family came the savior of mankind, a baby born in Bethlehem.

Thus did Ruth, the kindly Moabite woman who believed in the God of Israel, give life to an Israelite family that led down through the years to Mary, Joseph, and the gentle Jesus.

SAMUEL THE KINGMAKER

*T*here was a man named Elkanah who lived in the little hill town of Ramah on the slopes of Mount Ephraim, not far from Shiloh where stood the temple of the Lord and the holy ark. Every year he and his wife Hannah went to the temple with their offerings to worship God.

Hannah was a good woman whose husband loved her deeply. But she was sore at heart because she had no children. Year after year she prayed to the Lord to send her a son. As time passed and she remained without a child, she became more and more sad until she was overcome with grief and could not even eat for weeping.

Then she wept with bitterness in the temple of the Lord, and she made a solemn vow. "O Lord," she prayed silently, with the tears streaming down her cheeks. "Look on my sorrow, and remember me! Only give me a son and I will give him back to you to serve you all the days of his life."

The old priest of the temple, Eli, saw her tears and the silent movement of her lips. So strange and troubled did she look that he at first thought she had been drinking wine. Therefore he spoke sternly to her, and she answered humbly.

"No my lord," she whispered through her tears. "I have not

been drinking wine. I have poured out my soul to the Lord, for I am a woman of sorrowful spirit. Out of the depths of my grief have I spoken to him."

Old Eli saw his error. "Go in peace," he said to her, "and may the God of Israel grant you what you ask."

Peace stole into Hannah's heart. She rose and went away.

When she returned with Elkanah to their house at Ramah she wept no more, nor did she push aside her food untasted; and her face was no longer stained with tears nor marked by sadness.

Soon afterward the Lord remembered her. Hannah bore a son and called him Samuel, saying, "I have asked him of the Lord, and thus his name is Samuel." And in his babyhood the child was a great comfort and pleasure to his mother.

When Samuel was old enough to be of service to the priests in the temple, Hannah took many offerings to the house of the Lord in Shiloh. And she also took the child. When she had given up her gifts of wine and meat and flour, she gave the boy into the care of the old priest, Eli.

"O my lord," she said to Eli, "I am the woman who stood by you in the temple, praying to the Lord. For this child did I pray, and the Lord has given me what I asked of him. Therefore, as I vowed, I do lend him to my God, and as long as Samuel lives he shall belong to the Lord."

Then she prayed, and worshiped there in the temple with her husband and her son, and returned home with Elkanah. The boy Samuel stayed with Eli, and the old man taught him how to serve the Lord. And Samuel was happy in the temple.

Every year Hannah would make a new coat for her son and take it to him when she and Elkanah went to Shiloh to offer up their yearly sacrifice. Eli gave them good reports about their son and blessed them, for he was glad to have a boy like Samuel with him to grow up in the service of the Lord. Nor was Hannah left without a son in her own home, for as the years passed the Lord gave her three more boys and two lovely daughters.

Now Eli had two sons of his own who were also priests. But

they did not love the Lord and did many evil things, so that the people of Israel despised them. Eli spoke many times to his wicked sons, begging them to change their ways, but they would not listen to their father's voice. God warned Eli that their punishment would be terrible and that the honor of serving as high priest in the holy temple would be taken away from them and placed in more worthy hands. But still the sons of Eli went their way and sinned against the Lord.

Meanwhile the child Samuel grew, and found favor in the eyes of men and the Lord. Eli, watching him and guiding him, was more than ever glad to see the goodness of the boy, for the word of the Lord was seldom heard in those days and the Israelites needed someone of strong faith to come among them as their judge and leader.

One night, when all was quiet in the temple and Eli had lain down to sleep, a voice called Samuel's name.

"Here I am!" said Samuel, and he ran to Eli. "You called me; I am here."

"I did not call," said Eli. "Lie down, boy, and sleep."

Samuel went to his bed and lay down, but he did not sleep. The voice called again. "Samuel!" Samuel arose and ran to Eli.

"Here I am, for you called me," he said.

"I did not call, my son," said Eli. "Lie down again."

Samuel went back to bed. The voice called him again. "Samuel!" The boy arose and went to Eli.

"Here I am," he said, "for you did call me."

Then Eli realized that the Lord had called the child. "It was not I," he said. "Go, lie down. If you hear the voice again, say, 'Speak, Lord, for your servant hears.'"

So Samuel went and lay down once again. This time he lay wide awake and waiting, with great awe in his heart.

Once more the Lord spoke in the night. "Samuel, Samuel!"

And Samuel answered, "Speak, Lord, for your servant hears."

Then the Lord said to Samuel: "Behold, on an appointed day I will do in Israel a thing that will cause the ears of everyone that hears of it to tingle. On that day I will do to Eli all the things of which I warned him concerning his household and his sons. For I have told him that I will judge his house forever for the evil which he knows his sons have done, and from which he did not stop them. Therefore I have sworn to the house of Eli that the evil of his house shall not be cleansed by sacrifice or offerings, but shall be punished. And when I begin, it will be the end for them."

Samuel lay awake until morning, thinking about the strange voice in the night and its ominous message. At daylight he arose and opened the doors of the temple as he always did. But he did not seek out Eli, for his heart was heavy and he did not want to tell Eli what he had heard.

Eli waited for him, and still he did not come. At last the old man called for him. "Samuel, my son!"

Samuel went to him. "Here I am," he answered.

"What is it that the Lord told you last night?" the old priest asked him gently. "I pray you, do not try to hide from me anything he said."

Samuel sadly told him everything the Lord had said, hiding not a word.

Eli lowered his head in sorrow. "The Lord has spoken," he said. "So be it. Let him do whatever seems good to him."

But the time had not yet come, and the house of Eli was safe as Samuel grew to manhood. And the Lord was with him as he grew, so that Samuel spoke true words of prophecy and wisdom. All the land of Israel, from Dan even to Beersheba, came to know that Samuel was to be a prophet of the Lord.

Yet even though the Israelites trusted Samuel as a wise man who spoke the true words of the Lord, many of them disobeyed God and began again to worship heathen idols. And because they sinned, the Lord turned their powerful, land-hungry neighbors against them.

In the years after the death of Samson, the Philistines of the coastal plains had gradually built up strength until they were in control of the five great cities of Ekron, Ashdod, Ashkelon, Gaza,

and Gath, and with this great power and wealth at their disposal
they were prepared to attack the loosely scattered tribes of Israel.
And this they did: with all their great might they descended upon
the leaderless children of Israel and laid waste their land. Four
thousand men of the Israelite forces were killed in one terrible
battle, and God's country was again in the hands of Israel's arch-
enemies.

Afterward, when the remaining Israelites were gathered
together in their camp, the elders of Israel said: "Why has the
Lord let us be defeated by the Philistines? Let us fetch the ark of
the Lord out of Shiloh and carry it into battle with us. Then
surely we will win."

They would not understand that they had been defeated again
because they had been sinful and had turned away from God.
And instead of praying to their Lord before going into battle, they
took the ark of the Lord with them against the army of the Philistines. In their blindness they were sure that the enemy would be
terrified by the presence of the Lord among them. But they were
wrong; for, in truth, the Lord was not with his people, for they
were not with him.

And the Philistines did not allow themselves to be afraid. "Be
strong!" the Philistine leaders told their men. "See, God is in their
camp, and it will go hard with us if we do not battle mightily.
Acquit yourselves like soldiers, O ye Philistines! Do not become
slaves to the Hebrews because their ark is with them. Be men,
and fight!"

Trumpets sounded and the battle began. Eli's two sons themselves carried the ark of the Lord before them, convinced that by
merely carrying it they would win the day.

But the Philistines fought like men inspired; and they won.
Thirty thousand Israelites fell dead. Eli's two sons were killed, the
ark was captured, and the few Israelite soldiers who were left
alive ran screaming to their tents. A soldier from the tribe of Benjamin escaped from the dreadful slaughter and ran to Shiloh with

the news. Eli waited near the temple for word of his sons and the missing ark.

"Israel has fled before the Philistines," the man cried out. "Your two sons are dead, and many others as well, and the ark of God is taken!"

When Eli heard these awful words he fell back and died, an old man with a broken heart. He had judged Israel for forty years, and he had not done well.

Then Samuel became chief priest and judge of Israel in old Eli's place. Strange things began to happen to the Philistines. Wherever they took the captured ark, the people of the town became tormented by all manner of plagues. Horrible diseases spread from town to village and across the plains; boils and sores attacked both young and old; their fishlike idol, Dagon, toppled from his place. At last, in desperation, the tortured Philistines returned the ark to the people of Israel.

It was then that Samuel showed his strength.

"Gather together, all you children of Israel!" he cried. "Return to the Lord with all your hearts and put away the strange gods of the heathens. Serve the Lord only, and he will deliver you out of the hands of the Philistines!"

Then the children of Israel put aside their heathen gods and served their Lord. And on a day when Samuel offered up a burnt offering to the God of Israel in the presence of a multitude of his people, the armies of the Philistines drew near to do battle with the Israelites. A cloud rolled over the sun. And, that day, the Lord thundered with a great thunder against the Philistines; and the enemy from the coastlands fled in terror and complete defeat.

There was peace for a time. Samuel grew to middle years and to old age, and he judged Israel for the rest of his days. He was a wise man, and he was good, but like Eli he had sons who made false judgments and took bribes. And his people grew greatly concerned as Samuel aged.

The elders of Israel gathered together and came to Samuel with troubled hearts. "Behold," they said, "you are old and you will not always be with us. What of the future? Your sons do not walk in the ways of the Lord as you do, and we do not want them to judge us when you are gone. Therefore make us a king to judge us, like all other nations."

But this was displeasing to Samuel, for he did not think that a king would be right for his people. He prayed to the Lord for guidance.

"Give the people what they want," the Lord told him. "It is not you they are rejecting; they are rejecting me, so that I should not reign over them. Since the day I brought them out of Egypt they have been forsaking me for false gods. Therefore listen to them and do as they say, but warn them what manner of man shall reign over them as king."

Samuel went back to them. "So you will have a king!" he said. "Know, then, that he will take your sons and make them work for him as drivers of his chariots, and as horsemen, and as runners before his chariots. And he will make them servants in his armies, and servants in his fields, and servants to make his instruments of war. He will take your daughters to be cooks and bakers in his palace. He will take your fields, your vineyards, your olive groves, the best of everything you have, and give it all to his own officers and favorites. He will take your sheep, your asses, your finest young men, your maidservants, your menservants to be his own and put them to his work. And you will cry out because of the king that you have chosen, and the Lord will not hear you on that day!"

But the people refused to take heed of the warning voice of Samuel.

"We will have a king!" they demanded. "Let us have a king so that we may be like other nations, with a king to judge us, to go out before us and lead us into battle."

Samuel argued no more. "Go back to your homes," he told them, for he knew he would have to find the king they had demanded.

Now there was a man named Kish, of the tribe of Benjamin,

who had a son named Saul. And Saul one day went out looking for his father's asses that had strayed. In his search he came to the house of the wise man Samuel, and Samuel told him where he would find the wandering asses.

Samuel looked at tall young Saul, a strong and stalwart man of fine and handsome face. And the voice of the Lord told Samuel in his ear: "Behold, this is the man! Anoint him, for he shall be king and reign over the people of Israel!"

The old prophet took a vial of oil and poured it on Saul's head. And he gathered the people together, and all the people shouted: "God save the king!"

And so the proud young Saul, a noble warrior who stood head and shoulders taller than his fellow men, became the first king of the children of Israel at their demand.

It was not long before he proved himself. With great courage he led his forces into war against Israel's sworn enemies, the Ammonites and Philistines and Amalekites, and as he skillfully won battle after battle he also won the support of all the people of his land. As time went by, his young son Jonathan joined him on the battlefields to fight with equal bravery, and all Israel rejoiced because of their prowess in war. They were glad, then, that they had found a king so bold and strong, with so fine a son to be his heir.

King Saul went from one great success to another, and another. He pleased his people greatly. But he did not please the Lord.

Again and again he broke the Lord's commandments; again and again he caused grief to Samuel for his headstrong ways. Black moods came upon him and he turned away from God. He began to quarrel with the man who had made him king of Israel.

And at last Samuel had to tell him what the Lord had told him to say: "You, Saul, have disobeyed and rejected the word of the Lord. And therefore the Lord has rejected you from being king. Neither shall your son be king, for you are stubborn and sinful. The time will soon come when you shall no longer reign."

"I have sinned!" Saul cried out remorsefully. "Turn again with

me, I beg you, so that I may be honored in the eyes of Israel and
worship the Lord your God!" And bold, proud Saul clutched
desperately at Samuel's cloak as the old prophet turned away.
The cloak tore in his hands.

"It is too late," said Samuel sadly. "As you have torn my cloak
today, so shall the Lord tear the kingdom of Israel away from you
and give it to another man, a better man than you. To repent is
not enough; for a man who sins and lies and then repents cannot
be the strength of Israel."

Samuel went away, and he came no more to see Saul all the
days of his life. But he mourned in his heart for the brave young
man who had proved to be so great a fighter and so bad a king.

DAVID THE SHEPHERD BOY

I repent that I made Saul king of Israel!" said the Lord. "So rebellious and stubborn a man is not fit to rule my people."

Samuel knew this well, yet he had learned to love the tormented, sinful Saul almost as though the son of Kish had been his own son. Therefore he wept for Saul in the bitterness of his grief, and found no comfort anywhere.

Then said the Lord to Samuel: "How long will you mourn for Saul, seeing I have rejected him from reigning over Israel? Fill your horn with oil and go from here to Jesse in the town of Bethlehem, for I have provided me a king among his sons and you shall anoint him against the time when Saul shall cease to rule."

"How can I go?" said Samuel. "If Saul hears of it, he will kill me."

"Take a heifer with you as an offering," said the Lord, "and when you come to Bethlehem, say, 'I have come to make a sacrifice unto the Lord.' And call Jesse to the feast. When he is there with all his sons I will show you what you must do, and whom you shall anoint as king. Saul will not know of this, you need not fear."

Samuel did as the Lord had said. He prepared the offering,

filled the anointing horn with oil, and journeyed to the town of
Bethlehem where lived Ruth's grandson Jesse and his eight strap-
ping sons.

The elders of the town trembled at his coming, for the visit of
their high priest and prophet was usually a sign of God's displeasure and a warning of punishment to come. "Do you come in
peace?" they asked fearfully.

"Yes, I come peaceably," said Samuel. "I have come here to
make a sacrifice to the Lord. Therefore prepare yourselves, and
come with me to the sacrifice." Then he called for Jesse and his
sons to join him at the feast.

Now Jesse was a farmer and his sons were shepherds, and when
Samuel sent word that he wished them to be with him at the
sacrifice they came hurrying to him across the fields and pastures.
Seven of them, all tall and fine-looking young men, came with
their father Jesse; but one stayed with the sheep out in the
grazing lands.

He was young, no more than a boy and not yet as tall and well-
muscled as his brothers, but already he was known for his
courage. More often than not it was peaceful among the sweet
grasslands and cool, refreshing streams, but sometimes his lambs
would fall down a rocky hillside or climb too high to leap to
safety; and then the lad would risk his life to climb after them and
bring them back into the flock. Once a lion had leaped upon his
flock and dragged away a frightened lamb; the boy had gone after
the lion and killed it singlehanded. And once a bear had attacked
the sheep, only to be driven off and killed by the shepherd boy
with his simple, herdsman's weapons. He was brave among brave
men, for the shepherds of his time needed strength and courage,
and he was well known for his fighting skill.

There was something else about the boy that made him different from his fellow shepherds. He played the harp like a dream
with music in his heart and fingertips, and in his mind he
made up songs of praise to the Lord. As he watched his flocks,
always keeping his staff and sling beside him in case of attack

from any wild beast, he would draw his fingers across the strings of his harp and sing about the wonders of the Lord and all the sweet beauty of the hills and fields about him. And because he was a shepherd he sang as a shepherd would sing and thought as a shepherd would think:

"The Lord is my shepherd; I shall not want.

He maketh me to lie down in green pastures,

He leadeth me beside the still waters, He restoreth my soul;

He leadeth me in the paths of righteousness for his name's sake.

Yea, though I walk through the valley of the shadow of death,

I will fear no evil, for thou art with me;

Thy rod and thy staff, they comfort me.

Thou preparest a table before me in the presence of mine enemies;

Thou anointest my head with oil! My cup runneth over.

Surely goodness and mercy shall follow me all the days of my life,

And I will dwell in the house of the Lord for ever."

And on this day, while the lad was singing songs of glory in the fields, his father and his seven brothers were presenting themselves to the prophet Samuel and looking forward to the feast.

Samuel looked them over one after the other, seeking for the one who was to be the Lord's anointed. First, Eliab, Jesse's oldest son, came before him. Samuel gazed at his great, towering body and his handsome face, and approved of what he saw. "This, surely, is the Lord's anointed," he said to himself.

But the Lord said to Samuel, "Do not judge him by his face or by his height, because I have refused him. This is not the chosen one. The Lord does not see as a man sees; for man looks at the outward appearance, and the Lord looks into the heart."

Then Jesse called his second son Abinadab and made him pass before Samuel. He, too, was big and bold-looking; but the Lord made no sign to Samuel.

Samuel shook his head. "Neither has the Lord chosen this one," he said.

Then Jesse called his son Shammah. Again, Samuel shook his head. "Neither is this the chosen man," he said.

Jesse called another, and went on bringing his sons before Samuel until all seven had been scrutinized and turned away.

"The Lord has not chosen any of these," Samuel said to Jesse. "Are all your children here? Have you no other son?"

"I have one more," said Jesse doubtfully, "only David, the youngest. He is out in the fields, caring for the sheep."

"Send for him," said Samuel. "Bring him here, for we will not sit down and feast until he is among us."

So Jesse sent a messenger out into the green pastures to call young David from his flocks.

Samuel waited patiently. The Lord had said he would find a king among the sons of Jesse, and a king he knew he would find.

When he saw the boy leaping down the hillside and running swiftly toward him where he waited at the place of sacrifice, Samuel felt in his heart that his search was ended. David was young and vigorous and good to look at, and his fine, almost beautiful face was tanned and ruddy from his life outdoors.

The boy stopped in front of Samuel and gave him courteous greeting. In his clear eyes and his bright, open countenance, Samuel could see the goodness of young David's heart.

"Arise," said the Lord to Samuel. "Anoint him, for this is he who shall be king."

Then Samuel took the horn of oil and anointed David's head in the presence of his brothers. The spirit of the Lord came upon David from that day forward, and the lad knew that some day he would rule all Israel under the guidance of the Lord his God.

But that time was not yet come. Saul was still ruler in the eyes of the people, and David was still a youth with much to learn.

Samuel left Bethlehem and returned to his home with a lighter heart now that Saul's successor had been chosen; and David went back with his flocks into the green hills that he loved. And again he sang:

"Thou anointest my head with oil! My cup runneth over.
Surely goodness and mercy shall follow me all the days of my
    life,
And I will dwell in the house of the Lord for ever!"

And David was happier than he had been in all his life.

But the spirit of the Lord departed from Saul, and an evil spirit
from the Lord came upon him instead and troubled him deeply.
He knew nothing of the anointing of David as future king; nothing of the shepherd boy of the tribe of Judah who would rule and
whose sons would rule in place of Saul's own heirs; but he did
know that the Lord had turned away from him for his pride and
disobedience. Moods of black despair descended on him, and
there was no one in his household who could help him.

He suffered long and terribly. Then, at last, his attendants
thought of something that might ease his troubled mind. They
went to the king, for they loved him and wished him to be well,
and said: "We see that an evil spirit from God is troubling you.
Command us, our lord, to seek out a man who is a skillful player
on the harp. Surely it will come to pass that, when the evil spirit is
upon you, be will play soft music on his harp and you will then be
well."

Saul thought about it. Soothing music on a harp? It might be
pleasant. Nothing else had helped his misery; perhaps music
would.

"Do it, then," he said. "Find a man who can play well, and
bring him to me."

"Jesse of Bethlehem has such a son," one of the servants said. "I
have seen him myself, and although he is not yet a grown man he
is valiant and courageous, as well as being a musician of great
skill. Also he is wise, a young man both discreet and tactful. He is
good to look upon, a comely person, and the Lord is with him."

"Then he shall play for me," declared the king, and at once sent
messengers to Jesse with an urgent command. "Send me your son,
David, who is with the sheep," the messengers repeated when

they arrived in Bethlehem, and Jesse was proud that the king had sent for his son.

He called David from the pastures and told him to prepare for his journey while he himself made ready a gift for Saul. "Now take yourself and these presents to King Saul," he said to David, "and do whatever he asks of you."

David left Bethlehem with bread and meat and wine and traveled to the town of Gibeah. There he presented himself to Saul and gave the king his father's gifts. Saul looked upon him; and he liked the lad. To Saul's tired eyes the boy was good to look at and pleasant in his manner, and the music that he played upon his singing harp was soothing to Saul's uneasy soul.

The days passed and Saul came to love the boy as one of his own, for David was indeed wise and his music did much to ease the king's dark spirits. Saul therefore sent a message to Jesse, saying: "Let David, I pray you, stay with me, for he has found favor in my sight." Jesse was glad that David could be a comfort to the king, and he willingly agreed to Saul's request.

From that day on, David was always welcome in Saul's court. Saul was so pleased with him that he made the boy his armor bearer, which was a great honor for the shepherd boy who was destined to be king.

And whenever the evil spirit was upon Saul so that his heart was heavy with despair, David took up his harp and played his melodies upon it. Even though he knew that there would come a day when he would take the place of the man at whose feet he sat, he served Saul faithfully and with love. Saul was his king, and his king needed him. Saul's heart was eased as David made his harp sing between his skillful fingers, and the black despair fell away as the lad raised his clear young voice in songs that told of his faith in the Lord his God.

"I will lift up mine eyes unto the hills, from whence cometh
    my help.
My help cometh from the Lord, which made heaven and
    earth.

He will not suffer thy foot to be moved; he that keepeth thee
will not slumber.

Behold, he that keepeth Israel shall neither slumber nor
sleep.

The Lord is thy keeper; the Lord is thy shade upon thy right
hand.

The sun shall not smite thee by day, nor the moon by night.

The Lord shall preserve thee from all evil; he shall preserve
thy soul.

The Lord shall preserve thy going out and thy coming in
from this time forth, and even for evermore."

And Saul's dark spirit departed from him, so that he was
refreshed in his mind and strong in his body. The time came when
he felt he no longer needed David and his soft and soothing music
to be with him all his days, and he sent the boy back to
Bethlehem to mind his father's sheep. He knew that David would
come back whenever he was needed.

David sang in the fields as before, but with a new knowledge of
what it was to be king and a new understanding of how privileged
he was to be chosen by the God of Israel. His own faith grew
strong and sure as he tended his flocks and waited for the day
when he would be called to duty by the Lord.

"Make a joyful noise unto the Lord, all ye lands!" he sang.
"Serve the Lord with gladness;
Come before his presence with singing.
Know ye that the Lord he is God;
It is he that hath made us, and not we ourselves;
We are his people, and the sheep of his pasture.
Enter into his gates with thanksgiving,
And into his courts with praise;
Be thankful unto him, and bless his name.
For the Lord is good; his mercy is everlasting;
And his truth endureth to all generations!"

DAVID AND GOLIATH

*A*ll durings the days of Saul there was bitter war against the Philistines. Now once again the invaders from the coastal plains threatened to lay waste the land and destroy the cities. In great numbers, and with all their mighty weapons of war, they marched boldly into the land of Judah and pitched their war tents on a mountainside at Shochoh.

Saul and his warrior son Jonathan hastily gathered together the men of Israel and pitched camp on a mountainside directly across from the forces of the enemy. Between the two encampments lay the valley of Elah, and it was in this valley that the battle was expected to take place. Saul therefore drew up his forces into battle array and prepared to meet the foe.

But instead of any army, one man came out from the camp of the Philistines and cried out a scornful challenge to the men of Israel.

"Why are you arrayed for battle?" he boomed across the valley. "I am only one man, and one man only do I call to combat!"

Only one man; but he was a giant, and the men of Israel were afraid.

Goliath was the Philistine's name, and he was more than nine feet tall. Neither Saul nor Jonathan, in all their years of battle, had ever seen a man so huge and fearsome. He wore a great brass

helmet on his head and he was sheathed in a heavy coat of mail
the likes of which no man of Israel had ever seen before. Enormous plates of brass covered his shoulders and his legs, and there
was scarcely any part of his great body that was not encased in
armor. He carried a spear twice as big and weighty as any ordinary man could even hold; and a man walked in front of him
bearing a mighty shield.

King Saul stared down the mountainside at the giant and
repented that he had turned away from God and lost the prayers
of Samuel, for now he was in desperate need.

There was no man in the ranks of Israel who could match the
Philistine.

Twice each day, in the morning and the evening, the giant
Goliath came down into the valley and roared his challenge to the
armies of Saul, daring any man among them to leave the shelter of
the trenches and come out to fight him man to man.

"Choose a man," he shouted, "and let him fight with me. Am I
not a Philistine, and you the servants of Saul? There is no need for
battle. Let one man come down to me!"

But there was no man in the camp of Saul who dared to fight
him, not even Saul himself. The men of Israel watched the giant
and listened to the thunder of his voice, and their courage melted.

Day after day Goliath stalked the valley and roared his message
to the Israelites. "I defy the armies of Israel this day! Give me a
man, that we may fight together. If he kills me, then we will be
your servants. But if I kill him, you will submit to us and be our
slaves."

Saul trembled with dismay. He knew he had no chance against
this giant among Philistines.

Now David, at this time, was at home in Bethlehem minding
his father's sheep. Three of his older brothers were in Saul's army,
and one day his father Jesse sent him to the camp with supplies of
food for his brothers and their captain. David left his sheep in the
care of a keeper and went along his way with the corn and loaves
and cheeses.

For forty days the giant Goliath threatened the men of Israel, and each time he came out to challenge them the Israelites were more ashamed. And yet they still could find no man to go out and meet the challenge, for none of them were giants.

David reached the camp and greeted his brothers. As he spoke to them a great voice boomed across the valley. "Choose a man! I defy you, men of Israel!" Now David heard the challenge, but he heard no answer. Instead, he saw the men of Israel turn pale with fear and run back to their tents.

"Did you see the giant?" they asked David.

"Does no one dare to fight him?" he asked in turn. "Who is this Philistine, that he should defy the armies of the living God?"

"Goliath of Gath," they answered, their voices hushed with awe. "For forty days he has defied Israel, and we have no one to meet his challenge. The king has said that if any man will go out and kill the Philistine and save us from our shame he will be rewarded with great riches and high rank, and the king's own daughter will be given to him as his wife."

Young David wondered at their words. It was not that he was interested in riches; but he could not understand why any man of Israel should be afraid of any Philistine, giant though he might be. He was not impressed by Goliath's size or armor, and he said so.

David's brother Eliab heard him talking to the men, and was angry and embarrassed. "Why did you come here?" he asked roughly. "And who is looking after the sheep while you are gone? I suppose you have come here just to see the battle!"

"I see no battle," David said, "only a man who puts us all to shame. If no one else will go, then I myself will fight this enemy of God's people."

Eliab grunted scornfully and turned away. To him, David was only a younger brother speaking proud words that meant nothing. But there were others among the soldiers who took him more seriously, and soon David's words reached the ears of Saul. Saul sent for him at once.

Looking at him the king saw a handsome, clear-complexioned youth, not yet fully grown; a boy of whom he had thought highly enough to make him his own armor bearer, and who music had often soothed his troubled soul. But he had never thought of this poetic shepherd boy as a warrior. He eyed David doubtfully.

David spoke up. "Let no man's heart fail because of Goliath," he said earnestly. "I, your servant, will go out and fight this Philistine."

Saul smiled. "You, fight the giant?" he said gently. "You are but a youth, and he is a man of war with many years of battle behind him. How can you go out against him?"

"It is true that I have not fought men," said David. "But I have kept my father's sheep. And when the lion and the bear have come to take lambs out of my flock, I have gone out after them. And with my hands, I have killed the beasts and saved the lambs. This giant is the same to me as one of those wild beasts. The Lord delivered me out of the paw of the lion and out of the paw of the bear, and he will deliver me now out of the hand of this Philistine."

Saul gazed back at him. It seemed impossible, and yet the boy might have a chance. There was something about him that inspired confidence. He nodded slowly. "Go, then," he said, "and the Lord be with you."

But first he gave his own armor to the shepherd boy: a great brass helmet, a coat of mail, and a heavy sword to wear about the waist. David staggered under the weight. He was not used to the uniform of war, and he found it clumsy. "I cannot even walk with this," he said to Saul, and took off the armor. "I can only fight in my own way, with the things that I am used to."

So he took up his wooden staff, and chose five smooth stones from the nearby brook and put them in his shepherd's bag, and he carried his leather sling ready in his hand.

He walked down the mountain slope to meet the Philistine. The giant strode toward him; and they looked at each other across the valley of Elah.

Goliath, like Saul, saw a slim young lad, but he did not see the courage in the boy's heart nor the sling in his hand. All he saw was a boy with a shepherd's stick, and when he spoke it was with contempt for Israel's puny little challenger.

"Am I a dog, that you come at me with staves?" he roared, and cursed David by all the heathen gods. "Come, then! and I will give your flesh to the fowl of the air and the beasts of the field!"

There was still some distance between them. The slight boy walked calmly toward the giant of a man and called his answer to the Philistine:

"You come at me with a sword and a spear and a shield, but I come to you in the name of the Lord of Hosts, the God of the armies of Israel, whom you have defied! This day will the Lord deliver you into my hand. Not I, but you the Philistines, will be given to the birds of the air and the wild beasts of the earth, so that all the earth will know that there is a God in Israel. All here shall know that the Lord does not save by sword and spear, for the battle is the Lord's and he will give you into our hands!"

The giant roared with rage and lumbered forward to meet this impudent boy. Behind him, the great army of the Philistines watched and waited, sure that their champion would crush this slender, almost unarmed lad. Behind David, the men of Israel stood arrayed for battle; and Jonathan looked on and prayed.

David stepped forward and reached a hand into his shepherd's bag. Quickly, he placed a smooth stone in the sling. Then he raised the sling above his head, took aim, whirled it swiftly in the air, and threw with all his strength and skill.

The stone flew out of the sling, swift and straight as an arrow to its target, and struck the giant hard betweeen the eyes. Goliath swayed and fell like a great tree toppled by an axe.

The champion of the Philistines, the giant Goliath, had been dropped with a sling and a stone!

On one side of the valley, the Philistines gasped with disbelief and horror. On the other, the men of Israel saw the man who had terrorized them for forty days struck down by a pebble from a boy's slingshot; and they thought they had surely seen a miracle.

David ran toward the gigantic fallen body to make sure the duel was over. He pulled the giant's great sword from its sheath, brought it down with all his force, and cut off the Philistine's head.

And when the Philistines saw their champion would never rise again, they turned and ran away in terror. The men of Judah and Israel plunged after them with great shouts of joy and triumph, and pursued them deep into their own land, even to Goliath's town of Gath.

After the forty days of shame and fear, it was a glorious victory for the forces of Saul. David's name became known and praised throughout the land of Israel. When the conquering forces returned from the slaughter of the Philistines, women danced in the streets and sang their songs of praise to Israel's two greatest fighting men.

"Saul has slain his thousands," they sang joyfully, and Saul was pleased. "And David his ten thousands," they sang on.

But this did not please Saul.

THE ENMITY OF SAUL

*N*ow Israel had a new hero, and all the land rejoiced. Even Saul, stabbed by jealousy and tormented with black moods, still loved the lad David and admired his courage. After the battle with Goliath he took David home with him to his court and would not let him go back to his father's house.

Saul's son Jonathan had seen young David conquering the giant and he, too, had great esteem for a warrior so bold and youthful and yet so humble of spirit. And it happened, as he came to know David in the palace of Saul, that Jonathan came to love his new friend David as a brother.

"Let us make a covenant," he said to David. "May the Lord be between you and me forever, that we may be true friends as long as we shall live."

David took his hand and clasped it warmly. "You have my oath on it," he said. "We shall be friends forever in the sight of God."

And the friendship between the prince and shepherd boy was known throughout the land.

Saul himself was pleased with David and entrusted to him many important duties. David went wherever the king of Israel sent him, and behaved himself so wisely that Saul gave him command over all his men of war. David was soon accepted as a leader by all the people of the land and by all the nobles and attendants who served Saul. Everybody loved him; everybody praised him. As a warrior he was winning victory after victory, and as a man he was winning countless friends.

It was good for Saul that his bold captain should be so victorious in war, and at first he was glad that David was successful. But as time went by his jealousy grew within him and turned slowly into deep dislike. There came a day when he had seen enough of victory celebrations and heard too much of the women who played upon their taborets and sang their never-changing song:

"Saul has slain his thousands,
And David his ten thousands!"

On that day Saul's rage boiled over. "So they think he is greater than I, who am king!" he said angrily. "To him they credit *ten* thousands, and to me, only thousands! If he is ten times better than Saul, what more can he have but my kingdom itself?"

From that day forward Saul eyed David with growing hatred and suspicion. So jealous and outraged was he that, on the very next morning, the evil spirit from the Lord came on him once again and he acted like a madman before all the people of his house. David came to him with his harp and tried to soothe the troubled king.

But Saul could not bear the sight of him. David's very presence drove the king to greater frenzy. "I will kill this David. I will pin him to the wall!" he screamed, reaching for his javelin. With all his maddened might he flung the sharp-tipped spear across the room at David. But the lad was swift; he dodged and ran. Twice it happened; twice David moved away in time and saved himself from the flying javelin.

Then Saul became afraid. It was clear to him that the Lord had gone from him and was with David. And he began to plot other

ways of disposing of Israel's young hero. He removed David from
his post as commander over all the army and made him a captain
of a thousand only, and then he sent the youth away from the palace as a gesture of his great displeasure.

"Now," thought Saul, "the people will despise him. And
perhaps he will be killed in battle!"

But David was not killed, nor did the people of his land despise
him. He accepted his demotion humbly and behaved with
wisdom, for the Lord was with him all the time.

Saul was even more afraid. Within his troubled heart he knew
that this wise and brave young man would somehow take his
place, and he longed to kill David outright. Yet he knew, too, that
Judah, David's tribe, and all of Israel as well, loved David too
much to forgive his murderer. Therefore the king thought long
and hard until his cunning mind produced another plan. Some
time before, when he had been hard-pressed by the Philistines, he
had promised his elder daughter Merab to whomever killed Goliath. Thus far he had not fulfilled his promise. Now he said to
David: "Be valiant for me, and fight the Lord's battles, and you
shall have my daughter Merab as your wife." And to himself he
was thinking: "Let not my hand be against him; let him be killed
by the Philistines."

David went out against the enemy once more and battled
valiantly. But the Philistines did not kill him. And when the time
came that Saul's daughter should have been given to David for
his wife, Saul gave Merab to another man. Yet David did not concern himself over this insult, for he was a humble man and felt
himself unworthy of being son-in-law to the king. Saul was very
much displeased that David showed no anger.

Now it happened that Michal, Saul's younger daughter, was in
love with David. And, according to the king's advisers, David
looked with favor on Michal. This was pleasing to the king: here,
he told himself, was a better opportunity to get rid of David. "I
will offer her to him," he thought to himself, "and use her as a

snare! This time I will make sure that he falls by the hand of the Philistines."

He called David to him and forced himself to speak pleasantly, although hatred was eating at his heart. "You shall have my other daughter Michal," he said, in his most friendly manner. "You will yet be my son-in-law!"

David still thought he was not worthy of any daughter of the king. Then Saul commanded his servants to talk in secret with him and persuade him that the king wanted nothing more than that David should marry Michal. "Speak to him thus," said Saul. "Say: 'The king delights in you, all his servants love you, and it is good that you should be his son-in-law. As for the dowry, it does not matter that you are poor, for the king desires no dowry. All he wants is that you kill one hundred Philistines.'"

Saul sat back and waited, satisfied with his cleverness. Now David would certainly be killed!

But David was not killed. With a group of chosen men he went into battle and killed, not one hundred, but two hundred Philistines. Saul's heart sank and his spirit despaired for now he had to give Michal to David as his wife.

His hatred blazed into an even brighter flame as he saw his daughter with this man he feared. She was happy, she loved David, and this was more than Saul could bear. He was convinced now that David was being guided by the Lord and had been chosen as the future king. Within himself, in his great fear, he swore everlasting enmity. To persecute David without mercy became his one desire.

The Philistines attacked again. Once more David went out to meet them, and he fought more bravely and wisely than any of Saul's favorites. His fame continued to spread throughout the land of Israel, and Saul's rage knew no bounds. His dark mood descended on him even more heavily than before, and David, loving his king still, brought his harp into the presence of Saul and tried to ease his troubled spirit. When Saul saw David and heard the soft music that no longer soothed him, he picked up his javelin and again flung it furiously at the man he loathed. David nimbly stepped aside. The sharp weapon bit into the wall and hung there quivering while Saul raged and David slipped away into the night.

In his blind anger Saul sent men to lie in wait at David's house to kill him as he came out in the morning. But Michal heard of this and warned her husband. "You must go tonight, or in the morning you will die!" she told him urgently. So she let him down by rope through a window, and put pillows under his bedclothes to make it look as though he was still there, sleeping. When Saul discovered this deception he was even further outraged, yet angry as he was, he could not harm his daughter.

Now David sought out Samuel and remained in hiding with him for some time. Eventually he came back, hoping to make peace with Saul, and went at once to his friend Jonathan.

"What have I done?" he begged. "What is my sin before your father, that he seeks my life?"

"I do not know of any sin," said Jonathan. "My father would surely tell me if he had reason to want your life. But God forbid that you should die! Tell me what you want me to do and I will do it, for you know that I wish to do all in my power to help you."

It was agreed between them, then, that Jonathan should find out what Saul's feelings were and report his findings to David by means of a secret signal. The two young men again swore everlasting friendship, and Jonathan left his friend in hiding while he approached his father to sound him out about his intentions toward David. He was hoping, too, that he could reason with his father and convince him that the shepherd-warrior meant him no harm.

But it was useless. Saul's anger blazed and turned against his son. "You son of a perverse, rebellious woman!" he screamed at Jonathan. "Do I not know that you have chosen the son of Jesse as your friend, to your own downfall? And do you not know that as long as he lives you will not be king? Now bring him here to me, for he shall surely die!"

"But why should he die?" asked Jonathan. "What has he done?"

In answer, Saul's face darkened and he flung his javelin at his own son Jonathan with a cry of fury. Jonathan stepped aside and the javelin missed; but he knew then that his father was determined to kill David and would let nothing stop him. In an anger almost as fierce as his father's he left Saul's house to tell his friend that there was no hope of mercy from King Saul.

David came toward him from his hiding place.

"He has not repented," Jonathan told David sadly. "Go in peace, for we two shall be friends forever. The hand of Saul my father shall not find you, and you shall indeed be king of Israel, as he fears. Yet let nothing come between us, and may we always have our covenant before the Lord."

They clasped hands once again. Jonathan went slowly back to the house of Saul, saddened by the terrible enmity between his best friend and his father, and David went into the wilderness to seek refuge in the wild hills near the Salt Sea.

It was a time of wandering and persecution for him, for Saul would not relent. David was a hunted man. With no weapon but the great sword of Goliath, with barely any food, and with only a handful of loyal fighting men, he found refuge in the cave of Adullam, deep in the wilderness.

His place of hiding was not altogether secret. All his brothers and all the members of his father's house came to know about the cave of Adullam, and joined him there. All the men who were discontented under Saul, and all who were distressed by reason of debt or other hardship, gathered together and joined David in the hills. Yet not one of them, nor any of the people who knew where David and his band of outlaws had their camp, breathed a word to Saul. And Saul ranged desperately back and forth across the countryside with great companies of armed men, searching relentlessly for the man he hated.

Several times he came very close to David. More than once he inflicted dreadful punishments on people for not telling him where he could find his quarry. "You have all conspired against me!" he would scream. "Why does no one tell me where this man hides and lies in wait for me? Are you all in league with him?"

People died for David but David did not die. Hunted though he was, he moved safely through the wilderness from one stronghold to another while Saul sought him every day, yet could not find him, for the Lord was David's strength and safety. Saul's wild pursuit of an innocent man and his ruthless slaughter of David's friends caused the people of Israel to turn increasingly against him and begin to hope for his downfall. It was not only that they loved David, but also that they needed a king who would keep them strong against their enemies instead of stalking their greatest friend.

There came a day when Saul, in his never-ending search, did come dangerously close to where David and his men lay quietly in hiding. He knew that David was somewhere near him in the wilderness of Engedi, but he did not know exactly where. Weary from a battle with the Philistines and his endless pursuit of the son of Jesse, Saul went into a great cave to lie down and rest. While he slept, a silent figure came toward him from the dark recesses of the cave and stood looking down upon him. It was David; and Saul was in his power. He raised his sword and he brought it down swiftly and with one quick slash cut away a piece of King Saul's robe. But that was all he did, for he could not bring himself to take Saul's life. When Saul awoke and saw how he had been spared, he wept with remorse for his own wickedness and went away with shame and sorrow in his heart. For some time he gave up his murderous quest and left David in peace.

Then again the madness came upon him and he went out after David with a great company of men. And again David, who now knew the wilderness as if he had been born to it, saw Saul's forces from afar and kept his own men hidden while the king's men pitched their camp. In the dark of night David and his companion Abishai crept silently among the tents to the middle of the camp where Saul rested, his people pitched around him. Saul lay sleeping in a trench, his spear stuck in the ground beside him and a cruse of water near his head. No one stirred; no one saw the two men staring down at Saul.

"God has delivered him into our hands this day!" Abishai whispered triumphantly. "Let us kill him now, with one thrust of his spear."

David shook his head. "No, we must not kill the Lord's anointed. Leave him to the Lord; his day will come to die." And instead of plunging the convenient spear through the sleeping Saul, David pulled it quietly from the ground and carried it off. Abishai, disappointed but obedient, picked up the cruse of water that stood beside Saul's head. Then, as quietly as they had come, the two men left the camp, taking with them the trophies of their visit.

Saul awoke next morning to the sound of David's voice calling to him from the hills and begging Saul to give up hunting him like a partridge in the mountains. The king looked about him and saw at once that his spear and water cruse were missing; and when he discovered that he had again been spared, his conscience burned within him once more.

He called back to David: "I have sinned! Return to me, David my son. I will do you no more harm, for my life was precious to you this day. Blessed may you be in the eyes of the Lord, for you shall do great things!"

There was truce between them, then, though David did not go back with Saul to his palace. They went their separate ways in peace, but David knew in his heart that Saul would change his mind again, so he went to a far place called Ziklag to escape the king. Saul did indeed change his mind and did seek David, but when he heard that his rival had gone so far away, he gave up pursuing him and devoted his declining strength to fighting off renewed attacks by the forces of the Philistines.

By now the Philistines knew that Israel had been weakened by the poor leadership of the moody Saul. They knew, too, that Saul's own subjects and the men of his army had lost faith in him.

Therefore they massed all their armies on the soil of Israel, determined to crush the Hebrews during this time of opportunity. Saul saw their enormous forces and trembled with fear. David was not with him, old Samuel was dead, and Saul's own fighting spirit had been sapped by his bouts of hatred and madness.

Yet he rallied together his sons and his soldiers to meet the vastly stronger Philistine armies on the slopes of Mount Gilboa.

It was disaster from the start. Hundreds and thousands of Philistine arrows carried swift death into the Israelite ranks. Hundreds and thousands of Israelite warriors broke and ran down the mountainside or fell dead before the overwhelming onslaught. Brave Jonathan, fighting at his father's side, died with an arrow in his heart. Then his two brothers dropped to the bloodstained earth and died. At last great Saul, wounded almost to death by the enemy archers, fell upon his own sword and ended his tumultuous life. Now hordes of triumphant Philistines poured unchecked into the land of Israel. It was a terrible defeat.

When David heard the dreadful news he mourned for Saul as though the tortured king had been his lifelong friend instead of his sworn enemy. He and all the men with him wept and fasted until evening of that day, mourning for Saul and Jonathan and all the people of Israel.

In his sorrow David lamented with this song:

"The beauty of Israel is slain upon thy high places;
How art the mighty fallen!
Tell it not in Gath,
Publish it not in the streets of Ashkelon,
Lest the daughters of the Philistines rejoice,
Lest the daughters of the heathen triumph.
Ye mountains of Gilboa, let there be no dew,
Neither let there be rain, upon you, nor fields of offerings,
For there the shield of the mighty is vilely cast away,
The shield of Saul, as though he had not been anointed with
    oil.

Saul and Jonathan were lovely and pleasant in their lives,
And in their death they were not divided;
They were swifter than eagles,
They were stronger than lions;
Ye daughters of Israel, weep over Saul!
How are the mighty fallen in the midst of the battle!
O Jonathan, thou wast slain in thine high places;
I am distressed for thee, my brother Jonathan.
How are the mighty fallen,
And the weapons of war perished!"

Thus did David mourn for his lost king and for his good friend
Jonathan, while the land of Israel lay kingless and in ruins.

THE TRIUMPH AND TRAGEDY OF DAVID

*D*avid could not mourn long for Saul and Jonathan, for his land was sorely troubled and in great need of him. When he had done with weeping and lamenting he inquired of the Lord what he should do.

"Go back to Judah," said the Lord. "Go to Hebron, and dwell there."

So David journeyed back to his own land, taking with him his several wives, all the men who had been with him during his years of exile, and all the people of their households. The men of Judah came to welcome him; and there in Hebron they anointed David king over the house of Judah.

But to be king of Judah was not to be king of all Israel, and those who were left of the house of Saul were by no means ready to give up their claim. Abner, once captain of Saul's army, chose to support Saul's one surviving son as king, and succeeded in making him ruler over eleven tribes of Israel. Saul's son reigned for two years, but the house of Judah remained faithful to David.

Now there was long war between the house of Saul and the house of David. Abner fought hard for Saul; and David's nephew Joab gathered forces to destroy the armies of Abner. David gradually grew stronger and stronger while the house of Saul became weaker and weaker. When at last both Abner and the son of Saul were dead, all the leaders of the tribes of Israel came to David at Hebron. "Behold," they said, "we are your brothers. In time past when Saul was king, it was you who led the armies of Israel and brought us victory. The Lord then said to you: 'You shall feed my people Israel, and you shall be a captain over Israel.' Therefore make a league with us before the Lord, that you will rule us from this day on."

David vowed before the Lord to rule with all his might and wisdom, and the elders of Israel anointed him that day as king over all twelve tribes of Israel. Thus was Israel once again a united nation.

As king of all the land, David needed a great city for his stronghold. The fortified hill town of Jerusalem seemed ideal to him. It was occupied by the Jebusites, people of the land that had once been known as Canaan, and they boasted that their town was so strong that the blind and lame could hold it against any foe. But they were wrong; David drove them out and took their city easily, and from that time on Jerusalem was known as the city of David.

The city grew in size and wealth, and David himself grew powerful and great. He took more wives and concubines, and he had many sons. His fame spread rapidly to many lands, and their kings sent gifts to him. Hiram, king of the Phoenician city of Tyre, sent gift-laden messengers to David, as well as cedar trees, and carpenters, and masons; and they built David a royal palace. David thanked the Lord for his good fortune, for he saw that the Lord had indeed established him as king of Israel and that the Lord had exalted his kingdom so that the children of Israel might be great upon the earth.

But the Philistines were still strong in many of the cities of Israel, and when they heard that David had been anointed king of Israel they determined to destroy him. They marched their mighty armies toward Jerusalem and spread across the valley of

Rephaim south of the city. David looked down at their vast forces
and inquired of the Lord how he should meet this new threat.

"Shall I march against the Philistines?" he asked. "Will you be
with me, and bring me victory?"

"You shall not go out to meet them face to face," said the Lord.
"Instead, you must go around behind them so that they do not see
you, and array your forces beneath the mulberry trees. And let it
be that when you hear the wind blow through the tops of the
mulberry trees, you will go into battle and attack them from the
rear; for the sound among the trees will be a sign that the Lord is
moving before you to destroy the Philistines."

David did as the Lord commanded him. When he heard the
wind sighing through the treetops he launched a swift surprise attack that drove the Philistines out of the land of Israel and broke
their power for many years to come.

Now Israel truly was a nation worthy of respect, and Jerusalem
was a capital fit not only for a king but for the house of God.
David, in his gratitude and triumph, decided to bring the ark of
the Lord to the royal city. Therefore he built a small tabernacle to
house it until such time as he could build the magnificent temple
that he had begun to plan, and he gathered together all the
chosen men of Israel to join in a triumphal procession to carry the
ark to its new resting place. On that day he laid aside his kingly
robes for the simple garments of a priest, and as the great procession wound toward the hills of Jerusalem he danced joyfully
before the Lord with all his might. Trumpets, harps, cornets, and
cymbals sent their exultant noises to the skies. All the house of
Israel shouted out their gladness and sang songs of praise to the
Lord their God; and the priests of David set the ark down
reverently in the simple tabernacle.

"O come, let us sing unto the Lord!" the joyous voices sang.
"Let us make a joyful noise to the rock of our salvation.
Let us come before his presence with thanksgiving,
And make a joyful noise unto him with psalms!"

With renewed faith in God, and the ark in their midst, the people of Israel prospered mightily under David's rule. The scattered tribes were now one people, and in their new strength they successfully drove off invading hordes of Ammonites and Syrians and Moabites, until it was no longer necessary for David himself to lead them into battle. Joab, captain of the Israelite armies, was well equipped to handle the border skirmishes that still took place. David ruled long and wisely, and in his time Israel was great.

Yet David was not wise in everything he did. One evening he rose from his bed and walked upon the flat roof of his palace, and from the roof he saw a very beautiful woman whom suddenly he loved. He inquired after her and learned that her name was Bathsheba and that she was the wife of one Uriah, a soldier in his own army. Now David did a very sinful thing. He commanded Joab to send Uriah into the forefront of the battle so that he would be struck down and killed. And Joab did assign Uriah to the most dangerous part of the battlefield where fighting was at its hottest peak. Uriah fought valiantly, for he was a dedicated soldier, until he fell beneath an enemy sword and died there on the battlefield in the service of his king.

When word came to him of Uriah's death, David married the widow of the man whose death he had so cruelly arranged, and soon Bathsheba had a child.

But the Lord knew what David had done. In punishment to David he let Bathsheba's first child sicken and die. David was grieved, but since his remorse for the terrible thing he had done was greater than his grief, the Lord gave him and Bathsheba another son, whom they named Solomon.

David had many other sons by other wives, and among them he had one great favorite whom he dearly loved. His name was Absalom. In all Israel there was none so praised for his manly beauty as this princely youth: from the sole of his foot to the crown of his head he was perfect in every outward way. His own pride and joy was in the long flowing hair that he cut only once a year, when it was heavy on him and became a burden.

David did not realize, however, that Absalom had dreams of being king, and that he was already making plans to win the people to his side, preparing chariots and horses and fifty men to run before him so that Israel would take note of him and see his splendor.

Thus displaying himself to be admired, Absalom made it a practice to rise early in the morning and go to the gates of the city so that any man coming with a cause to lay before the king would see him first. Then the handsome prince would call out in a friendly manner and say, "Where do you come from, and what troubles you?"

The man would answer, and explain why he had come to the city of David seeking judgment to settle a claim.

"Your claims are good and right," Absalom would say. "What a pity it is that there is no one appointed by the king to hear and help you! If only I were judge in the land, then every man with suit or cause could come to me, and I would do him justice!"

His kind words and friendly manner had great effect on those who came to see the king. Not only did he always find their causes to be right and just and express a warm desire to help; he also treated them with courtesy, so that when they wished to bow to him he would restrain them gently and instead take each man by the hand and graciously bestow a kiss. In this way did he treat all those he met on their way to David; and with his courtesy and kindness he won the hearts of the people of Israel.

One day Absalom went to David and said: "Let me go, I pray you, to Hebron to fulfill a vow which I made unto the Lord, for I did swear that I would serve the Lord in Hebron."

"Go in peace," King David said, not knowing or suspecting that Absalom was using his vow as an excuse to leave Jerusalem and pursue his own plans for the kingship. Indeed, David knew nothing of what his son was doing.

Absalom took two hundred men with him from Jerusalem, innocent men who did not understand that he was making use of them. Upon his arrival in Hebron, Absalom sent spies throughout all the tribes of Israel, saying: "As soon as you hear the sound of the trumpet, then you shall cry out, 'Absalom is king in Hebron!'" For here in Hebron, too, Absalom had many friends, and he intended to gather his followers at this place and quickly build an army. Thus the conspiracy grew strong. The people turned increasingly toward the handsome, well-loved Absalom, and supporters flocked to his side in Hebron. Soon they would be ready to attack the city of Jerusalem and force David from his throne.

Then, just before Absalom's preparations were complete, a messenger hurried to David, saying "The hearts of the men of Israel are with Absalom your son." And the man told him what was happening at Hebron. David's distress was great. His favorite son, his Absalom! To war against him was unthinkable; to let him succeed in what he was doing would be sheer disaster. Scarcely knowing what to do, David decided that there was no way to save the city of Jerusalem from ruin but to leave it with all haste. "Arise!" he told the faithful followers who were still with him. "Let us flee, for we shall not else escape from Absalom. Quickly, get ready to depart, or he will overtake us here and destroy the city."

So the king left the city with his household and his men, leaving only the priests to guard the ark of the Lord, and a handful of women to keep the royal house in order. If the Lord was with him, David thought, he would return to the city of Jerusalem. And if not, it was better that the ark should remain in the tabernacle.

David and all the people with him crossed over the brook Kidron and gathered together in the wilderness. Then David climbed slowly up the Mount of Olives, weeping bitterly for the favored son who had turned against him and for the people who had conspired with Absalom for his downfall. Meanwhile Absalom, with his forces, entered into the city of Jerusalem only to find that it was almost empty. With his counselors he made cunning plans to seek out David and attack him.

Now David, saddened though he was, was still a king and still a fighting man; and although he did not want to harm his son he knew that he must stop this revolt or his country would suffer badly. Therefore when he had composed himself he led his forces by night over the river Jordan to the town of Mahanaim, where the people treated him with kindness and offered full support. There at Mahanaim he prepared for battle, dividing his army into three divisions with an experienced captain over each. One division came under the leadership of Joab, one under Abishai, and one under a man named Ittai who had volunteered his services to David after seeing the king's need. And David said to his people as they gathered in their strength: "I will go forth with you and lead you."

But the people answered: "No, you shall not go into battle. If we flee, it will not matter. Nor will it matter if half of us should die. But you are worth ten thousand of us, so you shall not either flee or die. Therefore stay here in the city and help us from this place."

"I will do whatever seems best to you," said David humbly, and he stationed himself beside the city gates. All the people came out by their hundreds and their thousands to hear his words and do battle for him. As Joab and Abishai passed by with their divisions he commanded them: "Deal gently for my sake with the young man Absalom." And all the people heard him when he gave these orders to his captains.

So the forces of David went out into the field against those who followed Absalom, and David waited at the gates of Mahanaim for news. The battle took place on the wooded slopes of Mount Ephraim and in the valley below, a vast stretch of forest land that was a tangle of great oaks and heavy undergrowth, and Absalom in his great confidence went forth ahead of his untried band of men.

The two forces clashed head-on, and one was far superior to

the other. David's three divisions of loyal and experienced fighting men quickly got the upper hand over the poorly led and ill-advised army of his son Absalom. The battle spread through the vast woods and over the face of the country; thousands of men fell by the sword and thousands more ran panic-stricken through the confusion of trees and vines to lose themselves in the great forest. There was a great and terrible slaughter that day of twenty thousand men; and the people of Israel, the followers of Absalom, fell in great numbers before the loyal followers of David.

Absalom, in his vanity, had not thought to cut his richly flowing hair before going into battle. Here and there he galloped on his mule, rallying his forces and demanding victory. And as his men scattered in retreat he rode behind them, searching desperately for a way out of the dark woods. On all sides he saw the soldiers of his father David, and he whipped his mule to greater speed so that he might ride between them. His long hair blew high as he rode; and his frightened mule darted beneath the trees and ran under the low-hanging, clutching boughs of a great oak. And suddenly Absalom was swinging between heaven and earth, the lovely long hair of which he was so proud caught on the branches of the tree. The mule galloped desperately away from under him and left him hanging there.

One of David's soldiers saw him dangling in mid-air. Remembering his king's words he did not harm the prince but hurried to his captain Joab. "Behold!" he said. "I saw Absalom hanging from an oak by his long hair!"

"You saw him helpless and you did not strike him to the ground?" Joab said roughly. "I would have rewarded you with ten shekels of silver if you had killed the traitor Absalom!"

"I would not put forth my hand against the king's son for a thousand shekels of silver," said the man, "for we all heard the king charging you and Abishai and Ittai not to touch the young man Absalom. You yourself would have been the first to blame me if I had."

"I cannot waste time with such as you!" said Joab, for he had no such scruples. With three darts in his hand he strode off to the oak from which Absalom hung, still alive and struggling painfully to free himself. And Joab thrust the three darts into the heart of David's son. Then he blew his trumpet, and his men returned from pursuing the fleeing forces of Absalom. They took his limp body from the tree and cast it into a deep pit in the forest; and then they filled in the crude grave and built a great mound of stones above it. Now all was over for the followers of Absalom. There was nothing left for them to fight for; nothing left for them to do but run and hide.

David still waited at the city gates of Mahanaim for word of the battle. A watchman on the roof above him lifted up his eyes and saw a man in the distance, running toward the city. The watchman called out and told the king. "If he is alone," said David, "he must be bringing news." And he waited anxiously.

Then the watchman saw another man running. "Behold, another man running alone!" he called out. "But the one in front looks like Ahimaaz, the son of Zadok the priest."

"If it is Ahimaaz he is a good man," said the king. "Therefore he must be coming with good tidings."

Ahimaaz called out as he drew near: "All is well! The victory is ours!" And he fell down to the earth upon his face before the king, saying, "Blessed be the Lord God, who has delivered into your hands the men who rebelled against my lord the king."

The king had but one question. "Is the young man Absalom safe?"

Ahimaaz knew the answer; but he loved his king and could not bring himself to tell David what had happened. So he turned his head away from the king's gaze, and he lied. "When Joab sent me on my way," he said, "there was great noise and tumult. But I knew not what it was."

The second runner came to a stop in front of David.

"Stand aside," the king told Ahimaaz, and turned his attention to the second messenger. Ahimaaz waited with a sinking heart as the man Cushi gave his message.

"News, my lord the king!" Cushi began. "For the Lord has given you vengeance this day against all those who rose against you."

Again the king had but one question. "Is the young man Absalom safe?"

Cushi hesitated, choosing his words carefully. Finally he said: "May the enemies of my lord the king, and all that rise against you to do you harm, be as that young man is now." Then David knew that Absalom was dead. And instead of rejoicing in his victory, he mourned bitterly for his lost son.

The rebellion had been broken and David needed only to return to Jerusalem and reunite his people, for now they needed him more than ever before. But for days he covered his face and wept, and cried out: "O my son Absalom, my son, my son Absalom! Would God I had died instead of you, O Absalom, my son, my son!"

And the great victory of that day was turned into mourning for all the people, for they heard how David grieved and cried out in his anguish: "O Absalom, my son, my son!"

THE WISDOM OF SOLOMON

*N*ow King David was old and his days were drawing to a close. In spite of occasional rebellion he had succeeded in welding his kingdom together so that it was strong and worthy of respect. His life had been full; apart from his sorrow over Absalom he had but one regret, and that was the Lord's refusal to allow him to build a temple for the ark. David's hands, the Lord had told him, were too bloodstained by war. Some day his son would build the holy house instead.

He had many sons, but his wife Bathsheba had made him swear that Solomon would be king. Therefore when David felt the day of his death to be drawing near he saw to it that Solomon was anointed king, and he told all Israel what the Lord their God demanded of a king.

Said David: "The God who is the Rock of Israel spoke to me and said, 'He that rules over men must be just, ruling in the fear of God. And he shall be as the light of the morning, when the sun rises, a morning without clouds; he shall be as pure as the tender grass that springs out of the earth in the clear sunshine after rain.' Let Solomon be such a king, for then the Lord will be a tower of salvation and will be merciful to his anointed."

Then David called Solomon to him and spoke to him for one last time.

"I go the way of all the earth," he said. "Be strong, therefore, and show yourself a man. Keep the commandments of the Lord your God and walk according to his ways. Obey his statutes, and his judgments, and his testimonies, as it is written in the law of Moses, so that you may prosper in everything you do. Then will the Lord fulfill the promise which he made to me, saying, 'If your children take heed of their ways and walk before me in truth with all their heart and with all their soul, then shall there always be a man among them of the throne of Israel.' Moreover, you know who has been faithful to me and who has not. Do therefore according to your wisdom; show kindness to those who have shown kindness to me, and do what you will to those who have done evil."

So David slept with his fathers, and was buried in the city of David. He had reigned over Israel for forty years: seven years in Hebron, and thirty-three years in the city of Jerusalem.

Now Solomon sat upon the throne of David his father, and under him a mighty kingdom was established. In accordance with his father's wishes he dealt out swift, stern punishment to those who had wronged David in his lifetime, and also to those who had threatened his own throne at the beginning of his reign. But he dealt kindly with those who were loyal to the house of David. To forestall war between Israel and the neighboring countries he made alliances with foreign kings, the first and most powerful of whom was Pharaoh, king of Egypt. Solomon married Pharaoh's daughter, making her the first of his many alien wives, and he brought her to live in the city of David. Then he devoted himself to securing his city and his kingdom. With the vast wealth inherited from David, he began to strengthen the great wall around Jerusalem, to build storehouses for storing grain against leaner times, and to build both a fine palace for himself and a temple for the Lord.

But until the house of the Lord was completed the people of

Israel worshiped and made their sacrifices on the tops of hills.
King Solomon loved the Lord and walked in the ways of David
his father; and he, too, sacrificed and burnt incense in high places
to the God of Israel. Often he would go to Gibeon to make his
sacrifices there, for Gibeon was a great high place, and there he
offered a thousand offerings upon the altar of the Lord.

In Gibeon the Lord appeared to Solomon in a dream by night;
and God said to Solomon: "Ask of me what you will, that I may
give it to you."

Solomon was humble of heart, and he knew that he needed
much wisdom and heavenly guidance to rule his kingdom well.

"You showed great mercy to my father David because he
walked before you in truth and righteousness," he said. "And in
your kindness you gave to him a son to sit upon his throne, as it is
this day. Now, O Lord my God, I your servant am king instead of
David. But I am like a little child and know not how to rule. I am
in the midst of your chosen people, a great people who cannot be
counted for they are so many, and it is for me to lead them. Give
to me therefore an understanding heart to judge your people, so
that I may know the difference between good and bad. For
without God's wisdom, who would be able to judge so great a
people as yours?"

It pleased the Lord that Solomon had asked this thing. He said
to Solomon: "Because you have asked for this, and not for long
life or riches for yourself, nor for the lives of your enemies, but for
understanding to make wise judgments, I will give you what you
ask. I give you this day a wise and understanding heart, so that
there shall never have been a man like you before you nor shall
there ever be in time to come. And I also give to you that which
you have not asked: both riches and honor, so that there will not
be anyone among the kings like you in all your days. And if you
will walk in my ways and keep my laws and commandments, as
your father David did, I will also lengthen your days."

Then Solomon awoke and knew he had been dreaming. Yet he
was sure that the Lord had indeed spoken to him in his dream.

He therefore went back to his city of Jerusalem to make offerings before the ark of the Lord; and he called all his servants and attendants to a great feast of thanksgiving.

It was apparent before long that the prayer of his dream had been answered, for there came to him one day two women, who stood before the king with a case for him to judge. With them they had brought a tiny baby.

"O my lord," the first woman said, "this woman and I live in the same house. And a child was born to me while she was in the house. It happened then that on the third day after I had my child, this woman also bore a son. Only we two were in the house; there was no one with us but the babies. And this woman's child died in the night, and she arose quietly at midnight and took my boy from beside me while I slept. Then she laid him on her bosom and put her dead child in my arms. When I rose from my bed in the morning to nurse my child, I saw that the child I held against me was no longer living. When I looked at him in the light of dawn I found that it was not my son that I was holding in my arms."

"It is not so," the woman said. "The living is my son, and the dead is yours."

"No, the dead is your son!" the first woman said again. "The living child is mine."

Thus they spoke in anger to each other before King Solomon.

The king listened closely, and then he said: "The one says, 'This is my son that lives, and yours is the dead.' And the other says, 'No, but your son is dead, and my son is the living.' Therefore let us see which of you is telling the truth."

He turned to his guards. "Bring me a sword," he ordered. They brought it to him. "Now," said Solomon, "divide the living child in two, and give half to one woman and half to the other."

"O my lord, no!" cried the woman whose son it truly was, for her heart yearned for her son and she wanted him to live. "Give her the living child and do not kill it!"

The other woman said only, "Let it be neither mine nor yours.
Let it be divided."

But Solomon had no intention of doing so cruel a thing. He had
been testing both women, and one of them had failed.

"Give the child to the woman who does not want the child
divided," he ordered his men. "By no means harm it; she is his
mother, for she would rather give him up than allow him to be
hurt."

All Israel heard of the judgment which the king had made, and
their respect for Solomon was great. They saw that the wisdom of
God was indeed in him so that he made judgments that were fair
and wise.

Solomon ruled well over Israel, and he had peace on all sides
round about him. The people of his kingdom lived in safety, every
man under his vine and under his fig tree from Dan even to
Beersheba for all the days of the son of David. God gave him
much wisdom and understanding and largness of heart, as much
as the sand that is on the seashore. His wisdom excelled that of all
the sages of the east and all the people of Egypt; he was wiser
than all men, and his fame spread to all the nations round about
the land of Israel.

It seemed that there was nothing that Solomon did not know;
nothing that he could not explain for everyone to understand. He
spoke learnedly of trees and herbs, of beasts and birds, of
creeping things, and of the fishes of the sea; and there were some
who said that he could even speak the language of the beasts and
talk to them in their own tongues. Like his father David, he made
songs about things of beauty under the Lord's sky, and he spoke
three thousand proverbs to guide his people in the ways of righteousness.

And these are some of the three thousand sayings:

Hatred stirreth up strifes,
But love covereth all trangressions.

A righteous man regardeth the life of his beasts,
But the tender mercies of the wicked are cruel.

The way of the foolish is right in his own eyes:
But he that is wise hearkeneth unto counsel.

A soft answer turneth away wrath:
But a grievous word stirreth up anger.

Pride goeth before destruction,
And a haughty spirit before a fall.

He that is slow to anger is better than the mighty;
And he that ruleth his spirit than he that taketh a city,

A merry heart is good medicine:
But a broken spirit drieth up the bones.

Even a child maketh himself known by his doings,
Whether his work be pure, and whether it be right.

A good name is rather to be chosen than great riches,
And loving favor rather than silver and gold.

And people of all lands came to hear the wisdom of Solomon, even the kings of the earth who had heard of his great knowledge.

Hiram, king of Tyre in the land of the Phoenicians, sent good-will messages to Solomon, for Hiram had been David's friend.

Solomon received his greetings gladly and sent back his own messengers, saying: "You know how my father David could not build a house unto the Lord his God because of the wars which were about him on every side. But now the Lord has given me peace so that there is neither enemy nor evil happening to prevent this work, and I intend to build a temple to the Lord my God. Therefore, I beg you, command your servants to cut me cedar trees out of Lebanon. My servants shall work with yours, and I will pay your men for help, for you know that there is none among us with the skill of your people."

When Hiram heard these words from the messengers of Israel he rejoiced greatly, and said: "Blessed be your Lord this day, who has given David a wise son over this great people."

So he sent to Solomon all the cedar trees and timbers of fir that the king of Israel wanted for the temple, and skilled workmen to help with the building of it. Solomon, in exchange, sent great quantities of wheat and oil for Hiram's household; and the two kings made a pact together that they would always live in peace.

It was in the four hundred and eightieth year after the children of Israel escaped from the bondage of Egypt, and in the fourth year of Solomon's reign, that he began to build the house of the Lord. And he commanded first that his servants bring great stones, cut stones and costly ones, to lay the foundation of the temple. In accordance with his wishes the stone was made ready before it was brought into the city of Jerusalem so that there would be no sound of ax nor hammer nor any tool of iron in the Lord's house while it was being built.

Now, though David had not been permitted to build the Lord's house himself, God had told him that his son would build it in his time. Therefore David had prepared many rich things and materials for the temple, and he had told his son Solomon: "Behold, I have prepared for the house of the Lord a hundred thousand talents of gold and a hundred thousand talents of silver; and brass and iron so abundant that it cannot be weighed; timber also and stone I have prepared, and you may add to it. Here also is pure gold for the candlesticks and bowls and basins; as well as onyx, and other precious stones of many colors, and marble in abundance." Then David had given to Solomon the pattern for the main building, the porch, and all the rooms, and for the inner holy chamber where the ark of the covenant would rest.

Therefore Solomon sent also for the riches stored by David, and proceeded to build the Lord's house according to the pattern laid out by his father. The outside walls were gigantic blocks of stone. The walls, floors, and ceilings of the temple were solid boards of cedar; and when the floors had been laid Solomon covered them with planks of fir. And the cedar of the house within was carved with knobs and open flowers: no stone showed inside, for all was cedar and much of it was carved into lovely, intricate shapes. Then Solomon covered the whole house, and the whole altar in the holy of holies, with the purest gold. And he carved all the walls of the house with figures of cherubim and palm trees and flowers in bloom, and covered them all with gold.

Solomon spent seven years in building the house of the Lord, and when it was done there was nothing like it for magnificence in all the earth. He brought in all the things that David had gathered and dedicated to the Lord: the gold and silver, the vessels and the candlesticks, the precious stones; and he put them among the treasures in the Lord's house. So ended his work.

Then he called together all the elders of Israel and the heads of the tribes so that they might bring the ark of the Lord into the beautiful new temple and give thanks unto the Lord for his many blessings. With their hearts full of praise and gratitude to God, the priests brought the ark of the covenant of the Lord to its new resting place. There was nothing in it but the two tablets of stone which Moses had put into it at Sinai, but it was the most glorious and holy thing in Solomon's temple.

And when the ark had been put in place, the glory of God filled the house of the Lord with so bright a light that the priests could not look upon it.

Solomon stood before the altar of the Lord in the presence of all the people of Israel and stretched his hands toward the heavens. "Blessed be the Lord God of Israel!" he said prayerfully. "I have built you a house to live in, a settled place for you to abide in forever, and a place where the ark of the covenant may rest eternally. Blessed be the Lord who has given rest unto his people Israel, as he promised. O God of Israel, hear your servant and your people when they pray toward this place, and may they trust

and honor the Lord all the days that they live in the land!" Then
Solomon blessed all the congregation of Israel, and held a great
feast of thanksgiving for all his people.

When all the feasting was over and the people had departed to
their homes, the Lord again appeared to Solomon in a dream by
night as he had done at Gibeon.

"I have hallowed this house that you have made," said the God
of Israel, "and I shall be within it as long as your heart is with me.
If you walk in my ways as your father David walked, being
upright and keeping always my commandments and my laws, I
will bless you and your children forever with the throne of Israel.
But if you or your children turn away from following me and go
to worship other gods, then I will leave this house that you have
built; I will cut Israel out of the land which I have given them,
and much sorrow shall fall upon the people."

Solomon would have done well to heed these words of the
Lord, for in them was not only a blessing but a warning.

THE DIVISION OF THE KINGDOM

*A*fter completing the house of the Lord, King Solomon devoted himself to further strengthening his kingdom and building up his capital city of Jerusalem. He had spent seven years in building the temple, but he was thirteen years in building his own palace.

It was a magnificent structure of cedar and great stones, with a throne of ivory overlaid with gold. Six high, wide steps led to the throne. On either side stood the gigantic figure of a lion; and twelve more lions stood upon the steps, six on either side. There was nothing like his glorious throne in all the kingdoms of the world. The drinking vessels of the royal house were of the purest gold, for silver was not rich enough for such a noble king. Solomon sent to sea a great navy that sailed to many far places and brought back to him much gold and silver, ivory and spices, apes and peacocks, and all the wonders of the world beyond the borders of the land of Israel. Soon he exceeded all the kings of the earth not only in wisdom but in wealth as well, as the Lord had promised.

Now there was a queen of the land of Sheba, a great and wealthy country on the other side of the Arabian sands across from Israel, who herself had much wealth and wisdom. When she

heard of the fame of Solomon, the wisdom given to him by the
Lord, and the wonders of his growing nation, she determined to
visit him and test him with hard questions. It was not easy for this
great queen to believe that Solomon could be so much greater
than she, and she wished to know if he were as wise as she had
heard it said.

So she traveled many miles across the desert from her own
country with a vast train of camels and attendants; and on the
camels' backs were stores of spices, gold, and precious stones, rich
gifts for a king who was already more than rich. When she came
to Solomon she talked with him of everything that was in her
heart, asking him many questions that she thought he could not
answer.

Solomon answered everything she asked, for in the Lord's
wisdom there was nothing that he did not know and nothing that
he could not tell her. She was amazed by his vast knowledge, for
it had seemed impossible that any man could be blessed with so
much learning and with such an understanding heart. Each question that she put to him was more difficult than the last, dealing with great mysteries of nature, science, and religion, yet
Solomon's wisdom was without end and he knew far more than
she could ask.

With eyes wide open in wonderment she surveyed the glorious
temple he had built to honor the Lord, and never had she seen
such magnificence in all her days. She gazed admiringly at the
great cedar pillars and overlays of gold in the house of the Lord,
and at Solomon's own throne of ivory and gold with the lions on
either side. She took note of his splendid chariots and many stalls
of spirited horses, and she saw the great array of food upon the
royal table. Queen though she was, she was impressed by the fine
manners of his multitude of ministers and servants and the
richness of their clothing, by the golden goblets brought in by his
cupbearers and by their costly robes; and the many beautiful
buildings he had built for his huge family struck her almost
speechless for their number and their elegance. Having heard so

much of his wisdom and seen the wonder and glory of Jerusalem, the Queen of Sheba no longer doubted that Solomon was all that people had said of him. Everything she saw and heard convinced her of the extraordinary might and learning of this king who ruled his nation under God's command.

"It was a true report that I heard in my own land about your great deeds and your wisdom," she told Solomon at last. "But I did not believe the words I heard until I came here and saw with my own eyes. Now I know that the half was not told me of the wisdom and glory of King Solomon. Happy are your men, and happy these your servants, who are with you all the time to hear your words of wisdom. Blessed be the Lord your God, who delights in you, for setting you upon the throne of Israel! It is because the Lord loves Israel that he has made such a man as you king over these people, to make judgments and do justice."

Then she gave the king a hundred and twenty talents of gold, and very great stores of spices and of precious stones. In return King Solomon gave the Queen of Sheba all she desired and whatever she asked, and many more wonderful things as well. And so she turned and went back to her own country with her servants, and with even more riches than she had brought to Solomon.

The king's wealth continued to increase. He built towns throughout his land: cities to store his treasures and his crops, cities to house his chariots, his horses and his horsemen. He had forty thousand stalls of horses for his tremendous fleet of chariots, and twelve thousand horsemen to ride them and to drive them. Tax money poured in from the Canaanites still living in the land, and gold flowed in from the foreign cities with which the king conducted trade. His merchants brought not only coin but horses, linen yarn, spices, and silverware from the far-off lands, and his treasure coffers were filled to overflowing. Yet he easily found ways to use the money, for he was always building and acquiring sustenance for his huge household.

Thousands of Israelites were put to work as builders of his cities, and as soldiers in the armies that never went to war because of his agreements with the neighboring lands. Twelve officers were set over all Israel to see that the king and his household were well provided with food, each officer making provision from his appointed district for one month out of the year. And Solomon's provision for one day alone was three hundred bushels of fine flour, and six hundred bushels of meal; ten fat oxen, and twenty other oxen from the pastures; one hundred sheep, as well as deer and buck and fatted fowl; and barley and straw for all his camels and his horses.

Solomon reigned over all the kingdoms from the river Euphrates to the land of the Philistines, and to the border of Egypt. All of them brought presents to him and served him all the days of his life. All the kings of the earth that sought his presence to hear his wisdom brought presents to him, too: vessels of silver and vessels of gold; fine wearing apparel and sweetsmelling spices; horses and mules, harnesses and armor, cedar trees and fir, and all manner of riches to make Israel the wealthiest nation in the world and Jerusalem its most magnificent city. The people of Judah, Solomon's own tribe, and the rest of Israel multiplied and became many. They worked long and hard but they profited by the wealth of the land. They were at peace, Solomon administered their national affairs with the firm hand that they needed; and they ate well, drank well, and made merry.

But King Solomon loved many women who were strangers to the land of Israel, and in making his political alliances he had married the daughters of a great many foreign kings. Beside the daughter of Pharaoh, he had married women of the Moabites, Ammonites, Edomites, Sidonians, and Hittites, heathen peoples whose women were expressly forbidden to the children of Israel. Of them the Lord had said: "You shall not take wives among them, nor shall your women take husbands, for surely they will turn your hearts toward their own gods." But Solomon did take them as his wives.

He had seven hundred wives, all princesses, and three hundred concubines. And, as the Lord had warned, they did turn away his heart. As he grew old he tried to please his wives by allowing them to worship in their own heathen ways, and with the passing of time they turned his heart toward their gods. Now Solomon, less wise than in his youth, built an altar to the evil Ashtoreth, goddess of the people of Sidon in Phoenicia, and worshiped at that heathen shrine himself. Then he built a high place for Chemosh, god of the Moabites, on a hill before Jerusalem; and then another for Molech, vile false god of the Ammonites. Thus he did evil in the sight of the Lord, building all these altars not only for his foreign wives but for himself. He still made offerings to the God of Israel three times every year; but far more often did he burn incense and make sacrifices to the strange gods of his many wives.

The Lord was angry with him because his heart had strayed away from the God of Israel. He said to Solomon: "Because you have not kept my laws and covenants I will take your kingdom from you and give it to your servant. For David your father's sake I will not do it while you live, but I will take the kingdom from the hand of your son. One part of it only will I give your son for David's sake, and for my chosen city of Jerusalem. The rest shall be divided from your house, from the house of David."

Now, though Israel was mighty and full of riches under Solomon's rule, there were many people who had become dissatisfied with the evil of his later days and with his vast extravagance. His own palace was even more magnificent than the temple of the Lord; his household consumed great quantities of food which the people had to provide; taxes were high, because of Solomon's costly buildings and the sacrificial edifices he erected for his wives. The treasury was being strained to danger point, and many people were forced to spend far too much time in building and repairing structures that were nothing more than luxuries. And so, when the Lord made adversaries to rise up against King Solomon, some were enemies from beyond the borders of Israel but one was a young Israelite named Jeroboam who had become displeased with Solomon's rule. The son of

Solomon's most trusted servant, Jeroboam was an industrious worker and a mighty man of valor. Solomon had taken note of his fine qualities, and had placed him in a position of some power. And now the Lord caused this young leader to lift his hand against King Solomon and gather followers round about him who were also discontented.

One day when Jeroboam went out of Jerusalem the prophet Ahijah met him on his way; for it was in Solomon's time that the great prophets began to speak for the Lord. When the two men were alone in the field the prophet caught at the new cloak he was wearing and tore it into twelve ragged pieces.

"Take ten pieces," he said to Jeroboam, "for the Lord God of Israel has said that he will tear the kingdom out of the hand of Solomon and give ten tribes to you. Thus said the Lord: 'Because Solomon and his house have forsaken the way of the Lord to worship heathen idols, I will give Israel to Jeroboam. Yet I will not take the whole kingdom away from the house of Judah but will give one tribe to the son of Solomon, for my servant David's sake. And Solomon shall be prince all the days of his life, but after him his kingdom shall fall. Only one tribe will stay with his son, so that David my servant may always have a light before me in Jerusalem, the city in which I have chosen to put my name.' But you, Jeroboam," the prophet Ahijah continued, "shall reign over the ten tribes of Israel, and if you walk in the ways of the Lord, he will be with you. But walk with care; the Lord has said that the house of David shall be thus afflicted, but not forever. There will yet come a great and powerful king from the line of Jesse, David, and the sinning Solomon."

Jeroboam went on his way and pondered the prophet's words. And when Solomon heard about the prophecy he tried to kill the rebellious young leader, but Jeroboam fled into Egypt until it was time for him to act.

Solomon reigned for forty years and then died, a great but sinful king who had wasted his wisdom as he had wasted the treasures of his kingdom. He was buried in the city of David; and Rehoboam his son reigned in his stead.

By this time all the people of Israel had become thoroughly dissatisfied with their lot under Solomon, and they hoped for less harsh treatment from their new king, Rehoboam. Jeroboam came back from Egypt on hearing of King Solomon's death, and went with the congregation of Israel to petition the new king.

"Your father made our burden grievously heavy," the people said to Rehoboam. "Our work was hard and our taxes were exceedingly high, so that we had little for ourselves. Now therefore lighten the heavy load he put upon us, and we will serve you well."

Rehoboam did not answer them at once. He had grown up in ease and wealth and luxury, and he knew nothing of what it meant to be a king. "Leave me for three days," he said. "Then come again to me, and I will answer you." When they had gone he consulted with the old men who had served his father Solomon, and asked: "How do you advise that I may answer the people?"

"If you want to serve your people well," they said, "then speak good words to them and answer their request. What they asked was right and fair. Be their servant, and they will be your servants forever."

But Rehoboam was not pleased with the advice of the old men; he had no desire to be the servant of his subjects. He went to consult with the idle young men who had grown up with him. "How shall I answer the people who have asked me to lighten the yoke my father laid upon them?" he asked these wealthy, indolent young princes.

"Answer them like a true king, harshly and with price!" they told him arrogantly. "Tell them that their load has not been heavy enough, and that you will make it worse."

Therefore, at the end of the three days the king went back to his people and spoke roughly to them, ignoring the counsel of the wise old men and following the foolish advice of his spoiled young friends.

"If my father made your yoke heavy," he said to the people of Israel, "I will make it heavier! My father punished you with whips; I will chastise you with the lash of scorpions!"

There was silence for a moment, then a rising murmur of horror and rebellion. Jeroboam arose in the forefront of his outraged countrymen.

"What share do we have then in the house of Israel and of David?" he cried out, and the people echoed him with angry shouts. "Go to your tents, O Israel! Depart from Rehoboam, son of Solomon and king of Judah, for he shall not be our king! And you, the people of David and Judah, see to your own house, for we will have no more to do with you!"

So, hot with rebellion, the ten tribes of Israel turned their backs on Rehoboam and followed Jeroboam. Only the people of Judah and the tribe of Benjamin stayed with Rehoboam, unworthy successor to the house of David. The land of Israel was torn apart like the prophet's cloak, so that the ten tribes of Israel were ruled by Jeroboam in the north and the two tribes of Judah were misruled by Rehoboam in the south. There were two Hebrew nations now; and the division of the kingdom was the beginning of the end of the Israel envisioned by Moses, captured by Joshua, and united by David and Solomon.

The land and people of Judah still had Jerusalem as their capital, so that all those in the southern lands who loved God could still worship at the holy place. But under Rehoboam's rule they did evil in the sight of the Lord, building heathen idols and altars on every high hill and under every green tree. Bad times came upon them, and the king of Egypt attacked Jerusalem while the strength of Judah was at its lowest ebb. There was nothing to stop the Egyptian invaders; they stripped both the king's house and the house of the Lord of all their treasures, even taking away the shields of gold which Solomon had made. And these lovely, priceless things never were replaced with anything of equal value, for Rehoboam did not have the resources of his father Solomon.

The northern kingdom of Israel established its capital at Shechem, and Jeroboam resolved to lead his people well. But he was afraid that his people would go up and make their sacrifices in the sacred city of Jerusalem, the city chosen by the Lord, and then be persuaded to turn against their leader in rebellion to rejoin Rehoboam and the house of Judah. Therefore he gave his people something to keep them satisfied in Israel: At the two strategic points of Bethel and Dan he placed two calves of gold for his people to worship, saying, "It is too much for you to go up to Jerusalem to worship and offer sacrifice. Here, O people of Israel, are the gods that brought you out of the land of Egypt!" And both Jeroboam and his people worshiped these false gods.

Thus, in the eyes of the Lord, there was little to choose between Judah and Israel, the two parts of what was once the promised land. United under a strong and godly ruler, the twelve tribes might have remained a mighty nation. Divided, each kingdom was weak, and both halves were in danger not only from their outside enemies but from each other. Civil war raged between Israel and Judah for all the days of Jeroboam and Rehoboam.

Years passed; the kings of both Hebrew countries died and were succeeded by their sons, and they in turn gave way to other kings. Among them, there were good kings and there were bad; there were weak and there were strong; there were those who worshiped the true God, and those who burned incense to strange idols. Brief periods of peace were shattered by the noise of battle. War followed war, defeat followed defeat. In spite of an occasional lull in the shedding of blood and the worshiping of graven images, both north and south sank ever deeper into sin and treachery and degradation.

ELIJAH AND THE PROPHETS OF BAAL

*O*f the two countries, Israel's disadvantage was the greater. Though it was twice the size of Judah to the south and had three times as many inhabitants, its geographical location placed it virtually in the midst of enemies and exposed it to their marauding expeditions. Judah, on the other hand, was a compact land, protected to a degree by Israel to the north and by such natural barriers as the Salt Sea and the desert of Arabia. Also, once the riches of its temple had been plundered, its empty treasure coffers and barren land were not as tempting to an invader as the storehouses and rich pastures of Israel. And although the people of Judah periodically turned to the worship of foreign idols, they still had a true national capital and religious center in their city of Jerusalem. Israel, however, had no permanent capital at all, either political or religious, to bind her people together. Each succeeding king chose his own favorite city for his capital; and each king, no matter what his early intentions, drifted into idol worship.

Ahab, the son of Omri, chose Samaria for his capital and reigned over Israel for twenty-two years. Those were bad years for all Israel, for Ahab did more evil in the sight of the Lord than any king before him. As if it were nothing to him to follow in the wicked ways of Jeroboam, who had built golden calves for his people to worship, Ahab took to wife the heathen woman Jezebel. She was the daughter of Ethbaal, king of the Phoenician city of Sidon, and in all the history of Israel there never had been nor ever would be a woman so vicious and sinful. Jezebel was an ardent worshiper of the idol Baal; and from her own land she brought hundreds of heathen priests so that the religion of Baal might be forced upon her husband's people.

Ahab made no attempt to turn her toward the God of Israel. He turned, instead, toward her false religion with a burning enthusiasm. He built a temple to Baal in the very heart of the city of Samaria. In the temple he placed an elaborate altar; and at the altar he worshiped the false god of the wicked Jezebel. But one altar to one false god, it seemed, was not enough: Ahab made a grove of trees where other false gods could be worshiped, and he did more to provoke the Lord to anger than all the kings of Israel who had gone before him. More altars sprang up throughout the land, so that the four hundred and fifty priests or prophets of Baal and the four hundred other prophets of the grove were kept well occupied with their evil work.

True believers, those among the men of Israel who had remained faithful to the one God, cried out against the excesses of Ahab and the terrible wickedness of Jezebel. But Ahab did not hear and Jezebel did not care. She meant to force her religion upon the people of Israel if she had to kill the lot of them. And many of them did die: she began a dreadful reign of terror in which all the old altars to the God of Israel were thrown down by her priests and soldiers, and faithful Israelites fell by the hundreds in a ruthless slaughter. God's priests and prophets ran into the caves and wildernesses of the land to hide from the wave of killing, and people who were not priests quaked before the onslaught and turned in fear to worship Baal. And so it was that the name of the God of Israel was no longer heard in Ahab's court nor even in the land.

And then one day a strange figure with ragged robe and

tangled beard and burning eyes appeared before King Ahab and gave him dire warning. The man was Elijah from the land of Gilead, the one true prophet with the courage to meet with Ahab face to face. His only garment was his shabby cloak of camel skin; his only food was what the Lord in his mercy provided in the wilderness; and he lived under no shelter but the trees of Gilead. And he was the first of the great prophets with the power to perform wonders with the help of God.

He stood before the weak and sinful Ahab and fixed the king with his burning stare. He spoke but once, and said: "As the Lord God of Israel lives, the Lord before whom I stand, there shall not be dew nor rain these years until I say there shall be!"

Then he was gone. To the astonishment of Ahab's court, it was as if the strange old man had vanished.

The word of the Lord came to Elijah, saying: "Get away from this place and turn eastward; hide yourself by the brook Cherith which flows into the Jordan. You shall drink of the brook while it yet flows, and I have commanded the ravens to feed you."

So Elijah went and lived beside the brook Cherith as the Lord had commanded him. It was soon clear to all that his prophecy had become an established fact.

Neither dew nor rain fell upon the land; drought and famine fell together upon Israel like a terrible plague. Ahab sought in desperation for Elijah to put an end to it, but Elijah was nowhere to be found. The Lord had safely hidden him and was caring for his prophet.

Elijah lived upon the bank of the brook Cherith and drank its waters. The ravens brought him bread and meat in the morning, and bread and meat in the evening, so that he always had enough. For months he lived there in solitude, and he drank what he needed until the brook dried up.

Then the word of the Lord came to him again. "Arise," said the Lord, "and go to Zarephath, which belongs to Sidon. I have commanded a widow woman there to care for you and give you food."

So Elijah left the dried-up brook and traveled through the

drought-stricken countryside to Zarephath in the land of the Phoenicians. When he came to the gate of the city he saw a woman gathering stray sticks for a fire, and he knew that she was the woman to whom the Lord had sent him. He could also see that she was poor and that she was in deepest despair.

He called to her and she turned to him. "Bring me, I beg of you," he said, "a little water in a vessel, so that I may drink." She nodded. As she was on her way to fetch it for him he called out again: "Bring me, I pray you, a little morsel of bread, for I am weak with hunger."

She looked at him. "I cannot," she said sorrowfully. "As God lives, I swear I have not the smallest cake in the house but only a handful of meal in a barrel and a little oil in a jar. I am gathering sticks now to make a fire, so that I may go in and prepare what is left for me and my son. It is very little; we will eat one last time and then we will die."

"Do not fear," Elijah said. "Go and do as you said, but first make me a little cake from what you have and bring it to me. Afterward bake cakes for yourself and your son, for there will be enough. The Lord God of Israel has said that the barrel of meal shall not become empty nor shall the cruse of oil run dry until the day that the Lord sends rain upon the earth."

The widow went into her house and followed Elijah's instructions. And she found that when she had baked a small cake for the prophet there was still meal and oil enough to feed herself and her son. Every day thereafter, for many weeks and months, there was enough in the widow's house for three people to eat. The barrel of meal did not become empty, nor did the cruse of oil run dry. And there was no longer any question of the small household dying for want of food.

But as time passed it happened that the woman's son fell sick. So very ill was he that the breath went out of him and it seemed that he was dead. The woman's heart was broken, and in her grief she turned upon Elijah.

"What have I to do with you, O man of God!" she cried. "Have you come to me to remind me of my sins and punish me by killing my son?"

"Give me your son," said Elijah gently. And he took the lifeless boy from her arms and carried him up to the loft where he was staying. Then he laid the child down on the bed and called upon the Lord.

"O Lord my God! Have you brought evil upon the widow who has been kind to me, by letting her son die? I pray you, let this child's soul come into him again; let him be restored to life." Then he stretched himself out upon the child three times, and three times prayed. The warmth of his body warmed the body of the child and the breath of his mouth entered the mouth of the child.

And the Lord heard the voice of Elijah. The soul of the boy came back into the young body, the breathing became deep and regular, and the child revived. Elijah picked the boy up in his arms and took him down to his weeping mother. "See!" he said. "Your son is alive."

The woman ceased her sobbing and grasped her child with loving joy and wonderment. "Now I know you are a man of God!" she said, reverent with gratitude. "By this miracle I know that the word of the Lord comes from your mouth and what you speak is the truth."

For three years there was meal in the barrel, oil in the cruse, and drought throughout the land. Neither dew nor rain fell upon Israel, and King Ahab was hard put to feed his household and keep his horses alive. His messengers went far and wide in search of the missing Elijah, hunting at the same time for far-off brooks that perhaps might have a trickle of water left and seeking pastures that might yet be green. They found nothing. But the misery and hunger in his land did not persuade the king to turn away from Baal and back to God. As for Jezebel, she persecuted the followers of the one true God even more relentlessly.

The word of the Lord came to Elijah in the third year of the drought, saying: "Go, show yourself to Ahab, and I will send rain upon the earth." So Elijah went to show himself to Ahab while the

famine was still sore in the land. There was every chance that
Ahab, in his anger, would try to kill the prophet who had brought
the drought upon him, but Elijah was strong in the knowledge
that God had sent him.

King Ahab scowled at the ragged figure of the elusive prophet.
"Are you the man who troubles Israel?" he demanded.

Elijah shook his head and answered calmly, "It is not I but you
who have troubled Israel, you and your father's house. For you
have forsaken the commandments of the Lord and worshiped
Baal, and thus you have made the trouble."

Ahab was astounded and mightily displeased. Yet he remembered that Elijah had spoken the truth three years before and he
knew that his land was desperately in need of rain, so now he listened to the prophet in silence and laid no hand upon him.

Elijah went on speaking, and he proposed a test: "Send out and
gather together all the people of Israel at Mount Carmel. Gather
also the four hundred and fifty prophets of Baal, and the four
hundred prophets of the gods of the groves, those who eat at
Jezebel's table. Then we will see which god is the mightier."

So Ahab sent messages to the children of Israel. Great crowds
of people and false prophets gathered together at Mount Carmel.

Elijah stood before them at an ancient altar that now lay in
ruins, as did all the altars of the God of Israel in his time.

"How long will you hesitate between two faiths?" he began. "If
the Lord is God, follow him and do not waver; but if Baal is God,
then follow him."

The people answered not a word.

"You must decide," Elijah said. "See, I alone remain a prophet
of the Lord, but Baal's prophets are four hundred and fifty men.
Let them therefore give us two bullocks. Let them choose one for
themselves, and cut it into pieces and lay it upon wood, but put
no fire under it. Then let the heathen call on the names of their
gods, and I will call on the name of the Lord. Whichever God answers, let him be the one God."

"It is well spoken!" said the people. But the prophets of Baal had nothing to say. They did not look forward to the test, but they could not refuse before the gaze of all the people. And there was Ahab, too, looking on and praying to his false god for rain to end the drought and famine. The challenge had to be met.

The bullocks were quickly provided for this strange contest between gods. "Choose yours first," Elijah told the heathen priests, "for you are many and I am only one. And call on the name of your god to put fire beneath your sacrifice!"

The prophets of Baal took their bullock and cut it into pieces. And they started praying to their god to send them fire.

From morning until noon they prayed with rising desperation for something that they knew within their hearts could never be.

"O Baal! Hear us!" they cried. But there was no answer from their idol: neither a voice crying out to aid them, not a flash of fire to burn the pile of waiting firewood. Their frenzy rose and their voices became louder and more wild, and they leaped upon the altar which they had made to Baal.

All their leaping and their shouting had no effect on Baal.

"Cry more loudly!" Elijah mocked. "He is a god; and perhaps he is already talking so that he cannot hear, or he has other business, or he is on a journey; or perhaps he is asleep and must be wakened."

They cried more loudly and cut themselves with knives according to their strange custom so that blood flowed out and stained their priestly robes. But no mysterious fire came to light the woodpile underneath their bull.

Midday passed, and afternoon; and evening came. But still there was no answer to their frantic pleas: no sign, no voice, no indication that their cries were heard.

"Enough!" Elijah said at last. "Your god does nothing for you." He turned to the waiting people of Israel. "Come near to me and see what I do now." They came close to him and watched his every move. First he rebuilt the ancient altar of the Lord, the fallen stones which had been disused for many years. He chose twelve large stones, one for each of the tribes of Israel, and made them into an altar in the name of the Lord. Next he dug a trench around it, deep and wide; and then he cut his bullock into pieces and laid his sacrifice on the wood upon the altar.

The crowd watched him expectantly. But Elijah was not ready yet.

"Fill four barrels of water," he ordered, "and pour it over the dry wood and the sacrifice until it is so wet that it is impossible for fire to burn it." Four barrels of water in a drought was a difficult request, but they obeyed in silence. "Again!" he said. They poured a second time. "Do it a third time," said Elijah. They poured again. The water overflowed the altar and ran about it so that it filled the trench up to the brim.

"Now," he said.

It was the time of the evening sacrifice; Elijah came near to the water-soaked altar and lifted up his hands in supplication. And he prayed: "Lord God of Abraham, of Isaac, and of Israel, let it be known this day that you are God in Israel and that I am your servant, and that I have done all these things at your command. Hear me, O Lord, hear me! Hear me, that this people may know that you are the Lord God, and that you have turned their hearts back to yourself again."

He looked up into the heavens, and the eyes of thousands followed his calm gaze. With a shocking suddenness, bolts of fire flashed down from the skies and fell upon the altar and the sacrifice. The water became a hiss of steam; the bullock, the wet wood, the drenched stones and the very dust itself went up in sizzling smoke and tongues of fire and the smell of the burning sacrifice rose toward the sky. The fire of the Lord ate down through the stones, licked up the water in the trench and left a ring of burnt-out soil. Finally it died out, leaving no trace of bullock, water, stones, or altar for the astonished multitude to gaze upon.

When the people of Israel saw this spectacular sign from heaven they fell upon their faces in awe. "The Lord, he is God," they cried. "The Lord, he is the only God!"

"Take the prophets of Baal!" said Elijah. "Let none of them escape." For he knew that this was his great chance to break the power of Baal in the land of Israel, and he meant to use it. So the people fell upon the sinful heathen prophets who had led them astray, and killed them all beside the brook of Kishon. When they had done their work that day there were no longer any priests to serve the evil Jezebel or minister at the altars of false gods.

Ahab looked on and said nothing, for there was nothing he could say. Even to him it was obvious that Baal and his priests had been completely routed and discredited by the God of Israel.

Then Elijah turned to Ahab on this dry and cloudless day. "Go now, and feast," he said, "for there is a sound of abundant rains."

Ahab heard no sound of rain, but he went to eat and drink as Elijah had said. Elijah himself went up to the top of Mount Carmel and cast himself down upon the earth to pray. One servant only waited near him while Elijah spoke to God.

"Go higher," said Elijah to his servant. "Look toward the sea and tell me what you see."

The servant climbed a high rock and looked into the distance.

"There is nothing," he reported to Elijah.

"Go again," said Elijah. "Go seven times, and tell me what you see."

Seven times the servant climbed to the lookout point and peered across the sea while the prophet prayed. The seventh time he came back and said: "Behold! A little cloud, no bigger than a man's hand, is rising from the sea."

This was the sign Elijah had been waiting for.

"Go to Ahab," he told his servant. "Tell him to prepare his chariot and hasten from here so that the cloud shall not overtake him."

The king looked at the tiny cloud, and doubted. But he prepared his chariot. The little cloud grew rapidly and came in swiftly from across the sea, and Ahab rode swiftly to the safety of his city while the heavens became black with heavy clouds and boisterous with wind. Great drops came pelting down. By the time King Ahab reached his palace gates the rain was falling down in torrents upon the thirsty land and running into small dry brooks that soon became wide life-giving rivers.

Now all the children of Israel knew that God had done what Baal and his sinful priests could never do. The Lord God had sent fire down from heaven, and he had sent the welcome rain. The years of drought and famine were over.

ELIJAH AND ELISHA

*J*ezebel was so far from being glad of the torrential rains that she flew into a violent rage. When Ahab told her what the prophet Elijah had done, and how he had ordered her own prophets slain by the sword, she snarled with fury and sent a messenger to seek out Elijah with an ominous yet foolish message: "Let the gods destroy me if I do not take your life as you have taken theirs, by tomorrow at this time!"

It was foolish because it gave Elijah a chance to run for his life, and he did so with all speed. Fed and guided by the angel of the Lord, he remained hidden in the wilderness for forty days and forty nights. While he hid from Jezebel's cruel hand he became increasingly despondent over the state of Israel. Nothing, it seemed, had changed. Even though Baal's prophets were dead, there were always more where they came from; and Ahab and Jezebel still ruled. While they lived the people of Israel would continue to be persecuted and would never find the courage to break away from Baal.

God let Elijah rest in a cave on Mount Horeb, which was also called Sinai, but at last he spoke. First there was a great and powerful wind across the mountains, which blew against the rocks and smashed them into crumbling pieces, but the Lord did not speak in the loud voice of the wind. After the wind an earthquake came and shook the earth beneath Elijah's feet; but the Lord was not in the thunder of the quake. After the earthquake there was a fire that swept through the trees and left a blackened trail; but the Lord was not in the crackling and the roaring of the flames. After the fire there was a still, small voice calling to Elijah to come out from the cave. When Elijah heard it he covered his face with his rough cloak, for even he was afraid to look upon the glory of the Lord. He went out to stand near the entrance of the cave to hear the word of God.

"Elijah! What are you doing here? Why do you hide?"

"I have loved the Lord God of Israel and done all things faithfully," Elijah answered sadly, "but I am downcast and discouraged. The children of Israel have forsaken your covenants, thrown down your altars, and killed your prophets by the sword. I, and I alone, am left, and now they seek my life."

"You are not alone," said the voice of God. "I have seven thousand people left in Israel who have never bowed before the false god Baal. Therefore take heart, and go from here. Syria will war with Israel; Ahab shall not forever be king but shall lose his house to one Jehu. And you must seek out Elisha, son of Shaphat, and anoint him to be prophet in your place when you are gone. For there are still good men in Israel."

Elijah took heart and left his cave in Mount Horeb. He found Elisha, son of Shaphat, plowing with twelve yoke of oxen in a field. Elijah went up to him and threw his mantle over the young man's shoulders, a sign both men knew to mean that Elisha was to continue the old man's work as God's prophet when the right time came. Elisha begged leave to say farewell to his mother and his father; and he killed the oxen to give a feast to the people he was leaving. Then he arose and went after Elijah, and served him faithfully for all the days of the old man's life.

Ahab, in the meantime, had mended his ways to some slight degree. God therefore gave him victory in a battle with attacking Syrians, northern neighbors of the people of Israel who had been

building up their strength throughout the years of the divided
Hebrew kingdom. Under Ahab's leadership the land of Israel was
temporarily spared from the doom that hovered over it. But
Jezebel had not improved by any means, and once again she
plotted with her husband to do a wicked and greedy thing. It was
a small thing, by her standards, but it was thoroughly evil.

It so happened that a man named Naboth owned a vineyard
that King Ahab coveted. The place was close to Ahab's palace,
and the king told Naboth, "I should like to have it as a garden of
herbs, for it is a pleasant place and near to my house." He offered
money; he offered a better vineyard; but Naboth respectfully
declined to give up the inheritance of his forefathers.

Ahab stalked back to his palace in a childish rage. He lay down
on his bed, turned his face to the wall, and refused to eat. When
Jezebel inquired what ailed him, he told her about Naboth's refusal to part with his family's vineyard.

"Ah, well, if that is all," said Jezebel, "it is easily remedied. Are
you not the king? Arise! Be merry! You shall have the vineyard of
Naboth."

And Ahab did acquire the coveted vineyard. The wicked
Jezebel bribed two men, almost as evil as herself, to accuse
Naboth of blasphemy against God and the king. And, exactly as
she had planned, the elders and nobles of the city took the innocent Naboth out of the city and stoned him cruelly to death.

"Arise now," said Jezebel to Ahab. "Take possession of the
vineyard of Naboth which he refused to give you, even for money.
For Naboth is no longer alive, and a dead man cannot possess a
vineyard." So Ahab took possession of it and strolled about it
proudly, planning his new herb garden.

Elijah found him there.

"Have you found me, O my enemy?" cried Ahab, alarmed by
the anger that burned in Elijah's deep-set, honest eyes.

"I have found you," said Elijah grimly. "And I tell you now that
I will bring evil down upon you and your house. Your sons shall
die, and another shall be king; and for Jezebel also shall there be

a fitting and most horrible end." And he proceeded to tell Ahab exactly what frightful things would happen.

And they did. Some time later Ahab was mortally wounded in battle with the Syrians, and he bled to death. The two sons who followed him to the throne died, each in his turn, by violence. The next king, Jehu, was indeed not of Ahab's house, for he gained the throne through bloody rebellion. And Jehu killed all Ahab's sons, all the great men of Ahab's court, all his kinsmen, and all the priests of Baal. When Jehu had done with slaughter there was not a man left of Ahab's family or followers.

But these things took place years after Elijah's prophecy, and the old prophet had other tasks in the intervening time. And he did not live to see all his words come true. There came a time when he was very old and had only one task left: to turn his work over to his young successor. The faithful Elisha went with him everywhere he went, learning from the old man and following in the ways of the Lord.

It was while Elijah and Elisha were together in Gilgal that the Lord made known his wish to take Elijah into heaven by a whirlwind. The two men set out together for Bethel and Jericho, where there were young priests studying to serve the Lord, and when they were along the way Elijah said: "Stay here, Elisha, for the Lord has sent me to Bethel."

But Elisha answered, "As the Lord lives, and as your soul lives, I will not leave you." So they went together to Bethel. And the followers of the prophets who were at Bethel came out to Elisha and said: "Do you know that the Lord will take your master from you this day?"

"I do know," said Elisha. "Hold your peace."

And Elijah said to him, "Elisha, wait here, I beg you, for the Lord has sent me on to Jericho."

"As the Lord lives and as your soul lives," answered Elisha. "I will not leave you."

So they came together to Jericho, and here also the young prophets spoke to Elisha saying, "Do you know that the Lord will take your master from you this day?" As before, Elisha answered, "Yes, I know it. Hold your peace."

Then Elijah said again to him: "Stay here, I pray you, for the Lord has sent me to the Jordan." Elisha answered again, "As the Lord lives, and as your soul lives, I will not leave you." For he knew very well that the old man's last day upon the earth had come, and he did not wish to be away from his beloved master at the end.

So the two prophets traveled on together until they reached the banks of the Jordan.

Fifty men of the followers of the prophets went after them and stood a short distance away to watch. Elijah and Elisha stood together upon the bank of the swiftly flowing river.

The old prophet took off his cloak, folded it together, and struck the waters; they divided to leave a path of dry ground upon which a man could walk. The two men crossed the Jordan by this miraculous ford, and the waters closed behind them.

When they reached the other side Elijah turned to his companion and said: "Ask, Elisha, what I shall do for you before I am taken from you."

"I pray you," said Elisha, "to let a double portion of your spirit come upon me."

"You have asked a hard thing," said Elijah, "for that is given by God. Nevertheless, if you are able to see me when I am taken from you, you shall have your wish. But if you cannot see me, it shall not be as you ask."

They walked slowly away together on the far side of the Jordan, still talking. And suddenly a chariot and horses blazing with strange fire swept across the sky and came down low between the two prophets. A great whirlwind swirled around and picked up old Elijah, lifting him toward the heavens on the fiery chariot.

Elisha saw it. "My father, my father!" he cried out. "It is the chariot of Israel, and its horsemen!" Then there was nothing more to see but Elijah's mantle fluttering to the ground. Elijah himself was gone, never to be seen again. Elisha tore his clothes in grief. When he had mourned and prayed he picked up the old prophet's mantle.

The young men watching from the other side of the Jordan saw him strike the waters of the river with the mantle, and they heard him cry out: "Where is the Lord God of Elijah?" And they saw that the Lord God was with Elisha, who had seen Elijah when he was taken from him by whirlwind and fiery chariot, for when Elisha struck the waters they parted for him even as they had parted for Elijah. The new prophet of Israel crossed over on dry ground.

"The spirit of Elijah has come to rest upon Elisha!" said the followers of the prophets, and they bowed low upon the ground before him.

It soon was clear to all the people of the land that Elisha was a worthy successor to his departed master. He, too, was capable of filling empty jars of oil, of raising children from the dead, of feeding many with small supplies of bread. And on one great occasion he even healed an enemy of the people of Israel. It happened during a brief truce in the intermittent warfare between Israel and the people of Syria, the invaders from the north who frequently crossed the frontier to raid Israelite towns and carry off their inhabitants into slavery.

Naaman, captain of the great army of the king of Syria, was honored as a great man by his master and his fellow citizens. To him the Lord had given much success in battle; and it was due to him that Syria was free. Naaman was a mighty man, and a man of valor, but he was a leper.

Under his bold leadership the Syrians had brought many captives from the land of Israel. One of them was a little maid, who became maidservant to Naaman's wife. Both her master and her mistress were kindly people, and she soon came to love them as her own. Naaman's terrible illness caused the young girl much grief. Her heart was sore because she knew that he was bound to die of it, and die horribly, unless some wondrous thing occurred.

One day she went to her mistress and said: "I would to God that my master were with the prophet that is in Samaria! For he, the man Elisha, would surely cure my lord of his leprosy."

The woman told her husband Naaman what the girl had said, and Naaman began to feel a glimmer of hope. He went at once to his king and asked if he might seek out this prophet with the gift of healing.

"Go, by all means go!" said the king of Syria, for he treasured Naaman. "I will send a letter to the king of Israel so that he will help you."

Naaman went off with the letter, ten talents of silver, six thousand pieces of gold and ten sets of beautiful clothing to offer as gifts to the king of Israel and the prophet.

He brought the letter to the king, at that time a man who knew little of the Lord and even less of the prophet Elisha. The king of Israel read the letter, and it said: "When this letter comes to you, you will see that I have sent with it my honored servant Naaman, that you may cure him of his leprosy."

When the king of Israel had read the letter he tore his clothes in great distress. "What is this?" he demanded. "Am I God, to kill and make alive, that this Syrian sends a man to me to be cured of his leprosy? Take heed! For it must surely be that he seeks a quarrel with me."

It did not occur to him for a moment to send for the prophet Elisha. But when Elisha heard that the king was troubled by the Syrian captain's visit, he sent a message to the king: "Why have you torn your clothes in such distress? Send the man to me, so that he at least shall know that there is a prophet in Israel."

The king sent Naaman off at once. The Syrian captain rode up to Elisha's dwelling place with his horses and his chariots, and waited outside the door for Elisha to come out.

Elisha did not come out. Instead he sent a messenger out to Naaman, saying, "Go and wash in the river Jordan seven times, and your flesh will become healed and you shall be cured of the leprosy."

But Naaman, the rich and mighty, was angered by these words, and said: "I had thought that he would surely come out to me himself and stand before me, calling on the name of the Lord his God and striking his hand over the diseased places to heal the leprosy! But no; he does not come out to me, and he tells me to wash in muddy Jordan! Are not Abana and Pharpar, rivers of Damascus in my own land, better than all the waters of Israel? May I not wash in them and be cleansed of this leprosy?"

And he turned and went away in a rage.

But his servants knew that simply bathing in a river was no cure for his illness; it was the prophet's very words that he must obey. They followed him, and said: "My lord, if the prophet had asked you to do some great and difficult thing to cure yourself, would you not have done it?" Naaman was silent for a moment; then he nodded. "Then why not do this easy thing?" they went on earnestly. "Is it not even better than a hard thing, only to obey when he says to you, 'Wash, and be made well'?"

Naaman listened thoughtfully, remembering what he had heard of this great man of the Lord. Then he went down to the river Jordan and removed his finery. Seven times he dipped himself into the waters of the Jordan, according to the advice given by the man of God, and seven times he looked at his body that was patched and shriveled with the dreadful leprosy. And then he rose from the muddy waters for the seventh and last time. His flesh was as clean and fresh as the flesh of a little child; his skin was clear, and all his leprosy was gone.

He went back then to the man of God with all his company of men, and he stood before Elisha with gratitude in his eyes.

"Now I know there is no God in all the earth but the God of Israel!" he said. "I beg you, take a gift from me, your grateful servant."

But Elisha shook his head. Naaman pressed him eagerly to accept a present that would show the feelings of his heart. Elisha still refused.

"As the Lord lives," the prophet said, "the Lord under whose blessing I stand, I will take nothing from you for what God has done."

"Then allow me to take something," Naaman said. "Will you not then give me two mules' loads of earth? For I will build an altar to God out of the soil of Israel, and from this time forth I will offer neither burnt offering nor sacrifice to any other gods, but only to the Lord."

Elisha was well pleased. "Take all the earth you want, and go in peace," he said.

So the Syrian captain departed from the land of Israel.

THE STORY OF JONAH

$\mathcal{I}$n time the great power of the Syrians decreased, leaving the lands of Israel and Judah free to fight each other. Elisha in his time had again and again helped the Hebrews to stave off enemy attacks, only to be rewarded by ingratitude and lack of faith. But the Syrians at last declined, and never again did they recover strength to terrorize the Hebrew kingdoms. One of their last acts of war had been to sack Jerusalem and inflict a staggering defeat upon the land of Judah. Israel had then taken advantage of this situation to invade Judah, plunder the temple of its treasures, and make hostages of their fellow Hebrews of the south.

This was the state of affairs when the great country of Assyria, once only a small part of the Babylonia in which Abraham of Ur had been born so many centuries ago, began to stir like a mighty giant and cast covetous eyes upon the neighboring lands. One of the Assyrians' first acts as a fighting nation was to invade Israel and force the king and all the rich men of the land to pay vast sums of money to the Assyrian king Pul. Not long afterward the Assyrians marched into the land of Syria, took its capital city of Damascus and carried its people away into captivity, and slew the Syrian king. Yet powerful as they were, the people of Assyria and

particularly of its capital Nineveh, did not believe in the God of
Israel, and they did much that was evil.

Now at about that time, in the reign of Jeroboam II of Israel,
there was a prophet named Jonah who was such a dedicated
Hebrew that he did not care at all what became of the souls of the
Gentiles of the world.

And the word of the Lord came to Jonah the son of Amittai,
saying, "Arise, and go to Nineveh, that great city of Assyria, and
cry out loud with preachings, for its wickedness rises up before
me." For the Lord God wanted his word to spread to the people
of other lands. They were his children, too.

But Jonah did not want to go to Nineveh, to turn the people
away from their sins. In the first place the Assyrians were Gentiles, and in the second place they were Israel's enemies. Jonah
very much preferred to let the people of Nineveh suffer and die
for their sins, worshiping their heathen idols and becoming more
wicked by the year, rather than go to their rescue by teaching
them to turn toward the true God.

And so, instead of going to Nineveh, he went down to the
seaport of Joppa and found a ship going to Tarshish, which was in
the opposite direction from Nineveh and twice as far away. He
paid his fare and boarded the ship, planning to hide out in
Tarshish and escape the presence of the Lord.

But it was not possible to avoid the Lord, who saw him board
the ship and knew of the rebellion in his heart. The ship sailed,
and Jonah went down below decks to get some rest. When the
wind rose he did not hear it, for he was fast asleep. But it was the
Lord who had sent the wind across the sea, and it blew into a
mighty tempest that churned the waters up to throw huge waves
against the ship until its timbers groaned and its decks were
awash with swirling seas. The little ship tossed and creaked like a
toy upon the waters, as if it would shatter into pieces at any
moment and take every man aboard down to the bottom of the
ocean. The sailors were terrified, for they had never in all their
lives seen such a frightful storm. Each member of the crew prayed

earnestly to whatever god he believed in, but no man's god could stop the storm. In desperation they threw the cargo overboard to lighten the load so that the ship might bob more freely on the raging waters. But nothing helped. And Jonah, fast asleep below, neither heard the wind nor felt the wild heaving of the ship.

So at last the master of the ship went down to him and said, "How can you sleep at such a time, O sleeper? Call upon your God, so that he may think of us, and then perhaps we will not perish."

Jonah arose, but he did not call upon his God as all the sailors had called upon theirs, for he was fleeing from his God and wished to have no speech with him. Therefore the storm went on raging bitterly about the ship until it seemed that the battered timbers would surely split into a thousand pieces.

The sailors talked among themselves with great misgivings. "Come, let us cast lots," they said, "so that we may know who is the cause of this evil that has come upon us." For they were sure—and they were right—that someone on board was responsible for their troubles.

So they cast lots, and the lot fell on Jonah.

They said to him, "You, who have caused this evil to come upon us, pray tell us why! What is your occupation? Where do you come from? What is your country? Of what people are you? And why did you bring this trouble?

"I am a Hebrew from the land of Israel," Jonah answered. "I serve the Lord, the God of heaven, who made the sea and the dry land." And he went on to tell them in all honesty why he was aboard their ship.

Then the men were exceedingly afraid, knowing that he had fled from the presence of the Lord and was being pursued. "Why have you done this to us?" they asked reproachfully. "And what shall we do to you, that the storm may be calmed?" For the waves were wild and thunderous, and the tempest raged with even more violence than before.

"You will have to take me up and cast me into the sea," Jonah said unhappily. "Then the sea will calm itself for you, for I know that it is my fault that this great tempest is upon you."

But the sailors, though they did not worship Jonah's God, were good men and they did not want to throw him overboard. They took up the oars and rowed with all their strength in a desperate attempt to race the storm and bring the ship to land. It was impossible; the strong winds roared and great waves rose like walls of water to crumble down upon the small ship and deluge it until it seemed that it must surely break and sink to drown the lot of them.

Then their cries of fear and anguish rose to the Lord God of Jonah, and they said, "We pray you, O Lord! We pray you not to let us die for the sake of this man's life. We beseech you, Lord: do not cause us to let the innocent die, nor blame us for their blood, for you, O Lord, have done as it pleased you."

And at last, when all their rowing and their praying failed, they took up the prophet Jonah at his own command and cast him forth into the sea. At once the wild wind died and the sea ceased from her raging.

The sudden calm was almost as terrifying as the storm. The men were struck with the fear of the Lord and his great might. They offered up sacrifices to the God of Israel and made vows to serve him. Thus had Jonah persuaded a boatload of Gentiles to turn toward the Lord without even preaching to them.

Now the Lord had prepared a great fish to swallow up Jonah as he fell into the sea, and the fish did swallow him without a bite. Jonah was alive inside the fish for three days and three nights, moaning with fear and praying to the Lord his God out of the fish's belly.

"I cried by reason of my affliction unto the Lord,
And he heard me," Jonah said hopefully.
"Out of the belly of hell cried I,
And you heard my voice.
For you had cast me into the deep,

In the midst of the seas;
And the floods surrounded me;
All your billows and your waves passed over me.
Then I said, 'I am cast out of your sight,
Yet I will look again toward your holy temple.'
The depth closed me round about,
The weeds were wrapped about my head,
I went down to the bottoms of the mountains.
When my soul fainted within me I remembered the Lord;
And my prayer came in unto you,
Into your holy temple.
I will sacrifice unto you with the voice of thanksgiving;
I will pay what I have vowed.
Salvation is of the Lord."

And the Lord spoke to the great fish, so that it opened up its huge mouth and spewed forth Jonah upon the dry land.

It was some little while before Jonah was ready to face the hazards of another journey. But eventually the word of the Lord came to him a second time, saying, "Arise, go to Nineveh, that great city, and preach there as I command you."

This time Jonah went to Nineveh. At least he did not have to go by sea. Yet still he went with resentment in his heart, for he hated Nineveh and all Assyria, and he did not want the Assyrians to repent and thus escape the wrath of the Lord. But the Lord had spoken, and Jonah had already had one unpleasant experience resulting from his disobedience. He was genuinely contrite.

Nineveh was an exceedingly large city housing many very wicked people. Jonah entered into the heart of it and began to cry out his message to the people: "Turn from your evil ways! Nineveh shall be overthrown at the end of forty days! Nineveh shall be destroyed! Turn from your false gods and believe in the Lord, the one true God!" Assyrians flocked after him as he strode along the streets; they stopped and listened with awe upon their faces as he talked in the market places and on street corners, and

they gathered round him in all their numbers to hear his vehe-
ment, warning words.

So inspired was his preaching, and so urgent was his warning of
destruction, that they came to believe in God and to repent of
their sins. From the smallest to the greatest of them, from the
beggar in the street to the king in his fine palace, they turned
from their heathen idols to the worship of the Lord. The king
himself rose from his throne and took off his costly robes. As a
symbol of his sorrow for his past wickedness he covered himself in
sackcloth and sat humbly among ashes. Then he and his nobles
sent a proclamation to all the people of the city:

"Let neither man nor beast, nor herd nor flock, eat or taste of
any food, nor drink a drop of water. Let every man and beast be
covered with sackcloth and cry mightily unto God for forgiveness.
Let everyone turn from his evil ways and from all the violence of
the past. If we repent, we may be saved. Who can tell if God may
not turn his fierce anger from us so that we will not perish as the
prophet says?"

And every man prayed, and put on sackcloth, and declared a
fast. The days passed into weeks, and still they served God with
all their hearts.

God saw their deeds, and how they had turned from their evil
ways, and he forgave them for their sins. Jonah looked on at
Nineveh and the works of the repentant people, and saw that the
city showed no sign of forthcoming destruction.

Now God's mercy displeased Jonah. He was very angry. That
the Lord could consider sparing the enemies of Israel so that they
might attack his land again seemed terrible to him. Then, too, he
had told the people of Nineveh that their city would be destroyed, and he did not wish to become known as a prophet
whose prophecies were false.

He complained bitterly to his Lord. "I pray you, O Lord," he
said, "is this not what I said when I was still in my own country?
That is why I fled to Tarshish, for I know you are a gracious God
and merciful, slow to anger and of great kindness, quick to forgive

when people seem to be repentant. And these Assyrians, it is not right that they be spared!" He was particularly resentful that it was his own eloquence that had turned the people of Nineveh away from evil to earn the forgiveness of God. "Therefore now, O Lord," he went on, "I beg you to take my life away from me, for it is better that I die than live."

"Is it right for you to be angry?" said the Lord, then was silent.

Then Jonah went out of the city and made a rough shelter for himself. It was hot there, and extremely uncomfortable, but he wanted to see what became of the city at the end of the forty days. So he sat down in the small shadow of his shelter, and waited.

Nothing at all happened to the city. Jonah was outraged.

Then the Lord made a gourd to grow, and caused it to become tall and large so that its leaves would shelter Jonah from the blazing sun. And Jonah was very glad of the shady shelter of its great green leaves, so much better than the crude roof he had made for himself. But early on the following morning God sent a worm to gnaw at the plant's heart, and the cool green leaves began to wither. When the sun rose there was nothing but a limp, dead plant to shield the prophet from its rays; and as the day wore on God sent a violent east wind that brought with it a terrible heat. The sun beat down upon the head of Jonah with such terrible, burning force that he fainted under its blaze, and when he recovered consciousness he wished again that he were dead. "It is better," he said mournfully, "for me to die than live."

"Is it right for you to be so angry about the gourd?" God asked his narrow-minded prophet.

"Yes, it is right for me to be angry, even unto death," said Jonah. "For why should this plant with its green leaves die? What has it done? And why should that wicked city be spared?"

Then said the Lord: "You have had pity on the gourd which was of use to you, though you neither planted it nor made it grow. It came up in a night, and it perished in a night, a mere plant that knows nothing and is nothing. Yet you wished it spared.

Therefore why should I not spare Nineveh, that great city in which there are one hundred and twenty thousand people, among them many little children, and also many herds and flocks? And all of them not knowing what is right from wrong until it is told to them?"

And thus did Jonah learn a lesson from a dead plant and a living city. All men, all women, and all children are beloved by the Lord whether they be Jew or Gentile, if they will listen to his words and choose to follow God.

BY THE RIVERS OF BABYLON

*T*he people of Assyria learned their lesson well, so well that they grew great and strong while Israel became weak and sinful.

Under King Hoshea the Israelites broke every commandment of the Lord and committed every sin of idol worship. And because of these sins the Lord permitted King Sargon of Assyria to sweep down upon Israel, capture its capital city of Samaria, and utterly destroy Israel as a nation. Then King Sargon, to make quite sure that this conquered people would never rise again, carried thousands upon thousands of them into exile in Assyria. All the leaders, all the nobles, all the few remaining wise men, all those who might have rallied their countrymen to revolt against their Assyrian masters were driven from Israel to Assyria, where they scattered like dry leaves in the wind.

Only a few Israelites, the poorest, most humble, and the least in learning, were permitted to remain in their ravaged land. The victorious Sargon looked upon his captive land and decided that it was not good to leave the cities empty and the fields untended. Therefore he sent families from Babylon and other heathen people of the east to take the place of those who had been transported forcibly to Assyria. In time the few remaining

Hebrews married among the heathens in their midst, and a new half-heathen, half-godly race resulted from the union. Its people became known as Samaritans, and because they were of mixed descent they came to be regarded with contempt by certain other peoples who themselves had little, if any, reason to feel superior.

As for the Israelites held captive in Assyria, they were allowed a measure of freedom that was more than they were capable of handling. Instead of uniting, they parted; instead of becoming a great new group within the alien land, they separated and dispersed into the far reaches of Assyria. Never again did they come together as a nation, and never again did they return to the land of their forefathers. From the day of their banishment until this very day they have been referred to only as the Ten Lost Tribes of Israel. For they are lost indeed: no one knows what has become of them.

Apart from the mere handful of Israelites left in and around Samaria, only the peoples of the land of Judah were left of the twelve tribes which had once been united into the one great nation called Israel.

The little, shrinking land of Judah struggled on as a nation for more than a century after the fall of Israel. Surrounded by enemies, it sometimes lost great bites of land to foreign armies, and sometimes it even succeeded in biting back and retrieving some of its lost soil. One or two of its rulers were upright, God-fearing men who tried to lead their people in the paths of righteousness. Once in a while, when they listened to the counsel of the prophets of the Lord, these kings did prevail upon their people to turn back to God, and at such times the land of Judah knew victory and prosperity. But there were not enough God-fearing kings.

Now it happened, in the reign of Hezekiah over Judah, that King Sargon of Assyria died. Sennacherib became Assyrian king in his stead and launched what promised to be an overwhelming attack against Jerusalem. But Isaiah the prophet interceded with the Lord his God so that the city held, and Sennacherib departed in defeat after a strange disease had laid low his forces.

Judah's fortunes waxed and waned. As the years passed, great changes began to take place in the country first known as Mesopotamia, then as Babylonia, and next as the Assyria of Sargon and Sennacherib. Within the land two mighty powers were constantly battling for supremacy: the Babylonians, also known as the Chaldeans, and the Assyrians. Under Sargon and several of the kings who followed him, the Assyrian empire reached great heights of might and splendor, but eventually the Babylonians regained the great power they had known centuries before. They revolted against their Assyrian masters, destroyed the city of Nineveh, and built up a new and even greater Babylonian empire. Nebuchadnezzar, the powerful, became king in Babylon. Thus the Chaldeans, or Babylonians, achieved supremacy over the Assyrians, and began to look around for other fields to conquer.

In the land of Judah the good kings had gone their way, giving place to those who were weak and sinful. Prophets and warnings came and went: Micha, Nahum, Habakkuh, Zephaniah, Jeremiah, and Ezekiel all tried to persuade their wayward people that they were heading for disaster, but to little avail. Some helped to stave off trouble, others prophesied inescapable doom, yet Judah learned no lesson from their words. Few men even listened.

Now the end came for the land of Judah.

King Nebuchadnezzar of Babylon attacked the city of Jerusalem with his vast army of Chaldean soldiers. They sacked and burned the city, carried away the treasures of the temple, and left the temple itself in ruins. And they took the king of Judah in chains with them to Babylon, and drove his people after him into captivity. Only a few remained amidst the crumbled stones that had been the city of Jerusalem. All the rest—the king's family, all the princes, all the nobles, all the wise men, all the young men of great promise, all the best among the people of the land—were made captives in the city of Babylon. The Chaldeans called their captives Jews because they had taken them from Judah, and since then all the people of the Hebrew race, all the descendants of Abraham, Isaac, and Jacob who was Israel, have been known as Jews.

In their captivity the Jews mourned for their lost city of Jerusalem. And they lamented:

"How lonely sits the city that once was full of people!
How like a widow she has become, that was great among the
    nations,
And a princess among the provinces.
Now she is a vassal.
She weeps sadly at night, and her tears are on her cheeks.
Among all her lovers she has none to comfort her."

And they sang sad songs for themselves also as they endured their captivity in the beautiful city of Babylon:

"By the rivers of Babylon,
There we sat down, yea, we wept,
When we remembered Zion."

Yet Nebuchadnezzar was not a cruel king compared with others of his times, and he treated his captive people well. As soon as his conquest of Judah was complete he gave orders to the master of his household to select certain of the finest young men among the captives so that they might be taught the language and sciences of the Chaldean people. "Choose from the king's family, and of the princes," he ordered. "Look for those of good health and pleasing countenance; young men who are skillfull in wisdom, cunning in knowledge, and able to learn."

His servant made a careful choice. And among those chosen were four young men who were not only wise but faithful to their Lord. Their names were Daniel, Shadrach, Meshach, and Abed-nego.

The king in his generosity served them with good food and wines from his own table, so that they would be well nourished and grow strong to serve him. But Daniel and his three friends were forbidden by the laws of their religion to eat such foods, and Daniel requested of the master of the household that they be supplied with simpler fare.

Now the master of the household had taken a great liking to Daniel, and therefore he said: "I fear my lord the king, who has given orders regarding your food and drink, will be much displeased. When you stand before him with the other children of your sort, he will be greatly angered if you are pale of face and unhealthy in appearance. The king will have my head if you do not look as strong and well as all the rest."

"Try us for ten days, I beg you," Daniel said. "Let us have beans and lentils to eat and only water to drink. Then look at us, and also at those who eat the food from the king's own table, and deal with us according to what you see."

So the king's man agreed to this request, and for ten days he allowed the four young men to eat the plain foods they had asked for. And at the end of that time he saw that they were fairer of face and stronger in body than all the young men who ate the king's meat and drank wine from the royal table. Therefore he took the meat and wine away and gave them instead the foods requested by Daniel.

As for the four young men, God gave them knowledge and skill in all learning and wisdom, so that they quickly learned the sciences of the Chaldeans and mastered the Chaldean language. And to Daniel, God gave understanding of dreams and visions.

When they had completed three years of study the king sent for the young Jews chosen for training, and he talked with them for many hours. Among them, Nebuchadnezzar found none like Daniel, Shadrach, Meshach, and Abednego. In matters of wisdom and understanding they were ten times better than the magicians and astrologers in the king's own realm.

Now it happened some time later that Nebuchadnezzar

dreamed strange dreams that broke his sleep and left his spirit
sorely troubled. He sent for the astrologers, the magicians, and
the sorcerers among his people and demanded that they help him.
"I have dreamed a dream that troubles me," he said, "but I do not
remember what it was. You are magicians; you tell me what I
dreamed, and what it means."

"O king," they answered, "we cannot tell you the meaning until
you tell us what you dreamed."

"I have told you, the thing is gone from me!" the king said
angrily. "Answer me, and you will be rewarded. If you do not,
you will be cut in pieces!"

"But we cannot answer," they protested. "Let the king but tell
his servants the dream, and we will show the interpretation of it."

The king's rage was mounting rapidly. "How will you be able
to interpret it if you are not even able to tell me what it was? If
you tell it to me I will believe your interpretation. But if you will
not make it known to me, there is but one decree for you!"

The Chaldean sorcerers shook their heads. "There is not a man
on earth, neither magician nor astrologer, who can answer such a
thing," they said. "Nor is there any other king, lord, or ruler on
this earth who would ask so rare a thing of his magicians. Only
the gods can answer you."

"Then you must die!" said the king, now wild with fury. "Every
wise man in this land shall die!"

Now Daniel was a wise man, and thus he also was in danger
though the king had not asked for his advice in the matter of the
dream. When he heard the king's decree he begged for time, and
with his friends he prayed to God for help. And the secret of the
king's dream was revealed to Daniel in a night vision. He went
quickly to the king before any of the wise men in the kingdom
could be slain.

"And are you able to make known the dream to me?" the king
demanded.

"I am able," Daniel answered. "Know first, O king, that no wise
man, astrologer, magician, or soothsayer can show the secret

which the king demanded. But there is a God in heaven who reveals such secrets, and who will make known to you what shall happen in the future. This is what you dreamed, O king."

The king listened closely so as to miss no word.

"The God of my fathers," Daniel said, "has made known to me that in your dream you saw a great image whose brightness was excellent and whose form was terrible to see. This image's head was of fine gold, his breast and arms of silver, his belly and his thighs of brass, his feet part iron and part clay.

"As you watched a great stone rolled against the feet of this fearsome image and broke the feet of iron and clay. And then the whole image shattered. The iron, the clay, the brass, the silver, and the gold became as dust, and the wind carried them away so that they were found no more. The stone that broke the image remained. It grew, until it became a great mountain that filled the earth."

At last the king remembered. That, indeed, had been his dream. "Now the meaning," he demanded.

"This is the interpretation," Daniel said. "You are the head of gold, a king of power and strength and glory, ruler of the greatest kingdom now upon this earth. After you will arise a lesser kingdom, one of silver; and then a third kingdom of brass, which shall rule over all the earth. Then there will be a fourth, a kingdom of iron that shall be strong in the beginning but will become as weak as clay.

"And in the days of these kings the God of heaven will set up a kingdom which can never be destroyed. It will fill the earth, and destroy all other kingdoms, and it will stand forever. That, O king, is the dream God sent to you, and that is the interpretation."

The king was amazed, but he believed in Daniel's words. "Of a truth," he said, "your God is indeed a God of gods, and a Lord of kings, and a revealer of secrets, seeing that he has given to you the power to reveal this secret."

Then the king gave Daniel many gifts and made him a great man in the land, setting him up as ruler over the whole province of Babylon and as chief of all the wise men. And at Daniel's request, the king gave Shadrach, Meshach, and Abednego much power in the affairs of Babylon.

All went well for many years. Nebuchadnezzar became great in conquest and in might. His power grew, his riches grew, his kingdom grew, and his pride grew also.

Forgetting all about the God of gods and the Lord of kings, he made a massive image of gold and ordered all the captains, judges, treasurers, counselors, sheriffs, and rulers of his provinces to come to the dedication ceremony and bow down to the golden idol he had made. And a herald cried aloud: "O people of all nations and all languages, to all of you it is commanded that when you hear the sound of the cornet, flute, harp, dulcimer, and all kinds of music, you will fall down and worship the golden image that Nebuchadnezzar the king has set up! And whoever does not fall down and worship shall be cast into the midst of a burning, fiery furnace."

When the music sounded all the officers and all the people of all nations and all languages fell down and worshiped the golden idol of their king. Daniel was not there, for he had business affairs elsewhere in the land, but his three friends saw the vast image on the plain. Their own hearts, not the herald or the king, told them what to do.

Then certain Chaldeans went to Nebuchadnezzar and accused the Jews. "O king, live forever!" they began. "You, O king, made a decree that when the music sounded every man must bow down and worship the golden image or be thrown into the midst of a burning, fiery furnace. Now there are certain Jews whom you have set over the affairs of the province of Babylon, whose names are Shadrach, Meshach, and Abednego. These men, O king, did not obey. They do not serve your gods, nor do they worship the golden image which you have set up."

Then Nebuchadnezzar, outraged and furious, commanded the three Jews to be brought before him. When he saw their calm, wise faces, his anger cooled slightly and he spoke in almost reasonable tones.

"Is it true, Shadrach, Meshach, and Abednego, that you do not serve my gods nor worship the golden image I have set before you? Did you not understand what I commanded? Now I shall give you one more chance. This time, when you hear the sound of the music, you will fall down on your faces and worship the image I have made. If you do, then all is well. But if you do not, you shall be cast within the hour into the midst of the fiery furnace. And who is the God who will then deliver you?"

The three men answered readily. "O Nebuchadnezzar, we have but one answer to give you. We do not want a second chance, for you must know that we will not serve your gods nor worship the golden image you have made. Our God is able to deliver us from the fiery furnace if it is his will. But if it is not his will, we would still gladly die rather than serve your gods or bow down to the image."

Then Nebuchadnezzar's fury knew no bounds and his face became twisted with rage. No longer was he reasonable when he spoke to these disobedient Jews. "Then the furnace shall be heated until it is seven times hotter that it has ever been!" he shouted.

And he sent for the most mighty men in his army to bind Shadrach, Meshach, and Abednego, and cast them into the burning, fiery furnace. The three men submitted without struggle and let their captors lead them to where the hot fire blazed as it had never blazed before. But the mighty men who led them were too hasty and came too close to the furnace that was blazing with a heat seven times hotter than usual; they flung their captives deep into the heart of the crackling flames, but in their zeal to fulfill the king's urgent command they allowed themselves to be caught by the furious heat and the leaping tongues of fire. And they died where they stood while the three Jews fell down, still tightly bound, into the midst of the burning, fiery furnace.

But the three Jews did not burn.

Nebuchadnezzar watched from a safe distance as they rose in the heart of the fire and began to praise and glorify and bless God in the furnace:

"Blessed art thou, O Lord God of our fathers;
And to be praised and exalted above all for ever.

O ye heavens, bless ye the Lord;
Praise and exalt him above all for ever.

O ye sun and moon, bless ye the Lord;
Praise and exalt him above all for ever.

O ye fire and heat, bless ye the Lord;
Praise and exalt him above all for ever.

O Israel, bless ye the Lord;
Praise and exalt him above all for ever.

O all ye that worship the Lord, bless the God of gods, praise
    him and give him thanks;

For his mercy endureth for ever."

Nebuchadnezzar listened, and watched with growing amazement. There was something remarkable about the furnace, and it was not only that the three men were not burning. He rose in haste and astonishment and said to his counselors: "Did we not cast three men bound into the midst of the fire?"

"True, O king," they answered.

"Then why do I see four?" said the king. "Look! Four men, unbound, walking about in the midst of the fire, and they are not even hurt! And see, the form of the fourth is like the Son of God."

Then he went close to the mouth of the fiery furnace and spoke into its depths: "Shadrach, Meshach, and Abednego, you servants of the most high God, come out! Come here to me."

The three men walked out of the heart of the fire, and there was no one left behind. And all the princes and governors, captains and counselors, gathered around to stare at the men, those men of God upon whose bodies the fire had had no power. Not a hair of their heads was singed, neither was there any sign of scorching on their clothes, nor was the smell of fire on them. Yet the ropes that had bound them had been burned away.

Then Nebuchadnezzar said, before all the nobles and rulers who were with him: "Blessed be the God of Shadrach, Meshach, and Abednego, who has sent his angel and delivered his servants that trusted in him! Blessed be these three men who defied the king's word and risked their own bodies that they might not serve or worship any god except their own! Therefore I make a decree: that any people of any nation or language, which says anything amiss against the God of Shadrach, Meshach, and Abednego, shall be cut in pieces and their houses leveled to the ground. For there is no other God who has such power to save!"

Then the king promoted Shadrach, Meshach, and Abednego to higher office in the province of Babylon, and they were respected by all men for the rest of their days.

DANIEL

When Nebuchadnezzar died, his son Belshazzar became king in his father's place. Now Belshazzar was a foolish and extravagant man who thought only of his worldly pleasures. Even though the mighty armies of the Medes and Persians were threatening the land of the Chaldeans, he made no preparations to defend his kingdom. In his pride and arrogance he was sure that Babylon was safe from any attack.

Belshazzar the king made a great feast to a thousand of his lords, and drank much wine before the thousand. Again and again were the wine cups filled, and when Belshazzar was flushed with drink he rose unsteadily to his feet and issued a command to his servants. "Go," he said to them, "and bring me the gold and silver vessels which my father Nebuchadnezzar took out of the temple which was in Jerusalem. Then shall I, your king, and my princes and my wives and all the other women of my household drink wine from these vessels of the Jews!"

So his servants brought the holy vessels which once had adorned the house of God, and all the people drank from them. As they drank the wine they praised the gods of gold, of silver, of brass, of iron, of wood, and the gods of stone, and the false gods despised by the true believers in the Lord.

But suddenly the noise and merriment died down. Every man and woman at the feast saw the king's eyes turn and stare at the wall of the banquet hall. They followed his gaze and gasped with astonishment and fear.

Near the great candlestick that shed its light upon the wall of the king's palace, the fingers of a man's hand had appeared. The fingers moved and wrote strange words upon the plaster of that wall, and the king saw the part of the hand that wrote. But no other part of the writer could he see, only the moving hand with the finger making letters on the wall beyond the candle. A great fear came upon Belshazzar. His face froze and turned pale with terror, and his mind troubled him so sorely that the joints of his legs were loosened and his knees knocked against each other. The finger wrote, moved on, and disappeared, leaving on the wall four mysterious words in letters that no man present could read, much less understand.

The king cried aloud for his astrologers and soothsayers. When his wise men came to him he said, "Whosoever reads this writing and tells me the meaning of it shall be rewarded with scarlet robes, and have a chain of gold about his neck, and he shall be the third ruler in the kingdom."

The wise men looked long at the writing, but they could make nothing of it. Belshazzar and his lords stood in the banquet chamber shaking with fear, not knowing what to do or where to turn for help.

Now the queen his mother came into the room where the feasting had been so merry only minutes before, and spoke soothing words to King Belshazzar.

"Oh king, live forever!" she said to her trembling son. "Do not let your thoughts trouble you, nor let your face be pale with terror. There is a man in your kingdom who has in him the spirit of the holy gods. In the days of your father this man showed himself to have wisdom and understanding like the wisdom of the gods. Nebuchadnezzar your father, the king, made him master of all the magicians, astrologers, and soothsayers. Therefore, because your father found in this Daniel such an excellent spirit, such knowledge and understanding, such wisdom to interpret dreams, and such skill in clearing up doubts, let Daniel now be called. He will show you the interpretation of this writing."

Daniel was brought in. The king said to him: "Are you that Daniel who is one of the captives from Judah? I have heard of you, that the spirit of the gods is in you, and that light and understanding and excellent wisdom is to be found in you. All of my wise men have been brought before me that they should read this writing, but not one of them is able to interpret it for me. Now it is said of you that you can make interpretations, and I say to you that if you can read it and explain its meaning, I will clothe you in scarlet and place a chain of gold about your neck, and you shall be the third ruler of my kingdom."

"Keep your gifts," said Daniel, "and give your rewards to another. I will read the writing for you and explain its meaning. But remember first, O king, that the most high God gave Nebuchadnezzar your father a kingdom and majesty, and glory and honor. And because of this majesty given by the Lord, people of all nations and languages trembled and feared before him, and his might was very great. But when his heart was lifted up and his mind was hardened in pride, he was deposed from his kingly throne. And they took his glory from him until he came to know that the most high God ruled in the kingdom of men, and that the Lord appoints over his kingdom whomsoever he will. And at last King Nebuchadnezzar blessed and honored the most high.

"But you his son, O Belshazzar, have not humbled your heart, even though you knew all this. Instead, you have lifted up yourself against the Lord of heaven, and have even sent for the vessels of his house. You and your lords and your wives and your concubines have drunk wine in them as you feasted in this place. And you have praised the gods of silver and of gold, of brass and iron, of wood and stone, which neither see nor hear, and you did this even while you drank from the holy vessels of the Lord. But the

Lord himself, the God who holds your life in his hands, this God you have not glorified.

"It was a part of God's hand that was sent from him, and his writing on the wall was written by that hand. And these are the words that were written: MENE, MENE, TEKEL, UPHARSIN. And this is the interpretation of them. MENE: God has judged your kingdom and numbered its days, and has finished it. TEKEL: You have been weighed on the balance scales, and you have been found wanting. UPHARSIN: Your kingdom is divided, and given to the Medes and Persians."

In spite of this dire warning, Belshazzar commanded his attendants to clothe Daniel in scarlet and place a chain of gold around his neck, and then he proclaimed to all his people that Daniel was to be the third highest ruler in the kingdom.

But it was too late for sudden belief in God's servants upon earth, too late for gratitude or lavish reward; and far too late for change.

That very night the city of Babylon was attacked. Belshazzar the king of the Chaldeans was slain by the soldiers who scaled the city walls while the rulers and the nobles feasted. The combined forces of the Medes and Persians swarmed through the city and the land of Babylon and made it all their own. And Darius, the Mede, took the kingdom and the throne.

Unlike Belshazzar, he took immediate note of Daniel.

It pleased Darius to set over the kingdom a hundred and twenty princes, and over these he set three presidents of which the wise Daniel was first. Thus Daniel, a Jew of captive Judah, was preferred above all presidents and princes because the new king thought so highly of his wisdom.

But the other rulers of the land were jealous of Daniel's high office. Time and time again they tried to find some fault in him, or some excuse for speaking evil of him to the king, but they could find no fault or error in him.

Therefore the presidents and princes gathered together and devised a plot against him.

"There is only one way we can find fault with him that will turn the king against him," they told each other, "and that is in some matter concerning the law of his God." In this they were correct, and soon they found a way. They had noticed that three times each day Daniel went into his house to pray in front of the window that looked toward the distant, ruined city of Jerusalem, and this was all they needed.

The nobles assembled before the king and humbly bowed down low.

"King Darius, live forever!" they said. "All the presidents of the kingdom, the governors, the princes, the counselors, and the captains, have consulted together so that you may draw up a royal statute. This shall be a firm decree that will require every man in this kingdom to acknowledge you, and only you, as the supreme being in this land."

What Darius heard was pleasing to him, and he told the speakers to continue.

"We ask you to establish a law," they went on craftily, "that for thirty days no one shall ask anything of any God or man but of you, O king. All prayers, petitions and requests must be addressed only to you. And if anyone should disobey your royal statute, he shall be cast into the den of lions. Now, O king, establish the decree and sign the writing of it so that it cannot be changed, for all the people of your kingdom know that no law of the Medes and Persians can be altered."

Darius saw no harm in this request, for it was flattering to him, and after all he was king of the great empire that had toppled the mighty Babylonians from power. Nor did he notice that his first president, Daniel the Jew, was not among the company that stood before him. Therefore he signed the writing and the decree they had prepared for him.

Now when Daniel heard about this harsh new law he went into his house as usual to kneel, three times a day, before the open window that looked toward far-off Jerusalem and the ruins of God's temple. He could see neither house of God nor ransacked city, but he knew that they were there, and in spite of the decree he prayed and gave thanks to his God as he had always done.

The envious presidents and princes saw him kneeling before the open window and heard him praying to his God and asking for guidance from the Lord. At once they hurried off to Darius to remind the king of his decree.

"O king!" they said, scarcely able to contain themselves, for triumph was now in sight. "Have you not signed a decree that for thirty days any man that asks a petition of any God or man but you, O king, shall be cast into the den of lions?"

The king nodded. "That is true," he said. "It was signed according to the laws of the Medes and Persians, which cannot be changed."

"Ah! Then know that Daniel, one of the people of the captivity of Judah, does not regard you, O king, nor does he respect the decree that you have signed. In his disobedience he prays three times each day to his God with his petitions and requests, instead of asking you."

Then King Darius saw the trap into which he had been led, and he was mightily displeased with himself. There had been no thought in his mind of the wise old Daniel, whom he truly loved, when he had signed the foolish law. He set his heart on trying to save him, and he thought and labored until sundown to find some way of keeping Daniel from the dreadful fate awaiting him. But it was useless. The stern law of the Medes and Persians left no escape for even the finest and most deserving of men.

At sunset the jealous nobles went back to the palace and stood again before their king. "Know, O king," they said, "that the law of the Medes and Persians is that no decree nor statute which the king has made may ever be changed, not in any way nor for any man."

It was true. With great reluctance King Darius sent for Daniel and commanded that he be thrown into the den of lions. When it was done he spoke down into the deep pit, where the innocent Daniel stood fearlessly among the growling lions, and said with both hope and sorrow in his voice: "Surely your God, whom you serve so faithfully, will deliver you from death."

Then a great stone was rolled over the mouth of the pit so that no man could look in nor any man climb out, and the king sealed it with his own signet so that the stone would not be moved until he himself gave the command.

King Darius went back to his palace and passed the night in torment and in sorrow. In his great anguish of spirit he could neither eat nor listen to music to soothe his troubled soul, and though he lay upon his bed of luxury he could not sleep throughout the long and terrible night. His every thought was with Daniel and how he must be faring in that dark pit with the snarling, hungry lions. After a night of torture and remorse he arose very early in the morning and went in haste to the den of lions, dreading what he might find when the sealed stone was rolled back.

In a voice full of grief he cried out to Daniel in the silent pit: "O Daniel, servant of the living God! Has your God, whom you have always served with faithful heart, been able to deliver you from the lions?"

Then to his great relief the voice of Daniel answered from the lions' den: "O king, live forever! My God has sent his angel and has shut the lions' mouths so that they have not hurt me, for I was innocent in the sight of the Lord. And I am innocent before you also, O king, for to you have I done no harm or wrong."

Then the king was exceedingly glad for him, and his heart rejoiced that Daniel had been spared. He called his servants and commanded that Daniel be taken at once from the den of lions, and it was done as soon as spoken. King Darius and his men looked with awe upon the living Daniel. There was no wound nor sign of any hurt upon him, because he had believed so firmly in his God.

The king was full of gratitude, but he was also angry. By his command the men who had accused Daniel were brought before him. And at a second command these false men and their families were thrown among the lions to suffer the fate that Daniel had so miraculously escaped. This time the lions did not spare their victims.

Then King Darius wrote and signed another statute which he sent out to all peoples and all nations of the earth. It was very different from the first, and it read:

> "Peace be multiplied unto you! I make a decree: that in every dominion of my kingdom, men shall tremble and fear before the God of Daniel, for he is the living God, and steadfast forever. His kingdom shall not be destroyed, and his rule shall be even unto the end. He delivers and rescues, and he works signs and wonders in heaven and in earth, he who has delivered Daniel from the power of the lions."

And from that time on Daniel prospered in the reign of Darius. And when Cyrus the Persian became king of Babylon he dealt with justice and kindness not only toward Daniel but to all the captive peoples of Judah.

For it had been said of Cyrus many years before when the prophet Isaiah had spoken God's words in the land of Judah, that the Lord had appointed him to do great things, saying:

> "I am the Lord that saith of Cyrus, 'He is my shepherd,
> And shall perform all my pleasure;
> Even saying to Jerusalem, thou shall be built;
> And to the temple, thy foundation shall be laid.'"

Daniel knew of this prophecy. He also knew the words of the prophet Jeremiah, who had written the Lord's sayings down in a book so that all Judah would know and remember that God had not forsaken them. And these were the words written down by Jeremiah:

"'For lo, the days come,' saith the Lord, 'that I will bring again the captivity of my people, and I will cause them to return to the land that I gave to their fathers, and they shall possess it. I will have mercy on their dwelling places; and the city shall be builded upon her own heap, and the palace shall remain after the manner thereof. And out of them shall proceed thanksgiving and the voice of them that make merry: and I will multiply them, and they shall not be few; I will also glorify them, and they shall not be small. Their children also shall be as aforetime, and their congregation shall be established before me, and I will punish all that oppress them. And you shall be my people, and I will be your God.'"

And because he believed in the Lord God of Israel and understood the sayings of the prophets, Daniel knew that the days of the captivity were numbered. Though he himself was old and the day of his death was drawing near, he was happy and he prospered in the reign of Cyrus. He might never see the new Jerusalem. But he knew that it would come.

THE HOMECOMING OF THE JEWS

*N*ow in the first year of Cyrus, king of Babylon and Persia, the Lord stirred up the spirit of the king so that the word of the Lord might be fulfilled according to the sayings of Jeremiah.

Cyrus made a proclamation throughout all his kingdom and put it into writing so that all his people would know of his decree. These are the words that he proclaimed:

> "Thus speaks Cyrus, king of Persia: 'The Lord God of Heaven, the most high Lord, has given me all the kingdoms of the earth, and he has commanded me to build him a temple at Jerusalem in Judah. If there be any here among you that are of his people, may the Lord your God be with you. May you go up to Jerusalem that is in Judah, and build the house of the Lord of Israel: for he is the Lord that dwells in Jerusalem. And whosoever remains of the people of Judah, let him be helped by the men of the place where he lives. Let him be given silver, gold, goods, and beasts, besides any offering which his neighbor may wish to give for the house of God in Jerusalem.'"

Great was the rejoicing among the captive people when they heard this proclamation by Cyrus and knew that their prophets' words were coming true. Not all the Jews wished to return, for now they had been in Babylon for seventy years and most of them had never seen the city of their forefathers. Many had become settled and prosperous in the land of their captivity. But many more exulted at the thought of going home.

The first to rise up and cry out his joy was the chief of the leaders of Judah and Benjamin. Then the priests rose up, and the Levites who remained of the scattered tribe of Levi, and then all the people whose spirits God had lifted up with the desire to go back to build the house of the Lord in the city of Jerusalem. At once they started preparations for the journey into Judah.

Their fellow Jews who were remaining, and their friends and neighbors in Babylon, poured gifts into their hands: gold, silver, goods of all kinds; sheep and cattle, donkeys, horses; vessels for the temple, precious things, and offerings for the house of God in Jerusalem. Cyrus himself brought forth the holy vessels which had been in the Lord's house, those which Nebuchadnezzar had stripped from the temple and taken out of Jerusalem to put into the house of his own gods, and gave these priceless treasures to one of the princes of Judah. When they were counted it was found that there were five thousand and four hundred vessels of silver and gold to adorn the temple when it was ready for adornment.

A great and joyous procession of men, women, children, and domestic beasts started out from Babylon and wound its way across the many miles of hills and plains to the land of Judah. Well over forty thousand people were returning to a home most of them had never seen. Among them were their handmaids and their servants, as well as two hundred singing men and singing women. The horses and the mules, the camels and the asses numbered more than eight thousand among the many families. And the treasures of gold and silver carried by some of the chief men among the elders of Benjamin and Judah were almost beyond counting.

Daniel was now a very old man and remained with Darius in Babylon instead of returning with his people to the land of his forefathers. He watched them go until the sounds of their singing faded into the distance and the clouds of dust settled behind the feet of their animals. Then he turned away and gave thanks to his Lord for delivering his people.

Zerubbabel of the family of David and Jeshua the priest led the vast cavalcade on its triumphal way. It was a long journey but a happy one, for not only were the Jews returning home but they were taking with them out of Babylon all the stolen treasures of their temple and mule-loads of precious gifts from generous friends. Surely it would not be difficult for them to start new lives in the city of their ancestors.

They came at last to the ruin of Jerusalem and looked at it with mixed feelings of deep gratitude and love and sorrow. Some hearts sank and others leaped, but to even the most uncritical eyes it was a pitiful sight. Imagination had not warned them it would be so devastated. The few half-Jews, half-heathens living in the city, and the foreigners who lived nearby, had done nothing to rebuild Jerusalem. Nebuchadnezzar's war had done its dreadful damage, and time and negligence had done the rest. The walls were crumbled piles of stone, the temple was a heap of rubble, and weeds grew among the ruins of what had once been a palace surrounded with fine houses. Those who had known the city in its days of glory and those who had been born in Babylon were horrified and heartsore.

But there was no time to mourn. Homes must be built, the city mended, the walls repaired, and above all the temple must once again be made into a house worthy of the Lord and be filled with its ancient treasures.

The Jews began at once to make homes for themselves within the city and in the small towns outside the walls. Zerubbabel and the priests built an altar to the Lord and made burnt offerings upon it every morning and evening. When all the people were settled in reasonable comfort they got down to the main task at hand. To the people of Tyre and Sidon they sent meat and drink and oil in return for cedar trees from Lebanon for the rebuilding of the temple, and they chose carpenters and masons to begin the work.

And when the builders were ready to lay the foundations of the temple of the Lord, the priests came with their robes and trumpets and the Levites came with cymbals so that they might praise the Lord. They sang together, as David and his priests had done so long ago, praising God and giving thanks for all their blessings. "For the Lord is good!" they sang, "And his mercy endureth forever toward Israel."

All the people shouted with a great shout when they praised the Lord, because their hearts were glad that at last the foundation of the house of the Lord was being laid. But many of the priests and Levites and leaders among the people were very old men who had seen and revered the first temple in Jerusalem, and now, with a new foundation before their aged eyes, their memories made them weep out loud while the rest of the people shouted for joy. Those who heard the great noise could not distinguish the cries of joy from the sound of the bitter weeping. And many people heard the noise, for it sounded far beyond the fallen city walls.

Work on the temple began in earnest then, with a vast flurry of activity and much cutting of cedar logs and blocks of stone. But the Samaritans and other people who lived in the land of the returned captives were not glad that the Jews were back, nor that the temple was to be rebuilt. Therefore they did all they could to harass the builders, troubling them in many ways and hiring counselors to defeat their purpose. It was not long before conditions became so difficult that the Jews were obliged to stop building, for the man who became king after Cyrus had listened to the pleas of the Samaritans and decided against the Jews.

But in time another Darius of Persia came to the throne. When he discovered how the Jews were being frustrated in their attempts to build the temple in spite of King Cyrus' decree that the Lord's house must be built, he himself issued a new and stern decree:

> "Let the work of this house of God alone! Let the governor of the Jews and the elders of the Jews build this house of God in his place. Moreover I make a decree that the goods and monies sent in tribute to the king be given instead to these men for the building. Also: young bullocks and rams and lambs, wheat and salt, wine and oil, and whatever may be required by the priests, shall be given to them every day without fail for the burnt offerings of the God of heaven. Whosoever shall defy this decree and hinder the building of the Lord's house shall have his own house torn to the ground and be hanged upon its timbers. I, Darius, have made a decree; let it be done with speed."

And it was done with speed. The Jews, no longer troubled by their enemies, went back to work with a will. And the house was finished in the sixth year of the reign of Darius the king. The children of Israel, the priests and the Levites, and all the people of the captivity kept the dedication of this house of God with joy and songs of thanksgiving to the Lord God, the God of Israel.

Yet there was still much work to be done in the city of Jerusalem. After the temple was finished there was little gold and silver left for other work, and indeed it was necessary for the people to spend the greater part of their time in tending to their lands to provide food for their families. The Samaritans and other jealous people again harassed the Jews of the city so that they became discouraged and weary, and left the ruined walls and buildings where they lay.

Now it happened that one Artaxerxes became king of Persia and its many possessions, one of which was the land of Judah. He

ruled his kingdoms from his capital city of Shushan in the land of
Persia, and he had in his Persian palace a young cupbearer. The
name of the youth was Nehemiah, and he was a noble young man
of Judah.

For years he heard no word of distant Judah. But one day
Nehemiah's kinsman Hanani and certain other Jews arrived in
Shushan from their homeland, and Nehemiah eagerly asked them
about the Jews who had left captivity and of conditions in the city
of Jerusalem. "Does all go well?" he asked.

They shook their heads sadly. "The people there are in great
difficulty and shame," they said, "for they are poor and troubled
by their enemies. Some have even married among the heathen
round about them. The temple is built, but the walls of the city
still lie in ruins and the gates are burned with fire as they have
been these many years."

When Nehemiah heard these words he wept and mourned for
several days. Then he fasted, and prayed before the God of
heaven. "Forgive us, Lord, for our many sins, and hear my
prayer. O Lord, I beseech you, grant me mercy in the sight of
the king so that I may help my people."

And it came to pass, on this day in the twentieth year of Artaxerxes the king of Persia, that Nehemiah performed his usual task
of taking wine before the king. For the first time in all his years of
service his face was sad and his manner expressed deep sorrow.

"Why do you look sad?" said the king, turning upon his cupbearer a penetrating gaze. "I do not think that you are sick,
therefore this must be nothing else but sorrow of heart."

Then Nehemiah was afraid that his cheerless look had angered
the king.

"Let the king live forever!" he said. "I grieve because the city of
my forefathers lies waste and the gates are burned with fire. How
shall I not be full of sorrow when the place of my fathers' tombs is
yet in ruins?"

The king looked at him shrewdly. "And what is your request?"
he said.

Nehemiah breathed a silent prayer to God that he should find words that would not displease the king. And then he answered: "If it please the king, and if I have found favor in your eyes, I beg that you will send me to Jerusalem in Judah where my ancestors lie buried so that I may help rebuild it."

Then the king, who was sitting with the queen beside him, asked the royal cupbearer: "How long will you be gone?"

This was difficult to answer, for Nehemiah could not judge how long it would take to rebuild the city walls he had never seen. But he set a time, and to his great joy the king granted his request.

"If it please the king," Nehemiah added, "give me letters for the governors beyond the river, so that they may give me safe conduct through their lands. And let me also have a letter to Asaph, keeper of the king's forest, that he may give me timber to make beams for the gates of the palace and for the walls of the city."

The king agreed to everything he asked, for the good hand of God was on his servant Nehemiah.

Accompanied by a small company of army captains and horsemen supplied by the king, Nehemiah made the long journey from the land of Persia and arrived safely in Jerusalem. He did not, at first, make known his presence to the people of the city, for he knew that there were enemies round about who had no wish to see the walls rebuilt and the city fortified.

He remained in hiding for three days, resting from his journey and quietly making plans. Then he arose and went out silently in the night to view the city by moonlight. And still he told no one what God had put in his heart to do. In company with some few chosen men he rode out upon his sure-footed donkey to inspect the ruins. He left the city by way of the Valley Gate, whose fortified tower had long since fallen into dust, and rode quietly past the Dragon Well to see the entire wall from outside.

For as far as he could see it was broken down and lay in useless heaps. The gates, nearly all of them, had been almost totally destroyed by fire. Piles of shattered stone lay everywhere about. He rode on, toward the Gate of the Fountain and the King's Pool,

hoping to re-enter the city at that point, but the rubble was piled
so high that his donkey could find no path. Any number of
enemies on foot, however, could easily climb across the stones if
they had a mind to.

Nehemiah rode on toward the brook Kidron and viewed the
section of the wall that faced the river. Then he turned back and
re-entered the city through the Gate of the Valley. It had not
been a heartening survey. Yet he was not dismayed.

In the morning he went to the priests and rulers and told them
what he had seen and why he had come. "You see the distress we
are in!" he said earnestly. "You see how Jerusalem lies in ruins,
and how the gates of the city are burned by fire. Come, let us
build the wall of Jerusalem so that we may no longer feel
shame, so that we may hold our heads up high!" He told them,
too, of God's answer to his prayers, and how the king of Persia
had encouraged him with words and deeds. And his listeners
were inspired.

"Let us rise up and build!" they cried.

And, led by Nehemiah, they started work at once upon the
walls. First they cleared away the fallen rubble and the debris of
the years of neglect. Then every man who was capable of working, and even every woman, set to work upon the walls.
Nehemiah parceled out the work according to the clans and families. Some men worked on the walls nearest their own homes;
others worked in groups to repair long sections of the walls and
replace the many broken, burnt-out gates.

Eliashib the high priest worked with other priests to repair the
Sheep Gate, through which the sheep for sacrifice were brought
into the city. The sons of Hassenaah built the Fish Gate, with its
great beams and solid doors and heavy locks and bars. Next to
them worked Meremoth, repairing the wall; and next to
Meremoth, Meshullah; and next to them worked Zadok; and next
to the men of Gibeon repaired Uzziel of the goldsmiths; next to
him worked Hananiah the son of one of the apothecaries, and so
on around the great circumference of the wall. Hanun and the in-

habitants of Zanoah repaired the Valley Gate and a thousand cubits of the wall. Shallun, ruler of part of Mizpah, repaired the Gate of the Fountain and the walls of the Pool of Siloah by the king's garden. Priests, merchants, nobles, gatekeepers, and all the people of Jerusalem worked together to rebuild their city wall and replace the devastated gates with sturdy beams and bars.

At first the Samaritans and other adversaries of the Jews mocked them for their efforts. "What do these feeble Jews?" they asked each other. "Will they fortify themselves against us? Will they make the wall in a day? Will they restore the stones out of the heaps of rubbish? What a poor wall it is! If a fox should leap upon it, their stone wall would break and fall."

But when they saw the great progress that was being made in filling up the breaches and raising up the walls, they became exceedingly angry. For the stone wall did not fall; it grew stronger every day. So now the enemies of the Jews conspired to come out and fight against Jerusalem before the wall was finished, for they knew that if they did not do it now they would never again have free access to the city.

But Nehemiah heard about these plans and made his own. From the moment the conspiracy came to his ears he set a guard to watch day and night for any sign of attack. During the workday, he set half of his builders to labor at the wall, and the other half to stand guard and hold spears and shields and bows in readiness. Even the builders and those who carried loads of stone and timber to the walls worked, each one of them, with one hand always ready to grasp the sword that was girded by his side. Nehemiah himself kept constant watch, urging his men on to even greater effort and yet never allowing his alert gaze to falter for a moment. A trumpeter walked always by his side, ready to sound an alarm if it were needed.

The threatened attack was never launched. It was obvious to the enemies outside the walls that there was nothing they could do to stop the work. Neither Nehemiah nor his kinsmen, nor any of the builders and servants, nor any of the guards, permitted themselves to rest beyond their barest needs. They did not so much as remove their clothes, except to wash, while the wall was being built.

And after fifty-two days of vigilance and unrelenting work, the wall was finished.

Great was the rejoicing when the work was done. Nehemiah gathered together all the people and the priests to dedicate the walls with gladness. They came with thanksgiving in their hearts, and with singing and with cymbals, and with psalteries and harps, and they sang joyful songs of praise to the Lord their God.

Their city, with the plains and countryside and towns around it, was all that was left of the land of Judah, and of the very much greater nation that had once been Israel. And even the small portion still left to them was ruled by a foreign king who counted them among his subjects.

But yet there was cause for happiness. The tribes of Benjamin and Judah had come back to the holy city of Jerusalem. They had rebuilt many of the damaged homes; they had repaired the city wall; they had built a great new temple to their Lord. As they sang they remembered God's promise, spoken through the mouth of the prophet Jeremiah: "For lo, the days come that I will cause my people to return to the land that I gave to their fathers. I will have mercy on their dwelling places; and the city shall be builded upon her own heap. And out of them shall proceed thanksgiving and the voice of them that make merry. Their congregation shall be established before me, and I will punish all that oppress them. And I shall be their God."

Thus had God's promise come true for the captive people of Judah. And they had yet another promise to remember: that some day a savior from the line of David, son of Jesse of the tribe of Judah, would come among them and cast his light upon the world.

So, that day by the city walls, they offered sacrifices and rejoiced: the priests and all the other men who had worked so diligently, the wives, the children, the scribe Ezra, the cupbearer-builder Nehemiah, the singers, and those who made music with the cymbals and the harps—all praised the Lord with love and gratitude. And the joy of Jerusalem was heard even afar off, across the plains and pastures of the land of Judah.

GOD'S PROMISE TO ISRAEL

*Y*ears passed into centuries. The land of the Jews became known as Palestine. Kings of many countries fought each other, and Palestine changed hands like any spoil of war. The Jews remained in their own land, sometimes suffering oppression and sometimes benefiting under the rule of their foreign rulers, but always clinging fast to Jerusalem as their holy city. The prophecies and promises of old were not forgotten, least of all the stirring words of the prophet Isaiah:

> "The people that walked in darkness
> Have seen a great light:
> They that dwell in the land of the shadow of death,
> Upon them hath the light shined.
> Thou has multiplied the nation, and not increased the joy;
> They joy before thee according to the joy in harvest,
> And as men rejoice when they divide the spoil.
> For thou hast broken the yoke of his burden,
> And the staff of his shoulder,
> The rod of his oppressor,
> As in the day of Midian.
> For every battle of the warrior is with confused noise,

And garments rolled in blood;
But this shall be with burning and fuel of fire.
For unto us a child is born, unto us a son is given;
And the government shall be upon his shoulders;
And his name shall be called Wonderful,
Counsellor, the mighty God, the everlasting Father,
The Prince of Peace.
Of the increase of his government and peace
There shall be no end,
Upon the throne of David, and upon his kingdom,
To order it, and to establish it
With judgment and with justice
From henceforth even for ever.
The zeal of the Lord of hosts will perform this."

And Isaiah also said:

"And there shall come forth a rod out of the stem of Jesse,
And a branch shall grow out of his roots:
And the spirit of the Lord shall rest upon him,
The spirit of wisdom and understanding,
The spirit of counsel and might,
The spirit of knowledge and of the fear of the Lord;
And shall make him of quick understanding in the fear of the
    Lord:
And he shall not judge after the sight of his eyes,
Neither reprove after the hearing of his ears:
But with righteousness shall he judge the poor,
And reprove with equity for the meek of the earth.
And he shall smite the earth with the rod of his mouth,
And with the breath of his lips shall he slay the wicked.
And righteousness shall be the girdle of his loins,
And faithfulness the girdle of his reins.
The wolf also shall dwell with the lamb,
And the leopard shall lie down with the kid;

And the calf and the young lion and the fatling together;
And a little child shall lead them.
And the cow and the bear shall feed;
Their young ones shall lie down together:
And the lion shall eat straw like the ox.
They shall not hurt nor destroy
In all my holy mountain:
For the earth shall be full of the knowledge of the Lord,
As the waters cover the sea.
And in that day there shall be a root of Jesse,
Which shall stand for an ensign of the people;
To it shall the Gentiles seek:
And his rest shall be glorious."

The Jews of Palestine waited: waited for a child to be born from the stem of Jesse and David, a child who would grow in wisdom and understanding until he became known as the Prince of Peace.

THE ANGEL GABRIEL

There was in the days of Herod, the king of Judea, a certain priest named Zacharias. He and his wife Elizabeth were both descended from Aaron, brother of Moses, and thus were both of priestly family. It happened, at this time, that Zacharias was to take his turn at serving in the temple at Jerusalem.

Now this temple was not that which had been built by Solomon, destroyed by Nebuchadnezzar, and rebuilt by the captives of the land of Judah on their return from Babylon. It was a great new temple, larger and more elaborate than ever before, and it had been built by Herod the Great to please the Jews so that they might not revolt against him and the harshness of his rule. And Herod, in his turn, was not truly the King of the Jews but the governor of the province of Judah or Judea, which was one fourth part of the whole land of Palestine. Each part had its own king or governor, and all four rulers were responsible to Caesar Augustus, emperor in Rome and powerful ruler of all the lands in the region of the Mediterranean Sea. Little Palestine was the smallest part of great Caesar's mighty empire. Yet it was a very much larger land than it had been in the days of Nehemiah, it was much more thickly populated, and it was more advanced in

many ways. The Jews had learned much from the learned Greeks
and conquering Romans, but they had not learned to free themselves from foreign rule. One day, they were sure, a leader would
be born among them, a man of God who would save them from
their sins and from their earthly bondage. He would be the one
true King of the Jews: the Messiah, he who would deliver them,
and the Christ, he who would be the anointed of the Lord. The
prophets of old had assured them that their Savior would come.

And still the Jews were waiting.

In the meanwhile they prayed. Those who were deeply
dedicated to the God of Israel made frequent pilgrimages to the
city of Jerusalem to celebrate the feasts and holy days with the
priests and wise men of the temple. Those who lived in Jerusalem
worshiped in the temple whenever the spirit came upon them.
There was always a priest in attendance at the altar.

One day Zacharias went as usual into the inner sanctuary of the
house of the Lord to burn incense upon the altar. Great crowds of
people were praying outside in the temple court as he went about
his priestly duties in the holiest of all the holy rooms.

Now Zacharias and Elizabeth loved the Lord and served him
with all their hearts, but like so many upright and faithful people
before them, they had one great cause for sorrow. They were old,
and yet they had no child. If there was any one thing that they
prayed for more than anything else, it was for a son of their own.

Zacharias lit the tiny flame upon the altar. The sweet smell of
incense rose in a cloud of smoke. And suddenly an angel of the
Lord appeared on the right side of the altar of incense. When
Zacharias saw this sudden apparition he was greatly startled and
troubled in his heart. He felt afraid, and he bowed his head.

"Fear not," said the angel gently. "Your prayer is answered.
Your wife Elizabeth will have a son, and you will name him John.
He shall bring you joy and gladness; and many will rejoice at his
birth, for he shall be great in the sight of the Lord. He will drink
neither wine nor strong drink and, filled with the Holy Spirit, he
will turn many of the children of Israel to the Lord their God. His

spirit and power shall be that of Elijah, so that he will go before
the Lord and turn the hearts of the fathers to the children, who
are without sin, and the disobedient to the wisdom of the just.
Thus he will make ready a people prepared to meet the Lord."

Zacharias was full of wonderment. "How can this be?" he
asked. "How shall I know that this is true? For my wife and I are
old, too old to have a child."

And the angel answered: "I am Gabriel, who stands in the
presence of God. The Lord has sent me to you to tell you these
glad tidings. But because you do not believe my words, which
nevertheless will be fulfilled when the right time comes, you shall
be dumb and not able to speak until the day that these things
shall be performed. Let that be your sign that what I say is true."

Zacharias looked again but the angel was no longer there. The
people in the temple court outside waited for the priest, wondering why he stayed so long within the inner sanctuary. When at
last the old man came out his lips were moving silently and his
hands made gestures in the air as if he had been taken with a sudden illness. As they stared at him, astonished, they became aware
that some strange and wonderful thing had happened to him. All
he could do was beckon to them dumbly and make signs that he
had lost his speech; yet on his face there was a radiance that they
had never seen before. It came to them, then, that he must have
seen a vision in the temple, and they were filled with awe. They
waited for some time to see what else might happen or what he
might say when he regained his voice, but there was no sign. The
old man remained speechless for all the time they waited, until at
last they went away and forgot what they had seen.

When Zacharias was finished with his days of duty in the
temple he departed to his own house in the rolling hills of Judea.
He still could not speak, nor did he speak for several months
thereafter. But soon after he came home his wife Elizabeth told
him that they were, at last, to have a child.

"Thus has the Lord dealt with me after these many years!" she said joyfully. And the old man gave thanks in the silence of his heart.

Six months later the angel Gabriel appeared again. This time the messenger of the Lord came to the city of Nazareth in Galilee, in the lakelands north of the province of Judea, and visited the maiden Mary who was betrothed to a carpenter named Joseph. Now Mary was cousin to Elizabeth, but she had heard nothing of the vision to Zacharias in the temple. Nor did she herself plan to marry her intended husband for some time to come, though all their friends and kinsfolk felt that she and Joseph had done well to choose each other. It was good, they said among themselves, that both Mary and Joseph were descended from the house of David, he who had once been king of all Israel.

It was a quiet day in Nazareth for Mary until the unexpected figure came to her as if from nowhere. And she looked up in surprise at the calm face of the stranger.

"Hail, Mary, you who are highly favored!" said the angel Gabriel. "The Lord is with you: blessed are you among all women!"

When Mary saw this sudden visitor, she was deeply troubled. What could this greeting mean? She could not understand it, and she trembled at his words.

"Fear not, Mary," the angel said to her, "for you have found favor with the Lord your God. You shall have a son, and you will call him Jesus. He shall be great, and shall be called the Son of the Highest. The Lord God will give him the throne of his forefather David, and he will reign over the house of Israel forever. Of his kingdom there shall be no end."

Mary was astonished and even more troubled, for her wedding day was still far off and Joseph was no king to be father to a king. "How can this be?" she asked the angel. "I am not yet married, and the man I am to marry is a good man but a carpenter. How then shall our son be king?"

"The Holy Ghost will come upon you," Gabriel answered. "The power of the Most High God shall cover you, therefore the holy child that will be born to you shall be called the Son of God. And behold! Your cousin Elizabeth is soon to have a child of her old age. For with God, nothing is impossible."

When she heard this Mary believed and no longer feared. "I am the handmaid of the Lord," she said humbly. "Let it be to me as you have said."

And the angel departed from her as suddenly as he had come.

Yet the news was so startling to Mary that she could not bring herself to tell it to her parents, nor to the man she was to marry. She therefore arose in haste and went into the hill country of Judea to visit her cousin Elizabeth.

Strangely enough, Elizabeth was not surprised to see her, for when Mary greeted her the older woman was filled with the Holy Spirit and the knowledge that came with it. She cried out in a joyous voice: "Blessed are you among women! Blessed am I that the mother of my Lord should come to me! And blessed is she that believes, for indeed those things will happen which were promised by the Lord!"

So Elizabeth already knew! Mary answered with joy in her own heart:

"Oh, how my soul does magnify the Lord,
And my spirit does rejoice in God my Savior.
For he has taken notice of his handmaiden in her lowly estate;
Behold, from henceforth all generations shall call me blessed.
For he that is mighty has done to me great things,
And holy is his name!
And his mercy is on those who love him from generation to generation.
He has showed strength with his arm;
He has scattered the proud in the imagination of their hearts.
He has thrown down the mighty from their seats of power,
And has lifted up those of low degree.
He has filled the hungry with good things,

And the rich he has sent empty away.
He has helped his servant Israel, in remembrance of his
   mercy,
As he spoke to our fathers, to Abraham, and to his children
   forever!"

Mary stayed with Elizabeth for about three months, helping
her cousin as the older woman grew heavy with the child, and
when the little one was born she returned to her own home in
Nazareth with the knowledge that she, too, was to have a baby.

When Elizabeth brought forth her son, her friends and family
gathered around to rejoice with her. The Lord had indeed shown
great mercy to the wife of Zacharias! And on the eighth day after
the birth they came to sanctify the child and offer suggestions for
his name.

"Let him be called Zacharias, after his father," they said.

But Elizabeth shook her head and answered: "Not so. He shall
be called John."

Now this was most surprising to them. "But there is no one in
your family by the name of John," they argued. "Why do you not
name him for your husband?" And they made signs to the father,
who was still incapable of speech, to ask him what he desired to
name his son.

Zacharias motioned for a writing tablet. When they brought it
to him he wrote these words upon it: "His name is John."

And they marveled, all of them; yet they marveled even more
when suddenly his mouth was opened and his tongue was loosed.
The power of speech came back to him and he praised God with
all his new-found eloquence. He was filled with the Holy Ghost,
and he prophesied, and said:

"Blessed be the Lord God of Israel!
For he has visited and redeemed his people,
And has raised up a horn of salvation for us
In the house of his servant David,

> As he spoke by the mouths of his holy prophets
> Which have been since the world began:
> That we should be saved from our enemies,
> And from the hand of all that hate us;
> To perform the mercy promised to our fathers,
> And to remember his holy covenant,
> The oath which he swore to our father Abraham!"

Fear came on all the people who heard him and on those who lived round about when they heard their neighbors repeat the words of Zacharias. "What manner of child is this?" they wondered to each other, and remembered the words within their hearts.

But Zacharias had no doubts about his child. He knew that the hand of the Lord was with him. And to the baby John, even before the little one could understand, he said:

> "And you, my child, shall be called the prophet of
>   the Highest,
> For you will go before the face of the Lord to pre-
>   pare his ways;
> To give knowledge of salvation to his people
> By the forgiving of their sins
> Through the tender mercy of our God;
> To give light to them that sit in darkness and in the
>   shadow of death,
> And to guide our feet into the way of peace."

And the child grew, and became strong in body and spirit. When he was of an age to leave his home he went into the desert where he fasted, studied the holy writings, and prayed until the day when he was ready to preach to the children of Israel.

In the meanwhile Mary had gone home to her parents and the man, Joseph, who was to be her husband. It was strange to him that she was already carrying a child within her although she was still a maiden and unmarried, but she told him all that she had seen and heard.

And one night, while he was thinking about all the strange things she had told him, Joseph fell into a restless sleep. An angel of the Lord appeared to him in a dream and said to him: "Joseph, son of David! Fear not for Mary's sake, or for your own for she has been visited by the Holy Ghost, the Spirit of the Most High. She will have a son and you shall call him Jesus, for he shall be the Savior of his people."

Joseph awoke, untroubled and refreshed in spirit. Soon afterward he took the maiden Mary to be his wife, and they lived together in Nazareth awaiting the birth of the baby who was to be called Jesus.

Elizabeth and Zacharias knew that their son John was to be a prophet preparing the way for a greater man than himself. And Mary and Joseph had been told that the boy Jesus was of his people. The young couple and the old looked forward with great eagerness to the days to come.

THE BIRTH OF JESUS

*O*ne day a proclamation was made throughout the land of Palestine and all the vast number of territories under the dominion of the Roman emperor. It said: "It is decreed by Caesar Augustus that a record shall be made of all the people in his possessions and lands so that each one may be taxed according to his property. Every man must place his name upon the tax list in the city of his fathers, from whence his family came."

Therefore every person in the land of the Hebrews, Roman subjects like so many hundreds of thousands of people throughout the world, went to his own city to put his name upon a register and pay his tax.

For Joseph and Mary, both of whom were of the house and family of David who had been born in Bethlehem, it meant a journey of seventy miles from Nazareth in Galilee to Bethlehem in southern Judea. Joseph was much displeased to have to travel at that time, for Mary his wife was soon to have her child. But they were obliged by law to go, and there was no delaying.

Mary made no complaint and they set off at once. Joseph walked by her side as she rode upon a slowly jogging mule along the rough road to the south. It was a long and tiring journey, and

by the time they reached the town of Bethlehem six miles south of
Jerusalem the place was already crowded with other citizens who
had come to register their names upon the tax rolls. Crowds
jostled through the narrow streets seeking lodgings for the night;
people pushed their way into the only inn and begged for rooms
in the private houses; and no one gave any thought to the plight
of the carpenter from Nazareth and his wife who was so soon to
have a child.

And because there was no room for them in the inn they sought
shelter in a stable, making beds for themselves amongst the
sweet-smelling straw in a clean and quiet corner that was separate from the animal stalls. Joseph made Mary as comfortable as
he could on a soft blanket of hay, and then he looked about to see
what else he might do to improve their simple shelter. There was
the child to think of; it would need some sort of bed. He found a
manger, one of the troughs from which the livestock ate their
fodder, cleaned it out with care and prepared it as best he could
for the coming of the child.

And so it was, while they were there in Bethlehem by order of
an emperor in far-off Rome, that it came time for Mary to deliver
her child. There in the stable she brought forth her firstborn son
and wrapped him tenderly in swaddling clothes; and Joseph
placed the baby gently in the manger he had so lovingly prepared.

The sun had set some hours before and the little town was very
quiet. Bright stars flecked the cloudless sky above the sleeping
folk in Bethlehem, and only in the fields nearby were there men
who stood awake and watchful. They were shepherds, keeping
watch over their flocks by night so that no wolves or thieves
might come upon their sheep and carry even one away. Sometimes they were silent, and sometimes they talked, but at no time
did they relax their guard over the least among their lambs. It
was a calm night, bright and peaceful; too bright for anything to
happen that might endanger the flock.

Then all at once it was even brighter than before: a great and wonderful light filled the sky, and the brilliant glory of the Lord shone round about the shepherds so dazzlingly, so suddenly, that their hearts leapt within them and they quaked with fear. And an angel appeared before them in the brilliance and cried out a message that brought them to their knees in prayer:

"Fear not! For behold, I bring you good tidings of great joy, which shall be to all people. For unto you is born this day in the city of David a Savior, which is Christ the Lord. And this shall be a sign to you: You will find the babe wrapped in swaddling clothes, lying in a manger."

The light that streamed down from the sky grew brighter yet, and suddenly there was with the angel a multitude of heavenly beings. They shone, themselves, in the brightness above the fields; and as the shepherds watched and listened with awe the heavenly choir praised God and sang:

"Glory to God in the highest, and on earth peace, goodwill toward men."

Then they were gone from the shepherds, away into the heavens, and the radiant light faded into the ordinary brightness of a cloudless, starry night. The shepherds rose in wonder and stared at one another.

"Let us go at once to Bethlehem," they said, "and see for ourselves this thing that has come to pass which the Lord has made known to us."

They went with haste, marveling at all they had seen and heard, and sought out the stable near the inn. There they found Mary and Joseph, and the newborn babe lying sleeping in the manger. And they knelt before this wondrous child of whom the angels had spoken, and they told Mary about the angelic host that had come to them. Then they left, and in their great wonder and excitement they told all they met about the awesome events of the night. And all who heard their story wondered, and talked of it among themselves. But Mary kept within her heart all the things she knew and all that she had heard, and she pondered them in silence as she tenderly watched over the baby in the manger.

The shepherds went back to their flocks, glorifying and praising God for all the things that they had heard and seen; and thanking him for sending them a Savior, who was Christ their Lord.

On the eighth day after the birth of the child, Mary and Joseph took him to be sanctified and named. As the angel had instructed them, they called him Jesus, a name meaning "salvation."

Now when Jesus was born in Bethlehem of Judea in the days of Herod the king, there were certain wise and noble men who lived in a distant country of the east and studied the stars. One night they saw a great new star appear in the eastern sky and blaze a path across the heavens toward the kingdom of Judea, where it disappeared from sight. Being learned men, they had heard of the prophecies that had been made among the Jewish people in a day long past, and when they saw the new star they felt at once that a great new king had been born in the land of the Jews.

"Come, let us go at once to see the newborn king!" they exclaimed to one another.

They loaded their camels with gifts for the wonderful child and set off on their long journey. And because Jerusalem was known to be the holy city of the Jews, the wise men from the east traveled to that famous city of kings believing that they would find the child in some royal palace there.

When they arrived they inquired of the people: "Where is he that is born King of the Jews? For we have seen his star in the east and have come to worship him."

But no one in Jerusalem had heard of the newborn "king" who was in Bethlehem.

When Herod the king heard of their questions he was deeply troubled, and all Jerusalem with him. After all, was Herod not King of the Jews? What child could claim his royal title? Then he, too, remembered the old prophecies, and sent for the chief priests and the scribes whose duty it was to record and interpret the teachings of the past.

"Now tell me," he demanded, "where this Christ, this new king of Israel, is supposed to have been born?"

"In Bethlehem of Judea, O King Herod," they replied, "for thus it is written by the prophet:

"'And you, Bethlehem, in the land of Judah,
Are not the least among the princes of Judah:
For out of you shall come a Governor,
That shall rule my people Israel.'"

Herod sent his priests and scribes away and thought about these sayings for some time. He did not like what they might mean to him. For he was king, and king he intended to remain no matter who was born in Bethlehem or anywhere else.

After a while he sent for the wise men of the east who were inquiring within his city about the newborn King of Jews. And he sent for them in secret, for he did not want his own priests and scribes to know what they might say to him. They came to him at once, thinking that he would surely be able to tell them what they asked.

Herod asked the first question.

"Tell me," he said genially, and with unfeigned interest, "what time did this new star appear in the eastern sky?"

They told him.

"And where is it now?" he asked them cunningly.

But they did not know.

"Then go to Bethlehem," he answered, "and search there diligently for the young child, for according to the scribes that is where he may be found. But no one knows where he is in the city, therefore I beg that when you have found him you will bring me word so that I may go and worship him also."

The wise men left Jerusalem and went upon their way to Bethlehem. Herod began at once to make his plans. It was true that he desired earnestly to know where the child might be, but not so that he himself might go and worship him. It was his own throne of which he was thinking.

The star which the wise men had seen in the east appeared again before them and led them on to Bethlehem. When they saw the star once more they rejoiced with great gladness in their hearts, knowing that they were soon to see the glorious child. When the star stopped above a humble dwelling place, they went in. All they saw was a simple carpenter and his wife Mary, and a child in Mary's arms. Yet they knew at once that the baby Jesus was the newborn king they had come so far to see, for the star was still hovering over the house where the young child was. In the fullness of their joy they bent down low and worshiped him, this child who would be not only King but Savior, and when they had done worshiping they opened up their sacks and chests of treasure. They gave the child gifts worthy of a king: gold for his earthly wealth, sweet frankincense and myrrh for sacrificial offerings to the Lord God of heaven; and they gave these precious things with wonder and thanksgiving in their hearts.

When they had blessed the child and given their gifts, the wise men thought it time to return to the city of Jerusalem and tell King Herod where this wondrous child might be found and worshiped by all the people of the land. But in a dream that came to all of them that night, God's angel warned them that they should not return to Herod with their news. Therefore they left Bethlehem, avoided Jerusalem, and went back to their country by another route.

Soon after the wise men had left, the angel of the Lord appeared to Joseph in a dream. "Arise," the angel said. "Take the young child and his mother and flee into Egypt for your safety: for Herod will seek the young child to destroy him."

Joseph arose at once in the night and gathered together the few possessions of his small family and the gifts brought by the wise men from the east. Swiftly, and in silence, he took the baby and its mother from Bethlehem by night and journeyed with all haste to the land of Egypt. And there the baby Jesus remained in safety while Herod lived out his last terrible months in the land of Judea.

King Herod waited for the wise men, but they did not come back. With growing impatience he watched for their return, waiting and yearning for their news so that he might find the child and rid himself of this threat to his kingdom; but still there was no sign of the wise men of the east. And then at last he heard that they had gone back to their own land without first coming back to him. Herod's anger knew no bounds. He knew he could not touch the wise men, but there was something he could do to destroy the child.

With the awful cruelty for which he was well known, he sent his soldiers out to Bethlehem and the surrounding countryside with orders to kill every child two years old and under. In this way he felt certain he would slay the one he wanted, in company with all those born at the time when the wise men saw the star.

His soldiers followed his terrible command. And after they had done so another prophecy of the prophet Jeremiah's was fulfilled:

"In Rama was there a voice heard,
Lamentation, and weeping, and great mourning,
Rachel weeping for her children,
And would not be comforted,
Because they are no more."

And they were no more, the children of Bethlehem who were two years old and younger. Only the baby Jesus was safe from Herod's senseless slaughter. Thus he, a child who was to be the Christ, the Savior, the Messiah of the Jewish people, began his life in a humble stable in Bethlehem and was now in hiding with his parents in the land of Egypt.

THE BOYHOOD OF JESUS

*T*he boy Jesus lived. King Herod died: old, sick in body and spirit, cruel to the last.

Then the angel of the Lord appeared again in a dream to Joseph, still in Egypt with Mary and her son. "Arise," the angel said. "Take the young child and his mother back into the land of Israel, for he who sought the young child's life is dead."

So Joseph arose and led his family back to their homeland. Egypt had been good to them, as it had been good to his forefathers Abraham and Joseph, but it was not meant that the King and Deliverer of Israel should grow up in a foreign land. It was toward Bethlehem, city of David, that the family now turned their steps.

Yet there were still obstacles in Joseph's path. When he came with Mary and Jesus into the land of Israel he heard that Herod's son Archelaus reigned in Judea in his father's place, and by all accounts the son was no less cruel than the father. Therefore Joseph was afraid to settle in Judea as he had intended, and while he wondered what to do he was told by God in a dream that he must turn aside from Judea and go north into the lakelands of Galilee. There another Herod ruled, one Herod Antipas, who was by no means a good and upright man but neither was he nearly so cruel as others of his family.

And so Joseph went back to the city of Nazareth in Galilee with Mary his wife and the little boy Jesus, and stayed there while the child was growing up. Thus another prophecy of old was fulfilled: "He that is the Messiah shall be called a Nazarene."

Joseph once again became a carpenter. Mary made a new home for the little family in Nazareth. The child Jesus grew, becoming strong in spirit and filled with wisdom, and the grace of God was upon him.

As time passed and the boy seemed to be no different from others of his age, Mary and Joseph thought less and less of the strange circumstances of his birth. They did not, and could not ever, forget, but he gave them no reason to treat him as anything other than a normal, healthy lad with all the usual interests of a growing boy.

Yet he was wiser than they knew, and nothing that he saw escaped him. As Jesus grew he came to know his town and everything about it, good and bad. He knew its people, old and young; its rich men and its poor, the kind people and the harsh, the tradesmen and the beggars. In his father's shop he learned much about the use of tools and the differences between various kinds of wood. And because a carpenter of those days was as much a builder as a maker of furniture, he also came to know something of the construction of houses. The boy Jesus could only watch when it came to the matter of building, but he was quick to learn the importance of a solid foundation, sturdy materials, and honest workmanship.

And because Nazareth was not a large town he also came to know the countryside around him as if it were the garden of his father's house. He knew the shores of Galilee and the fishermen who went out to cast their nets upon the waters. He knew the shepherds of the pastures, and came to share their feeling of concern and love for every lamb in every flock. He knew the farmers in the fields, and he watched them plow and reap. He knew the names of all the living things that grew in the hills and valleys: the crops, the trees, the fruits, the mustard seeds and weeds. He knew the birds and beasts and flowers, the thorns and thistles, and the grasses of the fields.

He also learned the history of his people and the commandments brought down by Moses from the top of Mount Sinai. Although the temple was in Jerusalem, and all devout Jews journeyed there for their special prayers and feasts, there was a synagogue in Nazareth where the people gathered for worship and to hear readings from the scrolls of wisdom left by the Hebrew prophets and poets of the past. Here in the synagogue Jesus praised the Lord on sabbath days, and here he studied the psalms and scriptures during the week until he could recite long passages by heart. Here, too, he learned to read and write, and to understand the words of wisdom that he had learned by listening to his teachers. Time and time again he heard the hopeful prophecies about the Messiah who would come to free his people Israel from the darkness of their own sins and the yoke of their oppressors. The yearning for yet more knowledge and understanding began to stir within him.

In accordance with the custom among the Jewish people, Joseph and Mary went to Jerusalem every year to celebrate the feast of the passover. And when Jesus was twelve years old his parents took him with them for the first time, for now he was on the verge of young manhood.

There was much for Jesus to see on the journey to the city of the temple, and much to interest him in the great city itself as crowds of pilgrims converged upon it from all sides. But it was the temple itself that stirred him more than the royal palace, the markets with their many wares, the noblemen in all their finery, or the impressive soldiers of the king. Instead of lingering in the streets with other boys his age he went each day to the temple and listened to the priests, and each evening he joined his parents as they praised the Lord and worshiped the Most High. He was fascinated by the altar and the sweet smell of burning incense, by the calm-faced priests in their flowing robes, and by the compelling words of the wise teachers within the temple court.

The feast of the lamb and the unleavened bread was celebrated by all, and much too soon the days of special prayers and fasts and feasts were at an end. The pilgrims who were going back to Nazareth gathered in a great company so that they might travel the long road together, and they set off from the city of Jerusalem in one vast but scattered throng.

But the child Jesus stayed behind in Jerusalem, unable to tear himself away and not even aware that his parents were already far distant while he sat listening and questioning in the temple. Strange new thoughts were working in his mind. He had been told the story of his birth, and more than once he thought of the words of one of the earliest of the ancient prophets:

> "There shall come forth a star out of Jacob,
> And a scepter shall rise out of Israel."

Was his the star? He could only wonder. But in his heart there was a feeling that the God of Israel was his Father and that he, the Son, had much to learn.

Joseph and Mary did not know that Jesus was not with them, for the group they traveled with was large and Jesus might have been anywhere within it with his young friends or his relatives. At the end of a day's journey they looked for him so that he might join them as they made camp for the night, and then at last they realized that he was nowhere to be seen. With growing anxiety they sought him among their kinsfolk and acquaintances, but they did not find him nor anyone who could tell them where he was. It came to them, then, that perhaps he had not left the city.

They hurried back at once and searched throughout the city, looking in all the places where they thought a young boy might have wandered. But still they did not find him, and their desperate questions met with no answer that could help them. No one had seen the boy.

And then, after three days spent in traveling and in searching, they went into the temple. And there they found their child sitting in the midst of the doctors and the learned scribes. He was listening to them with rapt attention and asking questions that showed so deep a knowledge and understanding that all who heard him were astounded. Both his questions and his answers showed a wisdom well beyond his years, and the learned men were talking to him almost as if he were one of them.

Joseph and Mary were themselves amazed, as much by his presence there as by his remarkable understanding. At the moment they were in no mood to congratulate their son upon his wisdom.

His mother said to him: "Son, why have you treated us this way? Did you not know that we were all to leave together? Your father and I have been seeking for you in sorrow, afraid that we might never find you."

He looked at them with surprise. "But I am in my Father's house. Why did you seek me? Did you not know that I must be about my Father's business?"

His parents did not understand. His father's business? What could he mean?

When Jesus saw that he had saddened them he rose at once and left the temple with them. Yet Mary grew thoughtful as they resumed their journey. Though the years had dimmed her memory of the visit of the angel, she had not forgotten that her son was no ordinary boy. Meanwhile Jesus went back to Nazareth with Joseph and Mary. From that time on, throughout his youth and early manhood, he was obedient to them in every way and never again gave them cause for hurt or sorrow.

But Mary thought often about the words he had used that day in the temple at Jerusalem: "Why did you seek me? Did you not know that I must be about my Father's business?"

And Jesus increased in wisdom as he grew in stature. As the years went by he grew in favor with both God and man. He lived a quiet life in Nazareth and gave no further sign that he was anything other than the son of a hard-working carpenter, except that he was perhaps more gentle and forgiving than most men and certainly more wise. To all who knew him then he was a kindly, ordinary Nazarene.

But his time was coming.

JOHN THE BAPTIST

The cousins John and Jesus grew to manhood, John in Judea and Jesus in the land of Galilee. In Rome, the emperor Augustus died. In Jerusalem, the cruel Archelaus was replaced as king of Judea by a procurator, or governor, named Pontius Pilate. Herod Antipas was still the tetrarch or royal administrator of Galilee; and Annas and Caiaphas were high priests of the temple in Jerusalem.

Now in the fifteenth year of the rule of the emperor Tiberius, when both John and Jesus were about thirty years old, John the son of Elizabeth and Zacharias left the desert country of his childhood and went into the wilderness to preach. The word of God came to him in the wild hill country of Judea, and he knew that his mission was to spread the word to all the people he could reach.

There were in Palestine, at that time, two main Jewish sects who worshiped the God of Israel with a great show of outward fervor. These were the Pharisees and the Sadducees, who were much alike in many ways. The essential difference between the two parties was that the Pharisees believed not only in the written Laws of Moses but also in laws and traditions that had been handed down by word of mouth, while the Sadducees, who were the priestly aristocracy, rejected all doctrines but those of the written Law. Both parties were powerful in the temple, both were deeply occupied with the rituals and ceremonies of their religion, and both were more concerned with strict observance of the letter of the Mosaic Law than with the spirit of it. They practiced all the rites with the utmost care, and they prayed all the required prayers with the greatest diligence; and in doing so they firmly believed that they were fulfilling all their obligations to God. But they were blinded by the trappings of their beliefs, and they forgot that godliness includes the everyday practice of neighborliness and love. In them there was more pride than faith, more knowledge of the outward form of their religion than understanding of its meaning.

John belonged to neither of these two sects. He cared nothing for rituals and formal prayers. His only concern was to pave the way for the coming Messiah, whoever he might be and whenever he might come, by persuading people to repent of their sins and turn their hearts to God.

And so he went into the country near the Jordan River, preaching; urging men to be baptized, to confess, to repent, to save themselves through sincere repentance, to prepare for the day when God would judge them according to their deeds on earth. It was John of whom the Lord God had spoken through the prophet Isaiah, saying:

"Behold, I send thy messenger before thy face,
Which shall prepare the way before thee;
The voice of one crying in the wilderness,
'Prepare ye the way of the Lord!
Make his paths straight.
Every valley shall be filled,
And every mountain and hill shall be brought low;
And the crooked shall be made straight,
And the rough ways shall be made smooth;
And all flesh shall see the salvation of God.'"

People came from far and wide to see this man who baptized in the Jordan and to hear his words. Among them were simple folk from the countryside of Judea, rich men from the towns, and scholars from the city of Jerusalem. With a zeal and fervor unmatched by any temple priest, John preached his message of repentance to all those who came to him. They confessed their sins and let him baptize them as a symbol of their cleansing; and they stared at him and wondered who he was.

He was like no one they had ever seen or heard before. His clothing was a robe of camel's hair with a leather cord about the waist, and his food was locusts and wild honey. He did not speak of the small, intricate details of the Law that were so important to the learned temple scribes, nor did he speak of altars, incense, or burnt offerings. His eyes burned with the light of earnestness as his tongue spoke strange words of a much greater Light that was to come, of a Being who would bring his listeners grace and truth and hope, of a Christ that was even now upon the earth.

Word of him continued to spread throughout the land. People told each other that a new prophet had come—a new Elijah, or perhaps even the long-awaited Messiah himself.

The Pharisees sent priests and Levites from Jerusalem to question him. They, too, marveled at his strangeness and his sayings.

"Who are you?" they asked. "Are you the Christ?"

"I am not the Christ," he answered.

"Who are you, then? Are you Elijah, returned to Israel?"

"No, I am not," he said.

"Or some other prophet? Tell us who you are, so that we may give an answer to those who sent us. What do you say of yourself?"

And he answered, "I am the voice of one crying in the wilderness, he of whom Isaiah spoke."

"Why do you baptize, then," they asked, "if you are not the Christ, or Elijah the prophet?"

"To prepare for another who is to come," he answered. "For there is one coming who is mightier than I, whose shoestrings I am not worthy to stoop down and unloose. I have indeed baptized with water, but he shall baptize with the Holy Spirit and with fire!"

And the people kept on coming to him, to be baptized in the Jordan and confess their sins. He was glad when they came, but he was angry when he saw Pharisees and Sadducees among the crowds. To him, they were hypocrites: righteous, zealous, self-denying on the surface, but self-righteous in their hearts and smugly certain that they had no need for baptism and repentance.

He looked at them and cried out angrily: "You brood of snakes! Who has warned you to come to me so that you might flee from the wrath to come? Bring forth deeds that show your true repentance! Do not boast and say to yourselves, 'We have Abraham for our father,' and think that that is enough to save you. For I say to you that God is able to raise up children for Abraham from these very stones! Therefore, what are you? And I tell you now that the axe is ready at the roots of the trees, to cut down those which do not bring forth good fruit. And they shall be cut down and cast into the fire! Repent, show good deeds while there is time."

The priests and Pharisees, the Sadducees and scribes, were outraged by John's words. But many people were moved and wanted to know what they should do to show their true repentance.

"Give," he said. "He that has two coats, let him give one to a man who has none. And he that has more food than he needs, let him do the same."

Then there came also certain publicans, or tax collectors, to be baptized by John. They were among the most hated of men, for the law permitted them to extort as much money as they could out of their fellow Jews and keep for themselves any sum above that which was required by the Roman emperor. Man, though not all of them, were cruel and greedy beyond words, and the Jews regarded them as the worst of sinners.

And when the tax collectors came to John they said to him: "Master, what shall we do to show ourselves worthy of forgiveness?"

"Exact no more than that which is appointed to you," answered John.

"And what shall we do?" asked the soldiers.

"Do violence to no man," said John. "Make no false accusations. And be content with your wages, instead of taking money in dishonest ways."

Thus did John baptize and preach and answer all their questions. Dozens, scores, and hundreds of people declared themselves his followers, and yet they did not know what to make of him. They wondered in their hearts whether John might not really be the Christ. Again they asked.

Again John answered: "No! But there is one among you, whom you do not recognize for what he is. He is the one who, coming after me, will be preferred before me. It is he who will baptize you with fire. His winnowing fork is in his hand, and he will clean his threshing floor. The wheat he will gather into his granary, but the chaff he will burn up with unquenchable fire. Will you be wheat? Or will you be chaff? Repent, I say to you!"

There were many other warnings he gave to the people who came to listen to him. No one was spared his warning words or the wrath of his rough tongue. Wherever he saw evil, he pointed at it and denounced it, no matter what the cost might be to him. Not even Herod escaped John's outspoken criticism. For Herod Antipas, tetrarch or governor of Galilee, had married his own brother Philip's wife. No common citizen would have gone unpunished for this crime, but no one dared to speak against a king. No one, that is, but John. John said whatever he wished about Herod's various crimes, particularly his illegal marriage.

Miles away in Galilee, Herod heard of this man whom other men were calling John the Baptist.

Jesus also heard of his cousin's work. Unlike Herod, he left Galilee and went to Jordan to be baptized by John. He had not yet begun to preach himself, but now his time was come and he was ready.

John looked at him as he came, and perceived something that

other men did not yet know and many more men would never believe. And when Jesus asked his cousin John to baptize him as he baptized all others who came to him, John at first refused him, saying: "It is I who need to be baptized by you. And do you come to me?"

And Jesus answered, saying, "It is fitting that we should do all righteous things."

Then John led him into the river and baptized him.

When Jesus had been baptized he rose up from the water, and as he did so the heavens opened above him and he saw the Spirit of God coming down like a dove to rest upon him. He heard a voice from heaven saying: "This is my beloved Son, in whom I am well pleased."

John saw the Spirit descending as a dove out of heaven and alighting upon Jesus. He knew, then, that Jesus was the Son of God.

And Jesus himself knew without a doubt that he had been born of God and appointed by God to be the Savior of his people.

JESUS IN THE WILDERNESS

After Jesus had been baptized he left Jordan and was led deep into the wilderness by the Spirit of God to be tempted by the devil. He was certain now that he was to spend the rest of his life doing God's work, but he felt the need to be alone with his own thoughts and test his own resolve. Difficult days lay ahead, and he wanted to think and pray in a quiet place before beginning his teaching mission.

For forty days and forty nights he fasted in the wilderness. And when the long days and nights had passed he was weak with hunger. The voice of the devil spoke in his mind.

"If you are indeed the Son of God," whispered the voice of the tempter, "why do you not command that these stones be made into bread?"

Jesus looked at the stones lying on the hillside, knowing that he could indeed turn them into bread if he so desired. But the divine power at his command had not been intended for his own satisfaction, nor was the provision of food for the hungry his major mission on earth. It was spiritual food that he was destined to provide.

"It is written," he answered, "that man shall not live by bread alone, but by the word of God."

And then it was as if the devil had led him to the holy city, and set him on the spire of the temple.

"If you are the Son of God," the voice said temptingly, "God will let no harm come to you. Cast yourself down from this height; show a great sign so that all may believe in you. For it is written that God will put you in the care of his angels to keep you from harm. In their hands will they bear you up, so that you shall not so much as strike your foot against a stone."

It would indeed have been a wonderful sign to all people. Such a miracle would surely make them wonder and listen to his words; they would have no doubt that Jesus had been sent by God. But it was not God's way, nor the way of Jesus, to convince people with spectacular signs. They must receive him because they loved God and believed in him, and not because they were impressed by wondrous signs.

"It is so written," Jesus agreed. "And it is also written: 'You shall not tempt the Lord thy God.'"

Again the devil took him up onto a high mountain to show him a vision of the kingdoms of the world and the glory of them.

"All these things will I give you," said the tempter, "and all the power and the glory of them. For all is mine, to give to whomsoever I choose. If you will fall down and worship me, it will all be yours."

But Jesus did not want earthly power and glory, for his was the kingdom of heaven. True, with his great powers, he was capable of taking possession of the entire world. But God's kingdom could not be shown to people by the tempter's way; it could only be shown by teaching them to love and serve and worship.

Then Jesus answered: "Get thee behind me, Satan! For it is written: 'You shall worship the Lord your God, and only him shall you serve.'"

At last the devil left him. After forty days and nights in the wilderness, tempted by Satan and with only the wild beasts for company, Jesus finished wrestling with his thoughts. And the angels came and ministered to him.

Now John the Baptist was still baptizing at the Jordan. Jesus went back to the place of his baptism and walked along the river bank toward John and his disciples.

John saw Jesus coming toward him. "Behold the Lamb of God!" he said. "This is he of whom I said: 'After me will come a man who is preferred before me.'"

Two of his disciples heard him say these words. They left John, then, and turned to follow Jesus.

Jesus saw them following. "Whom do you seek?" he asked.

"You, Master," they answered. "Where is your dwelling place?"

"Come, and you shall see," he said.

They went with him to the place where he was staying, and they spent hours listening to him talk. They asked questions, and he answered, and there was no end to what they asked. He talked of peace and love, of repentance and salvation; and the more they heard the more convinced they were that he was the man for whom Israel had been waiting for these many years. He did not look like a King, but he spoke like a Messiah.

One of the two who had left John to follow Jesus was a fisherman named Andrew. He became so carried away by the stirring words of this man from Nazareth that he went out to find his brother Simon.

"We have found the Messiah!" Andrew said. "Come with me; hear him for yourself."

Simon had heard much talk of a Messiah within recent days, for there was a feeling of expectation amongst the Jews. He, like many others, had thought that John might be the long-awaited one. Then John had said that he was not. Again Simon, like so many others, half expected the King of the Jews to appear in kingly regalia and quickly sweep their country free of the Roman rulers. No such man had appeared, and now Simon did not know what to believe or expect.

"Come! We have found the Christ!" his brother Andrew urged him.

"Perhaps," said Simon. He was a strong, rock-hard man of the sea, difficult to convince. But he followed Andrew to meet Jesus.

Jesus saw him coming. No one had told him that this large man was Andrew's brother, yet he knew who Simon was. He knew, too, what manner of man he would prove to be. He looked up and greeted the big man.

"You are Simon, son of Jona," he said to Andrew's brother. "But you shall be called Peter, which means stone. For you shall be my rock of strength."

Simon was astonished that Jesus should have known his name. He, too, sat down and questioned Jesus. As he listened he became more and more convinced that this wise and gentle man was the Christ predicted by the prophets of old. And, like his brother and his friend, he decided that he would follow Jesus.

The next day Jesus started back for his own homeland of Galilee. On the way he found a man called Philip, who came from Bethsaida which was the home town of Andrew and Simon Peter.

"Follow me," said Jesus. And Philip followed him.

As they traveled on, Philip listened to the compelling words of this man who surely must be the promised Messiah. And Philip sought out his friend Nathanael to tell him the good news.

"We have found him!" he said joyfully. "We have found the one of whom Moses and the prophets did write. It is Jesus of Nazareth, the son of Joseph."

Nathanael was skeptical. And he did not like Nazarines.

"Can any good thing come out of Nazareth?" he said scornfully.

"Come and see," said Philip.

Jesus saw Nathanael coming to him from a great distance. When the man drew near, Jesus said to him: "Behold, Nathanael! A true Israelite indeed, in whom there is no deceit."

"How do you know me?" asked Nathanael, surprised.

"I saw you under the fig tree," Jesus answered. "Before Philip called you, I saw you there."

Nathanael was even more astonished, for the fig tree under

whose shade he had been resting was so far away that no ordinary man could possibly have seen him there.

"Master, you are the Son of God!" he said reverently. "You are the King of Israel!"

"Do you believe that only because I said to you that I saw you under the fig tree?" Jesus asked. "You shall see much greater things than that. You will see heaven open, and the angels of God ascending and descending to the Son of man."

They wondered much at what he said. But whenever they were able to leave their work along the shores of Galilee, the men who had chosen to believe in Jesus left everything behind so that they could follow him.

THE BEGINNING OF THE MISSION

A few days after Jesus met his new
friends there was a wedding in the town of Cana in Galilee. Jesus,
his mother Mary, and his followers were all invited. A great feast
followed the marriage ceremony and many of the guests stayed on
for several days celebrating with much wine and food.

The wine supply ran dry before the feast was over. Mary was
helping to look after the guests, for she was a close friend of the
hosts, and she was the first to notice that the wine jars were all
empty. She quietly called her son Jesus aside, knowing that her
friends would feel disgraced if they failed their guests and
knowing, too, that Jesus would be able to help in one way or
another.

"There is no more wine," she said to Jesus.

"What would you have me do?" asked Jesus. "My hour is not
yet come." For he had not yet begun to show his wonderful
powers to the world, nor did he feel that they had been intended
for the use of thirsty wedding guests.

But Mary was sure that he would find a way to help. She said
to the servants, "Whatever my son tells you, be sure to do it."

Now there were six stone water jars standing there for the ceremonial cleansing rites of the Jews, each of them large enough to hold between twenty and thirty gallons of liquid.

And Jesus told the servants: "Fill the waterpots with water." For he had made up his mind to help his friends at this festive time. A beginning must be made sometime, somehow.

The servants filled the tall jars to the brim.

"Now draw some out," said Jesus, "and take it to the master of the feast." It was the custom for the master of the feast to taste each dish of food and each newly opened jar of wine before the guests were served. The servants did as Jesus told them and took a serving from the water jar to the master steward for approval.

He sipped, he swallowed with pleasure. Both the master of the feast and the servants were surprised: the servants because the water had been turned to wine, and the steward because the wine was so extraordinarily good. Now the steward did not know where this fine wine had come from, for the servants who had filled the waterpots had not told him. When he had sipped to his satisfaction he called the bridegroom, saying:

"Every man sets forth his good wine at the beginning of a feast and serves his poorer wine after his guests have already drunk freely. But you have kept your best wine for the last!"

The feast drew to a successful close, and for most of the guests it had been nothing more than a happy wedding party. Yet it was very much more than that. The turning of the water into wine marked the first time that Jesus had used his special powers to perform what is called a miracle. It was only the beginning of a series of unusual signs that were to make him known throughout the land. But it served, at this time, to show the wonder and glory of Jesus to followers who already wanted to believe in him. When they saw what he had done, they did believe.

After this Jesus went down to Capernaum on the shore of Galilee with his mother, his brothers, and his followers. They stayed for some days, and then Jesus went up to Jerusalem with his friends to celebrate the passover. They went together to the house of God to worship.

There they saw a sight that shocked Jesus to his very soul. The temple court was like a market place. Live oxen, sheep, and doves were being sold to the worshipers for sacrifices. Pigeons fluttered overhead; cattle lowed in their stalls; buyers and sellers bargained with each other within the walls of God's house. Money changers sat behind their tables clinking coins, ready to change foreign currency and large pieces of local money into the silver half-shekels required as contributions from the temple worshipers to the priests. It was supposed to be a place for prayer and meditation; instead it was a chaos of conflicting sounds and smells, part barnyard and part bank.

Jesus was outraged by this desecration of a holy place, the holiest place in all of Palestine. He looked about him and found several lengths of cord, and from these strands he made a little whip or scourge. In itself it was harmless against the thronging crowd, and indeed it was not meant to be a weapon. But Jesus knew how to drive a herd of cattle or a flock of sheep.

He raised the whip and advanced into the crowd of animals and people. Oxen started to move uneasily toward the temple gate and the sheep began to follow after them. The small whip flicked through the air as Jesus moved about the temple. People turned on him in anger; and then backed away when they saw the look of quiet rage upon his face and the determination of his manner. Money changers, salesmen and customers, oxen and sheep, sightseers in the temple court, fled in disorder before the relentless man with the tiny whip. They did not move quickly enough for Jesus. He overturned the tables of the money changers and spilled their silver on the floor. "Outside!" he commanded, snapping the small whip in the air. "Do your business where you will, but not within the temple." And to the people selling doves he said: "Take these things away! Do not make my Father's house a house of merchandise!" The startled salesmen picked up their goods, pocketed their profits, caught their doves, and swiftly left.

Now many Jews were angry with Jesus for having done these things. It had become their custom to barter thus within the temple court, for it was convenient for worshipers to have the animals for sacrifice, and the money changers with their half-shekels, so very near at hand. They could see nothing wrong with what they had been doing. Besides, this man who had driven them out was a stranger to them. Who was he, they asked each other, that he assumed authority to do such things?

No one seemed able to tell them who he was. They went to Jesus themselves. "What sign will you show to us, to prove you have a right to do such things?" they demanded angrily.

"This sign will I give you," Jesus said. "Destroy this temple, and in three days I will raise it up again."

"Three days!" said the Jews. "It has taken forty-six years to build this temple, and you will raise it in three days!"

Their anger changed to mockery, and they turned away. But Jesus had not been talking about the temple in Jerusalem. He had been talking about the temple of his body, and predicting his own death and resurrection. This was a sign indeed, if the Jews had only thought about it; but they did not think.

While he was at the passover festival in Jerusalem, Jesus began to teach and show other signs that made many people believe he must surely be the Son of God. The Pharisees, however, were not among his believers. Most of them were proud and stiff-necked people who were convinced that only they and the scribes of the priesthood were capable of understanding and interpreting the Laws of God. They refused to admit that either John or Jesus could have been sent by God to show not only the multitudes, but the Pharisees themselves, the error of their ways. To them, the teachings of Jesus were wrong, and the believers in Jesus had allowed themselves to be misled.

But among the Pharisees was a man named Nicodemus, a rich man and a leader in his community; and he came secretly to Jesus by night to talk to him.

"Master," he said, "we know that you are a teacher who has come from God, for no man could do these miracles that you do unless God were with him." And he told Jesus how strongly he desired to be a true believer and enter the kingdom of God.

"Unless a man is born again," Jesus answered him, "he cannot see the kingdom of God."

"I do not understand," said Nicodemus. "How can a man be born again when he is already old? Can he be a baby for a second time, and be born twice from his mother?"

That was not what Jesus meant. "To be born again is to become as pure as a child," he explained. "It is the spirit, not the body, which must be born anew, for that which is born of the flesh is only flesh; and that which is born of the Spirit, is spirit. I say unto you that, if a man is not born of water and Spirit, he cannot enter into the kingdom of God. But he that believes and is baptized shall be born again. Then shall the Spirit of God be in his heart, and then shall he be able to enter the kingdom. And I tell you, too, that God so loved the world that he gave his only begotten Son so that whoever believes in him shall not perish, but shall have everlasting life in the kingdom of God."

They talked on into the night and Nicodemus the Pharisee went away with much to think about. It seemed to him that this gentle Jesus must surely be the Son of God, and that his message of love and redemption was much more likely to be the truth than the rigid, ritualistic teachings of the Pharisees and Sadducees.

After these things had happened, Jesus went with his followers into the countryside of Judea. He stayed there with them for some time while they baptized certain newcomers to their ranks, for they had adopted John's practice of purifying by water. Jesus himself did not baptize, but taught among the people who came for baptism.

John was baptizing not far away at a place where there were many waters. A question concerning purification arose between some of John's disciples and a man of Judea, and this led to a discussion of the baptisms conducted by the followers of Jesus. John's disciples went to their leader and said to him: "Master, the man who was with you across the Jordan, the one to whom you yourself bore witness, behold, that same man is baptizing, and now everyone is going to him."

It was not quite true that Jesus was baptizing, but it was true that people were flocking to hear him teach and be baptized by his loyal followers, thus entering into the brotherhood of those who followed Jesus. John already knew about it, and was far from being jealous. He had known that this must happen.

"A man can receive nothing unless it is given to him from heaven," he answered his disciples. "It is not given to me to have what Jesus has. You yourselves bear me witness that I said, 'I am not the Christ, but he who was sent before him.' He has what I have not, but so it was intended, and I myself rejoice therefore. My happiness is now fulfilled. For he shall grow greater and greater, and I shall grow less and less."

It was true indeed that John's work was nearly done. He still preached against Herod Antipas for marrying Herodias, onetime wife of Herod's brother Philip, and though Herod himself was not greatly troubled by the prophet's words his wife Herodias was steadily stoking the fire of her rage and hatred. Word went out from Galilee to Judea that John must be found at once and seized.

Jesus, in the meanwhile, had left Judea and was traveling through Samaria on his way back to his own homeland of Galilee. Jews and Samaritans traditionally hated each other, yet Jesus the Jew spoke to the Samaritans as he spoke to everyone, and they listened to him when he told them how to love and worship God their Father. By the time he left Samaria there were many Samaritans who believed that he was the Messiah, the Savior of the world.

And by that time, too, John had been seized and bound. While Jesus journeyed into Galilee, John was lying in prison after once more saying to Herod:

"It is not lawful for you to have your brother's wife!" This statement he had added to a list of Herod's other evils, and it made Herodias boil with rage.

"Kill him!" she had screamed.

But Herod would not have John killed. He knew that John was not only a righteous man but a man with many followers, and he was afraid to put the prophet to death because of what the multitude might do. It was enough, he thought, to keep the man quiet in his prison cell.

As it happened, his wife Herodias did not think it was enough. But she kept her counsel and bided her time.

JESUS IN GALILEE

*J*esus came again to Cana in Galilee where he had made the water into wine. The people of Galilee awaited him with high hopes, for his fame was beginning to spread. They had heard of the miracle of the wine, and the many wonderful signs he had shown while in Jerusalem for the passover, and they looked forward with eagerness to seeing his wonders for themselves.

Now there was a certain nobleman, one of King Herod's officers, who lived in Capernaum. When he heard that Jesus had arrived in Cana he left his home at once and journeyed with all possible haste to meet him and ask for help. The nobleman's small son was dangerously ill, and there was not a doctor in the land who could cure him of his raging fever. The little boy was growing hourly worse, and now it seemed that he would surely die.

The man traveled hard until at last he reached Cana. There he sought out Jesus, finding him by the crowds that always gathered around, and implored the Nazarene to come with him.

"I beg you to come down and heal my son," he said anxiously, "for the boy is at the point of death."

Jesus slowly shook his head. Many people came to him in the

hope of seeing some miracle that would prove his powers. Yet he had not come to earth to show that he was a magician; he had come to lead his people into the kingdom of God, and he wanted their belief without first having to show some miraculous sign. If this nobleman was like so many others, he would want to see the miracle before offering his belief. Therefore, Jesus hesitated.

"Except you see signs and wonders done," he said to the nobleman, "you will not believe."

"Sir, I pray you!" the nobleman insisted earnestly. "Come down with me, before my child is dead!"

Jesus searched the nobleman's face, and he saw that this man's need was real.

"Go your way," he said. "Your child will live."

The man believed him. He turned away at once, not questioning, not doubting, and started on his long journey back to Capernaum. He had not even reached the city when his servants came out along the road to meet him. There was great joy on their faces.

"Your son lives! He is well!" they cried out gladly.

"I knew he would be," the nobleman said quietly. "What time was it when he began to get better?"

"It was yesterday at the seventh hour that the fever left him," they answered.

At that same hour, as the father knew, Jesus had said to him: "Your son will live."

Later, when the nobleman had seen his child, he told his household what had happened. From that time onward, not only he but all his family and all the members of his household believed that Jesus had been sent by God.

It was the second miracle that Jesus did in Galilee, and it was even more wonderful than the first. This man, who spoke so gently and with such inspired wisdom, was not only a powerful preacher, a worker of miraculous signs, but a healer as well.

Jesus traveled on through Galilee, talking to people at the wayside and teaching in the synagogues on the sabbath days. He came at last to Nazareth, where he had been brought up, and went into the synagogue on the sabbath day according to his custom. The people of his town had heard much about what he had said and done in other places, and now they wanted to see what he would do in Nazareth. The synagogue was crowded with the curious and devout, and there was silence as he stood up and opened the book written by the prophet Isaiah hundreds of years before. He found the place he sought, and read:

"'The Spirit of the Lord is upon me,
Because he has anointed me to preach the gospel to the poor;
He has sent me to heal the broken-hearted,
To preach deliverance to the captives,
And recovery of sight to the blind,
To set at liberty those that are bruised,
And to preach the chosen year of the Lord.'"

He closed the book and gave it back to the attendant, and then sat down to explain the meaning of the passage whose words they already knew so well. They knew that it referred to the Messiah. But they did not know when this Messiah was to come or what he would be like, although they did expect him to be a conquering king. All eyes were fastened on him; all his friends and neighbors waited with quickening interest for what Jesus had to say. They knew he was a healer, they had heard of his wisdom, but they still thought of him as a man very little different from themselves.

His next words astonished them.

He said: "Today has this scripture been fulfilled in your ears."

At first they did not realize what he meant. But then they stirred and whispered to each other, wondering at his words. For he had said that he was the one of whom the prophet had written, that *he* was the Son of God!

"Is this not Joseph's son?" they asked each other. "Is not his mother called Mary? Who is he that he should say these things?"

They looked at him resentfully. He was a healer and a teacher, yes, and perhaps a prophet; but still he was only their neighbor, only the son of a carpenter, only a man born on earth like all the rest of them. Now he was suggesting that he was the Messiah, the King and Savior of the Jews! Where was all the power and splendor that everyone expected of a divine King?

Jesus knew that they did not believe him, that they would expect him to perform some miraculous feat before their very eyes to prove his words. But that was not the nature of his teaching. Only those who had faith and accepted Jesus could receive his blessings. Even the Roman nobleman had understood that; but the Jews of Nazareth did not.

So Jesus said to them: "You will surely say to me, 'Physician, heal your own. What we have heard you to have done in Capernaum, do also in your own country.' But I say to you, no prophet is accepted in his own country or by his own people. There were many widows in Israel in the days of Elijah, when the heavens were shut for three years and six months so that no rain fell and there was famine in the land. But they did not believe in him; to none of them was he sent by the Lord. No, he was sent to a city of Sidon, to a Phoenician woman who was a widow. She cared for him, believed in him; and God cared for her through Elijah. And there were many lepers in Israel at the time of Elisha the prophet. None of them were cleansed, for they did not believe. But Naaman the Syrian was cured of his leprosy, for he believed and sought Elisha's help. And, like the people of Israel in those days, *you* do not believe!"

All the people in the synagogue were filled with wrath when they heard him say these things. Their admiration turned to sudden hatred and they rose up, shouting with rage. To this sort of teaching, to these words from a fellow Nazarene of all people, they surely would not listen! They laid rough hands on him and thrust him out of the synagogue and out of the city of Nazareth. Then they led him to the top of the craggy hill upon which the city was built so that they might cast him headlong over the side of it. Somehow he escaped them. They did not even notice until they were on the hilltop and ready to throw him down onto the rocks below that he had passed quietly through their midst and gone along his way.

Jesus went back to Capernaum and made his home there among friends. His followers went about their daily work while Jesus taught in the synagogues on sabbath days and preached the gospel of the kingdom of God to the people who lived near the shores of the inland sea of Galilee.

"Repent!" he would say. "The time is fulfilled, and the kingdom of God is at hand. Repent, and believe in the gospel!"

Then word came to him of John the Baptist's imprisonment, and he knew that it was time to make even greater efforts to bring salvation to his people. There were so many still to reach that he could no longer work alone. He had many followers who called themselves disciples because they had elected to believe in his teachings, but Jesus himself had not yet selected those among them who were worthy to spread his word abroad. The time to choose them, however, was drawing very near.

One morning, as he taught beside the sea of Galilee, the people pressing on him from every side to hear his words and to receive his healing touch, he saw two fishing boats drawn up on the shore. The fishermen worked nearby, washing their nets after a long night's work.

Jesus went on teaching, and the crowd grew even greater. Soon it became difficult for him to see any of them but those who pressed against him, and impossible for him to reach the ears and hearts of all. He made his way to one of the nearby boats, which was Simon Peter's, and stepped aboard.

"Put me out a little way from the shore," he asked his friend, and Simon Peter did so. When the boat stopped in the shallow water just offshore Jesus sat down and taught the people from it. When he had finished speaking he turned again to Simon.

"Put me out into the deep water," he said, "and let your nets down for a catch."

Now it was full daylight at the time, and not an hour at which the fishermen of Galilee were used to putting out to sea. Jesus knew as well as any man that the time for fishing was at night.

"Master," Simon answered, "we have toiled all night and have taken nothing." Jesus knew this; he had seen the empty nets they had brought in from the sea. "But," Simon Peter added as he looked at Jesus, "at your word I will let down the nets." He called to his brother Andrew to bring the nets, which were still drying in the sun, and the two brothers rowed out into deeper waters as Jesus had instructed them.

When they were some distance out they stopped and let down the nets. And in a matter of minutes the nets were filled with darting, glittering fish, a catch such as Simon had never seen in all his years of fishing. There seemed no end to the shining shapes that flashed around the boat. Simon and Andrew began to haul in with all their strength. But so great was the shoal and so heavy was the precious catch that the thick strands of their nets began to part. They shouted for their partners John and James, who were working in the other boat beached upon the shore, for they needed help with the tremendous haul. The two men came out at once and lent their willing hands to pulling in the sagging, tearing nets, and when at last they had brought the catch aboard both boats were filled so full that they began to sink.

When Simon Peter saw what was happening he fell down at Jesus' feet in the overloaded boat and cried out: "Leave me, O Lord, for I am a sinful man!" It had been almost too much for him; he was astonished at the great haul of fishes they had taken, and so were all the other men who had fished all night and caught not one.

"Do not be afraid," said Jesus. "From now on, you will catch men instead of fish."

They landed their boats safely and unloaded their huge catch.

And the next day when Jesus walked by the sea of Galilee and saw Simon Peter and his brother Andrew casting their nets into the sea, he said to them: "Come, follow me, and I will make you fishers of men."

They left their nets at once and followed him.

When they had gone a little further along the shore Jesus saw James and John in their boat with their father Zebedee, mending their nets. And Jesus called to James and John. "Come, follow me," he said.

And at once the brothers left their boat with their father Zebedee and his servants, and they followed Jesus.

Thus did Jesus choose the first four of his disciples. With them he went all about the land of Galilee, teaching in the synagogues and preaching the gospel of God's kingdom.

THE MIRACLES OF JESUS

*J*esus and his four disciples went together to Capernaum, and there Jesus entered into the synagogue and taught the people on the sabbath day. They were astonished at his teachings, for his words were full of power and he spoke as one who had authority from God, and not as the scribes, who did little more than repeat what they had read.

Now there was in the synagogue a man who was possessed by an unclean spirit, a demon that made him cry out in a loud voice:

"Let us alone! What have we to do with you, Jesus of Nazareth? Have you come to destroy us? I know who you are— the Holy One of God!"

Jesus rebuked the demon in the man. "Be silent; hold your peace," he said. "Come out of him."

The spirit made the man shake violently and fall down upon the floor. There was a loud cry, and then silence. The man got up, unhurt in his body and peaceful in his mind. The unclean spirit had left him.

The people who saw this were understandably amazed. They talked among themselves. "What thing is this?" they asked each other. "What new teaching can this be? See with what authority and power he gives commands to unclean spirits, and they do obey him!"

And immediately the fame of Jesus spread throughout all the region round about.

When Jesus left the synagogue that day he went into the house of Simon and Andrew, together with the brothers James and John. And Simon found that his wife's mother was lying ill, burning with a fever. Jesus went in at once to see her. He stood beside her bed, took her by the hand, and gently raised her up. Immediately the fever left her, and she arose from her bed. At once she went about her household in good spirits and good health, and within minutes she was preparing a meal for Simon Peter and his guests.

That evening, as the sun was setting on the sabbath day, the people of the neighborhood brought to Jesus all the sick folk among their friends and families and all those who were possessed by demonic spirits. It seemed as though the whole town had gathered at the door of Simon Peter's house: the diseased, the lame, the blind, and the troubled in spirit. Jesus laid his hands on every one of them, and healed all who were sick.

It was late before the throng of people left the house of Simon and Jesus was at last able to lie down and sleep. And yet it was very early in the morning when he rose and walked alone into the desert until he found a solitary place where he could stop and pray. It was peaceful for a time, but even here the people sought him out and eventually found him. Simon and his companions reached Jesus first.

"Everyone is seeking you," they said to him. "They want you to stay with them, but they are afraid that you will leave this place."

"They are right," said Jesus. "I must leave here. Come with me; let us go into the next towns so that I may preach in them as well, for I have been sent to proclaim the good tidings of the kingdom of God in other cities, too."

They left Capernaum then, and went together throughout all Galilee. Jesus preached in synagogues and cast out many demons

that were troubling people's souls; and the report of him went out
as far as Syria. He healed the epileptic and the palsied, the
diseased and the tormented; and great multitudes followed him
from Galilee and Decapolis and Jerusalem and Judea and from
beyond the Jordan.

While he was in a certain town a leper came to him and knelt
before him, worshiping. No man would touch a leper, and the sick
man knew it, for he had spent his life seeing people turn away
when he came near. Yet he knelt at Jesus' feet and begged for
help, and Jesus did not turn away.

"If you will," the leper said, "you can make me clean."

And Jesus, moved with compassion, stretched forth his hand
and touched him. "I will," he said. "Be healed."

As soon as he had spoken, the leprosy left the man and he was
clean.

Then Jesus said to him: "See that you say nothing of this to any
man. Go your way, show yourself to the priest, and make such offerings for your cleansing as Moses commanded so that the priest
will pronounce you clean of leprosy. But do not speak of me to
anyone."

The leper gave his thanks and went away. But instead of
obeying Jesus' request to be silent about his cure he went around
talking about the wonderful thing that had happened to him,
spreading his news abroad so widely that great multitudes flocked
to the town to listen to Jesus and be healed of their infirmities. So
huge were the crowds that Jesus could no longer enter the city
openly. Instead, he stayed outside in a desert place, hoping to use
it as a base from which he could move about freely. But even
there, people came to him from every quarter so that it was almost impossible for him to leave the place and go about his mission.

Several days later he managed to get back to Capernaum. It
was not long before the people of the city found out that he was
at home (for since his rejection at Nazareth he had made his home
in Capernaum), and they immediately gathered at his house to

hear his words and receive his healing touch. The friendly and the curious, the needy and the sick, all crowded in and filled the house. Even Pharisees, and scribes or doctors of the law, had come from every town of Galilee and Judea to listen to this man. In a very short time the place was so full that there was not an inch of space to spare, not even at the open door. And Jesus preached the word of God to them in that overcrowded room.

Now there was a man who was so ill and crippled with the palsy that he could not drag himself about in search of Jesus nor go up to him when he had found him. And when he did discover through friends where Jesus was, it seemed that there was no way to force the crowds to part and let him into the house. But he had four friends who were as sure as he that Jesus would be able to cure him, and they were determined that he should be healed. They carried him on his pallet to the house where Jesus was.

By now even the street outside the house was so packed with people that they almost despaired. The four friends looked about to find some other means of bringing the palsied man to Jesus, and at last they thought of a way. Carrying the sick man on the cot with the utmost care, they climbed onto the housetop and broke open a section of the roof. Then, slowly and carefully, they lowered their friend through the tiling and set him down, bed and all, in the midst of the throng pressing around Jesus.

Jesus looked down at the man, and up at the four friends on the roof. And seeing their faith, he said to the one who was sick of the palsy:

"Son, be of good cheer. Your sins are forgiven."

The sick man's heart was lightened. But certain of the scribes and Pharisees who were sitting there were thinking harsh things within themselves. In their hearts they questioned Jesus' right to say such words to any man. To them, those words were blasphemy. "Who is he, that he should speak such blasphemies?" they asked themselves. "Why does he say these things? Who can forgive sins but God alone?" Thus did they reason in their hearts, and they doubted Jesus, for they did not want to believe that

Jesus had been sent by God and that he, too, had the power of forgiveness. No, they would rather believe that he was an ordinary man speaking impiously of God.

Jesus could see what they were thinking. He answered their unspoken words at once. "Why do you think evil of me in your hearts?" he asked. "And what is it that you are reasoning within yourselves—whether it is easier to say to the man sick with the palsy, 'Your sins are forgiven,' or, 'Arise, take up your bed and walk'? Yes, it is easy indeed to pretend power, to talk rather than do. But do you think that forgiveness cannot be demonstrated? I will show you now that the Son of man does have authority on earth to forgive sins."

He turned to the palsied man, still lying ill and paralyzed on his pallet in the midst of the gaping crowd, and he said: "I say to you: Arise, take up your bed and go to your own house."

Immediately the man arose, took up his bed, and pushed his way through the crowd. He headed for his own house, praising God and talking excitedly to his four loyal friends, and all who saw him were amazed. They marveled, they feared, they glorified the God of Jesus; and they said: "We have seen strange things today."

Stranger things were yet to come.

Jesus went forth again by the seaside. The multitude followed him as usual, and he taught them as he walked. One day as he passed by, he saw a publican named Levi, also known as Matthew, sitting at the toll house where the tax money was collected. Matthew was hated by the Jews because he was a tax collector for the Romans. It did not occur to them that he might not be a sinner, for they had suffered from the dishonesty and greed of tax collectors through many years of Roman rule.

And to this man Matthew, hated tax collector, Jesus spoke two words:

"Follow me."

Matthew arose and followed him.

Some time afterward Matthew made a feast for Jesus in his

house, to which he invited a great company of fellow publicans and other people whom the self-righteous Pharisees regarded as unfit companions for all right-thinking Jews. When the Pharisees saw that Jesus and his disciples sat at meat with Matthew and the others, they murmured against Jesus and his friends.

"Why do you and your Master sit down with tax collectors and sinners?" they asked the disciples.

When Jesus heard the murmurings of the Pharisees he went to them and said: "Those who are well have no need of a physician, only those who are sick. And those who are without sin have no need of me. I did not come to call the righteous, but sinners to repentance."

Matthew, the tax collector, did not think he was so righteous that he had no need to repent. He knew that he had sinned, and he was humble. But the Pharisees could see no flaws in themselves, and they were proud. Thus they could not see that their need to repent was even greater than that of the self-admitted sinner Matthew.

For some time they were satisfied with Jesus' reply. Then they thought of something else to complain about. They went to Jesus and said: "Why do the disciples of John fast often and make prayers, and also the disciples of the Pharisees, while your disciples do not fast and seem always to be eating and drinking?"

"Can you expect the wedding guests to fast and mourn while the bridegroom is with them?" Jesus asked in return. "As long as they have the bridegroom with them, they cannot and should not fast. But the day will come when the bridegroom shall be taken away from them, and then will they fast."

The Pharisees did not know quite what to make of this, and they went away to think of further cause for complaint against Jesus and his followers. But what Jesus had meant was that he himself would one day be taken from his disciples, and then indeed would they pray and fast.

It was not altogether true that the disciples of Jesus were always eating and drinking, in spite of what the Pharisees had said, for they were simple men of scanty means and in their travels with Jesus through the countryside they often went hungry. Tax collectors did not often invite them home to dine, nor were there inns in the desert places where they often taught.

On a certain day it happened that their way led through some grainfields. The disciples had not eaten for some time. So they began, as they went through the tall grain, to pluck the ripe ears, rub off the chaff, and eat. The watching Pharisees, always with them, again had comments to offer.

"Behold!" they said to Jesus. "Why do your followers do on the sabbath day that which is not lawful to do?" For they regarded this simple action of the disciples as a crime, that of working on the sabbath day.

To Jesus, what the Pharisees had done to the day of rest was little short of ridiculous. Under their teachings the sabbath had become so enmeshed in a web of law and ritual that it was a day of torment rather than rest. But he answered patiently and with quiet logic.

"Have you never read in the scriptures what David did when he had need, and was hungry, as were those who were with him? How he went into the house of God in the days of Abiathar the high priest, and ate the sacred bread which is only lawful for the priests to eat, and also gave it to those who were with him? Or do you not realize that even the priests in the temple work on the sabbath, offering sacrifices in the morning and the evening? Yet you hold them guiltless, even though they work! And this I say to you: something greater than the temple is here, and something greater than the sabbath. The Lord desires mercy, and not sacrifice. If you would only understand! The sabbath was made for man, and not man for the sabbath. And the Son of man is Lord even of the sabbath."

That, indeed, was something that they did not understand. As the Lord on earth, Jesus was Lord of the sabbath as well as everything else. But this was beyond their understanding and always would be. To them, Jesus of Nazareth was only a man.

Jesus and his disciples made their way back to the city and went again into the synagogue. There was a man there who had a withered hand. The scribes and the Pharisees watched eagerly to see whether Jesus would heal the man on the sabbath day, so that they might once again accuse him.

And again Jesus knew their thoughts. He said to the man with the withered hand: "Rise up; stand forth in their midst." The man stood up and faced Jesus before all the silent watchers.

According to the Pharisees, even healing was work, and not the sort of work that Jesus could justify by quoting from the scriptures or pointing to the priests. And so they waited to see what Jesus would do on this sabbath day with the man whose hand was withered.

"I will ask you one thing," Jesus said to them. "Is it lawful to do good on the sabbath days, or to do evil? Is it good to save life, or to kill?"

They were silent, waiting. They could not answer him.

Jesus went on: "What man is there among you, that shall have one sheep which falls into a pit on the sabbath day, who would not lift it out? And of how much more value is a man than a sheep! Therefore, it is lawful to do good on the sabbath days. Stretch out your hand!"

Jesus looked around the hall, his heart grieving at the hardness of the Pharisees' hearts. But the man, believing, stretched out his hand. And in that moment it was restored to health and was as whole as the hand that had not been withered.

The Pharisees were filled with fury. They left the synagogue together to take counsel with each other, and with certain of the lords of Herod's court, as to how they might curb this dangerous lawbreaker. The best idea seemed to be to destroy him. But that seemed a little harsh. As for Jesus, he left the city before they had made up their minds, and withdrew with his disciples to the shores of Galilee.

Some time after these events there was a feast of the Jews, and Jesus went up to Jerusalem to celebrate it. Now there was at this time in Jerusalem, as in the days of old, a pool named Bethesda near the Sheep Gate. Around it, as Jesus saw, there lay a multitude of sick folk: blind, lame, diseased, and withered of limb; and all were waiting for the moving of the water. It was said among them that an angel of the Lord went down into the pool at certain times and stirred the waters, and that the first one who stepped into the waters after they had been troubled would be cured of whatever disease he had. So they waited, each one hoping and praying that he would be the first to move at the stirring of the waters by the angel.

There were some among them who could barely move, so that their chances of reaching the pool before the others were very slight. Thus there was a certain man lying beside the pool who had been ill for thirty-eight years. Each year he struggled to the pool to see the moving of the waters, and each year he failed to reach the water in time. There were always others before him.

When Jesus saw him lying there and knew that he had been in that condition for many years, he approached the man and said: "Do you wish to be made well?"

The sick man answered him: "Sir, I do, but I have no one to help me into the pool when the waters are stirred. Always, while I am on my way, another steps down into the pool before me."

"Rise, take up your bed and walk," Jesus said to him. And even as he spoke, the man was cured. He arose, took up his bed and walked away with gratitude in his heart.

Now it was the sabbath on that day, and those who saw him carrying his pallet stopped him and said: "It is the sabbath. It is not lawful for you to be carrying your bed."

The cured man, well and happy for the first time in thirty-eight years, looked at them and said: "He that made me whole again said to me, 'Take up your bed and walk.' And I did so."

The scribes and Pharisees among the Jews soon found out who had told the man to do this thing, and their outrage knew no bounds. Again, Jesus had healed upon the sabbath day, and this time he had even told a man to carry his own bed—to *work* upon the day proclaimed by God as the day of rest!

They taxed Jesus with this dreadful thing that he had done. He calmly answered, "My Father is still working, even on the sabbath, and I am working, too."

From that day on the Pharisees began to persecute Jesus without mercy. He had not only broken their Law by doing these things upon the sabbath day; but he had also claimed that God was his own Father, making himself equal with God.

They resolved, therefore, to kill him when they could find their chance.

THE SERMON ON THE MOUNT

There were those who followed the letter of the Law, and those who followed the spirit of it as expressed by Jesus.

When Jesus went again to the shores of Galilee, people flocked after him from Jerusalem and all the land of Judea; they came to him from the countryside and towns of Galilee, and from beyond the river Jordan. They heard of him in Tyre, and in Sidon, and in Syria, and they came to see him with their sick and their diseased and all those who were possessed by devils that tormented their souls.

Jesus cured them in their dozens and their scores and in their hundreds. He healed the palsied and the epileptic; he drove off pain and demons and even death itself. It became impossible for him to reach all those who came to him. A time came when he had to ask his disciples to have a boat always waiting for him just offshore so that he could preach from there in case the crowd pressed so heavily upon him that he could not teach or heal. By now his fame was very great, and he had healed so many people that countless numbers came to crowd upon him so that he might touch and cure them.

At last it became obvious that he could not do his work without others to help him not only with his preaching but his healing. Many men had followed him and were following him still, men who called themselves disciples because they believed in him and loved him, but of them all he had only chosen four to do his work. He knew, now, that he would have to make a further choice. One night, therefore, he went alone up into a mountain to pray; and he passed the entire night in prayer to God his Father.

When it was day he called all of his disciples to him and named the twelve whom he had chosen to be his apostles. These men were to be with him when they could help by being near at hand, and to be sent out at other times to preach in the many places he would not be able to reach if he worked alone. When they came to him he gave to them the power to heal all manner of sickness and disease, and the authority to cast out unclean spirits or demons.

Now the names of the apostles he chose are these: Simon, to whom he had given the name of Peter; Andrew, Simon Peter's brother; James and John, the sons of Zebedee; Philip, and his friend Bartholomew who was also called Nathanael; Thomas; and Matthew, who had been a publican; another James, the son of Alphaeus; another Simon, who was a Canaanite; Judas, also called Thaddaeus, who was the brother of the second James; and Judas Iscariot, who became a traitor.

When Jesus came down the mountain with the chosen twelve he once again saw crowds of people waiting for him. Goodness flowed out of him as the people pressed around and touched him, and he healed all those who were diseased and troubled with unclean spirits. But, seeing the great multitude and knowing that he would see many more like it in the months to come, he decided that he would wait no longer to teach his disciples all he could. He went up into the mountain again with his chosen twelve. There he seated himself. He began to speak, and even as he spoke the crowds came up to listen. But they did not distrub him as he taught the twelve.

"Know this," he said, "and remember always:

"Blessed are the poor in spirit, those who feel their spiritual need, for the kingdom of heaven belongs to them.

"Blessed are those who mourn, for they shall be comforted.

"Blessed are the humble, for they shall inherit the earth.

"Blessed are those who hunger and thirst for righteousness, for they shall be filled.

"Blessed are the merciful, for they shall obtain mercy.

"Blessed are the pure in heart, for they shall see God.

"Blessed are the peacemakers, for they shall be called the children of God.

"Blessed are those who are persecuted because of their righteousness, for theirs is the kingdom of heaven.

"Blessed are you when men shall abuse you, and persecute you, and say all manner of evil against you falsely, for my sake;

"Rejoice, and be exceedingly glad, for great is your reward in heaven; for so persecuted were the prophets who were before you."

For once the great crowd listened in absolute silence as Jesus went on speaking to his twelve disciples and explaining to them what manner of men he wanted them to be, for their own sakes and his.

"You are the salt of the earth," he said. "But if the salt has lost its flavor, how can it be made salty again? It is then fit for nothing but to be thrown away and trodden underfoot.

"You are the light of the world. A city that is built upon a hill cannot be hidden. Men do not light a candle and then hide it; they put it on a candlestick so that it gives light to everyone in the house. Therefore let your light so shine before men that they may see your good works, and glorify your Father who is in heaven.

"Do not think that I have come to destroy the law or the prophets; I have not come to destroy, but to fulfill. For whoever shall break the least of the commandments and teaches other men to do so, shall be called least in the kingdom of heaven. But whoever shall do them and teach them shall be called great in the kingdom of heaven. I say to you that unless your uprightness exceeds that of the scribes and the Pharisees, you will never enter the kingdom of heaven.

"You have heard that it was said to men in days of old that he who was harmed should exact equal harm in return. 'An eye for an eye, and a tooth for a tooth'; so it was said. But these are not the days of old. I say to you now, do not resist injury, and do not injure in return. If anyone strikes you on your right cheek, turn the other to him also. And if anyone wants to sue you in a court of law and take away your coat, give him your cloak as well. And if anyone compels you to go one mile, go two miles with him. Give to him that asks your help; and if anyone wishes to borrow from you, do not turn away. As you would have men treat you, so should you treat them.

"You have heard that it was said: 'You shall love your neighbor, and hate your enemy.' But I say to you: Love your enemies, and pray for those who persecute you. Then shall you truly be sons of your Father who is in heaven, for he makes his sun rise on the evil as well as the good, and he sends rain to the just and the unjust alike, and he is kind to the unthankful and the evil even as he is kind to the grateful and upright. Be you therefore merciful, even as your Father is merciful.

"For if you only love those who love you, why should you expect reward? Do not even the tax collectors do the same? And if you do good only to those who do good to you, why expect a reward? Even sinners do the same. And if you lend to those from whom you hope to receive, why think that you deserve thanks? Even the sinners lend to sinners, to receive as much again.

"I say to you, it is your enemies that you should love! Bless those who curse you; do good to those who hate you; pray for those who use you badly; and lend to those who need, hoping for nothing in return. Then shall your reward be great!

"Be therefore perfect, as your heavenly Father is perfect.

"And take care that you do not do your good deeds in public in order to be seen by others. If you do, you will get no reward from your Father in heaven. When, therefore, you give to charity, do not blow a trumpet before you as do the hypocrites in the synagogues and in the streets, so that they may be seen and praised. I say to you, the praise of man is all they will get! Instead, when you give alms, do not let your own left hand know what your right hand is doing, so that your charity may be secret. Your Father who sees what you do in secret will reward you openly.

"And when you fast, do not—as the hypocrites do—put on a gloomy look, for they disfigure their faces and make themselves look sad so that all men shall know that they are fasting. That, I say to you, is all the reward they will get. But you, when you fast, anoint your head with perfumes and wash your face, so that no one may know that you are fasting except your Father who is unseen. And your Father, who sees that which is done in secret, will reward you openly.

"And when you pray, do not be like the hypocrites, who love to pray standing in the synagogues and on the corners of the streets so that they may be seen at prayer. I say to you, the praise of men shall be their only reward. But you, when you pray, go into a quiet room, and when you have shut the door, pray to your Father who is unseen. And your Father who sees what you do in secret will reward you openly.

"And in praying, do not use idle repetitions and many empty phrases such as others do, for they imagine they shall be heard if they use many words. Do not be like them, for your Father knows what you have need of before you ask him. Pray, therefore, in this manner:

"Our Father, which art in heaven,
Hallowed be thy name.
Thy kingdom come;
Thy will be done
On earth, as it is in heaven.
Give us this day our daily bread,

> And forgive us our debts,
> As we forgive our debtors.
> And lead us not into temptation,
> But deliver us from evil:
> For thine is the kingdom,
> And the power,
> And the glory,
> For ever! Amen."

There was silence in the multitude. But they wondered at many of the things he said.

"If you forgive others when they do wrong," Jesus went on, "your heavenly Father will forgive you, too. But if you do not forgive others for their wrongs, neither will your Father forgive you for yours."

"And do not store up earthly treasures for yourselves, instead of the riches of the spirit. Rather seek out the kingdom of God, and all other things you need shall be given to you. I say to you, do not concern yourselves about the things of your daily life: what you shall eat, what you shall drink, what you shall wear. Is not life something more than food, and the body of more worth than clothes? Behold the birds of the air! They do not sow, neither do they reap, nor gather their food into barns. Yet your heavenly Father feeds them. And are you not of much more value than they?

"Which of you, by worrying about these things, can add one inch to his height or one minute to his life? And why should you be anxious concerning clothing? Consider the lilies of the field, how they grow; they toil not, neither do they spin. Yet even Solomon, in all his glory, was not arrayed like one of these. And if God so clothes the wild grass of the field, which grows today and is cast into the furnace tomorrow, shall he not more surely clothe you, O ye of little faith?

"Therefore do not be anxious, saying: 'What shall we eat?' or 'What shall we drink?' or 'How shall we be clothed?' For your heavenly Father knows that you have need of all these things.

Seek first the kingdom of God, and his righteousness, and all these things will be freely given you. Be not therefore anxious for the morrow, for the morrow will be anxious for itself. The evils of today are enough for the day.

"Ask, and it shall be given you. Seek, and you shall find. Knock, and the door will open to you. For he who asks of God shall receive; he who searches shall find; and to him who knocks the door shall be opened. And, as you would have other men do to you, do you also to them likewise.

"Each tree is known by its own fruit. No good tree brings forth bad fruit; no bad tree brings forth good fruit. Therefore, by the fruits of men, you shall know them."

Jesus said all these things and many more upon the Mount that day. And at last he said:

"Not everyone who says to me, 'Lord! Lord!' shall enter into the kingdom of heaven, but only those who listen to my words and do the will of my Father in heaven. I say to you now, you must be ready for the day when you are called to God. I will show you what the man is like who comes to me, hears my words, and acts according to them: He is like a man who, in building his house, dug down deep and laid the foundation upon a rock. When the rain fell, the floods came, and the storm winds blew and beat upon that house, it stood firm and did not fall because it was founded upon the rock. But everyone who hears these words of mine and does not act upon them shall be like a foolish man who built his house upon the sand. When the rain fell, the floods came, and the storm winds beat against it, the house upon the sand broke into pieces. Great was the fall thereof!

"But if you build your lives according to my words, you will be building on a rock foundation."

When Jesus had finished speaking the people were astonished at his words. For he taught them as one who had authority, and not as the scribes who quoted the old laws to them and never once said such strange things as: "Love your enemies. Bless those who curse you. Do good to those who hate you. Turn the other cheek."

These ideas were new to them. They did not sound at all like the preachings of the Pharisees. But to the thoughtful ones in the multitude the sayings of Jesus truly sounded as though they were the words of a merciful and loving God.

JESUS AND JOHN THE BAPTIST

$\mathcal{A}$fter he had ended all his sayings on the mountain, Jesus entered into the city of Capernaum. Now a certain centurion was there, a Roman captain over a hundred soldiers, who had a faithful bondservant of whom he was exceedingly fond. He was little more than a youth, this servant, but he lay ill with palsy to the point of death.

When the centurion heard of Jesus and discovered that he was in Capernaum even now he went to some of the elders of the Jews and asked them for their help. He was hesitant to approach the healer himself, for he was a humble man even though a captain of men.

"My servant lies at home, sick of the palsy and grievously tormented," the centurion told the elders. "I beg you, go to the healer Jesus and beseech him to come and save my servant."

The elders went at once to seek out Jesus, and earnestly requested him to go with them and heal the centurion's young servant. "This Roman is a worthy man," they said. "He is deserving of help, for he loves our nation and has himself built us our synagogue."

Jesus turned and went with them. When he was not very far from the house, the centurion sent friends out to him with a message. "Lord, do not trouble yourself," his message said, "for I am not worthy that you should enter under my roof. Neither did I think myself worthy to come to you. But only say the word, and my servant shall be healed."

When Jesus heard these words he marveled greatly. He turned to those who had followed him to the house and said, "I say to you, I have not found such faith in all of Israel—no, not among the Jews—as this Roman has shown!" And to the centurion's friends he said, "Go your way. As the man has believed, so shall it be done."

And when those who had been sent to speak to Jesus went back into the house, they found the servant cured of his sickness.

On the day after that, Jesus went into another city called Nain. Many of his disciples and other people followed him. When he came near to the gate of the city, Jesus and his disciples saw a funeral procession winding slowly toward them, and in the midst of it was the dead man being carried from the city in his coffin. The man was young, too young to have to die, and he was the only son of his mother who was a widow. The woman wept and mourned, and there were many people of the city with her as she walked along in sorrow.

The two groups met at the gate of Nain, the mourners with the bier and Jesus with his followers. Jesus looked at the woman. Her tears were bitter, for all she loved had been taken from her, and she mourned with all the sorrow of her heart. When Jesus saw her grief he felt a deep compassion for her. "Do not weep," he said to her. Jesus went up and touched the bier. The bearers stopped and stood still with their burden while this gentle stranger looked down at the dead face.

"Young man, I say to you, arise!" he said.

And the young man who had been dead sat up and began to speak. The widow woman ran to her son with tears upon her cheeks that now were tears of joy, for Jesus had given her back her only child. The cries of sorrow from those in the procession turned to cries of amazement and fear. Those who had seen what

Jesus had done praised God and glorified him, saying, "A great prophet has appeared among us! God has visited his people."

And this rumor about Jesus spread throughout all the region round about, which was southern Galilee, and throughout all Judea.

Jesus continued with his work in that part of Galilee, preaching his message of salvation and healing the sick, until word of his wonders reached the disciples of John. They went to him and told him all these things. Now John was still in Herod's prison, but the king on occasion permitted him to be visited by his friends. When the Baptist heard in prison about the works of Jesus he could not keep from thinking about his own plight. If it was indeed true that Jesus could do the marvelous things that were rumored of him, why did he not use his powers to free John? And although Jesus had referred to himself as the Son of man and the Son of God, he had never said directly that he was the Christ. Was he, or was he not, the long-awaited Messiah and King of the Jews?

Alone in prison, John's faith wavered. He had been the first to acknowledge Jesus as the Anointed One. But now he felt within himself a small doubt.

John thought long about these things. And at last he sent for two of his disciples. "Go to Jesus," he said to them. "Ask him this: 'Are you he that is promised, or do we look for another?'"

They went at once to Jesus with the questions John had instructed them to ask. Jesus understood at once that John had need of reassurance, yet he could not announce himself directly as the Messiah, for then not only the priests and Pharisees but Herod himself would have reason to condemn him. And for the same reason, he could not use his powers to free John. He still had work to do and little enough time in which to do it. Nevertheless, he must send a message to John that would convince him that the Messiah had indeed come.

While John's disciples watched, Jesus cured many people of their illnesses, and many of evil spirits; and to many that were blind he gave their sight. John's disciples saw lepers becoming clean, and saw cripples walk away, and they heard the gentle words that Jesus spoke. Eventually Jesus turned again to them.

"Go and tell John what you have seen and heard," he said. "Tell him how the blind receive their sight, how the lame walk and the lepers are cleansed, how the deaf hear and the dead are raised; and how the poor are being preached the good tidings of the kingdom of God."

Jesus knew that John would understand from these things that he truly was the Messiah, for they both knew the words of Isaiah concerning the One who was to come:

"Say to them that are of a fearful heart:
Be strong, fear not;
Behold, your God will come with vengeance,
God himself with a just reward;
He will come and save you.
Then the eyes of the blind shall be opened,
And the ears of the deaf shall be unstopped.
Then shall the lame man leap as a hart,
And the tongue of the dumb sing;
For in the wilderness shall waters break out,
And streams in the desert."

By these words would John be answered. Jesus sorrowed for his plight, but there was nothing he could do except send him that message. And Jesus knew that John had more need for reassurance about the Messiah than he had desire to be helped by miracles himself. "Say this also to him," Jesus said to John's disciples. "Say: 'Blessed is he who never doubts me.'"

The two men went back to John with a report of Jesus' works among the people and the things that he had said.

When they had gone, Jesus began to speak to the crowds about the prophet John. "When you went out into the wilderness to hear the words of John," he began, "what did you go to see? A reed swaying in the wind? No, that was not what you wanted to

see. And did you think you would see a man clothed in soft
raiment? No, for those who are luxuriously dressed live in the
houses of kings. Then what did you go out to see? A prophet?
Yes! You saw a prophet, and much more than a prophet. This is
the man of whom it is written:

"Behold, I send my messenger before your face,
Who shall prepare the way before you!"

"John is that man, and I say to you that among those born of
women, there is not a greater prophet than John the Baptist. Yet,
great though John is, he who is least in the kingdom of heaven is
greater than he. Those who listened and were baptized were ab-
solved of sin in the eyes of God. But the Pharisees and the scribes,
being not baptized, rejected for themselves the counsel of God.
Therefore I say, whoever has ears to hear, let him hear. Believe,
and act accordingly."

John the Baptist heard the news of Jesus' healing works, and
also of the tribute paid to him by the man he now believed un-
questioningly to be the Messiah. And this message was the last
one brought to him about the powers and sayings of Jesus.

King Herod's wife, Herodias, still nursed her hatred for the
imprisoned prophet. She would have had him killed the moment
he was seized, but Herod had denied her every plea. For Herod
feared John, knowing that he was a just and holy man, and he had
refused to harm him. Indeed, he spoke kindly to the prophet and
listened to his words. In the course of John's imprisonment he had
spoken often to him, learning much; and of late he had even
showed some signs of changing his evil ways.

But Herodias was still looking for revenge. Now she saw her
chance through her daughter, a dancer of much grace and skill,
who had been born to her when she had been Philip's wife. For
Herod, on his birthday, gave a banquet for his courtiers, high captains, and the leading men of Galilee, and this lovely daughter
came in at her mother's request and danced before the king and

his illustrious guests. All were delighted by her sinuous dance. When it was over the king, mellowed with wine, called to the girl and said: "Ask of me what you will, and I will give it to you. You have my oath upon it! Whatever you ask I will give, up to half my kingdom."

The girl had need of nothing for herself, but she knew her mother had a request to make. Therefore she left the banquet room and went to see her mother, who had chosen to wait discreetly in the background.

"What shall I ask for?" the girl said to her waiting mother.

The evil woman made no attempt to conceal her eagerness.

"The head of John the Baptist!" she replied triumphantly.

The girl went back to Herod. "My wish is that you will forthwith give me the head of John the Baptist on a platter!"

Herod was shocked into sudden sobriety. He had made a foolish oath before all the people of the crowded banquet hall, and the consequences of it were upon him. His heart was sorely troubled and he was exceedingly sorry for the rash promise he had made, for he still had no wish to kill the earnest Baptist from whom he had begun to learn so much. But because of his oath, and the guests who sat there watching him and waiting for his answer, he knew that he could not refuse her. He hesitated only briefly. Then he sent a guard with a message for his executioner: "Bring the head of John the Baptist into the banquet hall at once!"

The executioner went down into the dungeon and performed his grisly task. When he had done so, he brought John's head into the great hall upon a serving platter and gave it to the girl. She did not want it; she gave it to her mother. Her mother took it gladly, smiling exultantly at the pathetic sight. That tongue would never again speak harsh words against Herodias.

When John's disciples heard the dreadful news they came to the prison and removed the body so that they might give it the respectful burial John deserved. Then they went to Jesus and told him what had happened.

He sorrowed deeply for his cousin the prophet, he who had gone before to prepare the way. But with the death of John, Jesus' work had become even more urgent. He called together his twelve apostles to teach them all he could, and he urged them to redouble their efforts. He himself called on all his time and energy to travel about preaching and healing before time ran out altogether.

Jesus knew that his danger was increasing daily. It would not be long before Herod began to express an interest in him, and not a friendly interest; and at the same time the scribes and Pharisees were becoming more and more outraged by the doctrine that he preached. Already they had held meetings with the Herodians as to how they might silence what they thought of as his "blasphemy" and "heresy." Yet he continued working even harder than before and speaking to people with growing urgency.

He went about through cities and villages, preaching and bringing to his hearers the good tidings of the kingdom of God. With him went the twelve, and certain women, too, who had been healed of evil spirits and infirmities: Mary of Magdala, who was called Mary Magdalene, from whom he had cast out seven devils; Joanna, the wife of Herod's steward; and a woman named Susanna, and many others, who helped to look after the needs of Jesus and his disciples. Together they journeyed through Galilee to spread the gospel message.

PARABLES AND MIRACLES IN GALILEE

*O*ne day Jesus went out to teach again upon the shores of Galilee. At first he sat down at the seaside to talk to those who gathered, but as before the crowd pressing against him became so vast that it was difficult for him to talk to all and be heard. And again he got into a boat and sat down in it to teach the people while they listened from the shore.

This time he did not talk directly of the kingdom of God and man's need for repentance. Instead, he chose to teach in parables, short stories to illustrate the meaning of his lessons. Yet all the stories he told that day concerned the kingdom of heaven.

"Behold!" he began. "There was a farmer who went into his field to sow seeds of grain. And as he walked back and forth scattering the grain, some of the seed fell by the wayside, and the birds of the air flew down and ate it up. And some of the seed fell on rocky ground where there was not much earth. The plants grew quickly, because the soil was shallow; but when the sun came up the plants were scorched because they lacked both root and moisture. Therefore they withered away and died. And some of the seeds fell among thorns. They grew, but the thorns grew more quickly and choked the tiny seedlings.

"But other seeds fell on good ground. These seeds took root

and sprouted, growing into tall healthy plants that yielded up to a hundred times more seed than the sower had scattered in the first place. And I say to you, he that has ears to hear, let him hear."

Neither his disciples nor the rest of the listeners could understand what Jesus meant, although they knew that seeds would only grow in healthy soil. He explained his meaning to them. "Hear, then," he said. "The seed is the word of God, the sower is he who sows the message, and the soil is the people to whom the message is given. The wayside represents those who hear the message but do not want to act upon it. Then, as the birds fly down to eat up seeds that are scattered by the wayside, so does the evil one come to carry off the message that has been sown in their hearts.

"The stony places upon which the seeds fall and take root quickly, and then die, are like the people who receive the word with joy and gladness as soon as they hear it, but because they are shallow the word can take no root. For a while they believe, but in time of temptation or doubt they are quick to fall away.

"The thorny places refer to those people who hear the word of God and believe in their hearts, but allow the cares and riches and pleasures of this world to choke the word and crowd it out, so that their faith never ripens sufficiently to bear fruit.

"And the good ground that receives the seed represents the people who hear God's word, understand it, and obey it. When the words of God fall into willing hearts, they ripen into fruits of faith that increase like the grain that fell upon good soil."

He told them, next, a parable about good seeds and bad weeds.

"The kingdom of heaven," he said, "may be likened to a man who sowed good seeds in his field. But while he slept his enemy came and sowed weeds among the wheat, and went his way. When the blades of wheat sprang up and bore good grain, the weeds sprouted with them and quickly grew.

"The servants of the householder went to him and said: 'Sir, did you not sow good seeds in your field? Where did all the weeds come from?'

"'An enemy has done this,' answered the man.

"'Then,' said the servants, 'would you have us go out and gather them up?'

"'No,' the householder replied. 'Let both wheat and weeds grow together until the time of harvest. If you pull the weeds out now you may root up the good wheat with them. At harvest time I will tell the reapers to gather the weeds first and tie them up in bundles for burning; and then to gather the wheat into the barn.'"

When Jesus had finished telling this parable his disciples were just as puzzled as before. Although they had more understanding than the other listeners, they could not be sure what Jesus meant.

"Explain to us the meaning of the parable of the weeds," they begged.

"The sower of the good seeds is the Son of man," said Jesus. "The field is the world; and the good seeds are the people of God, the children of the kingdom. But the weeds are the children of the wicked one; the enemy that sowed them is the devil. The reapers are the angels, and the time of harvest is the day that God shall separate the good from the evil, even as the farmer burns the weeds and saves the good wheat in his barn. And the barn is the kingdom of heaven."

And then Jesus said: "You might also say that the kingdom of heaven is like a grain of mustard seed which, when it is sown in the field, is the smallest of all the seeds in the earth. But when this tiny seed is planted, it grows up and becomes greater than all the herbs. It shoots out great branches and becomes a tree so large that the birds of the air may nest in its boughs and rest under their shadow. So it is with the seed of the kingdom: it is small to begin with, but the tiny seed grows into the greatest of all things.

"Again, the kingdom of heaven is like a pearl, and the man who seeks it before all other things is like a merchant who, seeking perfect pearls and finding one of great price, sells all he has to buy the perfect pearl. Thus both the pearl merchant and the seeker of heaven give up all things for the one that is most important."

Thus did Jesus talk in parables that day by the sea of Galilee.

When evening came he said to his disciples: "Come, let us cross over to the other side."

The disciples sent away the multitude and took Jesus into a boat. As they cast off they saw that, even then, the crowds were trying to follow, for many of the people got into their own boats and rowed along behind them.

Jesus was weary after his long day of teaching and he fell asleep in the gently tossing boat. When they were far out from the shore a great wind arose and churned the waters, so that the boat rocked and plunged with the buffeting of the gusts and the boiling waves. Towers of water dashed against it and over the sides to drench the disciples and their Master, and the little ship began to fill. The storm raged on, and Jesus slept. His disciples pulled at the oars with all their strength, but they made no headway against the howling wind and lashing waves. The gusts slapped at them unmercifully; the boat was becoming dangerously full of water.

But Jesus slept on. His followers did not want to waken him, yet their plight was getting desperate. At last they came to him and woke him from his sleep. "Master!" they cried. "Do you not care that we are dying?"

Jesus rose up calmly and rebuked the winds, and to the sea he said: "Peace, be still." The wind ceased, and over the sea there was a great calm.

"Why are you so full of fear?" Jesus asked his disciples. "Have you still no faith?"

But now they were fearful for another reason. They had seen their Master heal, and they had seen him cast out devils, but the miraculous calming of a storm was something they had never seen before. They were filled with awe. "What manner of man is this?" they asked each other, marveling. "Even the winds and the sea obey him!"

Afterwards, the journey safely ended, Jesus and his disciples spent some time in Gadara on the far side of the sea, healing and teaching; and then they returned by boat to Capernaum. Crowds of people were waiting for Jesus on the shore and received him gladly, for they were eager to hear his words and ask his healing help. One of the people who most urgently wanted to see him was a man named Jairus, a leader in the synagogue at Capernaum. He threw himself down at the healer's feet and begged Jesus to come to his house, for his only daughter, who was about twelve years of age, lay dying on her sickbed.

"I pray you, come with me!" Jairus begged of Jesus. "My little daughter is lying at the point of death. Come with me, I beseech you, and lay your hands upon her so that she may be healed, and live."

Jesus turned at once and went with him. The crowd followed and thronged around him, pressing close upon him so that he could scarcely move. People jostled and clutched at him from every side. Jairus watched anxiously while Jesus made slow progress to his house, hampered in his every move. "Hurry, hurry!" thought Jairus to himself, although he did not speak the words aloud. "My daughter may be dead before we get there."

But it was impossible for anyone to hurry through the narrow, crowded streets. And even while Jairus waited, fighting back his anxiety, there was an unusual delay.

In the crowd there was a woman who had been trying desperately to reach Jesus and beg him for his help. For twelve years she had suffered many things from her illness and from all the doctors she had gone to, but she had grown worse instead of better. By this time she had spent all she had on physicians and medicines. When she heard the things concerning Jesus she followed after him, pressing her way through the crowd to get closer to the healer. "If I may but touch his clothes," she was saying to herself, "I will be healed." And she had no doubt at all that this was so.

At last she came close enough so that she could reach out and touch the border of his robe. Immediately she felt her illness leave her, and she let others in the crowd push past her to throng around the Master.

Jesus looked around. "Who was that who touched my robe?" he asked.

"It is not possible to say who touched you," his disciples answered. "You see the multitude pressing all around you. How can you say, 'Who touched me?'"

"I know someone with faith has touched me," Jesus answered, "for I felt the healing spirit flow from my body to another's." And he looked about to see the person who had touched him and been cured.

When the woman saw that she could not escape his notice, she came forward and threw herself down at Jesus' feet. Trembling with awe and wonder, knowing what had happened within her, she told him before all the people why she had touched his robe and how she had been healed immediately.

"Daughter, your faith has made you whole," Jesus said gently. "Go in peace."

Before he had finished talking to her a messenger came from the house of Jairus and pushed his way through the crowd toward the leader of the synagogue. "Your daughter is dead," the messenger said. "Trouble the Master no more, for she is gone."

Jairus cried out in his grief. But Jesus had heard what the messenger had said and he turned to the sorrowing Jairus. "Do not be afraid," he said. "Only believe, and she will be made well."

When at last he arrived at the house of Jairus he motioned the crowd to stay outside, for they were still following him and would have pushed in after him if he had permitted it, and he went inside with Peter, James, and John. Mourners had already gathered to bewail the little girl's death. The house was a tumult of weeping and wailing. Jesus looked around at all the moaning people and said: "Why do you weep and make this noise? Do not weep; the little girl is not dead, she only sleeps."

With that the mourners ceased their lamentations long enough to laugh scornfully at Jesus, for they knew the girl was dead. They had seen her lifeless body. But Jesus firmly sent them out of the house and went into the little girl's room with her father and mother and his three disciples.

He looked down at her where she lay and took her by the hand. And then he spoke. "Little maid, I say to you—arise!"

She opened her eyes and looked up into the smiling face of Jesus. And she got up at once and walked about the room.

"Now give her something to eat," said Jesus. Her parents nodded dumbly, for they were grateful and astonished beyond words.

Jesus left the house of Jairus and went back to the waiting crowd.

There were many more crowds awaiting him as he traveled through the cities and the villages, so many that he said to his disciples one day: "They are distressed and scattered, as sheep that do not have a shepherd. See, the harvest indeed is plenteous, but the laborers are few." And he called to him his chosen twelve apostles and began to send them forth two by two that they might do his work abroad. He gave them healing power, and authority over the unclean spirits that they might cast them out, and then he said to them:

"Go now, and preach that the kingdom of heaven is at hand. Heal the sick, raise the dead, cleanse the lepers, cast out demons; receive with thanks, and freely give. Take nothing for your journey save a staff, and the robe and sandals that you wear. Take neither wallet, silver, gold, nor extra coat. Stay wherever you are made welcome, and bless the house that receives you and is worthy. Wherever you are not made welcome and your words are not received, leave that house or town and shake off the dust of it from beneath your feet. Have faith, and fear not—but beware of men. For they will deliver you up to their councils, and in their synagogues they will scourge you."

When he had finished commanding his disciples he went his way to teach alone, and they went forth by twos to preach and heal in the countryside and villages.

Now at that time Herod the tetrarch heard of all these things that were being done by Jesus and his twelve disciples, and he was very much perplexed. He had heard of the so-called "King of the Jews" and wondered if this Jesus might not be the man. On the other hand, it was said by some that it was John the Baptist risen from the dead. Others said that Elijah had reappeared on earth, and yet others suggested the names of other old prophets who might have risen again.

Herod thought about it long and hard. At last he said: "It is John, whom I beheaded; he is risen again!" Yet he was not quite sure, and went on asking: "Who is this, about whom I hear such things?"

And he became increasingly anxious to see this man about whom he kept hearing such strange and wonderful things.

THE FEEDING OF THE MULTITUDE

*A*fter all these events and many others
the disciples gathered together and returned to Jesus. They told
him all that they had done, and he was pleased.

"Come, let us go into a desert place," he said, "so that we may
rest a while." For there had been so much coming and going of
people that neither Jesus nor his disciples had had time enough
even to eat.

They took a boat across the sea of Galilee to search out a place
where they might have some little time to themselves. But even in
the desert place they could not rest. When people discovered
where Jesus had gone they followed in their boats or hurried
around by land from all the neighboring towns and villages, so
that a multitude was gathered on the far shore even before Jesus
arrived.

And Jesus, when he saw them there, had compassion for them.
He bade them welcome and began to speak to them of the
kingdom of God. As the day wore on he answered those with
questions and healed all those who needed healing, and he taught
them many things. The afternoon grew late, and yet the people
stayed on, listening, in their hundreds and their thousands.

When it was almost evening his disciples came to him and said,

"There is no food in this desert place, and it is very late. Let us send these people away so that they may go into the farms and villages round about and buy themselves something to eat."

"They have no need to go away," said Jesus. "We will give them food." Then he turned to his disciple Philip. "Where shall we buy bread, that all these people may eat?" he asked. This he said to test Philip, for he himself knew what he would do.

Philip shook his head. The disciples had very little money between them, and the crowd was immense. "Two hundred pennyworth of bread would not be enough for all these people," he said, "even if each one only took a little."

"Then go and see how many loaves you can find among the people," Jesus said.

His disciples went through the crowd inquiring of the people. Finally Andrew, Simon Peter's brother, came back and reported what he had found.

"There is a lad here who has a basket with five barley loaves and two fishes," he said. "But what is that, among so many?"

"Bring the loaves and fishes here," said Jesus, "and have the people sit down on the grass in groups of fifty and a hundred."

Andrew brought the basket to him. And all the people, about five thousand of them, sat down upon the grass in groups. Jesus took the five loaves and two fishes and, looking up to heaven, gave a blessing. He broke first the loaves and then the fishes into small pieces and gave them to his disciples to distribute to the people. All the people ate, and all were filled. There seemed to be no end to the fragments of food.

When everyone had had enough to eat, Jesus said to his disciples: "Now gather up the fragments that remain, so that nothing shall be wasted." So the disciples gathered up the food that was left, filling twelve baskets with what remained after all the five thousand men, women, and children had eaten their fill.

Excitement ran through the crowd as they realized what had happened. Many of them said, "This is indeed the prophet who was to come into the world! It is he who is meant to be our king!"

As Jesus looked at them he saw what they were thinking, and he knew that they wanted to carry him off and make him their earthly king. But the kingdom of Jesus was not of this world and he could not allow them to do what they were thinking, so he told his disciples to get into the boat and cross before him toward Capernaum on the other side of the sea while he himself sent all the people away.

When all the others had gone, the multitude as well as his disciples, Jesus went up the mountain alone to pray.

When night came he was still praying alone, high on the mountainside. His disciples were well on their way across the inland sea to Capernaum. But high, gusty winds had come with the darkness, and the little ship was tossing about in the midst of a growing storm. Jesus came down from the mountain and stood alone on the shore, watching his disciples in their distant battle with the waves. After a while he went toward them on the sea, walking across the water as if it had been solid land beneath his feet.

The disciples looked up from their rowing when they saw the shadowy figure coming toward them through the night. And at the sight of someone walking on the water they nearly dropped their oars with fear. They had seen strange things, but none so strange as this, and at first they did not even think that the figure might be their leader Jesus.

"It is a spirit!" they cried out in their terror.

"Be of good cheer!" Jesus said at once. "It is I. Do not be afraid."

"If it is indeed you, Lord," said Peter, "then let me come toward you on the water."

"Come!" said Jesus.

Peter stepped bravely from the tossing boat onto the surface of the water and began to walk. But when the strong wind blew against him, and churned the seas beneath his feet, he suddenly became afraid. He felt his feet go under; he felt his big, strong body beginning to sink. "Lord, save me!" he cried out.

Jesus stretched out his hand and caught him.

"O ye of little faith!" he said. "Why did you doubt?"

And Jesus guided Peter to the boat across the foaming sea and helped him climb aboard.

The wind ceased at once, and they went along their way. Again his disciples were amazed by his extraordinary powers, for even the miracle of the loaves and fishes had not taught them what manner of being they had in their midst. Now they worshiped him, and said: "You are in truth the Son of God!" Yet they still said it more in awe than in true belief.

Nevertheless, they thought about these things as they crossed the sea on calm waters and continued with their mission on the other side; and they thought about them as they traveled with Jesus from Galilee to Phoenicia and back again to Palestine. Simon Peter, in particular, was very thoughtful while they journeyed. Finally, Jesus and the twelve made their way to Caesarea Philippi at the foot of great Mount Hermon.

On the way he questioned his disciples.

"Who do people say I am?" he asked.

"Some say you are John the Baptist," they answered, "and some say you are Elijah. Yet others say that you are Jeremiah, or another of the old prophets that has risen again."

"But who do you say that I am?" asked Jesus.

And Simon Peter answered, saying: "You are the Christ, the Son of the living God!"

Jesus rejoiced when he heard Peter's words. "Blessed are you, Simon, son of Jona!" he said. "For flesh and blood has not told you this, but my Father who is in heaven. And I say to you that you are Peter, the rock, and upon this rock I will build my church." Now he knew that his disciples, or at least one of them, believed him to be the promised Christ. But he also knew that other people did not yet believe it, and he wanted them to find out for themselves. So he commanded his disciples to tell no one that he was the Christ.

He began to teach them, then, about what the future held in store.

"I will go to Jerusalem," he said, "and suffer many things at the hands of the elders and chief priests and scribes. All of them will reject me and abuse me. I shall be killed, but after three days I will rise again."

They were shocked at what they heard. Peter took his Master aside and reproved him for saying such things, for he was convinced that Jesus could prevent the fate he was foretelling. It was true; Jesus had the power to prevent what lay ahead. But it was God's plan that his Son should bear the burden of man's sins.

"It can not be, Lord!" Peter said. "Such things must never happen to you!"

"You are talking like Satan the tempter," Jesus said to him. "It will be as I say. You shall not be a stumbling block to me in the things I have to do. Still you do not understand, for you are thinking man's thoughts, not the thoughts of God."

They traveled on in silence for some time. Then Jesus said to his disciples: "If any man wishes to come after me, let him deny all worldly desires, and take up his cross, and follow me. He is not to live selfishly, but for the Lord his God. For whoever wishes to save his life shall lose it, but whoever gives up his life for my sake, and for the sake of the gospel, will be saved. For what shall it profit a man to gain the whole world and lose his own soul? Or what shall a man give in exchange for his soul? Is there anything of equal value? I say to you, there is not! But God will reward each man according to what he does."

Six days later, Jesus took Peter, James, and John up Mount Hermon with him to pray. And as he prayed the expression of his face was changed and his whole appearance glowed. His face shone like the sun; his garments became as bright as white and glittering snow.

Two men appeared to talk to him: not his disciples, and not men of the earth, but Moses and Elijah in all their heavenly glory.

And they spoke to him about the death awaiting him in Jerusalem.

Peter and those who were with him were heavy with sleep and did not hear the talk. But when they awoke they saw the glory of Jesus and the two figures with him, and Peter knew who they were. He cried out: "Master, it is good that we are here! If you will, let us make three tabernacles; one for you, and one for Moses, and one for Elijah!" But he scarcely knew what he was saying, so dumbfounded was he by the amazing sight.

As he spoke a bright cloud came and overshadowed them, drawing them into its midst. Out of it there came a voice that said: "This is my beloved Son, in whom I am well pleased. Hear him!"

The disciples fell on their faces in fear. Jesus came to them through the brightness of the cloud and touched them. "Rise up," he said. "Do not be afraid."

When they looked up the cloud was gone, and they were alone on the mountain with Jesus. Of the two heavenly visitors there was no sign.

As they came down from the mountain Jesus told them to tell no one about the vision they had seen, not until after he had risen from the dead.

They kept it a secret to themselves, but they questioned among themselves what Jesus had meant by "rising from the dead."

He had said it before, and he would say it again. And in time to come they would find out what he meant.

DISPUTES IN THE TEMPLE

*J*esus and his disciples left Caesarea Philippi and made their way back to Capernaum in Galilee. As they traveled he tried again to teach them about the future and explain what had been talked about upon the mountainside while Peter, James, and John lay heavy with sleep.

"Let these words sink into your ears," Jesus said, "for the Son of man shall be betrayed into the hands of men, and they will kill him. But on the third day after his death he will rise again."

Yet the word did not sink in. The twelve could not bring themselves to believe that Jesus would allow himself to die; not with his great power to save and heal. They thought, therefore, that he was speaking in a parable, and they were afraid to ask him what he meant.

Jesus walked on, alone with his thoughts. His disciples drew apart from him and began an earnest discussion with one another, glancing now and then at Jesus as they spoke. He was not listening to them.

All this while they could have talked about the meaning of his saying, or what had happened on the mountain, or how it was possible for a man to rise after being three days dead; but they talked of nothing of the sort. They talked about themselves.

When they arrived at Capernaum they went at once to Simon Peter's house, which Jesus had called home ever since his own town of Nazareth had rejected him. After they had all refreshed themselves, Jesus sat down and called his disciples to him, for he knew what had been in their hearts while they were talking on the road to Capernaum. The twelve joined him where he sat.

"What was it that you disputed among yourselves along the way?" he asked. They were ashamed to answer, for they had been arguing about which one of them would be the greatest in the kingdom of heaven. They were still under the impression that it would be a kingdom similar to those on earth, and that Jesus would be appointing them to various high positions. And they were silent, for whatever else they failed to understand they did know that Jesus had no sympathy for worldly ambitions.

Jesus waited. Then he said: "If any man desires to be first in the kingdom, he must make himself the least of all and the servant of all. For if anyone is to be great, he must serve not himself, but others."

Now there were children in the household, and Jesus called a little child to come to him. The little one came gladly and Jesus put his arms about him. "Unless you change and become again like little children," he said to his disciples, "you will never enter the kingdom of heaven. Whoever, therefore, shall humble himself as this little child, shall be the greatest in the kingdom of heaven. And I say to you also, that whoever shall welcome one such child in my name, receives me also and makes me welcome. And whoever welcomes me receives not only me but also the Father who sent me. But whoever causes any one of the little ones who believe in me to waver in his faith, to turn aside and stumble, let that man beware: it would be better for him to have a millstone hung around his neck and to be sunk in the depth of the sea than to face the wrath of our Father in heaven. Do not despise one single little child! For it is not the will of my Father in heaven that any of these little ones should perish by going astray."

Jesus loved little children and their purity of heart. He sought them out to talk to them; and he welcomed them whenever they came to him. There was to come a time in Jerusalem when he would be so surrounded by children that he could scarcely teach their elders. On that day, it seemed that all the mothers in the city had brought their youngsters and their babies so that Jesus might put his hands on them and bless them. Then his disciples, exasperated by the endless procession of eager little ones, rebuked those who brought their children to see Jesus. Somehow they had decided for themselves that Jesus was much too busy to give his time to them. Yet they were wrong, for Jesus was never too busy to welcome children. He wanted them to come to him, and they themselves loved to gather around to touch his robe and listen to his stories. But the disciples reproved the mothers who had brought them. Jesus was much displeased when he saw them trying to keep the little ones away.

"Let the children come to me!" he said. "Forbid them not, for the kingdom of heaven belongs to such as they. I tell you again, whoever shall not accept the kingdom of God just like a little child, shall not enter into it at all. Now bring them here." And he took the little ones into his arms to bless them.

That, however, was later. At the moment, Jerusalem still lay ahead, for the feast of the tabernacles was at hand, and Jesus had decided to go to the temple to worship and teach. He did not want to call attention to his arrival, and he sent his disciples ahead while he himself visited his friends Mary, Martha, and Lazarus in the little town of Bethany on the outskirts of Jerusalem. When he did go into the city he went late and secretly.

The Jews therefore sought him at the feast. "Where is he?" they asked each other. No one knew but there was much murmuring among the multitudes concerning him. Some said, "He is a good man." Others said, "No, not so! He leads the multitude astray." No one of the masses spoke openly about him for fear of the leaders among the Jews.

In the midst of the festival Jesus went up into the temple and taught with the authority that made him so different from all other teachers. The Jews marveled at his sayings. "How is it that this man is so learned, never having been taught?" they asked each other. Jesus heard, and answered.

"The teaching is not mine," he said, "but his that sent me. Anyone who truly desires to do God's will shall know whether my teaching comes from God, or only from myself." And he went on teaching them.

His listeners were amazed at his logic and at the truths he spoke.

"Is not this he whom the leaders seek to kill?" one man asked another. "He speaks so openly, and they say nothing to him! Can it be that the rulers indeed *know* that this is the Christ? But no, he cannot be! We know this man, this Nazarene; when the Christ comes, no one will know where he is from."

Many of the multitude believed in him, nevertheless, and they murmured much among themselves. "When Christ does come," they said to one another, "can he possibly show more signs than this man has done?" The Pharisees heard what the masses were saying. Now, they thought, they would have their opportunity to arrest the man who spoke so unflatteringly of them and their strict adherence to the Law. They were still smarting over his comments on their public humility and private sin, and they had had enough. So, together with the chief priests, they decided to have him arrested immediately.

A band of officers therefore trooped into the temple to seize Jesus and take him to their masters. Instead of the fiery radical they expected, they found a calm-faced man speaking in a quiet but compelling voice to a crowd of fascinated listeners. "I will be with you for yet a little while," the man was saying. "And when I go, I go to him that sent me. You shall look for me, but will not find me. Where I am, you cannot come."

At this there was a discussion within the crowd. Where could he possibly go, that they would be unable to follow? Abroad, perhaps?

The officers who had come to take him hung back and listened, both to the crowd and to the words of this extraordinary man. They heard him say such things as: "If any man thirst, let him come to me and drink!" and, "I am the light of the world! Whoever follows me will not have to walk in darkness, but will live his life in the light."

They saw how eagerly the people listened, and they took note of the response of the multitude. Some said, "Of a truth, this is the prophet!" Others said, "This is the Christ." And others yet: "This is *not* the Christ, for this man comes from Galilee. Was not the Christ to have been born in Bethlehem?" So the people were divided in their opinions about Jesus, and the officers themselves did not know what to think. They tried to do their duty, but for some reason they were unable to lay their hands upon Jesus. Indeed, they found themselves not only interested but moved by his words. They went back to the chief priests and Pharisees without the captive they had been sent to get. Their masters were very much annoyed.

"Why have you not brought him?" they demanded.

"No man ever talked as he does!" the officers replied.

"Are you also led astray?" the Pharisees said angrily. "Do you now believe in him? Tell us: have any of the authorities believed in him, or any of the Pharisees? No! Only the common people, the multitude that does not know the Law, believe in him—and for that they are accursed! And this man, you can be sure, will be punished yet for his heretical teachings."

Now Nicodemus, the man who had gone secretly to see Jesus many months before and had been deeply impressed by what he heard, was sitting among his fellow Pharisees while they spoke thus about Jesus. And he did not like the things that they were saying.

"Does our Law condemn a man before he is given a hearing?" he asked.

"A hearing!" they said scornfully. "We know what he has done. What is the matter with you? Are you from Galilee, too? Search through the writings, and you will see that no prophet is to come from Galilee!"

After this they were even more determined to find some way of trapping Jesus into admitting that he was guilty of breaking their Law.

Jesus knew that his days were numbered. Yet he still came and went as he pleased, preaching as he knew he must preach and doing those things that he knew he must do.

One sabbath day, as Jesus and his disciples were walking in Jerusalem, they saw a beggar who had been blind from birth.

As they drew near the disciples said to Jesus, "Master, who sinned, that this man should have been born blind? Was it he who sinned, or was it his parents?" For the Jews thought that all misfortune was caused by someone's sin.

They stopped in front of the blind man.

"He did not sin, nor did his parents," Jesus answered; and the blind man raised his sightless eyes as if the better to hear the gentle voice. "He was born blind so that the power of God might be shown through him. And we must use this power, do God's work, while it is still day; for the night is coming when no man can work. As long as I am in this world, I am the light of the world."

When Jesus had said this he spat on the ground, and made clay from the earth and the spittle. Then he anointed the man's eyes with the clay and said to him, "Go, wash your eyes in the Pool of Siloam."

The blind man arose and made his way through the city streets and out through the gate of Jerusalem to the Pool of Siloam, knowing his way though he had never seen the road. He felt his way down to the water and washed as Jesus had bidden him. The clay came away from his eyes; he opened them; and for the first time in his life he was able to see. Incredulously, only half-believing even yet, he ran up the hill from the pool and hurried home to tell his parents the wonderful news. His heart sang as he ran, and his newly opened eyes looked with delight upon everything they saw.

He was well known in Jerusalem, this blind man, for he was to be seen every day begging in the street. And when his neighbors, and other people who had seen him sitting by the roadside with his hands outstretched, saw him running to his house with eyes wide open and a joyous smile upon his face, they were astonished.

"Is not this the man who used to sit and beg?" they asked each other.

Some said, "Yes, it is he!"

But others said, "No, it cannot be. It is someone like him."

The blind man spoke for himself. "I *am* he!" he said.

"How, then, were your eyes opened?" they asked, in their astonishment.

"The man who is named Jesus made clay," he answered them, "and put it on my eyes. Then I went to wash them in the Pool of Siloam, as he said I must, and I received my sight!"

His astounded neighbors brought him before the Pharisees, who questioned him. He repeated his story to them. And they muttered angrily because again the cure had taken place on a sabbath day.

Some of them said: "The man who did this is not a man of God, because he does not keep the sabbath."

But others said: "How could a sinner do such a miracle as this?"

And there was a division of opinion among the people who heard and talked about all this. Therefore they asked the once-blind man what he himself thought about the one who had opened his eyes.

"He is a prophet!" he answered.

Then the questioning Jews would not believe that the man had actually been blind and had been given his sight. They therefore sent him out of hearing and summoned his parents to question them as well.

"Is this your son, and was he indeed born blind?" they asked. "If so, how is it that he now can see?"

"Yes, this is our son, and we know he was born blind," his parents answered. "But how it is that he now can see, we do not know." They did know, for he had told them and they believed his words. But they denied knowledge because they feared the Jewish authorities, for the Jews had already announced that anyone who acknowledged Jesus as the Christ would be turned out of the synagogue. Therefore they said, "Ask our son. He is of age. Let him speak for himself."

Then the Pharisees again summoned the man who had been blind.

"Give the glory to God for what has happened to you," they told him, "for we know that the man you say has done this thing is a sinner."

"Whether he is a sinner or not I do not know," the man replied. "But one thing I do know: I was blind, and now I can see."

His answer displeased them mightily.

"What did he do to you?" they persisted. "How did he open your eyes?"

"I have already told you, and you would not listen," he said. "Why do you want to hear it again? Do you wish to become his disciples?"

"Pah! *You* are his disciple," they said angrily, "but we are disciples of Moses. We know that God spoke to Moses. But as for this man, we do not know that God has spoken to him; we do not know where he is from."

"Why, that is very strange," the man said. "You know nothing of him, you who claim to know so much, and yet he made me see! Now we know that God does not listen to sinners, but if a man worships God and obeys him, God does listen to him. It has never been heard, since the world began, that anyone has opened the eyes of a man born blind. If this man were not from God, he could do no such thing."

The Pharisees turned on him in anger. "You were born in sin

and you are altogether sinful! And do you now try to teach us, you sinner?" And they cast him out of the synagogue so that he would never again be allowed to worship there and be accepted as a true believer in their God.

But the man born blind did not need to worship there. When Jesus heard how the Pharisees had treated him he sought him out and spoke to him.

"Do you believe in the Son of God?" he asked.

"Who is he, that I may believe in him?" the man asked in return.

"You have seen him," Jesus answered. "It is he who speaks with you."

"Lord, I believe!" the man said joyfully. He fell to his knees and worshiped Jesus. And although from that time forth he was no longer welcome in the synagogue, he prayed within his heart and knew that his prayers were being heard.

THE GATHERING STORM

*I*n spite of the growing hatred and plotting of the Pharisees, Jesus went quietly on with his work. Soon after healing the blind man, Jesus spoke again in parables to the people of Jerusalem and the places round about.

He began with the story of the good shepherd.

"In truth, I say to you," he told his listeners, "that if anyone does not enter the sheepfold by way of the door, but tried to climb in some other way, he is a thief and a robber. The one who enters by the door is the true shepherd of the sheep. The watchman opens the door to him, and the sheep listen to his voice. The shepherd calls to his own sheep by name, for he knows them well, and leads them out to pasture. And when he has led out his sheep he goes in front of them to lead the way. They obey him and they follow him because they know his voice. But they will not follow a stranger. No, they will flee from him, because they do not know the voice of strangers."

His listeners did not understand this parable, so Jesus said: "I am the door of the sheepfold, and you, the people, are the sheep. All those who try to enter the sheepfold without waiting for the doorkeeper to open the gate are thieves and robbers; they are the false teachers who try to call my sheep. But the sheep, not knowing their voices, will not listen to them. Yes, I am the door, and the only door. Whoever enters through me shall be saved. He shall go in and go out, and he will find rich pastures. The thief comes to steal, and kill, and destroy; but I have come so that my sheep may have life, and have it in abundance.

"Or let us say, instead, that I am the good shepherd: the good shepherd lays down his life for his sheep. He that is hired, whose sheep are not his own, will not lay down his life for any of the flock. No, when the wolf comes, the hired shepherd leaves the sheep and flees; and the wolf snatches them and scatters them about.

"The false teacher is the hireling who cares not for the sheep. But I am the good shepherd: I know my sheep, and my sheep know me, even as the Father knows me and I know the Father. I will gather my sheep to me and guard every one of them. And other sheep I have, which are not of this fold. These are the Gentiles, and these, also, must I lead. They will hear my voice, and they will join the fold. Then shall there be one flock and one shepherd. And for my flock I will lay down my life.

"Therefore does the Father love me, because I am laying down my life so that I may take it back again. No one is taking it from me; I am giving it of myself. I have power to give it, and I have power to take it back. This is the authority I have received from my Father."

Again there arose a division of opinion among the Jews because of these words. They could not understand everything he said, but they did understand that he had spoken of God as his Father.

Many of them said, "He is possessed by a demon! He is mad! Why do you listen to him?"

But others said, "These are not the words of a man who is possessed. And can a madman open the eyes of the blind?"

Jesus went his way, leaving them to their argument.

One day, while he was teaching, a certain expert in the Law got up to test him with hard questions, hoping to be able to trick Jesus into saying something that the Pharisees might use against him.

"Master," he said, "what shall I do to inherit eternal life?"

"Can you not answer that yourself?" said Jesus. "You know the Law. What is written in it? How do you read it?"

The lawyer answered, "In the Law of Moses it is written: 'You shall love the Lord your God with all your heart, and with all your soul, and with all your strength, and with all your mind; and you shall love your neighbor as yourself.'"

"You have answered rightly," Jesus said. "Do this, and you shall have eternal life. For these are the greatest of the commandments."

His answer showed that he had come to uphold the Law rather than destroy it, but the lawyer was not satisfied.

"But who is my neighbor?" the man persisted.

Jesus answered with a parable.

"One day," he said, "a certain man was traveling the road from Jerusalem to Jericho. On the way he fell among thieves, who attacked him brutally and robbed him of everything he had. They stripped him, beat him, and departed, leaving him half dead.

"He lay there on the side of the road, bruised, bleeding, unable to move, and praying that help would come before he died.

"Now a priest chanced to be going that way, and he saw the wounded man lying by the side of the road. The man glimpsed the priest through his half-closed eyes, and he thought, 'Surely he will help me!' But the priest crossed the road and went past on the other side, making no move to help or even stop.

"And then a Levite came traveling down the road. He, too, saw the beaten man and heard his moans; and he, too, crossed over and passed by on the other side.

"At last there came a Samaritan." His audience stirred and made disdainful faces, for they despised Samaritans. "He rode up to the man," Jesus continued, "and saw his pitiful plight. And his heart was moved with deep compassion. He dismounted at once and bent over the wounded traveler. What the man was or where he came from made no difference to this Samaritan: all he thought of was that the man was suffering and desperately in need of help. He could see that, unless he were attended to at once, the man would surely die.

"Therefore the Samaritan dressed the wounds with wine and oil, and bound them up as best he could. Then he raised the man up with gentle, kindly hands and lifted him onto his own mule, for the man's mount had been stolen with all the rest of his possessions.

"The Samaritan led his mule and its burden along the road to Jericho until he reached the safety of an inn. There he lifted off the wounded man and gave him shelter; and he cared for him in the inn throughout the night. And in the morning, when he was ready to depart and attend to his own delayed affairs, he took money from his own wallet and gave it to the innkeeper. 'Take care of this man,' he said, 'and if you spend more on him than this, I will repay you when I come back.' And then he left.

"Now," said Jesus, "which of the three, do you think, proved himself a neighbor to that man who fell into the hands of thieves: the priest, the Levite, or the Samaritan?"

"The one who showed mercy to him," the lawyer said reluctantly.

"Yes," said Jesus. "Go, and do the same yourself."

And the lawyer departed from his presence, a little humbler and a little wiser.

It was some time later, in the winter, that Jesus again attended a festival in Jerusalem. He was walking in the temple during the feast of dedication when the people saw him and surrounded him on Solomon's Porch.

"How much longer are you going to keep us in suspense?" they demanded. "If you really are the Christ, then tell us plainly!"

"I told you," Jesus answered them, "and you would not believe me. The deeds that I do in my Father's name are proof of my words. But you do not hear me and believe, because you are not of my sheep, as I said to you. My sheep listen to my voice: I know them, and they follow me. I give them eternal life; they shall never die, or be plucked out of my hands. My Father who gave them to me is greater than all, and no one is able to snatch them out of my Father's hands. And my Father and I are one."

Now he had said it! He had as much as said he was the Father himself! The Jews in the temple were outraged. They shouted angrily and picked up stones with the intention of stoning him to death in the heat of their rage, but he stood calmly before them without a trace of fear.

"Why do you do this?" Jesus asked them. "I have shown you many good works from the Father. For which of those works are you stoning me?"

"We are not stoning you for any good work," they answered roughly, "but for you impious talk; and because you, a man, are making yourself out to be God. This is blasphemy!"

"How can you say I am blasphemous," said Jesus, "when my Father has sanctified me and sent me as his messenger to the world? If I am not doing my Father's work, do not believe in me. But if I am doing his work, even though you may not believe in me, then at least believe in the deeds. By these deeds you may come to know and understand that the Father is in me and I am in the Father."

They were not calmed by his words. They tried again to hurt and seize him, but he escaped from their hands and went away.

Again, he went across the Jordan to the place where John had first baptized, and there he stayed for a time. Many people came to see him and his miraculous signs; and many people grew to believe in him.

Now the Pharisees were still on the lookout for him, listening to his words and complaining about him to each other, but they did not dare to harm him as long as he was across the Jordan from Judea. Many publicans and sinners were drawing near to Jesus to listen to his words, so both the Pharisees and the accompanying scribes murmured angrily among themselves and said: "This man welcomes sinners. He even eats with them!"

"Yes, I welcome sinners," Jesus said. "It is the sinners who need me, every single one of them. And it is the sinners who shall be received when they seek me." Again, he began to speak in parables.

"What man among you," he began, "if he has a hundred sheep,

would be satisfied if one should stray and leave him with only ninety-nine? If one is lost, would you leave that one in the wilderness, or would you go out after it and search until you had found it? You search for it, I say; you do not leave it in the wilderness. And when you find it, you lay it across your shoulders and carry it to the fold, rejoicing. When you reach home you call together your friends and neighbors and you say to them: 'Rejoice with me! For I have found my lost sheep.' And I say to you, there will be more joy in heaven over one sinner who repents than over ninety-nine righteous people who do not need to repent."

He spoke another parable. "What woman who has ten pieces of silver, and loses one, will not light a lamp and sweep the house and look diligently until she finds it? And when she finds it, does she not call in her friends and neighbors, saying, 'Rejoice with me, for I have found the coin I lost!' In just that way, I say to you, there is joy among the angels of God over one single sinner who repents."

And then again he said: "There was a certain man who had two sons. The elder was righteous, and occupied with serious thoughts. The younger was carefree and reckless, eager to enjoy the pleasures that his inheritance would bring him. 'Father,' he said one day, when he could wait no longer, 'let me have my share of the property that is coming to me. Let me enjoy it now.' His father was not pleased, but he divided his property into two portions and gave his younger son the share that would have come to him in later years.

"Not many days afterward, the younger son gathered together all his possessions and new wealth and journeyed into a far country. There he spent gloriously and lived a riotous life with greedy new friends and woman companions. It was not long before he had squandered away all his inheritance. When all his money was gone his new friends left him too, so that there was no one to help him in his time of need.

"Then a mighty famine came upon the land, and he began to be in desperate want. He who had once lived in luxury and spent foolishly was now forced to accept the only work he could find, that of laborer to one of the citizens of that country. The man was a farmer, and he sent the youth into his fields to feed the swine.

"The new swineherd did his work, but though he worked he was given nothing in return. His hunger grew unbearable. After a while he would gladly have filled his belly with the husks that were given to the swine.

"Then he came to his senses and began to think. 'How many hired men my father has,' he thought, 'who have food enough and to spare, and I am dying here of hunger!' He thought about his home, and it became more and more attractive as he thought. Yet could he admit that he had been wrong and go back to his father? He decided that he could, for self-pride was not important to a man in his condition. And he truly repented of the foolish things that he had done. 'I will arise, I will leave here,' he told himself, 'and go back to my father. I will say to him, Father, I have sinned against heaven and against you. I am no more worthy to be called your son. Treat me, if you will, as one of your hired servants; only let me come home again.'

"He started on his journey home and eventually approached his father's house, worrying all the while about how he would be received and grieving for his foolishness. And his father, who had missed him and was concerned for him, saw him when he was still a long way off. As the youth drew closer the father saw that his son was ragged and dirty, completely without possessions and walking with his head bowed low. Love and compassion stirred within the older man. He ran from the house and threw his arms around his son, and kissed him with a joyous father's kisses.

"The youth was ashamed and drew away from him. 'Father, I have sinned against heaven, and in your sight,' he said. 'I am no longer worthy to be called your son. Let me be as one of your hired—'

"But his father would not let him finish. 'Bring forth the best robe!' he called to his servants. 'Put it on my son, and put a ring on his finger, and shoes on his feet. Bring the fatted calf; prepare a feast! Let us eat and make merry, for this my son was as if dead and is alive again; he was lost, and he is found!'

"The household began at once to make merry. The youth was brought fresh clothes, the finest in the house; the calf was prepared, and the wine jars opened. Now while all this was happening the elder son was working diligently in the fields. When he returned to the homestead after a long day's work he heard the sounds of music and dancing coming from the house. He called to one of the servants and inquired into the cause of the unusual merriment.

"'What is the meaning of all this?' he asked.

"'Your brother has come back,' the servant answered happily, 'and your father has killed the fatted calf because the youth has come back safe and sound.'

"But the brother was angry instead of being glad, and he would not go into the house to take part in the celebration. His father therefore came out to him and urged him to come in to welcome his brother and join the feast. Still the older brother could not feel happy for his father.

"'I have served you all these years,' he said angrily, 'and never once have I disobeyed a commandment of yours nor spent money foolishly. Yet you have never given me so much as an unfattened kid of a goat, that I might make merry with my friends. No, you do not rejoice over me! But as soon as your other son comes back, he who has wasted your money on loose women and riotous women, you kill for him the calf you have been fattening! Is this fair, is it right?'

"And the father saw that he was jealous. 'Son,' he said gently, 'you are always with me; you have not been away, you have not strayed. Everything I have is yours. But it is only right to make merry and be glad, for your brother who was dead has come back to life; he was lost, and now he is found! Come, rejoice with us.'

"And in this way," Jesus ended quietly, "does my Father welcome each sinner who repents and comes to him. And thus do I welcome all sinners who repent and come to me."

THE RAISING OF LAZARUS

While Jesus was still in the land beyond the Jordan he received an urgent call for help from his friends in Bethany. Mary, Martha, and their brother Lazarus loved Jesus dearly, and he loved them in return. He had made it his custom to visit them whenever he was near Jerusalem, for with them he always found friendship, hospitality, and true belief.

And now Mary and Martha had sent a message to him, saying, "Lord! Behold, Lazarus, whom you love, is very ill."

Now Jesus was many miles away from Bethany and it took time for the message to reach him. Indeed, when the messenger at last found Jesus where he taught, Lazarus was already on the point of death. Yet even then the Master did not hurry off to Bethany.

"This sickness is not unto death," he said. "It is for the glory of God, that the Son of God may be glorified thereby."

The messenger went his way and Jesus went on with his teaching. His disciples were glad that he was making no attempt to go to Bethany, for Judea was no longer safe for him. Therefore they made no objection as he continued preaching and healing among the people of the land beyond the Jordan.

Meanwhile, in Bethany, Lazarus grew sicker yet; and, while his sisters watched and wept, he died.

Two days later Jesus said to his disciples: "Let us go back to Judea."

"Master!" they protested. "The leaders of the Jews were but recently trying to stone you. And still you want to go there again?"

"Yes, I am going," he answered. "Our friend Lazarus has fallen asleep. I am going so that I might wake him from his sleep."

"Lord," the disciples said to him, "if he has fallen asleep, he surely will recover."

Now Jesus had spoken of his friend's death, but they thought he meant that Lazarus was taking rest in sleep and was therefore on the road to health.

"Lazarus is dead," Jesus told them plainly. "And I am glad for your sakes that I was not there, so that you may learn to believe in me. Come, let us go to him."

Jesus and his disciples arrived in Bethany two days later and found that Lazarus had been in the tomb for four days already. A number of Jews had come out from nearby Jerusalem to mourn with the weeping sisters and try to console them for the loss of their beloved brother. Jesus stopped at the wayside before entering the little town, and word of his approach soon reached the ears of Martha. As soon as she heard that Jesus was near she came running out to meet him.

"Lord!" she cried, as if with reproach. "If only you had been here, my brother would not have died." And then she added hastily, "But even now I know that, whatever you ask of God, he will give it to you."

"Your brother will rise again," Jesus comforted her.

"I know that he will rise again in the resurrection at the last day," said Martha sadly.

"*I* am the resurrection and the life," Jesus told her gently. "He who believes in me shall live, even though he dies; and whoever lives and believes in me shall never die. Do you believe that?"

"I do, Master!" said Martha. "I have believed and I do believe that you are the Christ, the Son of God, who was to come into the world."

And when she had said this she turned away and went back to the house where her sister Mary sat and mourned. She drew her sister aside and spoke to her in secret.

"Mary," she said, "the Master is here, and he is asking for you."

Mary sprang up quickly and ran out to meet him at the place where he still waited, hoping to talk to him alone. But the mourners who had been in the house with her saw her leave, and supposed that she was going to the tomb to weep. Therefore they followed her, saying to each other sympathetically, "She is going to the grave to wail and mourn."

But instead of coming to the tomb, they found themselves at the wayside watching the meeting between Jesus and Mary.

Mary fell down at his feet and wept. "O, Master," she sobbed, "if you had only been here, my brother would not have died." Now she was saying the same thing as her sister had said, but she was expressing deep faith rather than reproach; and a faith that was still unchanged even though her brother had died. Martha had not understood what Jesus had meant when he had talked of resurrection, even though he had explained to her. But Mary knew even without being told that Jesus could still help them if he wished. The one thing she could not know was whether or not it was the Father's will that Lazarus might be saved.

In spite of her great faith, therefore, she sorrowed and wept bitterly; and the Jews who had followed her were weeping bitterly as well. Jesus himself was deeply moved by their sorrow, and by the thought of the many people of Israel who did not have Mary's faith and would not rise again in the resurrection of the last day to enjoy eternal life.

But the immediate problem was not one of eternal life; it was the earthly death of a man who had believed in God the Father and in Jesus as the Son. While Jesus groaned within himself and his heart was troubled by his thoughts, he was not so troubled that he could not do what he had come to do.

"Where have you laid him?" he asked the weeping woman.

"Come and see, Lord," Mary said.

She and the mourners led him to the grave. Martha, watching from the house, saw the distant procession straggling toward the burial place, and she stopped her work to follow it.

Jesus still wept: wept for Mary and Martha in their sorrow; for the grieving friends of Lazarus; for all those who would not rise again. And the mourners saw his tears.

"See how much he loved Lazarus," they whispered to each other.

But others said, "Could not this man, who has opened the eyes of the blind and done even more wonderful things, have prevented Lazarus from dying?"

Jesus again groaned within himself and walked up to the tomb. It was a cave, and a heavy stone lay against it for a door. Mourners crowded around; Martha hurried from behind and joined them, wondering what Jesus could possibly do now.

"Take away the stone," said Jesus.

"But, Master!" Martha wailed. "He has been dead four days. Already his body is decaying."

Jesus turned to her. "Did I not say to you that if you would believe, you would see the glory of God?"

She nodded dumbly. Mary did not question him at all, for her faith was strong. At a sign from her, the mourners moved the great stone away.

Jesus lifted up his eyes to heaven and said: "Father, I thank you for hearing me. I know that you do hear me always, but I say this aloud to you now because of the people who are standing here, so that they may believe that you have sent me."

He lowered his eyes and looked into the open tomb.

"Lazarus, come forth!" he cried.

There was a quiet movement inside the cave. The mourners watched, speechless with awe and something close to fear.

A shadowy figure rose within the tomb. And Lazarus, who had been dead, came forth. His grave clothes were still on him and his face was covered with a cloth; but he moved, he walked.

Mary cried out with gratitude. The watchers gasped and paled.
"Loose him," Jesus said. "Take off the burial clothes, and let
him go."

The grave clothes came off.

Lazarus was indeed alive; startled, but in perfect health. The
watchers rejoiced and fell to their knees in reverence and thanksgiving. Martha and Mary wept tears of joy, and took their beloved
brother home again.

Many of the Jews who had come to mourn Lazarus came to
believe in Jesus because of the remarkable thing he had done
before their very eyes. But some of them went straight to the
Pharisees, and told them what they had seen.

The high priests and Pharisees at once called a meeting of the
priestly council, a religious high court empowered to try any case
involving Mosaic Law and pronounce any sentence but that of
death.

"What shall we do?" they moaned to each other. "This man
truly does many signs, or he seems to. If we let him alone he will
go on doing these things until all men believe in him. And then
the Romans will come and take away both our holy place and our
people. Yet it seems that there is nothing we can do!"

Caiaphas, who was high priest that year, snorted scornfully.

"You do not think at all!" he said sharply. "Nor do you consider
that it is better that one man should die for the people than that
the whole nation should perish on his account."

The Pharisees and priests were quick to see his point. So, from
that day forth, they began to devise various plans for capturing
Jesus and putting him to death.

Jesus, knowing their purpose, walked openly among the Jews
no more. He left Bethany, he left Judea; and he went with his disciples to a town called Ephraim in the country near the wilderness. Here they stayed until it was close to the time for another
holy feast in the city of Jerusalem. Slowly they started to make
their way back to the place which spelled so much danger for
Jesus. The usual crowd followed and listened to all they said.

There was much to talk about and much to do along the way, for time was running short.

They talked, first, of prayer, and Jesus told them a parable to show that they ought always to pray and never give up hope.

"There was once a judge," he began, "who neither loved God nor respected man. And in the same city there was a poor widow who had been wronged by an enemy. She went to see the judge, saying, 'Give me justice! Help me against that man.' But the judge brushed her aside. He had no interest in her troubles. The widow went to him again, and again, and then again; but he paid her no attention. Yet she kept going to see him and begging for justice, and after she had visited him many times the unjust judge said to himself: 'Why should I help her? I do not care for either God or man. But she keeps coming here to trouble me with her tale! I had better give her the justice she demands, or she will wear me out with her continual coming.' And so the judge did help her in the end.

"Learn from the story of this judge," said Jesus. "He did what the woman wanted because she came often to him. And shall not God, who is just and ready to listen, be much more willing to protect his chosen people when they cry to him by night and day? I tell you, he will do justice speedily! Pray often, therefore, and pray earnestly."

Now there were certain people in the crowd who were confident of their righteousness, and contemptuous of others whom they regarded as sinners. They were quite sure that they knew how to pray, even if no one else did.

To them, Jesus told this story:

"Two men went into the temple to pray. One was a Pharisee, and the other a tax collector. The Pharisee stood up boldly and prayed thus with himself: 'I thank you, God, that I am not like other men, the greedy and dishonest, the unjust, the adulterers, or like this tax collector here. I fast twice in the week, and I pay to the temple one-tenth of everything I get.'

"But the tax collector, standing at a distance, was so humble that he would not so much as lift his eyes to heaven. He stood with his head bowed and beat upon his breast, saying, 'God, be merciful to me, a sinner.'

"I tell you, it was this tax collector who went home with God's blessing, not the other. For everyone who exalts himself before God will be humbled, but he who humbles himself will be exalted."

A rich young ruler came to Jesus and asked what he might do to inherit eternal life. And when Jesus told him that he should sell his property and give his money to the poor so that he might have treasures in heaven, the young man went sorrowfully away. He could do anything but that, for he enjoyed his earthly wealth.

When he had gone Jesus said to his disciples, "Truly, I say to you, it is hard for a rich man to enter the kingdom of heaven." The twelve were amazed at these words, for, being poor themselves, they thought that the rich could do anything with greater ease than the needy. "Indeed," Jesus went on, "it is easier for a camel to go through a needle's eye than for a rich man to enter the kingdom of God. How hard it will be for those who trust in riches!"

"Who then can be saved, if not the rich?" his disciples asked.

"Those who truly believe," said Jesus. "The things which are impossible for men are possible with God, for with God all things are possible."

They were not far from the border of Judea when Jesus spoke again of his earthly destiny. He took his disciples aside, and as they walked along apart from the crowd he said to them:

"Behold, we go up to Jerusalem, and all things that are written by the prophets concerning the Son of man shall be accomplished. For he shall be betrayed into the hands of the chief priests and scribes, who will condemn him to death and deliver him to the Gentiles. And they will mock him, treat him shamefully, and spit on him. And then they will flog and crucify him; and on the third day he will rise again."

Even knowing this, he still turned his face toward Jerusalem.

THE WAY TO THE CROSS

*A*s they neared Jerusalem the disciples began to feel that they were on the eve of great events. They were sorely troubled by Jesus' words of death and resurrection, but they still supposed he meant the resurrection of the last day and that, therefore, the kingdom of God was immediately to appear. They still thought, too, that it would be much like an earthly kingdom, in which they would be offered positions of great power.

Yet they were wrong in this, and Jesus told them so with such bluntness that they became exceedingly disturbed by the prospect of entering Jerusalem. And they were right to be disturbed.

The Jewish passover was at hand, and many people had come up from the country to purify themselves before the festival. They looked for Jesus, and asked about him as they stood in the temple.

"What do you think?" they said to one another. "Do you think he will come to the festival? Or will he not, this time?"

For they knew that the chief priests and Pharisees had given orders that if anyone should find out where Jesus was, he should announce it to them so that Jesus might be seized.

Six days before the passover Jesus went to Bethany to visit Lazarus and his sisters, and make his home with them until the day of the feast. On the day that he arrived, Simon, who had been a leper, made a supper for him in his own house. Lazarus sat near Jesus at the table, the practical Martha served, and Mary sought to find some way to show Jesus her love and trust.

She therefore brought in an alabaster flask containing a pound of liquid spikenard, a fragrant ointment that was exceedingly precious and costly. This she took to Jesus. First she anointed his head with the rare perfume. Then she knelt low in front of him, anointed his feet with it as if caring for a travel-worn visitor, and wiped his feet with her hair. It was a gesture of great love and gratitude, and of much deeper meaning than most of those present could understand. Some of the people at the table murmured indignantly among themselves, saying, "To what purpose is this waste of precious ointment?"

Judas Iscariot, the disciple who was in charge of their small treasury, spoke up sharply against Mary.

"Why was this ointment not sold for three hundred pence and given to the poor?" he demanded angrily. "Why should it have been wasted in this way?" Now he said this, not because he cared for the poor, but because he was a thief. He had charge of the money bag and he used every opportunity to take whatever was put into it.

"Let her alone," Jesus answered him. "Why do you trouble her? When she poured this ointment on my body, she did it to prepare me for burial. You will always have the poor with you, but you will not always have me. She has done a good deed. I say to you that wherever the gospel is preached throughout the world, this woman will be remembered, and what she has done will be spoken of in memorial to her."

Judas smarted under this gentle reproof. He was already beginning to doubt that there would be any glory for him in the kingdom of which Jesus spoke, and he was interested above all in material things. So far he had gained nothing but some of the contents of the money bag. He fumed inwardly, and said no more.

Many of the people round about had heard that Jesus was at Simon's house, and they went there to see him, and not only to see him, but also to see Lazarus, who had been raised from the dead. They saw Jesus, they saw what Mary had done, and they saw Lazarus. And they were filled with wonder.

But the Pharisees, on hearing of all this, were driven to even further extremes of hate. Now they began to plot together so that they might also put Lazarus to death, because it was on his account that many of the Jews had come to believe in Jesus, and Judas Iscariot began to make certain plans of his own.

Meanwhile Jesus rested with his friends in Bethany on the sabbath day. Then he left them to go into Jerusalem. At Bethphage, near the Mount of Olives, he sent two of his disciples on ahead. "Go into the village yonder," he said. "As you enter it you will find an ass tied to a door, and next to it a colt that has never been ridden. Loose the colt and bring him to me. And if any man asks you, 'Why do you do this?' tell him that the Lord has need of the colt and will send it back soon. Then the man will let you take the colt."

The two disciples went to the village and found the colt where Jesus had said it would be. As they were untying it, the owner came up and said, "Why are you loosing the colt?"

"The Lord has need of him," the disciples answered.

The owner nodded, as if he had been expecting this, and willingly let them go. The disciples then brought the colt to Jesus and made a simple saddle from their coats. And Jesus mounted the colt, sitting as comfortably as he could on his disciples' garments, and rode toward Jerusalem.

In doing so he was fulfilling the words of a prophet of old:

"Tell the daughter of Zion,
'Behold, your King comes to you,
Meek, and riding on an ass:
On a colt, the foal of an ass!'"

As Jesus approached Jerusalem with his disciples, pilgrims coming for the passover fell in behind. When the people of the city saw the procession coming toward them led by Jesus riding on the colt, great multitudes of them went out to meet him and lead him in. Some of them spread their garments across the road so that he might ride in greater comfort over the rough cobblestones; some cut palm branches from the trees and laid them across his path like a carpet for a king. As he drew near to the entrance of the city his disciples and the whole multitude began to rejoice and praise God for all the mighty works which they had seen.

"Hosanna!" they cried, waving palm branches and crowding around him as he rode. "Hosanna to the son of David! Blessed is the King of Israel, who comes in the name of the Lord! Blessed is the kingdom that comes! Peace in heaven, glory on high, Hosanna in the highest!" And the twelve disciples rejoiced at this tumultuous reception, and praised God in loud, exultant voices.

The Pharisees looked on helplessly. There was nothing they could do to Jesus while the crowds thronged about him and acclaimed him. But they did manage to draw close enough to speak to him of their displeasure.

"Rebuke your disciples!" they said harshly. "They should not cry out and say such things."

"No, I will not rebuke them," Jesus answered. "I tell you, if they should keep their silence, the very stones would cry out instead of them."

And then he rode into the heart of the city, all Jerusalem was stirred. People came out from their houses and asked each other, "Who is this?" and others answered: "This is the prophet, Jesus, from Nazareth of Galilee." For, even though it seemed that all Jerusalem was with him, and crying out: "Hosanna to the son of David!" there were few who truly believed that Jesus really was the Christ. Jesus knew that the day would come when they would suffer for their sins and unbelief; and he wept for them as he looked upon the city. After a brief visit to the temple he went back to Bethany.

On the following morning he returned to Jerusalem and entered into the temple of God, where once again he saw the money changers and the sellers of sacrificial birds and beasts. And, as before, he cast out all those who bought and sold in God's house, driving away the sellers of doves and overturning the tables of the money changers. "It is written in the scriptures," he said to them, "that 'My house shall be called a house of prayer.' But you have made it a den of thieves!"

The sellers and the money changers went off in raging anger. But the blind and the lame came to Jesus in the temple, and he healed them.

The chief scribes and the Pharisees saw the wonderful things that he was doing, and they heard the children of the temple crying out joyously and saying, "Hosanna to the son of David!" Then they were even more indignant than before.

"Do you hear what these children are saying?" they said to Jesus angrily.

"Yes, I hear them," Jesus answered. "Did you never read, 'Out of the mouths of babes and sucklings you have drawn perfect praise'?"

When the priests and scribes heard this they decided that it was now time to destroy Jesus, for they feared that the multitude would cause such an uproar because of his presence that their Roman rulers would hear of it and be mightily displeased. Yet, because of that same multitude, they could find no way to do what they wanted: all the people seemed to be with Jesus, delighting in his teachings and hanging on his every word.

Therefore, because the Pharisees did not know what to do, Jesus was able to leave the city in safety and lodge once again in Bethany.

In the morning he came back to the temple, and the people came early to listen to his words. While he was teaching the people, the chief priests and the elders came to him and listened. Then they interrupted.

"By what authority do you do these things?" they demanded. "And who gave you this authority?"

But Jesus answered their questions with questions of his own which they could not answer, and they were silenced for a while. Yet still they watched him, and while they were not engaged in watching him they took counsel with each other as to how they might make use of his words to trap him and then turn him over to the ruling powers. They sent spies to him, Pharisees and men of Herod's party, who pretended to be honest men so that they might question him and twist his words. One unwise answer, and Jesus would be seized and handed over to Pilate, Roman governor of Judea. If the spies could only get him to say outright that he was King of the Jews, or persuade him to say anything against the Roman rulers, they would have him where they wanted him.

One of the spies approached Jesus with smiling face and honeyed words, and said: "Master, we know that you teach and speak the truth, regardless of what any man might think of you; and we know that you truly teach the way of God. Now tell us what you think: Is it lawful to pay the tribute tax to Caesar, or is it not?"

Now if Jesus said it was lawful, he would be admitting that Caesar was the rightful King of the Jews. And if he said it was not lawful, he would be saying something that the Romans could call treason.

But he saw their craftiness, and answered: "Why do you try to test me, you hypocrites? Show me the tribute money." They showed him a Roman coin called a denarius. Then he said to them, "Whose image is on this coin? Whose name is written on it?"

"Caesar's," they replied.

"Then give to Caesar what is Caesar's," Jesus said, "and give to God the things that belong to God."

They marveled at his answer. Their trick had failed, and so they went away to think of other traps. They hated everything he said: the things that they called blasphemy, and the things that they pretended to call treason. But the common people heard him gladly.

"Beware of the scribes," Jesus warned them even while the scribes themselves were listening. "Beware of the scribes and Pharisees who take widow's houses from them even while they make long prayers and pretend to be the most righteous of men. They shall receive the greater condemnation. They talk, but they do not act. They tie up heavy burdens and have them put upon men's shoulders, but they themselves will not lift a finger to move them. Everything they do, they do to be seen and praised by men: they love to have the chief seats in the synagogues and the chief places at feasts; they wear large tassels on their robes so that they will be admired, and the scripture texts they carry are twice as wide as those of anyone else; they desire deeply to be seen in long, flowing garments, and to be greeted with respect in the market places. Yet their long prayers are a pretense. All the things that they are seen to do are more important to them than prayers, for these things make them look important. But they are not important! I say to you that whoever exalts himself thus shall be humbled, and whoever shall humble himself shall be exalted."

He turned, then, from his friendly listeners to the others.

"Woe to you, scribes and Pharisees, hypocrites!" he said. "For you pay the tax of a tenth part of the herbs you gather and give it to the temple, thinking that you have thereby fulfilled your duties, but you leave undone the important matters of the Law—justice, mercy, and faith. Woe to you, you hypocrites! You clean the outside of the cup and the platter, but inside they are full of your greed and evil-doing. You blind Pharisees! You must first clean the inside of the cup and the platter, so that the outside may also become clean. Be clean within yourselves, not only on the outside.

"Woe to you, scribes and Pharisees, hypocrites! For you are like whitewashed tombs: outwardly, they appear beautiful, but inwardly they are filled with dead men's bones and all uncleanness. In the same way you also appear outwardly righteous, but inwardly you are full of hypocrisy and sin.

"You serpents, you offspring of vipers! How do you think you will escape the judgment of hell? I will send you prophets, wise men, and scribes to help you. But some of them you will kill and crucify; and some of them you will flog in your synagogues, and persecute from city to city; and upon your heads will come all their righteous blood!"

And it was true that, in the years to come, the apostles of Jesus would be stoned and flogged and persecuted, and driven relentlessly from one city to another. Again, the masses, the common people, would welcome them as they now welcomed Jesus, but the rulers of the synagogues would not. And Jesus knew that these things would come to pass in later years.

When he had finished his outspoken condemnation of the scribes and Pharisees, Jesus began to mourn for a Jerusalem that would never really listen and believe. He knew that even among the crowds that professed to believe in him, there were relatively few people who believed with all their hearts and souls. Many would turn away from him before the end; many would lose their belief when he had gone. And the people of Jerusalem would suffer greatly for their sins.

"O Jerusalem, Jerusalem!" he cried, in an agony of pity for the holy city and its people. "You who kills prophets, and who stones those who are sent to you! How often have I wanted to gather your children together, even as a hen gathers her chickens, and you would not allow me! Behold, your house is left desolate. For I say to you, you shall not see me henceforth until you say, 'Blessed is he that comes in the name of the Lord.'"

No, they would never learn, least of all the proud men in positions of power and authority, no matter how boldly Jesus spoke or how many wonderful signs he showed to them. Indeed, at that moment, the scribes and Pharisees were almost speechless with wrath over the things Jesus had said to them and about them in front of the enthralled crowds in the temple.

LAST HOURS IN THE TEMPLE

*J*esus did not hesitate to reprove the self-righteous and the proud, even when they happened to be people in a position to do him great harm. At the same time he was quick to appreciate goodness of heart, and praise those who did well.

A short while after he had rebuked the scribes and Pharisees he sat down near the temple treasury and noticed how the people were casting money into it for offerings to God. Many who were rich were putting in large sums and making no attempt to conceal the generous size of their offerings. Jesus watched them with a feeling of sadness because of their pride. But then there came a poor widow who put in two tiny coins called mites, which together were less than a penny. And he felt glad because of her.

Even as she stood there, Jesus called to his disciples and told them what the woman had done. "Truly," he said, for all to hear, "I say to you that this poor widow has given more than anyone else who is casting money into the treasury. All the others are giving what they can easily spare from their abundance. But she, in need though she is, has put in everything she had. Out of her want and misery, she gave all her living."

Then he went again to teach within the temple, and great crowds gathered to hear him. Even Gentiles asked to see him, bringing requests that he might come to their own lands and teach them as he was trying now to teach the Jews. But he had already taught both Jews and Gentiles what he could in the short time that had been allowed to him. His fate now was to leave them all, and he would not change that even though he could.

Before he left the temple that day he said to those who were with him:

"The hour has come for the Son of man to be glorified. Truly, I say to you, that unless a grain of wheat falls to the ground and dies in bringing forth new wheat, then it remains but a single grain. But if it dies, it yields a great new harvest. For he who loves his life shall lose it, and he who gives up his life in this world shall have eternal life.

"If any man serves me, let him follow me. Wherever I am, there shall my servant be also. For if any man serves me, he will be honored by my Father."

Jesus paused, thinking of the pain and sorrow of the days to come.

"Now my soul is troubled," he went on at last. "And what shall I say? 'Father, save me from this hour'? No! It was for this very reason that I came; for this hour I came into the world. Father, glorify your name!" He bowed his head.

There came a voice out of heaven like a roll of thunder, and it said: "I have both glorified it, and I will glorify it again!"

The murmuring of the crowd became a sudden silence, and then again a stirring of hushed voices. Some who had heard the sound said that it had thundered. Others said, "An angel has spoken to him!"

"This voice did not come for my sake," Jesus said to them. "It came for your sakes, that you might hear and believe. This is a time of judgment for the world. Through my death shall the prince of evil be cast out. And I, if I am lifted up from the ground, will draw all men to me." In saying this he was not only prophesying his own death to the multitude, but describing the manner of it, for he would indeed be lifted up from the ground to die. And in his death he would indeed draw men to him.

Voices from the crowd called out to him, saying: "We have learned from the Law that Christ shall endure forever. Therefore, if you are the Son of man, how can you say that you will be lifted up to die? Who, then, is this Son of man?"

Jesus did not answer them directly. "The light will be with you for only a little while longer," he said. "Walk while you still have the light, so that darkness may not overtake you, for he that walks in darkness does not know where he is going. Believe in the light while you have it, so that you may become the sons of light."

When he had said this he left the temple for the last time.

He and his disciples went together to the Mount of Olives. There they sat and talked, and Jesus told them that he would come to earth for a second time. And the day that he would come would be the last day of the earth, and all men would be judged according to their deeds.

"No man knows the day and the hour," Jesus said, "not even the angels of heaven. Only my Father knows. Watch, therefore, for you do not know when your Lord will come. If the master of the house had known what time the thief was coming, he would have been on watch and would not have allowed his house to be broken into. Be ready, therefore: do good, believe, and be prepared at all times for the coming of the Lord. Pray often, and be watchful of the things you do, for when the Lord comes he will expect you to have used the gifts he has given you, and used them well."

And he told a parable to illustrate his meaning.

"The coming of the kingdom of heaven may be likened to a man who was going on a long journey. Before he left he called his bondservants to him and gave them charge of all his goods. And to one he gave five talents, to another, two, and to another, one, each according to the servant's ability. Then he went upon his journey.

"The man who had received the five talents immediately went and traded with them, and made another five talents. In the same

way, the man who had received the two talents made another
two. But the man who had received the single talent dug a hole in
the earth and hid his master's money.

"Now after a long time the master of these servants came back
and settled his accounts with them. The one who had received
the five talents came and brought with him the other five talents
he had earned. 'Lord,' he said, 'you gave to me five talents. See, I
have made five more.'

"'Well done, my good and faithful servant,' his master said to
him. 'You have been faithful over these few things, therefore I will
set you over many things. Come, share with your master in his
good fortune!'

"Then the one to whom he had given two talents came to him,
saying, 'Master, you gave to me two talents; I have gained two
more.'

"His master said to him, 'Well done, my good and faithful servant. Come share with your master in his good fortune.'

"Then came the one who had buried his single talent in the
ground.

"'Master,' he said, 'I knew that you were a hard man,
demanding much from those who serve you. I was afraid of what
might happen if I were to lose the talent, and I hid it in the earth.
See, it is safe; I give it back to you.' And he gave the single talent
back to his master.

"But his master was greatly displeased. 'You wicked and idle
servant!' he said angrily. 'You say you knew that I was a hard
man, demanding much of those who serve me. Then why did you
not at least put my money into a bank? For then, at my return, I
would have received it back with interest. But you have made
nothing of it!'

"He turned to his other servants. 'Take the talent from this man
and give it to the one who has ten talents,' he commanded. 'For
everyone who has used what has been given him shall be given
more in abundance, but he who has not used it shall lose even
what he has. Now cast the unprofitable servant outside into the
darkness, where he may weep and gnash his teeth.'

"Therefore, I say, be ready always; for the Son of man is returning at a time when you do not think it. Blessed is the servant who shall be found doing his duty when the Lord comes. And blessed is he who does his best with what he has been given, instead of simply making the least possible effort to fulfill his duty. He who works for his Master shall be well rewarded.

"And I tell you further how you shall be judged. When the Son of man comes in all his glory, and all his angels with him, he shall sit on his glorious throne; and all the people of the earth shall be gathered before him. Then the Son of man will separate them as a shepherd separates his sheep and goats, and some shall stand on his right hand and some on his left.

"To those on his right hand the King will say: 'Come, you whom my Father has blessed, enter now into the kingdom prepared for you. For when I was hungry, you gave me food. When I was thirsty, you gave me drink. When I was a stranger, you took me into your homes. When I was naked, you clothed me. When I was sick, you visited me. When I was in prison, you came to me.'

"Then all those who have been welcomed by the King will wonder, and say: 'Lord, when did we see you hungry, and feed you, or thirsty, and give you drink? When did we see you a stranger, and take you in? Or without clothing, and give it to you? When did we see you sick, or in prison, and come to you? We fed beggars at the door, and drew water for thirsty travelers; we gave to those in need, and we opened our homes to those who had no shelter; but never did we do these things for the Son of man.'

"And the King will answer: 'Truly, I say to you, you did these things for me. Whatever kindness you showed to anyone, even to the most humble of these my brothers, you have shown to me.' Then the King will say to those on his left hand: 'Depart from me, you accursed ones, into everlasting fire, for you did not try to help me.' And they will say to him, 'But we did not see you, Lord!'

"Then the Lord will answer, saying, 'You have not helped the least of my brothers. When you saw the hungry, the thirsty, or the strangers in need, you gave nothing to them; when there were those who were naked, sick, or in prison, you turned away and did not help them. And inasmuch as you failed to help the most humble of people, you failed also to do it for me.'

"Those on the left," Jesus said finally, "shall go away into eternal punishment. But those on the right, who were kind and righteous, shall have everlasting life."

When Jesus had told them these things about the day of judgment and the kingdom of heaven, he said to his disciples: "You know that after two days it will be the feast of the passover. That is the time when the Son of man will be betrayed, and afterward crucified."

Even as he spoke the chief priests and scribes and elders of the people were gathering in the house of Caiaphas, the high priest, to discuss how they might take Jesus by stealth and put him to death. They agreed that whatever they did must be done soon, before Jesus could leave Jerusalem again, and that it must be done with guile and subtlety so that he could not escape their clutches. "But it must not be done on the feast day," they said, "or there will be an uproar among the people."

They were still pondering the problem when one of the twelve disciples, he who was called Judas Iscariot, entered stealthily into the presence of the chief priests and offered them his services.

"What will you give me if I deliver him into your hands?" he asked them slyly. "For I can find a way to betray him to you."

They rejoiced when they heard his evil words, for to have help from within the ranks of Jesus' own disciples was an opportunity that could not be bettered. Therefore they gladly agreed to give the traitor thirty pieces of silver. Judas, in return, promised to turn Jesus over to them in such a way as to cause no trouble in the city.

And from that hour he sought a convenient moment at which to betray his Master. It would have to be a time when Jesus was not surrounded by the multitude, so that there would be no disturbance among the people to arouse the anger of the Roman rulers. And Judas thought he knew when that time might be.

THE LAST SUPPER

*C*hen came the first day of unleavened bread, the day on which the passover lamb must be sacrificed and eaten with bitter herbs.

The disciples came to Jesus, saying, "Where would you have us go to make preparations for the passover feast, so that we all may eat?"

Jesus chose Peter and John and instructed them to go into Jerusalem, for they still stayed in Bethany whenever Jesus was not teaching in the temple or talking to the twelve upon the Mount of Olives.

"When you have come into the city," he told them, "you will meet a man carrying a pitcher of water. Follow him into whatever house he enters, and say this to the man of the house: 'The Master says, "Where is my guest chamber, where I may eat the passover with my disciples?"' Then he will show you a large upper room, furnished and ready, and there you will prepare for us."

Peter and John went into the city and found both the man and the house, as Jesus had said they would, and they made their preparations.

When evening came Jesus arrived and sat down with the twelve. As they all took their places at the table, Jesus said to them: "How greatly have I wished to eat this passover with you before I suffer! For I tell you, I shall not eat another until it is fulfilled in the kingdom of God."

Then he took the wine cup, and when he had given thanks, he said:

"Take this, and divide it among yourselves. For I say to you, I will not drink again of the fruit of the vine until the kingdom of God shall come." He passed the wine cup around the table and all the men drank of it in turn like companions at a farewell supper.

As they sat there an argument arose among the twelve. As before, the dispute was concerned with which of them should be called the greatest in the coming kingdom. Jesus listened for some time. At last he spoke, saying, "Whoever is the greatest among you, let him be as the least. And he who is chief must be the servant of all."

Soon after he said this he arose from the table, laid aside his cloak, and fastened a towel about him. Then he poured water into a basin and began to wash his disciples' feet, wiping them with the towel that was about his waist. This was something that was usually done by servants at the beginning of a feast, but the disciples had no servants. And not one of them had thought to do this service, not even for their Master. Shame kept them silent until Jesus came to Simon Peter.

"Lord, Lord!" Peter protested. "Why do you wash my feet?"

"You do not understand now what I am doing," Jesus answered, "but you will understand hereafter."

"You shall never wash my feet," said Peter, and tried to pull away; for he did not want the Lord to do so humble a task for him.

"If I do not wash you, you have no share in my kingdom," Jesus said.

"Lord!" said Simon Peter. "Then wash not only my feet, but also my hands and my head!"

Jesus smiled gently. "Anyone who has already bathed needs only to have his feet washed to be wholly clean," he said. "You are already clean. But not all of you are clean." He said this because he knew that one of his disciples would betray him. And he knew which one it would be.

When Jesus had finished washing their feet he returned to his place at the table.

"Do you understand what I have done to you?" he asked. "You call me Master and Lord, and you say well, for so I am. If I then, your Lord and Master, have washed your feet, you ought also to wash one another's feet. For I have given you an example, so that you may also do what I have done to you and be my true disciples. Truly, I say to you: a servant is not greater than his lord, nor is he that is sent greater than he who has sent him. If you know and understand my commands, you will be blessed if you do them. But I know that you will not follow my example.

"I do not speak of all of you. I know whom I have chosen. But the scripture must be fulfilled that says:

> "'He who is eating bread with me
> Has raised his heel against me.'"

The disciples looked at one another doubtfully, wondering what he meant. Jesus himself was deeply troubled, for he loved his twelve disciples. Yet he knew that there was one among them who did not love him. He saw their wondering glances, and he sadly said: "Yes, it is one of you who will betray me; one of you who is eating with me at this very table."

Again they looked at each other back and forth across the table, feeling great sorrow in their hearts. Each man knew that he had weakness in himself, and each man feared that he might make some terrible mistake that would betray his Lord.

"Is it I, Lord?" each one said in turn. "Is it I?" And they began to question among themselves as to which one of them it was that would do this dreadful thing.

"Tell us who it is!" Simon Peter begged.

Jesus answered, "He that dips his hand with me in the dish, the same shall betray me." Now all of them had dipped in the same dish with him, so they still did not have the answer to their question. But then Jesus dipped a piece of bread into the dish in the middle of the table and handed it to Judas Iscariot.

"Is it I, Lord?" Judas whispered, so quietly that only Jesus could hear him.

Jesus nodded. "You have spoken. Whatever you do, do quickly."

No one but Jesus and Judas understood the meaning of this quiet exchange of words. The rest of the disciples thought that, since Judas held the money bag, Jesus had asked him to go out and buy extra things needed for the feast, or perhaps to give something to the poor. So they thought nothing of it when Judas, having received the piece of bread dipped in the bowl, left the room immediately and went out into the night.

There was no more talk of betrayal after Judas had gone, for as soon as he had left Jesus said to the rest of his disciples:

"My children, for only a little while longer shall I be with you. You will seek me when I have gone; but where I am going, you cannot come. I give to you now a new commandment: Love one another, as I have loved you. By this will all men know that you are my disciples—by your love for one another."

They continued with the meal, although all felt a heaviness of heart they had not known before.

It was almost over now.

Jesus took bread, blessed it, and broke it into small pieces.

"Take; eat," he said to his disciples. "This is my body, which is given for you. Do this in remembrance of me." They each took a piece, and ate.

And when the meal was over he took a cup of wine. He gave thanks and passed the cup to them. "Drink of it, all of you, for this is my blood and the new promise which I give to you. It is shed for you and for many, and it shall be poured out for many, for the forgiveness of their sins. Take it and share it among you. For I tell you again that I shall not drink of the vine until the day I drink it anew with you in my Father's kingdom."

They drank silently.

Then Simon Peter asked the question that had been troubling him.

"Lord, where are you going, that we may not come?"

"I have said to you that where I am going you cannot follow me now," said Jesus, "but you shall follow me afterward."

"But why cannot I follow you now?" asked Peter. "I will go anywhere; I will lay down my life for your sake. With you I am ready to go to prison and to death."

"Will you lay down your life for me?" said Jesus, in a voice of infinite sadness. "Truly I tell you, Peter, that before the cock crows tonight you will deny me three times."

"No, even if I die with you, I will not deny you!" Peter said vehemently. And all the other disciples, except for the missing Judas, said the same.

Jesus let it rest for the time being. Then he said:

"Let not your hearts be troubled. You believe in God; believe also in me. In my Father's house are many rooms. If it were not so, I would have told you. I go now to prepare a place for you. And if I go to prepare a place for you, I will come again to take you back with me, so that where I am, you may be also. You know the way to the place where I am going."

"But, Lord," Thomas said to him, "we do not know where you are going. How, then, can we know the way?"

"I am the way," said Jesus. "I am the way, the truth, and the life. No one comes to the Father but through me, even as no one comes into the sheepfold but through me. And whoever has known me has known my Father also, for the Father is in me.

"And I go soon to my Father. Yet a little while here, and the world will see me no more. But I will not leave you desolate: the Holy Spirit shall be with you. And peace I leave with you; my peace I give to you, and not as the world gives it do I give it to you. Let not your heart be troubled, neither let it be afraid. You have heard me say that I am going away and coming back to you, yet you sorrow became I leave. But if you love me, you will be glad and rejoice, because I go to the Father and my Father is greater than I. I have told you all this before it comes to pass, so that you will believe me when it happens.

"I shall not talk much more with you. Arise, let us leave here."

And when they had sung a hymn, they went out into the Mount of Olives to find peace in the garden of Gethsemane.

Judas, in the meanwhile, was following their movements and reporting to the high priests and the elders.

As Jesus and his disciples went along their way in the darkness toward the garden, Jesus spoke another parable.

"I am the true vine," he said, "and my Father is the farmer of the vineyards. Every branch in me that does not bear fruit, he takes away. And every branch that does bear fruit, he prunes clean so that it will bring forth more fruit.

"Now you are the branches, and I am the vine. You are clean already, as the branches that have been pruned, because of the words which I have spoken to you. Abide with me in your hearts, and I shall abide with you. As the branch cannot bear fruit of itself unless it remains on the vine, neither can you bear fruit unless you abide with me in your hearts and I abide with you. He that abides with me, and I with him, will bear much fruit. But if your hearts are apart from me, you can do nothing.

"If you keep my commandments you will always keep my love, just as I have kept my Father's commandments and have always kept his love. This is my last commandment to you now: Love one another, as I have loved you. Greater love hath no man than this, to lay down his life for his friends. And you are my friends, if you do as I command you. No longer shall I call you servants, for the servant does not know what his master is doing. Now I call you friends, for all the things that I have heard from my Father I have made known to you.

"Until now you have asked for nothing in my name. But ask, from this time forth, and you shall receive so that your joy may be full. The Father himself loves you, because you have loved me, and have believed that I came from God.

"I say these things to you so that, through me, you may find peace. In the world you shall have tribulation. But be of good cheer, for I have overcome the world!"

Then Jesus raised his eyes to heaven. "Father! the hour is come," he said. "Glorify your Son, that your Son may also glorify you. You have given him power over all men on earth, that he should give eternal life to as many as you have given him. And this is life eternal: that they should know you as the only true God, and know that Jesus Christ is the one whom you have sent. I have glorified you on earth; I have finished the work which you gave me to do."

They came, then, to the brook Kidron, and there Jesus said to his eleven disciples: "All of you will forsake me this night. For it is written, 'I will smite the shepherd, and the sheep shall be scattered abroad.' But after I am raised to life I will go before you into Galilee."

Again, Simon Peter protested. "Even if they all desert you, I will not!" he swore.

And again Jesus answered, "I tell you truly, Peter, that the cock shall not crow tonight until you have denied me three times over."

Then they crossed the brook and went together into the garden of Gethsemane. They all knew it well, for Jesus had often gone there with his disciples.

And Judas also knew the place.

THE BETRAYAL

*A*s they entered the garden of Gethsemane Jesus drew three of his disciples to his side and said to the rest of them: "Sit here, while I go yonder and pray."

The eight men sat down beneath the trees at the entrance to the garden. Jesus took Peter, James, and John with him and walked along some little distance. And as he walked he began to think again of how he was being betrayed, of how he would be seized and beaten and led away to die. It would not be long now before the dreadful ordeal would begin. And at the thought of the betrayal and the suffering that was to come, Jesus' heart grew heavy and he was sorely troubled. He said to the three men with him, "My soul is exceedingly sorrowful, even unto death. Stay here, and keep watch over me while I am praying."

He walked on a little further into the grove of trees. Then he stopped, still in sight of the three on watch, and knelt to pray. "O my Father," he began, "if it yet may be, let this bitter cup pass away from me so that I do not have to drink of it. All things are possible for you; take from me this suffering, if you are willing. Nevertheless, let not my will, but yours, be done."

He prayed. But no sign came to him that he would be spared. After praying for a time he rose up and walked slowly back to his three waiting disciples; and found them all asleep. He awakened them and said to Peter, "What, could you not watch with me one hour? Watch now, and pray that you do not fall into temptation. The spirit indeed is willing, but the flesh is weak. Sleep not."

He went away from them a second time and prayed, saying, "My Father, if this cup of suffering cannot pass me by without my drinking of it, then let your will be done."

Again he went back to his three disciples, and again he found them heavy-eyed with sleep. Nor did they know what to answer him when they awoke, even though he had so great a need for their love and support.

He left them and went away to pray a third time. In his agony of suffering and loneliness he prayed with even greater intensity than before, and the sweat rolled off his face to fall like great drops of blood upon the ground. Then there appeared to him a bright angel from heaven, to give him strength and comfort in his agony. Peace came into his heart. He rose, strong and ready for whatever was to come.

For the third time he went back to his disciples. "You may as well sleep on now, and take your rest," he said. "There is no longer any need to watch. Behold! the hour has come, and the Son of man is betrayed into the hands of sinners. He who betrays me is at hand."

And even before he had finished speaking there was a clamor of startled cries from the eight disciples at the entrance to the garden. Lights flickered through the trees and harsh voices gave commands. The sounds of clinking metal and heavy footfalls filled the night. And then the bright glow of lanterns and torches swept the grove and came to rest on Jesus.

In the gloom beyond the lights he could see a great band of soldiers, accompanied by officers from the chief priests and the Pharisees. The group came closer, and in the brightness that now was almost in their midst, Jesus and his disciples could see the clubs and swords carried by the intruders.

One man went slightly ahead of the group, leading the officers forward.

And then this one man, the betrayer of Jesus, gave a signal to the others saying: "Whomsoever I kiss, that is he. Take him!"

Judas stepped forward and stood before Jesus with his arms outstretched in a gesture of false friendship.

"Hail, Master!" he said, and kissed Jesus on the cheek.

"Why have you come, my friend?" said Jesus. "Would you betray the Son of man with a kiss?"

The soldiers advanced upon him.

Jesus walked toward them. "For whom are you looking?" he asked.

"For Jesus of Nazareth," they answered.

"I am he," said Jesus calmly. They drew back, soldiers, priests and Pharisees, disconcerted by his manner.

He therefore asked again: "Whom do you seek?"

"Jesus of Nazareth," they repeated.

"I told you that I am he," said Jesus. "If it is I whom you seek, let these other men go their way without harm."

It was as if he himself had given a signal, for at these words the chief captain gave an order and the whole band rushed forward to lay rough hands upon him. For a moment there was a great confusion of clanking swords and milling men, even though Jesus stood there without moving, and in the turmoil Simon Peter drew a sword and slashed at one of the servants of the high priest. The blow struck savagely at the man's head and cut off his right ear. The man screamed with pain.

"Put up your sword!" said Jesus, already firmly bound with sturdy cords. "All who draw the sword shall die by it. Do you not know that I could beseech my Father to save me, and he would send more than twelve legions of angels to vanquish this band of men? But how then would the scriptures be fulfilled, which say this thing must happen?" Jesus turned then to the man whom Peter's sword had struck. "Let me first do this," he said. He touched the man's ear, and at once it was healed.

The soldiers clawed at Jesus, dragging him away. Chief priests, elders, and captains of the temple gathered around in triumph and shouted abuse while the armed men waved their weapons threateningly at a band of disciples who had no further thought of fighting back.

Then Jesus said to the ugly crowd:

"Do you come out with swords and staves to arrest me, as though I were a robber? I sat daily with you in the temple, teaching, and you did not stretch out a hand against me then. But this is your hour, the hour when the forces of darkness are in power. All this is happening now in fulfillment of the scriptures of the prophets."

The crowd fell upon him then to push and drag him from the peaceful garden to Jerusalem. And each and every one of Jesus' disciples turned, left their Master, and fled into the darkness. As for Judas, he had already gone his way.

The enemies of Jesus led him first to the house of Annas, father-in-law of Caiaphas the present high priest, and onetime high priest himself. He was still very influential among the priests and Pharisees, who deferred to his age and experience and often consulted him in cases involving serious breaches of Mosaic Law. Therefore, although their respect for him was hardly justified, they now brought Jesus to him for preliminary questioning.

Jesus stood in bonds before the old high priest. Annas heard the furious charges against him, and then began to question him about his disciples and his teachings.

Jesus told him nothing about his disciples. Now would he say anything about his teachings. Instead, he said: "Why do you need to question me? I have spoken openly to the world. I have always taught in synagogues and in the temple, where all the Jews meet together and have heard me. I have said nothing in secret. Why, then, do you ask me? Ask those who heard me when I spoke; they know what I said."

One of the officers struck Jesus across the mouth. "Is that the way you answer the high priest?" the man said roughly.

"If I have said anything evil," Jesus answered calmly, "then say what evil I have spoken. But if what I have said is true, why do you strike me?"

Annas tried again. But he could get nothing out of Jesus that he could use as evidence against him. The old priest sent him, therefore, to Caiaphas the high priest, who had already called together certain chosen members of his council. They sat there waiting, the inner circle of priests, elders, and scribes, eager to see the Nazarene standing bound before them.

The officers brought Jesus into the council chamber.

And Simon Peter, who had fled with all the others, came back from hiding and followed at a distance as far as the court of the high priest. It was late by now, and chilly winds blew outside in the courtyard. Some of the servants and officers had built a fire to warm themselves against the chill of the night, and Peter went to share its warmth while he waited for the end of the scene within.

Inside, the chief priests and all the present members of the council sought false witnesses to offer evidence against Jesus so that they might put him to death. Many came forward, and many gave false statements, but none of the false statements agreed.

At last two false witnesses stood up confidently and declared:

"We have heard him say, 'I will destroy this temple built by the hands of men, and in three days I will build another, which shall be made without hands.'"

But this was not what Jesus had said; and even the testimony of these two men did not agree.

Caiaphas the high priest stood up and faced Jesus. "Do you answer nothing?" he demanded. "What is this, that these witnesses say against you?"

But Jesus gave no answer. It was useless to explain what he had really said, or what he had meant by it. And in any event, what he had said would soon become a fact.

Caiaphas spoke again. "I demand that you tell us, on your oath by the living God, whether or not you are the Christ, the Son of God."

And Jesus said: "I am. And you will see the Son of man sitting on the right hand of the Almighty, and coming upon the clouds of heaven!"

The high priest tore his clothes with rage and triumph. "He has spoken blasphemy!" he cried. "What further need have we of witnesses? We ourselves have heard the blasphemy from his own mouth! What do you say now, you priests and elders?"

"He is worthy of death," some answered at once, and others took up the cry: "Yes, he deserves to die!" And they all condemned him to death.

Then some began to spit upon him and to strike him. Those who were holding him mocked him and beat him with their fists, saying, "Prophesy, you Christ!" Then they blindfolded him and struck him again with evil glee. "Show us that you are a prophet! See if you can tell us who it was who struck you!" And they all struck him and abused him without mercy.

The long night wore on and still they treated him unmercifully, shameful in their actions and shameless in their vindictive triumph. When it was almost dawn the chief priests, scribes and elders of the people, all the members of the council, held a final consultation over Jesus. It was formally decided by them now that he should be put to death. Yet they could not effect the sentence without first convincing the Roman procurator that it must be done.

Meanwhile, Peter was still waiting in the outer court, sitting there and warming himself by the fire in the cold first light of dawn. A maidservant at the courtyard door saw him where he sat. She looked at him searchingly. Surely, she thought, she had seen this man before. Of course she recognized him! She went to him and said: "You were with this Jesus of Nazareth. Are you not one of his disciples?"

Peter was suddenly filled with the fear he had felt earlier in the garden of Gethsemane. And all he could think of was the violent death that he might suffer if he admitted to being a follower of Jesus.

"No!" he said. "I do not know what you are saying."

Nervously, he moved from the courtyard to the porch.

Shortly after that a second woman saw him. "This man is one of those who were with Jesus of Nazareth," she said to others who stood nearby; and she looked accusingly at Peter.

Again he denied it with an oath. "I do not know the man!" he said.

Next one of the servants of the high priest, a kinsman of the man whose ear Peter cut off, came up to him and stared him in the face. "You! You Galilaean!" he said. "You are one of them; I know you by your speech. And did I not see you in the garden with him when we came to seize him?"

"No!" said Peter. And he began to curse and swear. "I do not know the man; I do not know what you are talking about."

And immediately, the cock crowed in the blue light of the morning.

At that moment Jesus came out from the high priest's house, bound with tight cords and pushed rudely by the attendants of the priest. He turned and looked at Peter with compassion as he passed. Peter saw him and turned his eyes away. He remembered, now, those words of Jesus: "Before the cock crows, you will deny me three times."

And Peter had denied him thrice. He went out from the courtyard, weeping bitter tears.

THE TRIAL

*T*he death sentence had been passed by the council of the Jews, and now all that remained to be done was to obtain the official approval of their Roman ruler. A great company of people led Jesus to Pontius Pilate, procurator of Judea, for final judgment. High priests and chief Pharisees took up the lead. Behind them came the false witnesses who had spoken against him, various hirelings who had been persuaded to shout abuse against the man whom others called King of the Jews, and numbers of people who had little understanding of what was happening but had been attracted by the crowd. In the midst of all was Jesus, still bound and pushed along by soldiers who did not care what he had done but knew that he must not escape.

Pontius Pilate came out into the courtyard of his palace and stared at the multitude. There were high priests there, he saw, and elders of the people, and many others whom he did not know. In the midst of all there stood a man who clearly was their prisoner. The man's wrists were tightly tied together, his simple robe was soiled, and he had evidently been beaten without mercy. Yet he seemed serene and unafraid.

Early though it was, Pilate was ready to listen to their case. It must surely be important, or they would not have come at this hour, least of all with their high priests in the lead looking both outraged and triumphant.

"What accusation do you bring against this man?" asked Pilate.

"He is an evildoer," Caiaphas and Annas answered him, "or we would not have brought him to you. He has been corrupting our nation, forbidding people to give tribute to Caesar and saying that he is Christ, King of the Jews." Now in saying this they were not bringing up their own charge of blasphemy, for they knew that Pontius Pilate had no interest in their religious laws. But they were sure he would be interested in a Jew who claimed to be a king and refused the tribute to Caesar, for this was treason against the Roman rulers.

Yet they had not read Pilate as accurately as they thought. The Roman ruler caught the phrase, "King of the Jews," and decided at once that this was a Jewish religious question and therefore none of his concern.

"Then try him yourselves," said Pilate, "and judge him according to your own Law."

"We have tried him," they answered. "But we have no authority to put any man to death."

Pilate knew that very well. But he had not expected them to ask the death sentence.

He looked again at the captive Jesus and saw a most unlikely looking king, and a most unlikely looking criminal. And as he looked the chief priests and the elders shouted accusations against the prisoner, accusing him of many things; yet the prisoner himself said nothing. Pilate found this very strange, for he had seen many prisoners before and they had always been vigorous in their own defense.

"Do you have no answer for them?" Pilate said to Jesus. "Do you not hear how many things they charge you with?"

But Jesus made no answer to any of the accusations. He only stood there, dignified and calm; so calm that Pilate marveled greatly, turned away, and went back into his palace, for he knew nothing of this prisoner and realized he would find out nothing while the mob was screaming accusations in the courtyard.

From the judgment hall of his palace he there sent for Jesus.

Jesus came in and stood before him; still bound, still unafraid.

And Pilate the governor asked him: "Are you the King of the Jews?"

"Do you ask me this because you think it yourself?" said Jesus. "Or have others told you this about me?"

"Am *I* a Jew?" answered Pilate. "Your own people and the chief priests handed you over to me. What have you done? Do they accuse you rightly?" For he wanted to know if Jesus really claimed to be their king.

"My kingdom is not of this world," Jesus answered. "If it were, my men would have fought to keep me from being delivered into the hands of the Jews. No, my kingdom is not here on earth."

"Then you *are* a king?" said Pilate.

"You say rightly. I am a king," Jesus answered. "It was for this that I was born, and for this that I have come into the world: to testify to the truth. Everyone who is on the side of truth listens to my voice."

Pilate stared at him. "What is truth?" he asked.

With these words he arose and strode out into the courtyard once again to face the Jews. He had heard all he needed to hear: Jesus had said, "My kingdom is not of this world," and to Pilate that did not sound like treason against the Roman emperor.

"I find no fault in this man," he said.

The priests were thunderstruck that Pilate should have found Jesus innocent. Mutterings broke out in the crowd they had gathered to lend weight to their false cause, and the priests themselves became increasingly urgent in their demands.

"He is stirring up the people!" they cried fiercely. "He has been teaching his radical doctrines throughout all Judea, beginning in Galilee, going all over the countryside, even coming here to Jerusalem!"

"Oh?" said Pilate. "Galilee? Is this man a Galilaean?"

"Yes, he is from Nazareth."

"Ah." Pilate was glad to hear it. The whole affair was becoming a nuisance to him. If this Jesus was a Galilaean, he came under Herod's jurisdiction. And Herod could take care of his own.

So Pilate sent Jesus and his accusers to Herod Antipas, who also happened to be in Jerusalem at that time because of the festival.

Now when Herod saw Jesus he was exceedingly glad, for he had long been interested in seeing this man. He had lost his earlier desire to send out soldiers to seize him, for by all acounts the man Jesus was not John the Baptist risen again, nor had he spoken out against Herod as had John. Nevertheless, Herod had heard many extraordinary things about the Nazarene, and he was most anxious to see some miracle performed by him.

Therefore he greeted Jesus with enthusiasm, though without cordiality, and questioned him at length. But Jesus gave no answer to Herod's questions, nor any sign of his miraculous powers. Herod soon tired of him; this was poor sport indeed. He let the chief priests and scribes have their turn to speak. And they were only too willing. Vehemently they accused Jesus of inciting rebellion among the people, of refusing to pay tribute to Caesar, of claiming to be the Messiah, the King of the Jews. But Herod was not interested. He had only wanted to see signs, and he had seen none. Certainly he could see no evidence of treason, and obviously the man was no threat either to the Romans or to Herod himself.

The only thing that caught the tetrarch's interest was that this quiet man before him could claim to be the King of Israel, or the King of the Jews. And that in itself was Judea's problem, not Herod's. Still, it was an amusing thought and Herod smiled. A king, was he? And Herod laughed as he struck upon an idea that entertained him greatly. At least he would have some enjoyment from all this!

"Bring robes!" he ordered his palace guards. "If this man is a king, then let him look like a king!"

So they dressed Jesus mockingly in regal robes, laughing at their own cleverness, and they ridiculed him as he stood there in the finery they had forced upon him.

But soon they tired of this, too, for Jesus seemed untouched by their mockery; and they stopped their jeering and sent him back to Pilate.

Pilate was not pleased to see the Jews returning with their captive. He called together the chief priests and the leading members of the council, and all the people who had demanded that he pronounce sentence upon Jesus.

"You brought this man to me," he said, "as one who has misled the people with false claims. I have examined him before you and have not found him guilty of any of the things of which you have accused him. Neither has Herod found him guilty, for he sent him back to us. This man has done nothing to deserve death. I will therefore have him flogged, and then release him."

The crowd stirred restlessly. Flogging with the metal-tipped scourge was a terrible punishment, but it was not death. And they wanted Jesus dead. Certainly they did not want to have him released.

Now at the time of festival it was customary for the governor to release to the people any prisoner they chose; and at this particular time a notable prisoner named Barabbas was lying bound in a dungeon. Barabbas was a revolutionary who had stirred rebellion among the people, in addition to being a robber and a murderer; and while Pilate himself definitely preferred to have such a man languishing in jail, the people themselves had no great interest in Barabbas either in prison or out, until Pilate now gave them a choice.

"Shall I then release the King of the Jews, in accordance with your custom?" Pilate asked. "Or whom would you have me release—Barabbas, or Jesus who is called the Christ?" He hoped that the crowd would call for Jesus, for he knew that the high priests had delivered Jesus to him out of envy and he did not wish to condemn the Nazarene to death.

But the mob gathered by the priests and Pharisees cried out together: "Not this man! Away with Jesus! Release not him, but Barabbas!"

Pilate was deeply disturbed by their answer. And while he sat there on the judgment seat, hesitating, he received a message from his wife. It said: "Have nothing to do with harming that good man, for I have suffered many things this day in a dream because of him." At this, Pilate was even more worried than before. He mulled the problem over in his mind. Even while he was doing so the chief priests and elders were arousing the multitude to cry out for Barabbas so that Jesus might be destroyed.

In spite of the rising tumult, Pilate asked again: "Which of the two would you have me release?"

"Barabbas! Barabbas!" they shouted back.

"Then what would you have me do to Jesus, who is called Christ?" Pilate asked them.

"Crucify him! Crucify him!" the people screamed.

"Why? What evil has he done?" asked Pilate. "I have found nothing in him to warrant his death. I will therefore chastise him and release him."

"No! Crucify him, crucify him!" screamed the crowd. "Give us Barabbas instead!"

But Pilate sent for his guard so that Jesus might be flogged, for he thought that, once the crowd saw the dreadful punishment inflicted upon Jesus, they would relent and no longer demand his death.

Pilate's soldiers flogged Jesus brutally. When they had done, they led him into the common hall and gathered about him with glee upon their faces. They stripped him of his tunic and dressed him in a purple robe such as a very great king might wear; and they wove a wreath of thorns and placed it on his head as if it were a crown; and they thrust a tall reed into his hand as if it were a scepter. Then they bowed low and knelt before him as though in worship of a mighty king.

"Hail, King of the Jews!" they mocked.

When they had had enough of this they took the sturdy reed and struck him with it, and they spat upon him. Then they led him back to Pilate.

Pilate once again went out into the courtyard and said to the waiting priests and multitude: "Behold! I bring him out to you, so that you may know that I find no fault in him." Surely now, he thought, the council and the people would have had enough.

Jesus came out wearing the crown of thorns and the purple robe.

Pilate pointed at him. Jesus was gaunt and bleeding, a travesty of a king in his mock-regal raiment; but still he stood upright and moved with quiet dignity.

"Behold the man!" said Pilate.

Whipped into yet greater frenzy by the high priests and their officers, the crowd cried out: "Crucify him! Crucify him!"

"Take thim and crucify him yourselves, then," Pilate said, frightened by their ferocity. "I can find no crime in him."

But the Jews, under Roman law, were not permitted to execute a man themselves. The Romans had to do it for them. And it was clear to the high priests and the Pharisees that Pilate was still trying to avoid pronouncing an official sentence.

"We have a Law!" the Pharisees shouted. "And by our Law he deserves death for declaring himself to be the Son of God!" The crowd roared again, and this time there was a note of menace in their cries.

Pilate, hearing it, became even more afraid. He led Jesus to one side and asked him, almost desperately, "What *are* you?"

But Jesus made no answer.

"Do you refuse to speak to me?" said Pilate. "Do you not know that it is my power to release you, or have you crucified?"

"You have no power against me that is not given to you from above," Jesus answered. "The man who betrayed me to you has committed the greater sin."

At this, Pilate tried again to release him, but the Jews cried out:

"If you free this man, you are no friend of Caesar's! Anyone who pretends to be a king commits treason against Caesar!"

"Then shall I crucify your king?" said Pilate.

"He is not our king!" the high priests shouted back. "We have no king but Caesar! Are you not Caesar's friend?"

By now their threat was obvious, and Pilate really was afraid. If what they were saying came to Caesar's ears, he himself would be in jeopardy. Already it looked as though a riot might develop, and this in itself would be enough to endanger his position.

He therefore sent for a bowl of water and washed his hands before the crowd. "I am innocent of the blood of this just man," he said. "You must see to it yourselves."

Then all the people answered, "Let his blood be on us, and upon our children!"

Pilate pronounced sentence. He released Barabbas to them, and he called his soldiers to give them their instructions. When they had finished mocking Jesus in his purple robe, they took it off and dressed him once again in his own simple garment. Then, leaving the crown of thorns upon his head, they led him away from the governor's palace to be crucified.

And Pilate, having washed his hands of the whole affair, left them to it.

Now Judas Iscariot, the betrayer of Jesus, was hovering on the fringes of the crowd as it neared the city gate, and soon discovered that Jesus had been condemned to death by crucifixion. Suddenly he was stricken with terrible remorse for the treacherous thing he had done. With a greatly troubled heart he went back to the chief priests and elders with his thirty pieces of silver.

"I have sinned!" he said. "I have betrayed an innocent man."

They looked at him with scorn. "What is that to us?" they said. "That is your affair; answer for your own sin."

In an agony of repentance the traitor threw the pieces of silver on the temple floor. Then he ran out of the temple to a lonely place outside the city.

The chief priests picked up the pieces of silver. At this moment even they felt some slight sense of shame. "It is not lawful for us to put this money into the treasury," they said, "because it is the price of blood."

They therefore took counsel with each other, and after some discussion they decided to use the money to buy the potter's field for the burial of penniless strangers. The ground they afterward purchased with the blood money has been called the Field of Blood to this very day. And because it was a potter's field, any piece of ground used as a graveyard for unknown persons or the very poor is still, today, known as a potter's field.

The crowds, with Jesus in their midst, milled through the northern city gate.

And Judas, in the lonely place, hanged himself upon a tree.

THE CRUCIFIXION

*I*t was still early on that long morning of trial and condemnation when Jesus started his last and most painful journey.

The Roman soldiers led him through the north gate of the city to the place of death, called Calvary by the Romans and known as Golgotha in the Hebrew tongue. Both names mean "The Place of the Skull." Jesus staggered up the hillside carrying the heavy cross upon which he was later to be nailed, for it was the custom among the Romans that those who were about to die by execution should carry their own crosses.

His back was bowed beneath the weight of the great wooden beam as he walked, and his feet stumbled on the rough road. A great company of people gathered and followed him as he slowly climbed the hill to Calvary. Some were enemies who mocked him, some were passing strangers who joined the throng through curiosity or chance, and some were his friends who longed to help him but could not. The women among them wailed and wept, lamenting Jesus and beating their breasts with sorrow as they saw his suffering and knew that worse was yet to come.

And even with the racking pain in his body and the cross upon his back, Jesus saw their sorrow. He turned his head to them and said: "Daughters of Jerusalem, do not weep for me. Weep rather for yourselves and for your children, for a time is coming when it will be said, 'Happy are the childless, who have no little ones to be slain, and happy are those who never will have children.' For when Jerusalem suffers for its sins it will be well for those who have no young ones, for not even the youngest will be spared. And at that time the people of the city will say to the mountains, 'Fall on us!' and to the hills they will cry, 'Cover us!' so that they might escape their fate. But there will be no escape, for if this is what they do when I am here, what will they do when I am gone?"

He stumbled on beneath the cross, carrying it upon his wounded shoulders. But he had been so badly beaten that his strength was almost gone, and at last he fell and could not rise. The soldiers cursed and prodded him. But still he could not manage to struggle to his feet with the weight upon his back.

"You, there!" the soldiers shouted, and they seized upon a man in the crowd who knew nothing of what was happening. The man was Simon of Cyrene, who was coming in from the country; and they laid the cross upon his back and compelled him to carry it after Jesus. Jesus therefore rose and walked on slowly.

The procession continued. Now two other doomed men, common criminals, were brought into it to be led with Jesus to the place of death.

At last they all reached the Place of the Skull. When they came to the hilltop the soldiers ordered Simon of Cyrene to lay the cross down flat upon the ground. Then they removed Jesus' clothes and made him lie upon the cross. They nailed him to it through his hands and feet. Now they raised the cross and planted it firmly in the earth. Meanwhile, other guards were preparing the two criminals for crucifixion, and when the three crosses were raised Jesus was in the center with one robber on his right hand and the other on his left.

The soldiers offered Jesus a drink of sour wine mixed with bitter gall, but he refused it. And as he hung there on the cross awaiting death, Jesus called out: "Father, forgive them, for they know not what they do."

There was little to do but wait. While they waited, the soldiers divided up the clothes that Jesus had been wearing into four parts, one for each man guarding him while he slowly died. But when they came to the tunic and saw that, instead of having a seam, it was woven in one piece from top to bottom, they decided that it could not be divided. Therefore they said to one another, "Let us not tear it, but cast lots among us to see who shall have it." They did so, and in doing it they fulfilled the psalm in the scriptures, which read: "They divided my garments among them, and for my clothing they cast lots." All these things the Roman soldiers did, without knowing that what they were doing had been predicted centuries before.

Now Pilate had written a sign in letters of Hebrew, Latin, and Greek, saying: "THIS IS JESUS THE KING OF THE JEWS." When the soldiers had finished their business of dividing up the clothes they set the sign over Jesus' head and settled back to watch him die.

The people stood there staring at him. Others, passing by along the road, stopped to jeer at him and shake their heads in scorn.

"You who would destroy the temple and build it up again in three days, save yourself!" they mocked. "If you are the Son of God, save yourself and come down from the cross." The chief priests, with the scribes and elders, mocked him in the same way, saying: "He saved others, so we hear, but he cannot save himself. He is the Christ, the King of Israel and the chosen one of God! Therefore let him now come down from the cross, and we will believe in him. He trusted in God; let God now deliver him if he wants to. For this man said, 'I am the Son of God.'"

But though Jesus could have come down from the cross he would not, for death on the cross was his destiny.

The soldiers mocked him, too. They came to him offering him sour wine to moisten his dry lips, and said: "If you are the King of the Jews, let us see you save yourself!"

Even the robbers who were being crucified alongside him abused him. One in particular mocked and cursed at Jesus. "Are you not the Christ?" he said. "If you are, save yourself and us!"

But as the time passed and the first man received no answer, the second man began to see in Jesus a quiet strength he had not seen before. He therefore rebuked the other, saying, "Have you no fear even of God, when you are suffering the same penalty as this man? We two are suffering justly, for we deserve to die for what we have done, but this man has done nothing wrong." Then he turned his head to look at Jesus. "Lord," he said, "remember me when you come into your kingdom, for I believe in you."

And Jesus answered him saying, "I tell you truly, today you will be with me in Paradise."

Then he looked down to see those who stood near him. Close to the cross stood his mother, his mother's sister, and Mary Magdalene, and only one of his disciples. Both Lazarus, whom he had raised from the dead, and the eleven men who had been his most devoted followers, were still in danger from the vengeful priests and Pharisees. Most of them, therefore, were afraid to be seen near him even while he was dying on the cross. But John at least, whom Jesus dearly loved, was there with the wailing women.

When Jesus saw John standing at his mother Mary's side and trying to comfort her, he called down from the cross. To his mother he said: "Woman, behold your son John!" And to John he said: "John, behold your mother! Care for her." And from that hour John took Mary into his own home and cared for her as if she were his mother.

The painful hours dragged by. High noon came, and the sun blazed overhead. Then suddenly the sun was covered by black clouds, and darkness fell over all the land. A strong wind swept the hill upon which the crosses stood, an eerie sound in the strange darkness of the day. Many of the people shook with fear and many of them left the place of death, trying to escape their fear. But many others, friends and enemies alike, stayed to see the end.

Three hours later, under a sky still ominously dark, Jesus cried out suddenly: "My God, my God, why have you forsaken me?" His hearers recognized the words, for they were also in the scriptures that had foretold the manner of his death. There was a brief silence, and the sky began to brighten.

Then Jesus spoke again, once more fulfilling the scriptures.

"I thirst," he said.

There was a bowl of the sour wine standing by. One of the watchers took a sponge and soaked it in the wine, then put it on a reed and held it up so that Jesus might drink. And some of the others jeered, saying: "Let us see whether Elijah comes to save him!"

Jesus moistened his lips with the sour wine. His work was now accomplished and he was ready to free his spirit. He cried out again in a firm, clear voice:

"It is finished!"

And to his listeners it sounded not like a cry of despair, but a cry of victory.

Now Jesus spoke his last words on the cross. "Father, into your hands I entrust my spirit."

When he had said this, he bowed his head, and died.

At the very moment in which he yielded up his spirit the curtain that veiled the inner sanctuary of the temple in Jerusalem was torn in two from top to bottom. The earth quaked, great rocks shattered; tombs opened, and saints rose from their sleep to leave their graves.

The Roman centurion in charge of the guard saw how Jesus had yielded up his spirit; he saw the earthquake and many other strange and wonderful things that happened in the moment of Jesus' death, and he was so frightened and amazed that he cried out in glory of God. "This surely was a righteous man!" he said in awe. "Truly he must have been a Son of God!" And others echoed him.

But now it was all over. The crowds that had gathered to watch the spectacle turned away, beating their breasts, and went back to the city. But the friends of Jesus, and his mother, and many women who had followed him from Galilee, stayed there watching from a distance. Among them were Mary Magdalene, and Salome the wife of Zebedee and mother of James and John, and Mary the wife of Alphaeus and mother of the other James. All had loved him deeply; and all were overcome with sorrow for their Master and for his weeping mother.

It was now mid-afternoon, and the beginning of the sabbath would come with the setting of the sun. And because the bodies could neither be removed from the crosses or allowed to remain upon them on the sabbath day, least of all during the passover season, the Jews went to Pilate and asked that the bodies be removed at once. Pilate agreed to their request and sent his soldiers back to Calvary.

First they made sure that the two robbers were dead. Then they came to Jesus. They knew he was already dead, yet one of the soldiers thrust a spear into his side; and from the wound there flowed both water and blood. They stared at the limp body in surprise, not knowing that they were fulfilling yet another prophecy: "They shall look upon the man whom they have pierced."

When it was close to evening there came a rich man from Arimathea, named Joseph, who went to see Pilate to ask for the body of Jesus. Now Joseph was a Pharisee and a respected member of the council, but like Nicodemus he was a good and righteous man who had vehemently objected to any suggestion that Jesus might be harmed. In fact, when the council had held their hasty pre-dawn meeting, they had taken good care to exclude both Joseph and Nicodemus. They knew that these two men were sympathetic toward the Nazarene. What they did not know was that both of them were actually disciples of Jesus, and were themselves looking for the kingdom of God through the man from Nazareth.

And now Joseph of Arimathea stood boldly before Pilate,

asking for the body of Jesus so that he might bury it. Pilate granted permission.

Joseph therefore went to the place of death, taking with him fine linen cloths to wrap around the body. Nicodemus went also, taking a mixture of myrrh and aloes to perfume the grave clothes. Ordinarily the body would be carefully washed and anointed before burial, but there was no time for that. Together the two men took Jesus down from the cross. Together they bound his body in the linen cloths with the spices, in accordance with the Jewish custom. Then, with the help of friends, they gently carried Jesus to a tomb in a garden near the place of the cross.

It was Joseph's own new tomb, one that he had hewn from rock for the day of his own burial, and no man had ever yet been laid in it. Now Joseph was using it as a resting place for Jesus so that the Master might be buried before sundown, and in a place where his body would be safe from enemies who might wish to steal or desecrate it.

The eleven disciples were hiding in Jerusalem. But the women who had come from Galilee followed the small procession and saw Jesus being gently placed within the tomb. Then Joseph rolled a great stone against the mouth of the tomb and departed for his home. When this was done the women left, too, and went off, mourning bitterly. And they rested on the sabbath day, according to the commandment.

The first night of sorrow passed. Very early in the morning the chief priests and Pharisees hurried off to Pilate and made another request. For during the night they had been struck by a thought that had not even occurred to any of the followers of Jesus.

"Sir," they said to Pilate, "we remember that when the deceiver Jesus was alive he said, 'In three days I will rise again.' We ask, therefore, that you give orders to have the tomb closely guarded and secured until the third day. For it may be that his disciples will try to come at night and steal him away, afterwards saying to the people that he has risen from the dead."

"Take the guard," said Pilate. "Make the tomb as secure as you can."

So they went off with the officers and made the grave as secure as they could by sealing the stone and leaving a guard on watch.

This was the second day of Jesus' death.

When the sabbath was over at sunset of that day, Mary Magdalene and Mary the mother of James, and Salome who had followed Jesus through Galilee, went out and bought sweet spices and ointments so that they might properly anoint the body of Jesus whom they loved. When the night had passed and the early morning hours had come, they would go to the tomb and make the burial preparations for which there had been no time before. So the women made plans to go to the garden first thing in the morning.

But the eleven disciples remained behind closed doors, afraid for themselves and full of sorrow over Jesus. They had wanted a king and they had dreamed of glory, and now the dream was gone with the death of Jesus. They had loved him; they had learned much from him; but they had never really understood all he had told them about the nature of the kingdom of God, or what he had meant when he had said that he would rise again. Now they sat there without hope, staring silently at each other and not even thinking to count the days.

The morning of the first day of the new week dawned. It was the third day of the death of Jesus. The Roman soldiers still stood on watch outside the tomb. With the coming of the dawn the ground began to tremble and shake, and a great earthquake racked the garden where Joseph of Arimathea had laid Jesus in the cave. An angel of the Lord came down from heaven and rolled away the stone from the mouth of the tomb, and calmly sat upon it. His face was as bright as lightning, and his raiment as white as dazzling snow; and his watchers gaped and turned pale with fear. They stared at the angel, quaking, and so overcome with shock were they that they fell to the ground like men who had been struck dead.

When they recovered themselves they got up and fled into the city to report what they had seen. They ran very quickly, and they did not look back.

It was very early when Mary Magdalene and the other women came with their spices to anoint their beloved Jesus. The guard had gone, but this did not surprise them for they had not known that any soldiers had been posted. As they walked into the garden they were saying to one another, "Who will roll back for us the stone from the doorway of the tomb?" for the stone was much too heavy for the women to handle alone. Then they reached the tomb. And what they saw then did surprise them.

The stone had already been rolled back from the cave. And when they looked in through the open doorway they saw that the body of Jesus was no longer there.

HE IS RISEN!

*T*he women stared amazed into the tomb. They could scarcely believe their eyes, for they had seen Joseph laying Jesus in the tomb. But it was true: Jesus was not there.

Mary Magdalene gasped with shock and fear. Her only thought was that the enemies of Jesus had come and taken him away from the place where he had been so lovingly laid. In her misery she turned abruptly and ran back into the city to find John and Simon Peter.

"They have taken the Lord away from the tomb," she gasped, "and we do not know where they have laid him!"

They were disturbed and puzzled. Not knowing what to do, they did nothing. Mary left them and wandered slowly back toward the garden.

Meanwhile, the Roman guards who had run from the tomb had gone straight to the priests to tell them what they had seen. They knew nothing of the visit of the women, but they did know that the body of Jesus was gone. The priests were angry and alarmed, although they could not blame the soldiers. After a quick consultation with the elders they decided on a course of action: they

would lie. They gave the soldiers a large sum of money to hide
the truth and tell a different version of their story.

"We will not have it said that Jesus is risen," they announced.
"Tell people that his disciples came in the night and stole away
his body while you slept. If news of this comes to Pontius Pilate
and he accuses you of failing in your duty, we will persuade him
that you were not to blame and see that no trouble comes to you."
The soldiers therefore took the money and began to spread the
false story among the people. And those who heard, believed
them.

Now the other women who had been with Mary Magdalene
were still within the tomb. But while they looked about it they
saw that they were not alone. Jesus had indeed gone, but now
they saw a young man in dazzling white apparel sitting at the
right. There was a glow about him that amazed and frightened
them.

"Do not be afraid," the angel said. "I know you are looking for
Jesus of Nazareth, who has been crucified. He is not here, for he
has risen. Remember, he said that he would be crucified and on
the third day rise again." Then they did remember, and their
hearts rose joyfully.

"See," said the angel, "here is the place where he was laid."

The women looked again, and saw the linen cloths that had
been wrapped about his body. If they had thought, like Mary,
that his body had been stolen, they saw now that it could not be
so.

"Go quickly now!" the angel said to them. "Tell Peter and the
rest of the disciples that he is risen, and say to them: 'He is going
before you into Galilee, and you will see him there just as he told
you.'"

The women hurried off, still awed and frightened yet overjoyed. They went at once to the place where Peter and the rest of
the disciples were waiting for they knew not what. "He is risen!"
the women said. The men stared blankly at them. Women! First
Mary Magdalene, and now the rest of them.

But the women went on with their story. All they had seen and heard they told to the eleven disciples. And to the men their excited words seemed only to be idle tales, and they did not believe what they were hearing.

Yet when the women were gone Peter thought about their words. He rose, then, and ran quickly to the tomb with John. They stooped and looked inside. There was no body; neither was there a young man in shining white. There were only the linen grave clothes, and the face handkerchief neatly rolled up in a place by itself. This was not the work of vandals. But what was it? The two disciples turned and left, full of wonderment yet still without understanding of what had come to pass.

Now Mary Magdalene came walking through the garden, unseen by them and not seeing them herself. She stopped outside the tomb and quietly wept. And as she wept she, too, stooped and looked into the cave, for even through her tears she could see a bright glow coming from it. Inside she saw two angels dressed in dazzling white, one sitting at the head and one at the feet of the place where the body of Jesus had lain.

They said to her, "Woman, why are you weeping?"

"Because they have taken away my Lord," she answered sorrowfully, "and I do not know where they have put him."

When she had said this she turned away, too grief-stricken to realize that she had been talking to no ordinary men. Through her tears she saw a figure standing outside the tomb. It was Jesus, but she did not know that it was he.

"Why do you weep?" asked Jesus gently. "For whom are you looking?"

Mary looked at him through misted eyes and still did not know who he was. Supposing him to be the gardener who cared for Joseph's garden, she said to him: "Sir, if you have taken him away, tell me where you have laid his body, so that I myself may take him and place him somewhere else."

Jesus looked at her with love and said: "Mary!"

She turned and saw him anew. Now she knew the voice; now

she knew the face. It was like the face of Jesus, and at the same time strangely unlike; and yet she knew that this was he.

"Master!" she cried. Full of joy and gladness, she reached her arms toward him in a gesture of worship and devotion.

"No, do not touch me yet," Jesus said in kindly tones, "for I am not yet ascended to my Father. But go to my brothers, to my friends, and tell them that I will soon ascend to my Father and your Father, to my God and yours. And I will see them before then."

As Mary looked upon him, he was gone.

She went at once to see the disciples to tell them that she had seen the Lord, and found them mourning and weeping still. She said that he was alive; she told them the things he had said. But they, sorrowing for his death and puzzled by the disappearance of his body, could not believe that he really was alive and that she had seen him. It was a woman's dream, they thought: she had wanted it to be true, and so she had believed. But they could not believe.

Now it happened that same day that two of Jesus' followers had left Jerusalem after the sad passover and were traveling along the road to Emmaus, a village about seven miles from the city. As they walked they talked sadly together about all the strange and terrible things that had happened. They had heard that Jesus had risen from the dead but they did not believe what they had heard. All their bright hopes of a Messiah who would save Israel had been cruelly shattered, and only despair and misery were left.

While they walked, Jesus drew near to them in the form of a stranger, and they did not know him.

"What is it that you are discussing so earnestly as you walk?" asked Jesus. "And why are you so sorrowful?"

They stopped and stood on the road, looking sad.

One of them, whose name was Cleopas, answered him, saying: "Are you a stranger in Jerusalem? You must be, for surely you are the only man in the city who does not know the things that have been happening here these last few days!"

"What things?" asked Jesus.

And they answered, "Why, the things concerning Jesus the Nazarene, who was a prophet mighty in deed and in word in the eyes of God and all the people. The chief priests and our rulers delivered him up to be condemned to death, and the Romans crucified him. We had hoped, and we believed, that he was the Christ who would be the Savior of Israel, but now he is dead. Besides all this, it is now three days since these things came to pass, and certain women of our company have astounded us. They went early to the tomb this morning but they did not find his body where it had been placed. No, they came back saying that they had had a vision of angels who had told them he was alive. Therefore some of us went to the tomb to prove what they were saying. We found it empty, as the women had said, but nowhere did we see our Lord."

"Ah, you are foolish," Jesus said. "And how slow of heart you are to believe all that the prophets have said! If you had believed, you would have known that all these things were to happen. Do you not remember that the Christ would have to suffer all these things before entering into his glory?" And then, beginning with the books of Moses, and going on to all the prophets, he interpreted for them all the passages in the scriptures that concerned himself. They listened eagerly, and much was made clear to them that they had not understood before.

When they drew near to Emmaus, where the two men lived, Jesus bade them farewell and would have gone on further. But the two men urged him not to go. "Stay with us," they begged him warmly, "for it is getting toward evening and the day is almost over."

He thanked them and accepted.

They went into the house together and sat down to dine. Jesus took the bread and blessed it; then he broke it, and gave it to the other two. And all at once their eyes were opened, and they knew him. As they gazed at him in startled recognition, he vanished from their sight.

Then they rejoiced within themselves as they realized that their hopes of a redeemer had not been dashed, but had come true. He was alive! With great excitement they said to one another, "Were not our hearts glowing within us while he spoke to us along the way and explained the scriptures to us? We should have known then that he was the Christ!"

They rose that very hour and hurried back to Jerusalem, to the house in which the eleven disciples were accustomed to gather together. They were all there but one, and they welcomed the newcomers mournfully and firmly locked the door for fear of the Pharisees. The two men told the others everything they had seen and heard that day.

"The Lord is risen indeed!" they said. "We have seen him for ourselves." And they explained what had happened on the road, and how the stranger had come with them to their house to eat with them, and how they suddenly came to know him with the breaking of the bread.

As soon as they had finished their story, Jesus himself suddenly appeared in the midst and said to all: "Peace be with you!"

But his disciples felt by no means at peace. They were startled and terrified by this sudden apparition, for the door had been securely bolted in case of a surprise visit by any of their enemies, and they had been quite certain that no one could possibly get in. This sudden visitor must surely be a spirit! And they trembled with fear.

"Why are you so troubled?" Jesus asked. "And why are doubts and questions arising in your hearts? I am no ghost. See my hands and feet! It is I, myself. Touch me yourselves and see; feel me and find out that I am real. A spirit does not have flesh and bones, as you can see I have." And as he said this he showed them his wounded hands and feet, and his side where the soldier's sword had pierced him.

They believed and yet at the same time did not quite believe, for it was too wonderful to be true. They gazed incredulously at his living body and the deep, dark scars, amazed at what they saw. But he had died, they knew; this could not be he!

And while they wondered still, disbelieving through sheer joy, Jesus said to them: "Have you anything here to eat?"

One of them managed to pull himself together to find food. Jesus sat down at the table and they brought him broiled fish and a piece of honeycomb. He took the food and ate before their staring eyes. They watched as though they had never before seen a man at dinner. Yet when they saw him eat they knew he was indeed no spirit but a man; that he was Jesus, in the living flesh.

Then he said to them again, "Peace be with you! Now you see that all things concerning me, that were written in the Law of Moses, in the books of the prophets, and in the psalms, have been fulfilled." Then he opened up their minds so that they might more fully understand the scriptures, and he said to them: "It is written that the Christ should suffer, and rise again from death on the third day; and that repentance and the forgiveness of sins must be preached in his name to all the nations, beginning in Jerusalem. As my Father sent me, so will I send you."

And when he had said this he breathed on them and said: "Receive the Holy Spirit: if you forgive the sins of any man, those sins will truly be forgiven. And if you do not release any man from his guilt, the sins of that man will be retained."

They listened now as they had listened to him in the years before his death, and they knew for certain that he was Christ returned to them.

He left them, then, and they rejoiced that he had risen and come back into their midst.

But Thomas the Twin, one of the eleven, had not been with them when Jesus came. When he joined the others they told him at once and with great joy: "We have seen the Lord!" Thomas was a doubter; he still would not believe. He said to them, "Unless I see for myself the marks of the nails in his hands, I will not believe; and until I put my finger into the marks and my hand into his side, I will not believe." And there was nothing they could do to convince him that Jesus was alive.

Eight days later the disciples were again together in the house with the door firmly closed and locked. This time doubting Thomas was with them. Jesus appeared as suddenly as before and stood there in their midst.

"Peace be with you!" he said. And Thomas still looked doubtful.

"Thomas," said Jesus. "Come to me." Thomas went to him.

"Reach out your finger," Jesus said. "Look at my hands and touch the marks." Thomas did so. The expression on his face began to change. "Now," Jesus told him, "place your hand into my side." Thomas felt the wound. "Have faith; believe!" said Jesus.

"My Lord and my God!" said Thomas then. "I do believe." And he was filled with joy.

Jesus said to him, "Only because you have seen me, do you believe. But blessed are those who have not seen me, and even so, believe."

Now all eleven of them knew that Jesus had indeed risen from the dead as was written in the scriptures and as he had said he would.

JESUS ASCENDS INTO HEAVEN

Some time after the events in Jerusalem, Jesus did show himself to his disciples at the sea of Galilee as he had promised. The way it happened was this:

Simon Peter, with Thomas who was called the Twin, and Nathanael of Cana, and James and John the sons of Zebedee, and two others of the disciples, were together one evening on the shore of the inland sea.

Simon Peter said to the rest, "I am going fishing."

"We will go with you," said the others.

So they got into the boat and took it out into the midst of the sea. But though they lowered their net and hauled it in time and time again, they had caught nothing by the time the first dim light of dawn appeared in the sky. They turned back toward the shore with not a single fish to show for their long night's work.

At daybreak Jesus appeared on the shore. They saw him standing there in the soft and shadowy light of morning, but they did not know that it was he. As they brought the boat in toward the land he called out to them: "Children, have you any fish?"

"No," they answered with regret.

"Then cast your net on the right side of the boat, and you will find some," Jesus said.

Supposing that he was a fellow fisherman kindly offering them good advice, they cast again at once. And this time they could not haul in the net for all the multitude of fishes that it held.

Then John realized who stood upon the shore. "It is the Lord!" he said to Peter.

When Simon Peter heard that it was Jesus he quickly put on his fisherman's cloak—for he had taken it off while he worked—and sprang into the sea to go to Jesus. The other disciples followed in the boat, dragging with them the net full of fish. They were quite close to land, no more than a hundred yards away, so it was not long before they pulled the boat up on the shore. And as soon as they landed they saw a charcoal fire burning, with a fish already laid upon it, and some bread nearby. But the man whom John had said was Jesus did not look like their Lord. It puzzled them, but nevertheless they went toward him on the beach.

"Bring some of the fish which you have caught," Jesus said to them.

Simon Peter went back to the boat and hauled the net ashore. It was full of huge fish, a hundred and fifty-three of them, and even though there were so many of them the net was still unbroken.

"Come and break your fast," Jesus invited his disciples.

And though he did not look the same as he had looked before, they did not dare to ask him who he was. This time they were sure, because of the miracle of the fish, that he must be the Master.

They joined him at the fire. Jesus took the loaf of bread and gave it to them with the fish.

When they had eaten, Jesus turned to Simon Peter and said:

"Simon, son of Jona, do you love me deeply, even more than these others do?"

"Yes, Lord," Peter answered. "You know that I love you."

"Then feed my lambs for me," said Jesus. And then he asked a second time, "Simon, son of Jona, do you love me deeply?"

"Yes, Lord," Peter said again. "You know that I love you."

"Then tend my sheep for me," said Jesus. And then he asked a third time, "Simon, son of Jona, do you love me deeply?"

Peter was grieved because Jesus had asked him three times if he loved him; for he had momentarily forgotten that he had once denied his Lord three times and required his forgiveness. "Lord," he said, "you know all things. You know that I love you." But he did not understand that Jesus was speaking of divine love, a love that would sacrifice all things for his Lord.

"Then be my shepherd; feed my sheep," said Jesus. And with these words he was assuring Peter of forgiveness and entrusting him with the task of carrying on his own work. "You know that when you were young," Jesus went on, "you used to clothe yourself and go wherever you pleased. But I tell you truly that when you are old you will stretch out your hands for help, and someone else will clothe you in another way, and take you where you do not want to go." In saying this he was telling Peter that the manner of his disciple's death would not be of Peter's choosing, but that in dying as he was to die he would be glorifying God.

With these words Jesus ended their meeting. This was now the third time that Jesus had showed himself to his disciples after he had risen.

For forty days after he had risen from the dead he appeared among them many times to prove to them that he was indeed alive, and to speak to them about the kingdom of God.

One day he talked to them upon a mountainside in Galilee, and said:

"All authority in heaven and earth has been given to me. Go, therefore, and make disciples of all the nations, baptizing them in the name of the Father, of the Son, and of the Holy Spirit. Teach them to observe all the commandments that I have given you. Preach the good news to all the world. He who believes and is baptized will be saved, but he who does not believe will be condemned. And these signs will accompany those who believe: in my name they will cast out demons; they will speak in many new tongues; they will take snakes into their hands and not be hurt;

and if they drink any deadly poison, it will not harm them; they will lay hands on the sick, and the sick will recover. And I say to you that I will be with you always, even to the end of the world."

When he saw them the next time they were together in Jerusalem. And when he met with them there he commanded them to stay in Jerusalem until they received a promise from the Father. It would come in the form of a visit from the Holy Spirit, and they would know when it came that they were ready to go out and tell the gospel story.

"John baptized in water," he said, "but you will be baptized in the Holy Spirit not many days from now. You will receive power when the Holy Spirit comes upon you, and you will be my witnesses to tell the story of the truth in the city of Jerusalem, and in all Judea, and in Samaria, and to the uttermost ends of the earth. But do not leave Jerusalem until the Holy Spirit is given to you, for only then will you be ready for your work. Now let us go to Bethany, and then you must come back to the city."

So then the Lord Jesus, after he had spoken thus to them, led them out as far as Bethany.

When they were at a quiet place on the outskirts of the village he lifted up his hands and blessed them. His face was radiant and peaceful.

An unusual brightness came into the sky. And even as he blessed them he was taken up before their eyes and carried into heaven where a white cloud hid him from their sight.

And he sat down at the right hand side of God.

The disciples stood there looking upward in amazement as he disappeared. For long moments after he had gone they gazed into the heavens and wondered to themselves. And they they became aware that two men in white robes had appeared beside them.

"You men of Galilee," the strangers said to them, "why do you stand there, gazing into heaven? This same Jesus, whom you saw being taken up into heaven, will come again in the same way as you have seen him go."

Then the disciples bowed down before the wonder of it all, and they worshiped Jesus. Afterward they returned to Jerusalem with their hearts full of joy, and they spent much time in the temple praising God.

Now Jesus was gone, but his going was not the end of his story nor of his mission to the world. He left to his disciples, and to everyone on earth, a doctrine of love and a promise that he would come again. And he had also left concrete instructions for his apostles to follow. They were to wait for the promise from the Father, and then they were to go out into the world and teach what they had been taught.

While they waited they all met together with the women, including Mary the mother of Jesus, and prayed earnestly to God. And then they chose a twelfth man, Matthias, to take the place of Judas Iscariot. Now there were twelve apostles again, but many more disciples who came to join them and help them spread the word of God. Altogether there were about a hundred and twenty of them as the day of pentecost approached.

It was ten days after Jesus went to heaven that the Jews celebrated the festival of the harvest, called the feast of pentecost. On that day all the disciples gathered together to take part in the celebration.

And suddenly there came a sound from heaven, like a mighty rushing wind, and it filled all the house where they were sitting. And there appeared to them a blaze, as if of flame, that parted into tongues of fire that rested upon each one of them. All at once they were filled with the Holy Spirit, with new strength and power, and they began to speak in other languages as Jesus had said they would.

They began to preach in the temple and on the streets, and they spoke to people in the words that Jesus himself had used. When word of what had happened was noised abroad, people came to hear them from far and wide and were amazed because each man heard the disciples speak in the language which he himself understood. "Are these men not Galilaeans?" they said to one another. "Behold, they speak every language of the world!"

And it was true. The disciples spoke in many tongues, so that they could talk to all the people of the world and tell them all the glad news of the gospel. They went forth from Jerusalem with new courage and great powers, no longer afraid of the high priests and the Pharisees and determined to be Jesus' witnesses and tell the story of the truth wherever they might go. For indeed the death of Jesus was not the end; it was only the beginning.

The apostles of the Lord spread the gospel message from Jerusalem to the uttermost ends of the world: teaching, healing, suffering, gaining some enemies and many converts wherever they went. There was Peter, the rock upon whom the Christian church was founded. There was John, who carried the message far across the sea. There was Stephen, who was stoned to death for his beliefs, yet died forgiving those who killed him. There was Philip, who preached and healed in the city of Samaria. There was Paul, once a Pharisee, who became converted to Christ and taught the message of salvation in the east and in the west among the Gentiles. And there were others, more and more of them as the years passed and the story of Jesus Christ became known throughout the world. Through them the message of love and brotherhood became the new hope of the nations.

And that hope will never die.